Land of Lost Content

'The Cloth Dresser' from George Walker, *The Costume of Yorkshire* (1814).
Reproduced by permission of The British Library.

Land of Lost Content

The Luddite Revolt, *1812*

Robert Reid

HEINEMANN : LONDON

William Heinemann Ltd
10 Upper Grosvenor Street, London W1X 9PA

LONDON MELBOURNE TORONTO
JOHANNESBURG AUCKLAND

First published 1986
© Robert Reid 1986

SBN 434 62900 6

Printed in Great Britain by
St Edmundsbury Press Ltd
Bury St Edmunds

For Penelope

Contents

	Introduction	1
1	The Stage	5
2	The Gentlemen	10
3	The New Men	24
4	A Man of the People	31
5	The Workers	38
6	The Power of the Worker	46
7	A Question of Technology	51
8	1811	56
9	Decision	63
10	Trouble	69
11	The Power of the Law	78
12	Preparing for the Worst	84
13	The Enemy Within	91
14	Lines of Communication	99
15	Rawfolds	108
16	The Tide of Sympathy	118
17	Shots in the Dark	127
18	Awful Times	132
19	Radical Reformers	140
20	Maitland	147
21	In Manchester	153
22	Death of a Minister	156
23	Officer in Command	163
24	'The Doctor'	172
25	Raynes	182
26	Goodbye, Grey	187
27	On Oath	196

28	An Anonymous Letter	208
29	King's Evidence	215
30	The Turning Tide	220
31	Retreat and Retrenchment	227
32	Defence	232
33	Trial	238
34	Retribution	249
35	This Deluded County	256
36	The Last of the Luddites	266
37	The Law of Technology	272
38	Ever After	285
	Notes	297
	Bibliography	315
	Index	321

Into my heart an air that kills
  From yon far country blows.
What are those blue remembered hills,
  What spires, what farms are those?

That is the land of lost content,
  I see it shining plain,
The happy highways where I went
  And cannot come again.

A E Housman

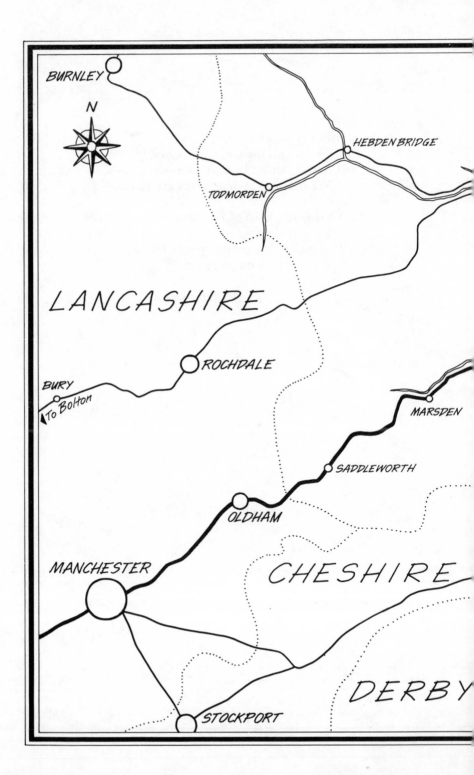

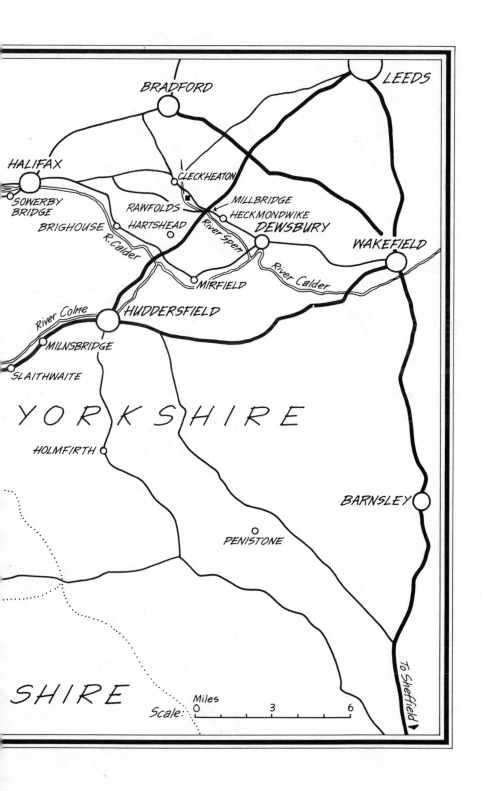

BRADFORD

LEEDS

HALIFAX

SOWERBY
BRIDGE

CLECKHEATON

RAWFOLDS

MILLBRIDGE

BRIGHOUSE

HARTSHEAD

HECKMONDWIKE

DEWSBURY

River Spen

R. Calder

WAKEFIELD

MIRFIELD

River Calder

River Colne

HUDDERSFIELD

MILNSBRIDGE

SLAITHWAITE

Y O R K S H I R E

HOLMFIRTH

BARNSLEY

PENISTONE

S H I R E

Scale:

Miles

3

6

To Sheffield ▼

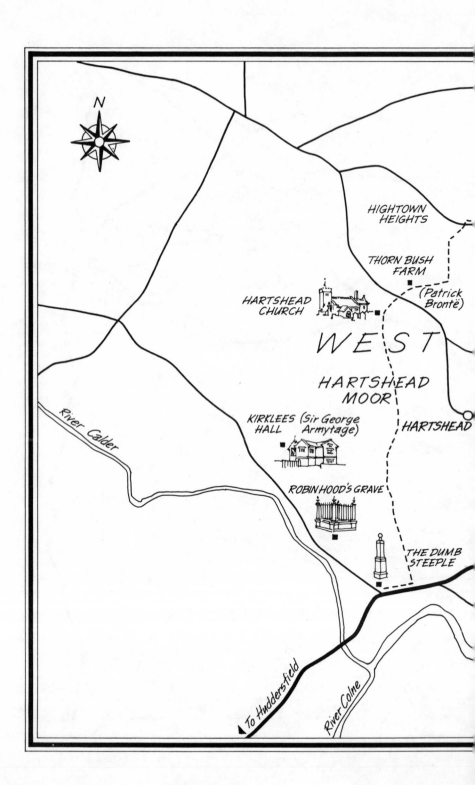

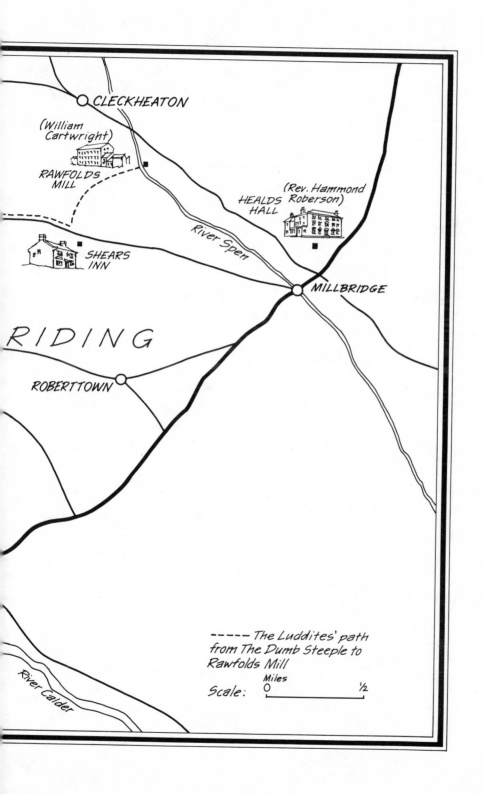

CLECKHEATON

(William Cartwright)

RAWFOLDS MILL

HEALDS HALL
(Rev. Hammond Roberson)

SHEARS INN

River Spen

MILLBRIDGE

RIDING

ROBERTTOWN

River Calder

----- The Luddites' path from The Dumb Steeple to Rawfolds Mill

Scale:

Miles

0   ½

Introduction

The incident at the centre of this story, though unusual, immediately affected a trivial number of people in one small community. But its consequences are considerable. Among other things, it securely etched the word Luddite into the language and on to history and gave its present meaning uncomfortable ambiguity; it also directly influenced the thinking that led to the policies which built the present welfare state.

As a child, I went twice each day to and from the school built in the early nineteenth century by one of the characters involved in this incident, the Reverend Hammond Roberson. It was possible for me to make this journey of not much more than half a mile by walking almost the whole of the distance on the stone farm walls which kept the dairy herd in the meadows surrounding Roberson's house. I needed to put my feet on metalled road only once each journey – when I crossed the valley bottom to reach the industrial village. The capsule which had preserved this odd rural enclave from 1800 until 1940 has long since been broken. Though the Georgian house still stands, the school is now occupied by a fibreglass company and the meadows are covered from end to end with little modern houses. However, it is necessary to add an unsentimental observation which is not without relevance to the technological as well as the social implications of this story. Not only are the interiors of these ranks of new dwellings immeasurably more comfortable and civilised than the cottages of the industrial village of 1812, they are infinitely better provided for than the grey terraces with their cold flagstone floors which even forty years ago stood alongside the beck in the valley bottom.

I cannot claim that as a child I was aware of the importance of the tragedy which, in the early nineteenth century, struck the people of the valley in which I was born. Only much later when I became interested in the extraordinary power of applied technology did I begin to appreciate this. However, when young I was conscious of the ambivalent attitude of those who lived there to the influence technology held over their lives, and I was also aware of their conflicting memories of the people who had been alive when that technology first remoulded existence in the valley. This story deals with some of these people, among whom Hammond Roberson is one.

More novelists than historians have used this incident as a quarry for material. Charlotte Brontë, who met Roberson, is among the best known. The key episode in *Shirley* is based on what happened in the valley.[1] Two sentences from her novel summarise the dilemma central to the real-life events. They are spoken to the character she based on the Rawfolds mill owner, William Cartwright. 'Invention may be all right,' a worker tells him, 'but I know it isn't right for poor folks to starve. Them that governs mun find a way to help us.'[2]

A phrase from *Shirley*, 'misery generates hate', was adopted in 1944 by Sir William Beveridge as the clarion call of his book, *Full Employment in a Free Society*. There is therefore a visible link between the incident at Rawfolds and the modern welfare state of which Beveridge was architect.

Charlotte Brontë's account is engrossing and, within novelistic licence, accurate enough. However, her assessment of the characters involved and their motivations does not coincide with mine, though the documentary source she used is the first I should acknowledge. The *Leeds Mercury* was at the height of its influence in 1812. Its radical editor, Edward Baines, kept a conscientious and concerned record in his paper of the events which were tearing at the heart of northern England. I have relied particularly heavily on his account of the York Special Commission of 1813 which is certainly as accurate as and often fuller than that of the official reports which I have also used.

I am equally in debt to a second journalist, Frank Peel, the editor of the *Heckmondwike Herald* in the late nineteenth century. Peel collected and published local memories and stories in *The Risings of the Luddites* (1888). His book has been an inspiration. E P Thompson (whose exhaustive *The Making of the English Working Class* places any writer on this period in his debt) commends Peel's account as 'generally accurate, even in detail.'[3]

Alas, wherever I have been able to check Peel in detail, I have found he is generally inaccurate – even to the extent of inventing dates and reshuffling the order of the Luddite trials to give them more dramatic effect. It also should be noted that Peel recognised good source material when he saw it. He used as his own long sections of Edward Baines's work. But his errors are of no great importance. Without Peel's diligence in gathering together eye-witness accounts the flavour, the drama and the pathos of the affair might have died. Nevertheless, since he makes no attempt to filter out some of the taller stories enthusiastic local folk fed him, I have used his work sparingly.

I have treated the work of two other local historians with much greater caution. D F E Sykes and G H Walker say of *Ben o'Bill's, the Luddite* (1898) that their story 'is mostly true, and the authors have not felt called upon to vary in any material respects the story as it was gleaned in part from the lips and in part from the papers of the narrator.' In spite of their assurances, I have found their tale, which since its publication has been widely used as a histori-cal source, not only inaccurate but positively misleading. Having said this, as a scientist walking in historians' tracks, I have to add that I have found the scholarship of F O Darvall, J L and Barbara Hammond and E P Thompson unimpeachable when dealing with the period of this book and I have profited greatly from them.

The stores of information which I have used as original sources have been chiefly those of the Home Office files of the Public Record Office, the Radcliffe Papers of Leeds District Archives and the Wentworth Woodhouse Papers of Sheffield City Library. I am grateful for the help given me by the librarians of these institutions, and I am also grateful to the Royal Institution Library which provided so much other material for my use. For their comments on parts of the manuscript, I am in considerable debt to Dr John Belchem, Professor Geoffrey Best, His Honour Judge Nigel Curtis-Raleigh, John Nussey and J E Stanfield.

In the period in which this book was written several violent episodes involving workers organised on a national scale took place. The brutality shown in some of these even began to approach that related here. A persuasive case has been made for the poverty of historicism. Nevertheless, a knowledge of the events of 1812 made it possible to predict the course of a remark-able number of these modern episodes. The comparisons make it seem probable that there is still something to be learnt from the incident at Rawfolds.

1

The Stage

One August day early in the eighteenth century, Daniel Defoe set off on one of the steep tracks heading out of Lancashire. The weather was bad and he had to put up for the night at a Pennine inn. Rising early and starting his climb down into Yorkshire from Blackstone Edge, as the sun began to rise over the mist-covered valleys below, he was suddenly overwhelmed by the pastoral scene which lit up before him.

Everything about the valley he now began to walk through enchanted him. His admiration for it was boundless. It was not simply the exquisite natural beauty of the tumbling streams and the wooded hillsides, there was everywhere for him to see an extraordinarily successful marriage between man and the things man had made from the countryside. It was faultless. Defoe felt the urge to commit to paper a fulsome description of this idyll and the people who were a part of it. Ever one to reach for a hyperbole whenever the least opportunity presented itself, he did so.

> This whole country, however mountainous, and that no sooner we were down one hill but we mounted another, is yet infinitely full of people; these people are full of business; not a beggar, not an idle person to be seen, except here and there an alms-house, where people ancient and decrepit and past labour might perhaps be found; for it is observable, that the people here, however laborious, generally live to a great age, a certain testimony to the goodness and wholesomeness of the country, which is, without doubt, as healthy as any part of England; nor is the health of the people lessened, but helped and established by their being constantly employed,

5

and, as we call it, their working hard; so that they find a
double advantage by their being always in business.[1]

He so fell in love with the way of life he had found that eventually
he hid away in this valley to write and to share its peace and
industry, and probably completed *Robinson Crusoe* there. But
if Defoe's uncritical phrases defy belief, there are many other
writers of the time to testify that these valleys in the foothills of
the Pennines were, if not Shangri-la, then at least something
exceptional in the land: contented as well as industrious, generously populated as well as picturesque. Bishop Pococke, when he
looked down on them, compared the hillsides to the Mount of
Olives. The modern visitor can still see a great deal of what
inspired the traveller in the landscape when, viewed from the
same vantage point, something of its purity has been restored by
a light, early morning snowfall, covering the worst of the nineteenth century's industrial blight.

Defoe had accurately noted what made the hum of creative
activity audible in the valleys: power – natural power from two
sources

> and that in a situation which I never saw the like of in any
> part of England; and, I believe, the like is not to be seen so
> contrived in any part of the world; I mean coals and running
> water upon the tops of the highest hills. This seems to have
> been directed by the wise hand of Providence for the very
> purpose which is now served by it, namely, the manufactures
> which otherwise could not be carried on.[2]

There were many, not least the people of the valleys themselves,
who saw divine guidance in the way elementary technology had
been applied to what could be produced on this only modestly
fertile land. It had made wealth – wealth which, unlike so much of
the rest of England was noticeably well distributed among the
inhabitants of the houses which dotted the landscape.

Another of the things Defoe observed as he went over from one
valley and into the next was that there was hardly a house out of
speaking distance with its neighbour, each one fed and powered
by the stream diverted alongside it. As the sun rose, he saw
brightly reflected from the patch of ground in front of practically
every homestead a piece of white cloth stretched into a great
horizontal rectangle by the hooks of a tenter or wooden frame.
Before him was the product of the greatest industry of England
nearing its last stage of manufacture: wool.

6

Wool was the solid base of British industry and had been for more than two centuries. It was not for comfort alone that the highest judicial officer in the land, the Lord Chancellor of England, sat on his woolsack. Neither was it a religious nor a sanitary measure that an Act of 1678 provided that 'no corpse of any person shall be buried in any shirt, shift, sheet or shroud, or anything whatsoever made of or mingling with flax, hemp, silk, hair, gold or silver, & etc., or in any stuff or thing other than what is made of sheep's wool only' on pain of a penalty of £5. Relatives were required to produce a certification of the use of a woollen shroud within eight days of a burial. Thus was the place of importance of wool in the national economy both enshrined in symbolism and strictly protected by parliamentary decree.

Some idea of the dominance of wool in British trade can be got from the fact that in the first ten years of the eighteenth century imports of raw cotton amounted to less than £35,000; the woollen industry in the same period was consuming £2,000,000-worth of fleece.[3] Defoe, as he found his way to the cloth markets of small places such as Halifax and Huddersfield was amazed to find that in any one of them £10–20,000 value of finished cloth was being bought and sold in little more than an hour of business, and this in an area where the trade was still if not in its infancy, not out of its youth.

Worsted – the cloth made from combed long-fibre wool – had been taken by Yorkshiremen for their own, gradually leaving high and dry the Norfolk parish which gave the stuff its name. Within about fifty years of Defoe's tour the small valley towns of the West Riding, rather than the great city of Norwich, were becoming the most important centres of the industry. By 1774, the trade employed 84,000 men, women and children in this area of Yorkshire involving 20,000 families.[4] By the end of the century the eastern county's worsted trade was to be in serious decline. And the east was not the only area to find its trade leeched by the north country. The south-western counties were discovering there was damaging competition from Yorkshire for their coarser woollen cloths while a depressed Adam Smith noted in *The Wealth of Nations* that 'the wool of the southern counties of Scotland is, a great part of it, after a long land carriage through very bad roads, manufactured in Yorkshire, for want of capital to manufacture it at home.'[5]

The extraordinary and infectious atmosphere of prosperity in this community was made even more unusual, as Defoe had seen, by an apparent absence of class stratification – of obvious rich and of obvious poor – which was so evident and so distressing in the great centres of population of England, the cities. The egalitarian character of the place persisted well into the next century in spite of events which were beginning to overturn the way of life of so many of the people of the country. Southerners were forever taken by surprise by it. Mrs Gaskell, walking through Keighley one day on her way to Haworth, for all her familiarity with Cheshire and Lancashire, was nevertheless struck by the fact that 'nearly every dwelling seems devoted to some branch of commerce. In passing hastily through the town, one hardly perceived where the necessary doctor or lawyer can live, so little appearance is there of any dwellings of the professional middle-class such as abound in our old cathedral towns.'[6] The possibility of a society where the individuals were not distinguishable by their class of house and style of occupation had until that moment not occurred to Chelsea-born Mrs Gaskell.

But in the Calder valley and in the quiet, wooded valleys which were tributaries of this river, those of the Holme and Colne and the small but busily trickling Spen, there existed that egalitarian idyll, or at least something approaching it – and it delighted the radical sentiments of Defoe. As elsewhere, the gentry existed. But it nowhere dominated. The local population was not dependent on and therefore not subservient to the family which lived in the great house on the hill. Instead, the farmsteads which patterned the sides of the valley were remarkably self-sufficient units. Each one of these, in the middle of four or five acres, usually housed a Master and his family, and with them lived a handful of workmen or apprentices, their numbers depending on the acreage. There was neither class nor social division between Master and worker. The land, which they all worked for part of the time, fed them, and the hillsides nearby and the dales to the north provided the wool which they spun, combed or carded, then wove before stretching it across the great tenters in front of the house. There, as Defoe had seen, the white surface shone as it reflected the sun's light: a symbol not simply of prosperity but of contented activity which permeated these valleys.

And the idyll, or as near as reality would allow, was to persist almost to the end of the century. There is no question that it would have persisted longer had it not been for the fact that unprecedented technological invention began to sweep over Britain. It was to these West Riding valleys that the new inventors would look for the power sources – the water and the coal to drive some of the most productive of their new inventions. The result would eventually be to change radically, sometimes for the better, more often brutally for the worse, the character of the lives of the inhabitants of the valleys. Nevertheless, so established in its even, prosperous, satisfied and self-satisfied pattern was this way of life that it had the momentum and the inner strength to resist change far longer and far more resolutely than any other area in Britain affected by the Industrial Revolution. The conflict was to threaten the stability of the nation from within as it has never been threatened since.

2

The Gentlemen

People in these valleys never acquired the habit of doffing their caps in a gesture of inferiority. However, there was no way in which they could avoid the presence of the local gentry. As elsewhere in the nation, those who felt confident enough to claim high birth and, more important, who had the cash and the real property to give substance to the claim, lived in the prime countryside sites. In the Spen valley there was no doubt as to who was established in the pride of place.

The Armytage family lived over the brow of the hill on a splendid site once occupied by Benedictine nuns. It was called Kirklees. Directly in the path of everything that had seemed most perfect to Defoe, it overlooked both the Spen's neighbouring valleys, the Colne and the Calder, at the point where the rivers joined. But for all its prominent position the house at Kirklees and the people who lived there at the beginning of the nineteenth century succeeded in remaining aloof, remarkably insulated from the valleys around and from the way of life of the ordinary people below. The social separation was little different from what it had been 150 years earlier, and little different from what it is today, with the same family still occupying the same house.

There was more than an insularity which set the mansion apart. There was a mystery about it which local people only reluctantly tried to penetrate. The mystery was helped physically by the thick shroud of trees that surrounded the place, and was sustained spiritually by local tales of the ghosts of prioresses and nuns and of the death of Robin Hood whose grave is so imperturbably marked by maps as lying within Kirkless' grounds in spite of any facts history might suggest to the contrary.

The Armytage family had taken no part in the woollen trade which, in the late eighteenth century, was making these valleys rich. The result was that their power over the people who were living so comfortably and confidently in the farm workshops was strictly circumscribed. Sir John Armytage, the baronet who had inherited Kirklees and its limited local acreage nevertheless used that power, as his predecessors had done in the seventeenth century,[1] to further the family prejudices which had persisted since the Civil War. It was, he felt, the duty of the supporters of King and Country, whenever they were able, to show their displeasure towards Quakers and Nonconformists; he played his part in no uncertain terms.

Once, not long before, John Wesley had stood in these valleys and local families had poured from their homes to listen to him. 'Thousands and thousands filled the vale and the side of the hill,' Wesley wrote.[2] Their response deeply moved him, just as his message strongly and permanently influenced his open-air congregations. The gulf separating the Armytage family and many of the valley families therefore widened as Methodist and Baptist sects took root in a community where Established Churches could be discovered only after a long trek over difficult roads and packhorse tracks.

One of Armytage's tenants was a farmer, Joseph Priestley, a strong character with dissenting beliefs whose son, John, was eventually to become a ruling elder of a local Independent chapel.[3] The clash between landlord and tenant was inevitable and Armytage eventually evicted Joseph Priestley from house and land. The only consolation Priestley could draw from this experience of the age of enlightenment was that he did not end up in the cells of York Castle, convicted of 'riotous assembly', as did some other victims of the Armytages' defence of established religion.

The bitterness of the Priestley family (which included the more celebrated dissenter, the chemist Dr Joseph Priestley) was to last for several generations. It was also to provide the link between the Armytage baronetcy and the other character who, by the turn of the nineteenth century, though not a man of means in the conventional sense, was a man of considerable substance: one who with the latest heir to Kirklees, George Armytage, was the only other resident in the valley who could write 'Gentleman' after his name in the certainty that he would be taken seriously. His name was Hammond Roberson.

*

It was inevitable that this place with its simple natural beauty and with an industry beginning to open like a flower in the sun of the early years of the Industrial Revolution should attract others besides neutral observers such as Daniel Defoe and Bishop Pococke. Over the twenty years which spanned the turn of the nineteenth century several men, a few of them exceptional, looked into these little valleys and saw potential there. Some looked as visionaries and some with greed, just as some looked as social planners and some with the eyes of decision-makers and rulers. What each saw was a way of turning the flower's nectar into a honey pot. All these men had one thing in common – a well-defined ambition: ambition which in its sweep might beneficially embrace the local people, but which in most cases was fuelled by a powerful wish only for self-advancement. What good and what harm was done by each outsider in turn who pushed himself forward is of course much easier to assess in retrospect. The judgement of by far the greater number of Hammond Roberson's contemporaries in the Spen valley was harsh. History, however, may yet learn to look on him with a kinder eye and ask whether he really was the insensitive and loathsome bully woven into the stories passed down the valley from children to grandchildren, or whether he deserved the epithet 'Gentleman'.[4] Whatever else can be said of him, his personal ambitions were not hidden. He wrote them large, and in the end, what he achieved would surprise even those who loathed him.

Hammond Roberson's origins were entirely alien to the north country. It says something of his unusual character therefore that once he had arrived in the West Riding, for all that he differed from the local inhabitants by birth, breeding, accent, education and bearing, during the rest of his life he never expressed any wish to live and die anywhere other than in this place of his adoption.

He was born in 1757 at Cawston in Norfolk of yeoman stock, educated at Magdalene College, Cambridge, and then persuaded by the evangelical vicar of Huddersfield, Henry Venn, who had seen something extraordinary in the character of the 22-year-old, to become curate of the church at Dewsbury in the Calder valley.

He was a vigorous and striking young man. Charlotte Brontë had a glimpse of him when she was ten years old and he in middle age on the point of reaching the heights of his ambitions. For all that she saw him only once she was unusually impressed, in particular by his stern military bearing.[5] This, coupled with both

12

his admiration for, and his uncanny likeness to Wellington, led to his nickname, the Duke Ecclesiastic. Charlotte Brontë was to hear a great deal more about Roberson as the years passed and, like many others, was to become confused about the qualities hidden behind the aquiline nose and the patrician voice. She turned him into a character for a novel:

> a personage short of stature, but straight of port and bearing on broad shoulders a hawk's head, beak and eye, the whole surmounted by a Rehoboam, or shovel hat, which he did not seem to think it necessary to lift or remove before the presence in which he then stood . . . despite his clerical hat, black coat and gaiters, more the air of a veteran officer chiding his subalterns, than a venerable priest exhorting his sons in the faith.[6]

This was her description of Mathewson Helstone in *Shirley*. The novel was to be her version of the events leading to the most traumatic year of Hammond Roberson's life, and of the lives of many others in these valleys.

That is not to say that the rest of Roberson's life was lived in low key. The incident which brought him into contact with the Armytage family's affairs was nothing if it was not dramatic. It took place in the last weeks of 1787, within days of the first production of Mozart's *Marriage of Figaro*; and if some audiences sense that what creaks in this masterpiece is the unlikelihood of its famous plot, then all that is necessary to restore faith in the unlikelihood of real life is a consideration of the marriage of Hammond Roberson.

He had taken up his duties as curate in Yorkshire with the vigour with which he attacked all his involvements. The little woollen towns, built where streams joined rivers, as at Dewsbury, had less charm than the valleys themselves: the poor were more in evidence, so was their ignorance; and worse, Roberson was appalled by the Methodist activities he found there. All this gave him the first glimpse of a mission, to educate those who could afford no schooling and restore them to the proper established faith of the nation.

Within a short time of his arrival at Dewsbury he had organised what was claimed as the first Sunday School in the north of England[7] and soon had several hundred pupils attending make-shift schoolrooms at different places in the nearby district in houses and halls which he rented for a few pence. Children were not his only target. A substantial number of illiterate adults made up the classes. There they got the only education in their lives. A forerunner of Baden-Powell and some of his methods, Roberson also had the ability to marshal by his enthusiasm vast Sunday School processions and, with banners unfurled, he would lead great crowds singing from one village to the next.

It was inevitable that Roberson's evangelical activities should take him to the old parish of Birstall, four miles along an easy road from Dewsbury. Not only did the village have a well-established Anglican community, it was a centre for dissenters and the home of the by now famous family of Priestley. It was nearby at the village of Gildersome that Hammond Roberson fell passionately in love with John Priestley's grand-daughter, Phoebe Ashworth.

Roberson was by no means the only young man in search of the hand of the attractive Phoebe. One story had it that his grey mare was one in a row of three horses put up at Gildersome stables whilst their three dismounted owners converged simultaneously on Phoebe. But Phoebe's choice was clear and as far as her family was concerned, disastrous. Hammond Roberson, the 'clerical Cossack' as Charlotte Brontë called him, was firm favourite in the race. Phoebe's mother, Mary, was dying and bitterly opposed to the marriage of her daughter to Roberson He was, after all, as active in his dislike of dissenters as had been the Armytage who had evicted her grandfather. 'God knows,' wrote Phoebe, 'what agonies I passed through in the concluding days of my Mother's life; and I did love her, *better* than my own soul. I avoided promising, but I felt as if I never could join hands with my Hammond in defiance of the dying sentiments of my Mother.'[8]

It was shortly after Mary Ashworth's death that a successful Birmingham businessman, a Mr Wareham, was introduced to the family as yet another suitor for Phoebe. A psychologically somewhat less than stable young man according to Phoebe, he nevertheless saw his main chance. Mary Ashworth's will was yet to be read, but it was believed that Phoebe, one of three daughters, stood to benefit little from it. Wareham begged to speak to her and told her that should the will reveal that she had no fortune to offer a husband, and should Hammond Roberson therefore change his mind about her attractiveness, then he, Wareham, his business success and all, would be at her disposal.

Hammond Roberson was not so shallow as Wareham hoped. In the breathless style which went with her character, Phoebe told a friend of what happened, extracting every drop of romance from the experience.

> Mr R, when I told him of the will affair, said if I were left with but a shilling he should wish my hand. The recollection of my Mother's uniform opinion, her *dying* sentiments, the united view of all my Baptist friends ... I was for some weeks near insanity. Mr R rose on me in every visit; his exquisite tenderness ... [9]

Nevertheless, notwithstanding her Hammond's gentle concern, Phoebe allowed herself to be persuaded by the unstable, though rich, Mr Wareham to set off on a journey of somewhat carelessly unspecified destination. It turned out to be Birmingham. Soon a side-trip to Lichfield was arranged by one of Wareham's friends. En route, however, the conversation quite took Phoebe's breath away when it was revealed that,

> they intended that I should marry Mr Wareham that morning. I declared I would not. While he was gone to the clergyman, I wandered thro' a great Inn, and found at last an empty garret, in which I fastened myself, and would not open the door till they assured me all thoughts of that sort were at an end. Mr Wareham was told a month's residence only could make the marriage practicable. [10]

Safely back in Birmingham, Phoebe locked herself in her bedroom in the hope that Hammond would do something about her plight. Wareham, meanwhile, banged at her door, begging to be let in. When she made no response the message was shouted through the door that a note had been delivered for her. Phoebe had no doubts as to who had sent it. When she flung open the door, there was Wareham holding a letter addressed in Hammond's neat military hand. As Phoebe, overjoyed, read her lover's announcement that he was at an Inn but a few doors away, and offering to sweep her away in a chaise, Mr Wareham fell at her feet in a fit of convulsions. Worse, he began to pass in and out of consciousness. She took the opportunity to write a note to Hammond. She later described to a friend the depths of her emotions as she gazed at Wareham's body:

> Oh, what a day! He seemed frequently dying. I stole a moment to say to Mr Roberson, I wished him to have some conveyance ready in the evening, for I did wish to see Mr

Wareham better before I left him forever. Oh! what hours. His eyes fixt, and his hands convulsed, and his friends weeping over him, and I the undesigned cause![11]

Then during one of Mr Wareham's lucid moments Phoebe made her exit. 'We all thought it best that Mr Roberson and Mr Wareham ... should not meet,' she added as something of an understatement. At last she reached the inn where Hammond Roberson was waiting. And when she saw him, she swooned for, she said, 'my emotions were too powerful for my strength, and for some time I was insensible. Mr Roberson ... used every means to recover me, and a gentle pressure on my cheek from my Hammond ... first brought me to sensibility.'[12]

And here the man of action took command. Hammond swept his love into the chaise, whipping its horse through the night to remove her as far and as quickly as possible from the Midland danger zone. Phoebe had no doubts about either his commitment or his determination. He had with him, she noticed, pistols which he clearly would not have hesitated to use in her, or his own defence. They stopped for only an hour's rest at Chesterfield. Over breakfast Hammond bluntly put forward the view that the proper thing to do was to set about 'consummating the business directly'. She, meanwhile, had already made up her mind while locked in her Birmingham room that, 'if I ever saw Mr Roberson again I would be his for life immediately.' And so she was.

Back in Yorkshire, deliriously happy, she slept for eleven hours while Hammond, once more on his own grey mare, rode in and out of Dewsbury making all arrangements necessary for the business he had in mind. Next day Hammond married his Phoebe.

This was the man Charlotte Brontë portrayed as cold, unfeeling and lacking in much common humanity, whom Phoebe's relations swore had married her only for her money, and who local detractors whispered had treated her cruelly. All these assessments were based on hearsay. None seems to tally with the character of the man Phoebe married.

By the spring of the following year Roberson had resigned his curacy and moved with Phoebe to Squirrel Hall, a house overlooking the Spen valley near the untidy little town of Heckmondwike. There, with his own and with Phoebe's money – her mother's will had left her modestly well-endowed – he was able to indulge even better his passion for education by setting up a boys' school.

He had fallen in love with Phoebe and he had also fallen in love with this valley. He had not yet found his ideal place in it but, more important, through it he had already begun to crystallise his ambition.

Two miles north-west of Squirrel Hall, near the mill bridge where the Huddersfield to Leeds coach road crossed the stream, was the geographical centre of the district. Above it lay the main township of the valley, Liversedge; a mile or so to the east was Heckmondwike; and to the north-west, Cleckheaton. If Hammond Roberson stood at this point in the valley, on the one side he could see a substantial stone-built, symmetrical-fronted house standing above its own meadow, and facing it on the other side, a green wooded knoll. If he looked up beyond that little hill, over Liversedge, he could see the crest at Hartshead, behind which lay Kirklees. Charlotte Brontë would later describe this view in as colourful, if not as breathless, a fashion as Phoebe herself might have done: ' . . . the distant hills were dappled, the horizon was shaded and tinted like mother of pearl; silvery blues, soft purples, evanescent greens and rose-shades, all melting into fleeces of white cloud, pure as azury snow, as with a remote glimpse of heaven's foundations.'[13]

Roberson, the clerical Cossack, would perhaps have been embarrassed by such romanticism. Nevertheless, the natural charms of the place can only have attracted him. It was true that the woollen mills which had by now been built in the valley bottom were beginning to taint the little river. Soon manufactories – or factories as they came to be called – would add more seriously to the pollution. But there were plenty of trout still in its upper reaches, and woodcock, judcock, snipe and partridge were still being taken as game. But objectives other than those of sampling the simple valley excited Hammond Roberson more. He realised that from that spot, for several miles in any direction, there was no established church. Heckmondwike had its Independent chapels where the Priestleys worshipped, but no Anglican church; Liversedge was served by the tiny Norman stone building at Hartshead, two miles up bridle paths and almost out of the valley; and standing in an isolated field, more than a mile from the village, Cleckheaton had its White Chapel[14] – the young sporting curate who took charge of it shortly after Roberson's arrival in the valley, the Reverend Thomas Wilson, never lived at the place, seldom came near it and infinitely preferred his other parish in the Dales, from the steps of which he could announce the next meet of his personal pack of harriers to his congregation of foot-followers.

Roberson had no doubts about the disastrous consequences of this situation for the local population, now growing rapidly as the woollen trade grew. For all its physical attractions and its contented spirit of industry, it was far from having reached spiritual perfection: indeed, as far as he was concerned, the nonconformity which now gripped the lower classes of the valley was to be equated with godlessness. He wrote:

> The best disposed people were scattered to seek religious means for themselves and the ignorant, the young and the vicious had been left to the operation of native depravity and the influence of wicked counsellors. The due effects are but too visible. Our population is lamentably degraded. To the vice of ignorance and ferocity of heathenism is superadded the pestilential gloom of atheism.[15]

When at last the hillside stone house, Healds Hall, fell vacant, Roberson recognised it as the place from which he could launch his ambition. He would build churches for this atheistic valley; if necessary he would build them on the scale of the wool churches of his native Norfolk; he would fill them with the old and the ignorant as well as the young. What is more, he would make sure that those who flocked to his churches would be educated in the way he chose.

Healds Hall was perfectly placed. On the wooded knoll opposite he would build his first great church and be able to see it rise stone by stone. Above it, hidden in the trees, he would put a modern vicarage suitable for himself and for Phoebe and their family. Below the meadow in front of the house he would build a school on the edge of the stream for workers' children.

In 1795 he moved with Phoebe and his boys' school to Healds Hall.

*

Joseph Radcliffe's ambition was no less patent than that of Hammond Roberson. Whereas Roberson planned to move nearer to God, Radcliffe planned to move nearer to the King – feeble-minded as George III now was.

Kirklees Park overlooked not the Spen valley, over which the aloof and retiring Armytages were *de facto* if not titular lords of the manor, but the Colne valley where it joined the Calder. Three miles up the Colne was Huddersfield and three miles beyond that on the way to the Lancashire border was Milnsbridge.

There was no retiring aspect to the character of the man who dominated Milnsbridge.* Joseph Radcliffe's beautifully proportioned, small, neo-classical mansion *was* the village. Its symmetrical façade was surmounted by a splendidly carved, ornate apex in the centre of which was a circular window that stared down the valley like the eye of a benevolent Cyclops. Respectfully placed at some distance from its gardens, ornamental ponds and plantations were the few cottages that made up the village community on land mostly owned by Radcliffe. Spread in the hills, from Huddersfield below to the border above, were the farmsteads of small Masters and the cottages of the cloth workers. The whole was a scene of eighteenth-century industry as tranquilly settled as any English gentleman might wish. And Joseph Radcliffe most certainly looked the part of the fine old English gentleman, which is what his friends called him.[16] He was short-legged and portly, with a Punch-like face and a long nose set between white mutton chop whiskers. The result was a benign and grandfatherly appearance.

But all was not quite what it appeared on the surface. For a start Joseph had not been born a Radcliffe at all. As the locals well knew, until 1795 he had been Joe Pickford, born at Ashton-under-Lyne. It was in that year that his 85-year-old unmarried uncle, William Radcliffe, had died. William, a man of considerable property, elected to leave it and much else besides to the now middle-aged and portly son of his greatly loved sister, 'subject only to the condition that he should assume the name of Radcliffe in lieu of, or in addition to, his proper patronymic'.[17]

That is not to say that Joseph was not already a man of some substance. At Royton, near Manchester, where he lived, he had already been – as his contemporary, Jane Austen, described the process with approval – 'rising into gentility and property'. The tremendous windfall which fell into his lap was simply added fuel to the already burning ambition for that which alone could raise him to the level of the Armytages and their like: ennoblement.

---

* Milnsbridge, the home of Joseph Radcliffe, should not be confused with Millbridge, the village 6 miles north-east of Huddersfield near which was Hammond Roberson's house. Both place names emphasise the importance of water power and transport to the woollen economy of the district.

The problem he had to face, as with all ambitious men, was to create or discover the opportunity to realise that ambition.

So far he had done what he could in the public service by taking on magistracies at Royton and at Oldham. There he had put considerable fear of summary justice into the minds of the local inhabitants. 'I'll take thee before Pickfort', became a catch-phrase for a threat of punishment which stayed in Lancashire long after the stimulus for it had left the county.[18]

Pickford naturally aligned his loyalties with the class to which he aspired. With both the latest in line of the baronets, Sir George Armytage, and with Hammond Roberson he shared the same unswerving approval of both the Established Government and the Established Church and took every opportunity which presented itself to advertise that support.

Political reformers and nonconformists were first in the firing line when loyalty needed to be actively demonstrated. The wrecking of Dr Joseph Priestley's house by a Birmingham mob had the united support of the nation as represented by such men as Armytage, Roberson and Pickford. The act itself was carried out by a gang of workers.

When, in 1794, a similar attack was carried out on a public house where reformers were holding a meeting a few score yards from Pickford's home at Royton, the place was wrecked and the reformers savagely beaten up. The local parson stood outside the pub pointing out every reformer who tried to escape so that the mob could identify each victim more easily. One report of the affair said, 'the constables of the place had been called upon by the peaceably disposed inhabitants to act but they declined to interfere and the mob had their own way.'[19] Yet although Joseph Pickford was reported to be in his house during the whole of the violent incident, he took no step whatever as magistrate to prevent it and never appeared on the scene. When, in a short time, the cloth workers were to change their loyalties, Pickford's tolerance of working-class violence would change accordingly.

Before the end of the next year, on December 19th, he had obtained the Royal Sign Manual authorising him to change his name. It was as Joseph Radcliffe that he moved into Milnsbridge House. It was a most suitable base for him to further his ambitions.

Thirty years earlier he had lost his young wife. Now, married again, he could throw himself into the affairs of his newly adopted county with the confidence of a rich man getting richer. Between

1800 and 1810, with the canal companies eager to provide transport for both the woollen and cotton industries, he acquired interests in the Leeds and Liverpool, the Manchester, Ashton and Oldham, and the Rochdale canal companies. In those years he was able to put by very tidy sums both from land sales and from arbitration awards as a result of property cut and taken, when the Huddersfield canal was navigated through long stretches of the parts of the valley he owned.[20]

Radcliffe had every intention of carrying out his public duties in the West Riding of Yorkshire with all the zeal that had given him his reputation in Lancashire. Now appointed magistrate for the district which was his new sphere of influence, he lived by the letter of the law and intended to see that others did the same. Before long he was applying his summary justice to cases in which a lighter hand might have been equally effective. One cloth worker was hauled before him after what can only have been a heavy evening's drinking in a Huddersfield public house. The man, James Jubson, according to the evidence given by a trooper of the 18th Light Dragoons, had turned up at a late hour outside the entrance to the regimental barracks and shouted, 'them that were a friend of the King were no friends of his.' He then pushed his way past the sentry into the Guard House and 'damned the King and his Ministers as he returned from thence'.[21]

For this offence Radcliffe committed the politically disillusioned, but undoubtedly tipsy and undoubtedly unimportant Jubson to the cells of York Castle. He recommended to the Home Office that proceedings should be taken against the cloth worker because of the threat he presented to the state.[22]

Radcliffe intended to make his public presence well felt by the lower orders and well known to the higher orders of society, particularly if these last had a channel of communication to government. In this case his most obvious link, as the holder of an unspectacular north of England magistracy, was through the Lord Lieutenant of his county.

The West Riding was presided over by an extremely wealthy, conscientious and conspicuously soft-centred aristocrat. Earl Fitzwilliam was unusual among Lord Lieutenants in any case because he actually lived for a substantial part of the year at the place for which he was responsible to government. He had once again taken up residence at his great house, Wentworth Woodhouse, near the south Yorkshire border. Also, unlike most other Lords Lieutenant, he was far from being a high Tory. His liberal attitudes had already once led to his political downfall. He had been recalled as Viceroy of Ireland for the support he gave to the movement which wanted to allow Catholics access to political power. It was not to be the last time that his highly refined conscience had him fall from grace.

Fitzwilliam's conscience was his strength and his weakness. He wanted to be all things to all men. He wanted, for example, as a Whig, to give his loyal support to a Tory government at a time when he was unhappy about the effects of its policies on the workers of the West Riding.

Joseph Radcliffe saw this soft centre and was prepared to exploit it. Now one of the Lord Lieutenant's Justices of the Peace, he established a regular correspondence with Fitzwilliam. His letters left no doubt as to how effective a magistrate he was becoming. When in 1801 there were workers' riots against manufacturers in Lancashire there was no question of his remaining quietly and inactively behind the curtains of his house in Milnsbridge. Radcliffe was determined, he told Fitzwilliam, to put on a display: a really 'formidable appearance of military' to frighten off any Yorkshiremen who felt inclined to imitate the behaviour.

He personally rode out to check that the regular cavalry stationed at Halifax and the local volunteer militia regiment which Sir George Armytage commanded, was ready to support him if he decided to take action in an emergency.

But no emergency arose. He therefore made sure to emphasise to Lord Fitzwilliam that this part of the county was never more secure than as it was now – in his hands: 'I am happy to see the spirit shown by the Huddersfield and Halifax Volunteers, and I am confident no other force is wanted to keep the peace of this western part of the Riding. I think there are but few of the disaffected united Englishmen in this neighbourhood.'[23] His letter showed how little he knew of the undercurrents in the affairs of the people around him.

But with Sir George Armytage himself, Radcliffe signally failed to build the familiar and frequent communication of the kind he had begun with Fitzwilliam. Armytage had already shown his resentment at the newcomer's imperious ways. He had had a sharp note addressed to Radcliffe warning him against interfering in his militiamen's activities.[24]

However, Radcliffe could withstand a rebuff. He was settled in the peaceful, industrious Yorkshire valley, he owned much of it and he was virtually in legal and military command of it. All he now needed was the title which would be a proper reflection of his status in the community. Already he had established a sound dialogue with the Lord Lieutenant who, given the circumstances, had the power to make the wish come true.

3

The New Men

Both Hammond Roberson and Joseph Radcliffe were reaching their prime during the rise of one of the most phenomenal episodes in the history of Western civilisation. The subject of the Industrial Revolution arouses passions. It means different things to different people. There is not even consensus on the meaning either of the word Industrial or of Revolution.[1] The facts relevant to the events soon to grip the way of life of the valleys to which Roberson and Radcliffe had now moved, however, are inescapable. In a period lasting from just before the middle of the eighteenth century to just after the middle of the nineteenth, mechanical inventions – relatively simple pieces of technology – began to be applied in houses, workshops and then factories, and began to have unforeseen effects.

Previous civilisations could offer magnificent technological achievement for comparison, but until that period none had produced so much in so short a span of time as that which appeared in Britain. The twenty years beginning in 1750 is an example of just one short phase of this extraordinary fertile burst of creativity. In those two decades crucible steel was established as a commercial process, the Carron iron works was opened, Harrison's no. 4 chronometer was tested, Hargreaves invented his spinning-jenny, the first iron rails were cast at Coalbrookdale, Arkwright patented his spinning machine, Wedgwood established his pottery at Etruria, Ramsden invented the screw-cutting lathe, Wilkinson established his boring mill, Bramah invented his water closet, Crompton perfected his mule and Watt's steam engine came into use. In the same twenty years the Westminster Bridge and Smeaton's Eddystone Lighthouse were completed, the

Worsley–Manchester canal was opened and the first iron bridge was built at Coalbrookdale.

But this was not all. These were simply the grander achievements visible above the surface. Beneath it an unusual amount of vigorous activity on a smaller but most effective scale was taking place.

Many of those who lived through some part of this unusual period of invention realised full well that an unprecedented spirit was stirring at all levels in the nation. In 1757 Josiah Tucker was astonished by what he had seen on his travels in the workshops of the Midlands and the North. He wrote, 'In the metal industries of Birmingham and Sheffield, almost every Master Manufacturer hath a new invention of his own, and is daily improving on those of others.'[2]

The Industrial Revolution was not a chance event. By the end of the seventeenth century technology had given birth to its greatest single creation: modern science itself. Science – the ability to measure, to predict – had been the consequence of the invention of simple but accurate instruments: the ruler, dividers, compasses, the vernier scale, the telescope, the microscope, the clock. And science was to enter into an incestuous relationship with technology. It was to fertilise new techniques by the thousand of which James Watt's steam engine was only one.

It was not chance that Watt's revolutionary separate condenser followed hard on the heels of James Black's purely scientific discovery of the latent heat of steam – the energy stored in steam when boiling water turns to the gas. How much or how little Watt relied on this discovery is debatable. What is not debatable is that he knew of it and that he knew that there was a quantifiable relationship between the energy of steam and the power it could generate. The fact that Watt's engine would not be widely directly applied in industry for many decades is not important. It was this discovery, more so than any other single piece of technological invention, which spelled out unambiguously the potential of harnessed power.

Watt actually wrote it out for his customers in terms of money: in exact sums of pounds, shillings and pence. His 'new Method of Lessening the Consumption of Steam and Fuel in Fire Engines' was a technique for getting more work done by the same amount of coal. He and his partner, Matthew Boulton, showed their absolute confidence in their new product by writing an equation. On the one side was coal used and on the other money saved.

They launched themselves into the entrepreneurial spirit of the age by offering to take their fees as a percentage of this money which their machines saved each of their clients. By 1785 Watt and Boulton reckoned they had been cheated of £300,000 in premiums from Cornish mines alone where they estimated that owners had saved as much as £1 million and where some slippery customers had squeezed out of the precise terms of the contract.

Watt's steam engine was a primary source of power fuelled by coal. At first it was not a rotary engine and was simply used to pump water to a height where it could work water mills. However, once the increased possibilities for natural power had been seen, it did not in the least matter whether its source was coal, wood or water, any more than in the twentieth century the source was oil or the atom's nucleus. The potential was limitless.

The steam engine was a catalyst. It caused yet more inventions of power to pour out of England in a torrent and these, for a time, turned the whole world into Britain's market.

The spirit of change, however, had been slow to move through the traditional industries of the valleys of West Yorkshire, though by the time Hammond Roberson settled there some of its consequences were visible. At much the same time that he moved in to Healds Hall, William Peabody Cooke began to use as a factory a mill by the stream not much more than a quarter of a mile down the coach road from the Hall. Roberson and Phoebe could look down at the counting house window lit by a tallow candle at which Cooke father, then in later years Cooke son, would work late into the night.

The new industrialists who were moving into the valley chose to build their capital on one of the two classic processes of sound economics by which wealth has consistently been created by those looking for profit: the division of labour by product and the division of labour by process. William Cooke looked to the product. He decided to use his mill solely for the manufacture of carpets, a woollen product in which nobody in the valley had until then specialised. The looms he introduced to weave the carpets were from Brussels – an innovation to the district.

Because Cooke introduced a new product and created employment founded on no traditional practices whatever, his mill flourished – and the result is that Cooke himself has not much further part to play in this story. During the next few years the apprentices from the farmsteads and the poorly paid from the shops of the small wool Masters migrated to his factory floor. It continued

26

to produce its carpets and its profits into the 1960s when industrial competition from countries Cooke had never heard of over-whelmed it.

It was nothing much more than chance that made William Cartwright decide to use his capital to specialise not in a single product of the woollen industry, but in a single process. Had he not done so he might have ended his days as a wealthy, worthy and dull man – which Cooke unquestionably was. Instead, Cartwright was to become a figure at the centre of an unusual incident of history, romantic enough to be taken as one of the key characters for the novel which Charlotte Brontë hoped would be her greatest.

Cartwright moved into the Spen valley shortly after the turn of the nineteenth century. Charlotte Brontë probably met him on the day she saw Hammond Roberson. She told Mrs Gaskell that he was tall, dark-skinned, perhaps with foreign blood, and that he had gentlemanly habits.[3] To many of the local people he was a distant figure. The fact that he spoke French fluently inevitably must have made him an object of suspicion. It is certain that his accent was different from that of the people of the valley, but there is no evidence that he spoke other than standard Georgian English. Charlotte Brontë saw enough romance in him to have his fictional character fall in love in *Shirley* with the girl into whom she wrote so many of her own feminist qualities. His Yorkshire workers, however, saw him in a different light from the aspiring young authoress. What evidence there is suggests that he was respected, but not much liked by them.

In 1809 he rented a mill less than a mile upstream from William Cooke's factory at a place called Rawfolds on the edge of marsh land. From the hill at Healds Hall Roberson could just see the light in Cartwright's counting house burning late at night like that of Cooke.

Rawfolds was a pretty, well-wooded spot. The mill was powered by water from the Spen which was held in a dam run-ning along the full length of one side of the factory. Two white-painted cottages stood within a quarter of a mile of the mill. In one of these Cartwright had installed his young wife and family. Above them, scattered across the slopes of the valley were the farmsteads, each with its tenter displaying the cloth like a badge, the result of the previous week's industry. A few larger buildings here and there, both at the valley top and bottom, had begun to mark out where men such as Cartwright had begun to specialise in one of the techniques used to produce that cloth. The small Master, the new manufacturers and their workers continued to live in reasonable and prosperous harmony. One Master living nearby still described the conditions of work as providing 'a greater Happiness than any other Branch of Manufacture in the Kingdom'.[4]

The factory system, which both these young manufacturers adopted, was one by which one man controlled in an entirely new way the working lives of many men and women. The power of this system had not yet been fully appreciated. Nor had its revolutionary influence on the people on whom it depended. In the next few decades observers with violently opposed views would pronounce on what it was capable of doing for the human condition. Friedrich Engels, himself the son of a manufacturer, would write in *The Condition of the Working Class in England*: 'The slavery in which the bourgeoisie holds the proletariat chained, is nowhere more conspicuous than in the factory system. Here ends all freedom in law and in fact.'[5]

On the other hand, the historian of the worsted industry, John James, writing at almost the same time as Engels, would speak of:

> This grand instrument of labour – the factory system, nay not merely an instrument, but containing within itself powers for its own direction – the joint result of the genius, skill and perseverance of Arkwright, Watt, Cartwright and a host of others, who almost simultaneously sprung up to contribute, as by one magic influence, to its perfection, unlike some of the inutile creations of the moderns, comes home to the first necessities of life, and supplies in abundance, and at little cost, beautiful and durable materials of apparel for all the civilised nations of the earth.[6]

The one believed the system itself was inseparable from abuse by wicked capitalists. The other denied this. Engels, in sentences carrying the unmistakable smell of truth, could point to the poverty and misery into which children as well as men and women would be dragged by the system. He would use the degrading conditions of the woollen valleys as well as the cotton towns to provide some of his most shaming and politically powerful examples. James, with equal conviction, could point to the material benefits which increased productivity must inevitably bring to the workers themselves. To the incredulity of those who had only needed one glimpse of the interior of a factory to know that the system was a social evil, he could argue that there were vast numbers of people spending large portions of fulfilled lives in these buildings, taking pride in their work. Demonstrating inexplicable loyalty, generations of local workers would keep the machines of William Cooke and his descendants turning for 150 years.

In these woollen valleys the paradoxes of the system and its violent consequences were to show themselves in an unusually graphic fashion. But the factory system William Cartwright established at Rawfolds Mill in 1809 produced none of the degradation Engels was to see. Some, at least, of the people of the valley welcomed it as an alternative form of employment. Cartwright appeared to be doing little more than one of the small Masters higher up the valley had already begun to do: that is, specialise in cloth finishing. The fact that he was preparing to do it on a bigger scale than anybody else meant, not unnaturally, that some of the small Masters would begin to look over their shoulders. But many of Cartwright's workers not only approved of what he was doing, some would be willing to put their lives in line for his right to do it.

Like his small-scale competitors, Cartwright could not afford not to look over his shoulder. In the next valley, the Colne, William Horsfall was already finishing cloth on a bigger scale than Cartwright could begin to contemplate. Horsfall had taken over the management of the large Ottiwells Mill in Marsden from his father Abraham and from his uncle John. Like Cartwright, Horsfall lived right alongside the mill in Ottiwells House, a substantial residence suitable for a successful man. It overlooked the little town to which he owed his success.

Marsden was a busy place nestling then as confidently as it does today under the wing of the Pennines. Joseph Radcliffe, whose Milnsbridge House was only 4 miles down the valley, had land there and he owned the plot on which the Horsfalls had built their factory. The town had already attracted several of the new breed of vigorous industrialists such as the Horsfalls. Enoch and James Taylor were a pair of ambitious blacksmiths who had seen that the new inventions being turned into wooden machines for the woollen trade, could be made stronger, cheaper and quicker, and to more exact specifications, from cast iron. Enoch Taylor's great hammer, which he carried with him from his days in the blacksmith's shop, became famous as his and his brother's firm prospered. It symbolised the strength and the success of the work of their brothers' foundry. In honour of the elder it was called by the local people simply 'Enoch'.

The Taylors were powerful allies for William Horsfall. A bustling workshop next door manufacturing any kind of machines he could specify, was an advantage William Cartwright badly wanted. As things stood in 1809 he had to import most of his new machinery from neighbouring valleys. The parts were carried by pack-horse or cart over the rough moorland tracks, a hazardous journey at the best of times in these years when coach roads ran only between large towns and cities.

The booming market town to which both Cartwright and Horsfall had to ride every Tuesday over the rough roads in order to do business, was Huddersfield. In the old Cloth Hall there Defoe, just as he had at Halifax and Leeds, had watched goggle-eyed as manufacturers unrolled great lengths of finished cloth for the touch of traders from Europe as well as from every major city in Great Britain and Ireland. In not much more than a whisper, men such as Cartwright and Horsfall would make their bargains. Before the bell rang at thirty minutes after midday to signify the end of trading,[7] tens of thousands of pounds' worth of business would have been struck. It was there that the two men could see the precise nature of the competition from the small Masters as well as from each other.

The finished cloth was the coinage of the Woollen District. As the new specialists in the trade, Cartwright and Horsfall were key men whose movements in and out of the cubicles of the great circular building were watched with care by those who saw them as competitors.

But not only were their financial dealings minutely observed. These men were among the most receptive to the series of technological changes which had taken place in their industry. And workers as well as other manufacturers were carefully noting the innovatory manufacturing methods on which they were building their success.

4

A Man of the People

One other character – and that is probably as appropriate a word as any to describe him – now added himself to the unusual social mix of these valleys. Much the same age as Cartwright and Horsfall, he had alien interests and contrasting aspirations. Whatever motivation spurred him, it was based in a different culture from that of the two young manufacturers.

He is not much more than a comma in this paragraph of history and as punctuation he tends to confuse rather than enlighten the sense of the issues. But this is true of much of his Irish impact on life.

He was a man of the people; he had had intimate experience of the problems of the poor worker; he was a convert from Methodism to the Established Church who could sympathise with the conflict of the dissenter; and he was a scholar who had had to struggle for the Cambridge education designed to give him the abilities to counsel wisely the people he would be sent to serve. He was therefore uniquely qualified to take a decisive and involved role in a community needing help. He could have been – literally perhaps – a godsend to the people of the woollen valleys. No man, as it happened, could have turned out to be farther from fulfilling the expectations with which his upbringing seemed to have so providently provided him.

His name, in 1809, was Patrick Brontë, though it had been successively, indecisively, Pruty, Prunty, Brunty, Bronte, Brontê, Brontē, Brontè and Brontĕ. He had not yet lighted on the Brontë which his daughters' novels were to make permanent and famous.

He travelled to Dewsbury at the age of thirty-two to take up the curacy Hammond Roberson had left several years earlier. The vicar he was to serve under was the Reverend John Buckworth who, with his young wife, provided rooms in the vicarage in which Brontë could begin work in the wool town.

The couple would find that their tall, thin lodger with auburn hair and thick Ulster accent was a peculiar mixture. For a start he had a curiously high-flown romantic view of himself. He passed this view on to his daughters. In *Shirley*, which is set in these valleys, Charlotte reflected it when she described the Irish curate, Malone, as having:

> the high featured, North American Indian sort of visage which belongs to a certain class of the Irish gentry, and has a petrified and proud look, better suited to the owner of an estate of slaves, than to the landlord of a free peasantry.[1]

Physically this was an accurate description of her father by Charlotte. Socially it represented his dream of his origins rather than reality. He was born the son of a farm labourer, the eldest of ten, in a mud-floored, thatched cabin in County Down. It was as a child that, whilst working for a blacksmith, he had overheard his employer tell an old man that his young assistant, Patrick, was 'a gentleman by nature.'[2] He never forgot the incident nor the implication that his origins were fixed on a higher plane than those of ordinary men. He told this story, as he did many others, many times to his daughters. In these tales he not infrequently ranked as a noble and sometimes a heroic figure.

Although he was an odd character, there was no question of his intelligence. Seven years before reaching Dewsbury he had entered St John's College, Cambridge. With the help of scholarships and grants, some from Methodist sources and some from William Wilberforce's Church Missionary Society's Fund[3] he had taken a degree and been ordained in the Church of England. He had, en route, rubbed shoulders with the great, the rich and the famous. Lord Palmerston, whom he once met at Cambridge, was all of these. For that relationship he claimed a considerable degree of intimacy. Whether it was quite as intimate as the young Patrick maintained, however, was doubted by at least one of several young ladies he courted, Mary Burder – 'those great and affluent friends that you used to speak of', she later wrote in a stinging letter of rebuff.[4]

One of the stories Patrick Brontë told his daughter Charlotte and which she told Mrs Gaskell concerns an incident which occurred in Dewsbury not long after his arrival there. It is supposed to have taken place on the Sunday School Whitsuntide walk, the leadership of which Brontë inherited from Hammond Roberson. A drunk – a tall, well-built man, so the story goes – sprang out in front of the procession and regaled the banner-holding young ladies leading the group with a rich vocabulary of foul language. Patrick is then supposed to have stepped in front of his flock, to have grabbed the bully and flung him into the gutter before leading the procession on. In one telling of the tale not only is the drunkard large, he is a local boxer and cock fighter.[5]

The story begins to wilt a little, however, when an early biographer reveals the source of the story as an old man who, as 'a little lad', was at the back of the procession and, though he did not actually see the incident, heard tell of it. And it withers when yet another tale, almost identical in drama, and with Patrick still its hero, takes place in Drumballyroney ten years earlier.[6] It is not unreasonable to suspect that more than one tale involving Patrick Brontë originated in his own fertile imagination.

Mrs Gaskell, when she met him, typically saw him through a pair of clear and analytical eyes. Sitting in his bare room – it had nothing but a desk, two hanging shelves, two pipes and a spittoon – she was not swayed by his 'rather elaborate old fashioned compliments, but I was sadly afraid of him in my inmost soul: for I caught a glare of his stern eyes over his spectacles at Miss Brontë once or twice which made me know my man'.[7]

He was touchy, insecure, self-centred (that 'selfish old man' one of his daughter's friends called him in later years[8]) and even by his own admission, 'eccentrick'.

But as a young man Patrick Brontë's eccentricities were, certainly to many of the population he had now joined, not only acceptable, they were even lovable. Hammond Roberson, when they met some time after Brontë's arrival in Yorkshire, was amused by the tall Ulsterman's habit of carrying a shillelagh under his arm wherever he went, and he nicknamed him 'Old Staff'. In return for whatever attention Roberson paid him, Brontë faithfully returned the compliment. He was inordinately impressed by the dynamic Tory parson and began to mould some of his habits and attitudes on Roberson as he set about his clerical duties in the valley.

There is one incident involving Patrick Brontë which was to have a serious bearing on the ultimate fate of many of the working class of these Yorkshire valleys. There is no doubt about its authenticity; its main events are well documented. There is some doubt as to the sum of the influence Brontë had on its outcome, but this is irrelevant to the influence the affair had on his parishioners.

The story has a rollicking beginning. On August 2nd, 1810 – less than a year after Patrick Brontë had arrived in Dewsbury – his vicar, John Buckworth, was standing in the pulpit of the parish church. The daily service was proceeding quietly and normally, when suddenly the doors of the church were flung open. Through them came a horse. Unsteadily astride was its aggressively drunk owner, the local apothecary, Samuel Jackson, shouting at the top of his voice. It took the efforts of the vicar, churchwardens and a good part of the congregation to turn the horse and shoo it with its hollering rider back through the doors and into the street.

The misbehaving druggist was soon sent to cool his heels in the local gaol. But here the rich, bucolic overtones of the tale fade and tragedy sets in. Jackson was now visited by his pregnant young wife, Martha. Undoubtedly shocked as a result of seeing his shameful condition and hearing of his shaming behaviour, Martha, within hours, went into premature labour and died in childbirth. When the news was taken back to Samuel Jackson he too took sick. Shortly afterwards he died of what was described as 'a convulsive fit'. He was buried by Patrick Brontë on August 14th, not much more than a week after his wife.

Rumour began to spread in Dewsbury, however, that Jackson had poisoned himself and an exhumation order was sought and granted. The date of the disinterment of the body was fixed for September 18th, and a sizeable crowd of voyeurs gathered to see the coffin raised. Brontë took his right and proper place close to the grave when it was opened.

Examination of the body showed that the death of poor Samuel Jackson had not been by his own hand but by natural causes, probably brought on by the terrible short sequence of events following his escapade. It was returned to its grave and would quickly have been forgotten had it not been for a second incident which impinged on it.

Two days after the exhumation a weaver named William Nowell was interviewed at his home at Dawgreen, Dewsbury, by a corporal of the 30th Regiment then serving in the district. He accused Nowell of having been offered and having taken the King's Shilling from a private soldier of the Regiment, James Thackray, at the nearby Lee Fair on September 18th, and that he,

Nowell, was therefore now a deserter. Next day he was put under arrest.[9]

On September 25th, Nowell was arraigned before the Wakefield magistrate, Mr Dawson, who listened to Thackray's evidence against him. Dawson, however, refused to wait for witnesses to be collected for the defence. He convicted Nowell of desertion and committed him immediately to the infamous Wakefield House of Correction.

This case of summary justice caused a sensation in the small community. Several of its leaders, including John Buckworth his father-in-law, Mr Halliley and Patrick Brontë himself took up the case of Nowell. Brontë fired off letters in several directions. One went to the acquaintance of his Cambridge days, the young Lord Palmerston. The old friendship was not acknowledged by the Secretary at War, but the letter was. Halliley even managed to enrol the support of the county Members of Parliament, William Wilberforce and Lord Milton, Earl Fitzwilliam's son.

Repeatedly Wilberforce took the matter to the War Office and eventually Palmerston forced a rehearing of the case on the unrepentant magistrate. Dawson had no alternative but to reassemble witnesses in the affair and to submit it to new evidence for the defence. By this time Brontë and several other gentlemen had gathered no fewer than fifteen of Nowell's friends together. Each of them obligingly provided him with a firm and consistent alibi. The case collapsed. After having spent ten weeks in the House of Correction Nowell was made a free man and returned to his trade. James Thackray was subsequently found guilty of perjury and transported for seven years.

The news of the weaver's triumph over the local magistracy went to every part of the woollen valleys. His name and his fame spread as the *Leeds Mercury* gave over more than fifty column inches to its correspondent, 'Sydney' – a pen-name providing a thin disguise for Patrick Brontë. This letter revealed the part he had played in putting to rights this evident miscarriage of justice.[10] But equally what placed itself in the minds of the cloth workers who absorbed the newspaper's detailed retelling of the trial's nuances, was the power of the alibi.

Fifteen men had sworn to having seen Nowell standing in the crowd which had stood around the grave-diggers who had raised the coffin of Samuel Jackson at its exhumation. It had been lifted at the precise time that James Thackray claimed to have given William Nowell the King's Shilling at Lee Fair. Yet Brontë, whose self-publicity had made him a key figure in the case, could not himself testify to having seen Nowell that day. But this scarcely mattered. He had helped make a large number of people familiar with the case. Irrespective of whether Nowell was guilty or innocent – and there is even less chance today of knowing with certainty which was the case – they were to remember it for some months to come, as they were to remember the effect of the well-rehearsed and well-presented alibi.

There was one other incident of personal drama to involve Patrick Brontë before his departure from Dewsbury. In the part he plays in it he runs histrionically true to form.

Shortly after Hammond Roberson and Phoebe moved into Healds Hall, Roberson took charge of the nearest available church. It was the little stone-built Norman building at Hartshead next to Sir George Armytage's village of Clifton:

Hartshead-cum-Clifton,
Two cracked bells and a snipt 'un.

It took Roberson an hour to walk from his house in the bottom of the valley at Millbridge to his church, and not much less than that by horseback. Fortunately he was well enough off from the income from his boys' school and from Phoebe's inheritance to afford two curates to help him run the parish. But by 1803 he had decided to resign and to dedicate himself to the first of his great ambitions – to build the church in the valley near his home. But he had another reason for trying to centre his activities nearer Healds Hall. Phoebe was ill and gradually becoming an invalid.

In the few years since Roberson had left it, the Hartshead church, isolated on the edge of the moor from both its own small village and its own extensive parish, had had a dwindling congregation under a sickly vicar. Since Hartshead was a daughter church to that at Dewsbury, the responsibility for the continuation of the services there fell to the Dewsbury vicar, John Buckworth. He now delegated that responsibility to his curate, Patrick Brontë.

For several weeks early in 1811 Brontë had to make the difficult 5-mile journey on the back of a hired cob to read a brief service to an uncertain congregation whose only regular member was the young clerk, Joseph Tolson, who came with him from Dewsbury on a second hireling.

One Sunday when Brontë was due to conduct the Hartshead

morning and afternoon services, Buckworth had approached him to say that he intended to spend the evening with his wife's parents, the Hallileys. He asked Brontë, therefore, to take on the Dewsbury evening service in addition to his curate's duties at Hartshead.

It was on the lonely journey back from Hartshead Moor that the weather on the hills turned bad. Brontë and Tolson were caught in a thunderstorm and soon soaked to the skin. When he reached Dewsbury, Brontë rode to the Hallileys' house and, dripping at the door, spoke to its owner. He asked Mr Halliley if his son-in-law, John, considering the state Brontë was now in, would after all take the parish evening service. 'What!' said Halliley. 'Keep a dog and bark himself?'[11]

If the remark was made as a joke, the wet and cold Patrick Brontë was in no mood to appreciate it. He turned and left. Later he appeared at the church as he had agreed and conducted the first part of service as he normally would. When the time came for the sermon, he mounted to the highest stairs of the three-decker pulpit and announced, according to the young Tolson, who had followed him to the church, that 'it was not his intention to preach again after that evening, giving as his reason that he had been most grievously insulted.'[12]

Brontë then preached his sermon, left the pulpit and never returned to it. If there was now a minor crisis within the Established Church, providence provided the gap through which it could evaporate. Within days the sick vicar of Hartshead died. The sensible Buckworth grabbed the opportunity to put distance between passions and immediately appointed Brontë to the church.

At thirty-four Patrick Brontë had at last reached the living for which the years of study, training and service had prepared him. Spiritually, he was in an interesting position. In a vibrant community on the edge of troubled times he needed to restore faith to a scattered flock and to lead them together again. Geographically too he was advantageously placed. His church lay directly between the Colne and the Spen valleys. Any traffic seeking the shortest route from one place to the other would need to pass alongside where he worked and lived. He would be able to influence that traffic too if he chose.

5

The Workers

History has always been in the main a record of the upper classes, by the upper classes, for the upper classes. The chronic failure of the poor to put pen to paper because they did not know how to write, rather than because they had nothing to write about, has of course robbed historians for ever of a true record of how most people lived during most of history. It is only at this period – the beginning of the nineteenth century – that, for the first time, substantial documents appear signed by the hands of the working people who wrote them, rather than with the 'X' that testifies to somebody else's written version of events.

Even this story has to rely on many records at the bottom of which is a cross interpolated as a name by the hand of Joseph Radcliffe or some other magistrate. Nevertheless, there are sufficient pieces of paper ending in a signature – demonstrating the hard-won skill of a working man – to make it possible to put more than a skeleton structure – sometimes the feel of flesh and blood – to a name. Some of the men who worked in the finishing shops of the West Riding were among the first of whom this can be said. Finishing is the process by which a piece of woollen cloth is given its smooth surface. When done by hand, the final part of this process requires the use of a huge pair of shears and is known as cropping. The pages which a cropper, George Mellor, wrote and signed a few days before his violent death tell us a great deal more about him than most of the many thousands of words written by others to describe his activities during the last months of his life.

Mellor was twenty-three years old at the time, good-looking with close curled auburn hair and with the imposing build necessary to make the most of his craft skill. Like all croppers his right wrist carried a mark: a permanent hoof of skin caused by the to-and-fro motion of the *nog* or wooden handle of the shears. The stigmata made it possible instantly to recognise the work he and all other croppers did.

But there was a great deal to distinguish Mellor from the other tough young men he worked alongside. Apart from the fact that he could write well, he had travelled. He had even anticipated the journey of the revolutionaries of the next century by having been to Russia, probably as a young seaman. Many croppers in both the West Country and the North had served in either the army or navy before returning to the wool trade. Mellor was also extrovert and articulate; but what gave him particular power in the establishment in which he worked was the special relationship he had with its owner.

John Wood's finishing shop was at Longroyd Bridge, a mile down the Colne valley from Joseph Radcliffe's Milnsbridge House and on the very edge of Huddersfield. It was a useful site for the trade. William Horsfall and every other merchant further up the valley, on their way to the Tuesday cloth market, had to ride across the bridge which led to the town. Near the bridge, on the edge of the Colne, several small Masters, including John Wood, had set up shops specialising in finishing. Wood's trade had prospered and he now had two or three small adjoining shops, each one housing three or four croppers.

George Mellor was on far more familiar terms with his employer's attitudes, his business dealings, his profits, his relations with other Masters and his relations with the shop floor for the reason that his widowed mother, Mathilda, was remarried to John Wood. Mellor himself, far from reacting against his father's replacement, got on well with Wood and continued to live in the household along with other young croppers and apprentices. The respect which other workmen showed him was partly shaped, therefore, by the knowledge that he was the boss's stepson. Notwithstanding, all subsequent evidence showed that he was a natural and exceptional leader to whom older men deferred. What is lacking in evidence is how much or how little Mellor allowed himself to be manipulated by Wood to act on his behalf.

The character of Wood, as some of those who were involved with the events of that year found, remains hidden in shadows. Perhaps as an act of self-preservation, he gave as little information to his contemporaries as he did to history. What is certain is that he would observe the same customs and hold the same values as his workmen.

These small Masters were remembered as

> men who doffed their caps to no-one, and recognised no right in either squire or parson to question, or meddle with them. ... Their brusqueness and plain speaking might at times be offensive. ... If [he] rose in the world high enough to employ a few of his neighbours, he did not therefore cease to labour with his own hands but worked as hard or perhaps harder than anyone he employed. In speech and in dress he claimed no superiority.[1]

Years later, Mrs Gaskell took a careful note of the kind of individuals who lived in the area when she recaptured the characters and the atmosphere in the houses and woollen establishments that surrounded the young Charlotte Brontë's home. It is likely than John and Mathilda Wood would have matched her description.

> Such dare-devil people, – men especially, – and women so stony and cruel in some of their feelings and so passionately fond in others. They are a queer people up there. Small landed proprietors – dwelling on one spot since Queen Elizabeth, – and lately adding marvellously to their incomes by using the water power of the becks in the woollen manufacture which had sprung up during the last 50 years:– uneducated – unrestrained by public opinion – for their equals in position are as bad as themselves and the poor, besides being densely ignorant are all dependent on their employers.[2]

Mrs Gaskell adds as the next sentence, 'Miss Brontë does not what we should call "visit" with any of them.' Nevertheless, this gap in her experience did not deter Charlotte Brontë from writing in detail about these small employers, the croppers, their improvident activities, their unreal expectations and, as she saw it, their brutal politics.

Wood, for all that he was close to his stepson, gave away no favours as far as living and working conditions were concerned. George Mellor had to follow the young croppers' custom of sharing beds. His sleeping companion, William Hall, came from Liversedge and knew William Cartwright's mill well. In another bed in the same room an apprentice, Thomas Smith, slept. Other croppers lived nearby with their families. Benjamin Walker was one. He was nicknamed Ben O'Buck's[3] because his father had been a well-known dandy in the district. Now he lived alone with the mother who doted on him. One local story which was passed down the years was that Walker was in love with a girl named Mary Bamforth, who planned to marry George Mellor.[4] Whether this was true or not, there was no love lost between Walker and Mellor: 'our Master's wife's son,' as Walker called him.[5]

Mellor's bosom companion did not work at John Wood's, but at an adjoining finishing shop owned by a Mr Fisher. Nevertheless this cropper, William Thorpe, spent much of his spare time in and around the Wood household. He was good-looking, like Mellor, and bigger and taller. 'Lusty' was the description of him given by George Mellor's cousin Martha.[6] Together Thorpe and Mellor made a forceful, intelligent and dominant pair.

But it was not simply physique and an above-average mental skill which put Mellor, and along with him young men like Thorpe, in the dominant role which they had achieved in the valley. What secured this was the state of the technological development of woollen cloth weaving and the part they played – or failed to play – in it.

The history of this technology is a paradigm for many another industry. At each stage of its development the progressive decrease in the number of craftsmen required to produce the same volume of product can be both easily seen and quantified. When cloth production was entirely a hand craft, a skilled weaver could weave in a day as much yarn as twenty spinners could spin by hand in a day. It was inevitable, therefore, that the earliest machines invented for the woollen trade should have been in spinning. The foot treadle was an enormous breakthrough in the mechanisation process which now made it possible for only five spinners to supply one weaver.

The fully mechanised spinning machine powered first by horses, then by water and eventually by steam, pushed the process to extremes, increasing productivity well beyond levels necessary to supply the hand weaver. In doing so it created a new pattern of social behaviour: the factory system.

With this kind of invention as its example, the weaving process kept pace. It too was influenced by another seminal invention, the flying shuttle. This ran on wheels carrying the weft back and forth between the warp and so eliminated the need for an apprentice, whose job had been to retrieve the shuttle. It instantly doubled the output per man. But still it was only one step on the road to full mechanisation. The most notable single contribution came from Edmund Cartwright, a Leicestershire clergyman brought up in the woollen district and educated at Wakefield Grammar School. In spite of the fact that he had spent all his formative years in a place where some of the best worsted cloth in the world was manufactured, running true to the form of his English class origins, he was entirely ignorant of the techniques used to make it.

On holiday in Derbyshire in 1784, he listened to some Manchester cotton manufacturers arguing over the problems now caused by over-production in the spinning trade. A parson and a poet and with a poor mechanical sense, he now set about thinking how weaving could keep pace with the output of spun yarn.

He had heard that a chess playing machine had been recently on show in London. He therefore argued that the weaving process, which involved only three basic movements, should be relatively easily automated. Perfecting the invention bankrupted him. Nevertheless, there were many examples of his weaving machine operating in the north of England by the first decade of the new century. In 1809 Cartwright was voted £10,000 compensation by a House of Commons made uncharacteristically perceptive to technology's consequences by the climate of invention now sweeping the nation.

Worsted, which is made from long fibres which lock closely together, has no gaps in the cloth at the completion of the weaving stage. Woollen cloth, produced from shorter fibres, no matter whether it is produced by one of the improved versions of Cartwright's loom, or woven by hand, in its unfinished state has an uneven texture with gaps needing to be filled. The actual process of 'fulling' the cloth was done by soaking it in water to which Fuller's Earth powder had been added, and then gently pounding it. Until the Middle Ages this was done by bare human feet walking on the wet cloth. The addition of a wooden hammer to the cam of a rotating shaft was a relatively simple technological application of the water wheel. It accounted for the siting of thousands of woollen mills, such as that of William Cartwright at Rawfolds, on the banks of dammed streams such as the Spen.

The next step was to return the cloth to its original shape. This was done by stretching it across the tenterhooks of wooden frames set up in the open air.

The production of cloth to this stage had, until the middle of the seventeenth century, been the basis of Britain's great export trade in woollen cloth. The final finishing process had become a speciality in a number of European cities such as Leyden and Sedan, but eventually English manufacturers got hold of both the process and the workers with the necessary skills – which were probably greater than in any other single speciality of the trade.

Finishing, besides giving the cloth its smooth surface, creates its individual final texture. It was done by stretching the cloth, then brushing it with teasels – wire brushes which replaced the prickly plant originally used in the trade. This raised a 'nap' of wool on the surface of the cloth which was then thoroughly damped with water. It was now brought to a smooth finish by the cropper and his enormous pair of metal shears. A really fine piece of cloth would be tentered again to dry it and given three more close croppings by a skilled craftsman.[7] The technological improvements to this process were the strings on which not just the livelihoods, but the very lives of William Cartwright and William Horsfall would eventually dangle.

The shears which for centuries had been used for cloth cropping were of the simplest design: a pair of metal blades were squeezed together for cutting and when released were returned by the spring of the metal which joined them, to their original position in the hands. As skills with the shears improved, so did the size and weight of the tool. Bigger and heavier blades gave a smoother finish. Some weighed more than 50lb so that any man who in the first place was strong enough to manipulate the blades, would eventually develop extraordinarily large arm muscles and tendons of the hand and wrist – so much so that some fascinated doctors carried out autopsies of croppers' bodies.[8] Some apprentices who had worked alongside the croppers had been known to collapse, their hands running with blood, after only a few hours of the work.

A simple enough device introduced into the seventeenth-century English woollen trade gave the cropper a much less brutal technique. It also made it possible for him to work with a much smoother, quicker rhythm and so improve substantially the quality of his work. All it consisted of was a handle fixed to the upper blade to which was attached a cord. This helped him put the blade under traction before letting it spring back to its original

43

position. When they were introduced to Holland the new shears were violently opposed by the Guilds. Their members' jobs were under threat not simply from a reduction of the available work because of the speed at which the new tools could operate, but because they opened the trade to less burly operatives.

In England the introduction of the new shears had an easier passage. By the end of the eighteenth century they were universally used in all woollen finishing shops by croppers who were the cream of the industry – big men who needed to take a pride in their work. George Mellor, at twenty-three at the height of his physical skills, was well able to handle a piece of equipment weighing up to half a hundredweight. After a long apprenticeship and two years of experience in one of the most prominent finishing shops in the district, he was in – and well knew it to be the case – the pivotal position of the industry. It was his abilities, and those of the other young men alongside him, which could make or mar the finished product.

But the two basic processes of finishing – raising the nap by teasels and cropping the cloth by shears – were, in the fervent atmosphere of invention of the nineteenth century, too simple not to be mechanised.

A teaseling machine had in fact already been sketched out by Leonardo da Vinci in one of his notebooks. It simply required a wheel to rotate two cylinders fitted with teasels and between which the cloth passed. It was ideally suited to be worked by either a water wheel or a steam engine. It was also ideally suited for observation of the social and economic effects of machine technology – the gig-mill was the name preferred for it by Karl Marx. What previously took one man eighty-eight hours – a standard working week – to perform, raising the nap on a piece of cloth by hand, could now be done by a man and a boy in twelve hours.[9]

Also hidden in Leonardo's sketches was a machine for cropping cloth. By 1787 a device not unlike da Vinci's had been invented and was in use in England. By the beginning of the nineteenth century workshops all over Europe, of which Enoch and James Taylor's at Marsden was one, were able to produce cropping machines. In the Taylors' case they were machines which could be powered by water wheel such as the one at William Cartwright's Rawfolds mill.

The Taylors simply attached several pairs of croppers' shears on to a frame across which was stretched a roll of cloth. As a rotating cylinder took up the cloth and moved it under one fixed blade of the shears, the other blade was automatically opened and closed by a cam attached to a shaft power-driven by a water wheel. Nothing could be simpler, and so long had all the constituent parts of the technology been known that the surprise is that it had not been introduced earlier. One of these new machines could now crop in eighteen hours what a skilled cropper using hand shears took eighty-eight hours to do.[10]

And so, long before the end of the eighteenth century, the main technological problems preventing the mechanisation of every one of the main processes of woollen cloth manufacture had been overcome. Yet, so deeply entrenched were conservative attitudes to life and work there, that not one had been successfully introduced into the Colne and Spen valleys. Spinning remained firmly a home occupation done by the cheap hand labour of women, in spite of the fact that it took five of them to supply one weaver; weaving itself, which in its mechanised form could easily keep pace with mechanised spinning, was to remain a handloom operation, even in factories, for several decades to come. And machines for both the finishing processes which could increase up to sevenfold the productivity of one man stayed where they had first been nervously tried: outside the woollen valleys.

When, in 1809, William Cartwright took the lease on his factory at Rawfolds and first considered whether he should buy from the Taylors and import their shearing frame into his valley – so introducing mechanisation to it – he was well aware that any such move would face opposition. What was uncertain was the form that opposition would take, and how well organised it might be. The recent experience of some factory owners with establishments only a few miles from his was enough to cause any ambitious young manufacturer to be wary of the croppers.

6

The Power of the Worker

The potential power of local workers' organisations had first been demonstrated less than ten years earlier. One morning in late September 1802, Benjamin Gott, the Leeds manufacturer, had appeared in a shaken state in front of the government's representative in the county, the Lord Lieutenant, Lord Fitzwilliam. Gott was the biggest single factory owner for many miles. He had taken his new modern factory system much further than any Yorkshire mill owner. He could now employ under one roof eighty croppers, along with ten times that number of workers to prepare the cloth for them.

That day, he told Fitzwilliam,[1] every one of his croppers had handed in his notice. Not only had they said they would not work for him, they had spelled out precisely how far they intended to stretch their power. They had made it clear they would not allow any other croppers to work for him, would not allow him to set up business anywhere else, and would prevent any other manufacturer taking on the work on his behalf. Gott had little doubt of their ability to carry out the threat.

The dispute was the result of his having taken on two apprentice croppers who were above the age permitted by an Elizabethan statute: fourteen years. This meant they would not complete their apprenticeships until well beyond their twenty-first birthdays, and that Gott would then be using a cheap source of labour.

Eighty croppers had united to bring to a halt a factory employing 1,000 people simply on a question of principle. Fitzwilliam was staggered. 'Was this measure,' he asked, 'the consequence of harsh treatment or ill usage – was it for the purpose of extorting increase of wages?' And to his bewilderment he had to come to the conclusion that it was 'for no such causes'.[2]

Gott might have been willing to try to break the strike if other manufacturers had supported him but, as both he and Fitzwilliam knew, besides being big, tough men, the croppers had other highly significant advantages on their side. As Fitzwilliam told the Home Office when he reported the affair:

> They are the tyrants of the country; their power and influence has grown out of the high wages, which enable them to make deposits that puts them beyond all fear of inconvenience from misconduct.[3]

By the turn of the year they were victorious: Gott backed down. He got rid of his over-age apprentices, 1,000 people returned to work and he returned to the business of selling his finished cloth. 'The Masters have yielded, till they have lost all authority: the journeymen are the Masters,' said Fitzwilliam.[4]

There was no doubt in the Lord Lieutenant's mind what the correct course of action by employers should be under these circumstances. They should, he told the Home Secretary, replace the croppers with machinery. Gig-mills and cropping machines were available and would instantly cut the power base from beneath the croppers' feet. But no manufacturer moved to take this bold step and Fitzwilliam knew well enough why this was so. People in the district were scared of the likely consequences. Only a few weeks earlier he had had an uncomfortable communication from the Mayor of Leeds, William Cookson.[5] A wool merchant himself, and ever ready to tremble at the possibility of violence within his town's boundary, Cookson had become so frightened by the news of machine-wrecking in the west of England, that he had done the rounds of local manufacturers to plead with them not to set up either gig-mills or shearing machines in their factories.

The peaceful victory of the eighty croppers employed by Benjamin Gott acting as a Combination was until that time probably one of the most smoothly successful actions ever taken by a combination or union of workers in one trade. It came about in spite of the fact that the organisation that made it possible was proscribed by law. The Combination Acts of 1799 and 1800 had been written to prevent the associations of workmen precisely of the kind formed by the Leeds croppers; yet they were so difficult to enforce that the croppers had made no attempt to hide their activities. On the contrary, they had advertised them well. Gott had closely questioned each of the eighty croppers in the presence of two witnesses and discovered that some had been forced to join the Combination in order to secure a closed shop. Nevertheless, not one was prepared to repudiate his membership. Gott maintained, and it might well be so, that this was from fear of retribution by the other seventy-nine.[6] There had already been examples of blacklegs having been dragged through the streets by their hair and of their families being ostracised or beaten up.

The effects of the Combination Laws had been to drive other workers who wanted to take what ought to have been perfectly proper means to safeguard their jobs and wages by negotiations, into forming the alternatives allowed by law: Friendly Societies and Sick Clubs. Some of these had taken to meeting by night in unlikely places. For local middle- and upper-class residents these groups on the moors, in fields and in pubs, inevitably presented a sinister threat because they wafted afresh over the countryside the frightening odour of the French Revolution and its excesses of only a few years earlier.

With surges of activity, periods of quiescence, occasional strikes and sporadic violence, the activities of the cloth workers and particularly the croppers in favour of their rights under the law as they interpreted it, had continued for several years. The agitation increased when manufacturers succeeded in introducing a Parliamentary Bill to suspend a number of statutes which were favourable to the workers. So threatening was the situation becoming that by 1806 the government decided to establish a Committee on the Woollen Trade. One Halifax cropper, John Tate, who was clearly most articulate and intelligent, told the Committee that since 1803 Yorkshire croppers and weavers had raised and spent more than £10,000 in legal fees to put the case for the preservation of the statutes to Parliament.[7] The sum translated into modern values is enormous. And the Committee, rather than seeing this as the price of commitment of men who believed themselves to be in the right, interpreted the cash spent as a manifestation of wealth of a group with worrying potential political power. Its fears of a Combination of croppers was not even veiled in what it had to tell the House of Commons: 'Your Committee need scarcely remark that such Institutions are, in their ultimate tendencies, still more alarming in a political, than in a commercial view . . .'[8] But Parliament was becoming increasingly preoccupied during this period not with internal threats from the north of England rather with external pressures from across the Channel. Napoleon, whose jibe of 'a nation of shop-keepers' accurately described the country's source of wealth and therefore strength, had now set about undermining the source. One of several decrees he introduced effectively barred from France any vessel, no matter what its country of origin, which had touched a British port.

Parliament's response, beginning in 1807, was the Orders in Council. These twenty-four Orders were introduced initially under a Whig, but then under a Tory government by a Chancellor, Spencer Perceval, who was saved from notoriety only by the fact that he was mercifully unknown by the people of the nation he eventually was to lead. Characterless and retiring to the point of disappearance, Perceval allowed Orders to be framed which closed off not only neutral European ports to British trade, but eventually began to threaten the ports of what was already on the way to becoming one of the biggest markets in the world, America. As Order followed Order, Britain's vast export trade began to dwindle. In reprisal the Washington government had introduced its Non-Intercourse Act.

Both governments' actions were exceptionally successful. And the consequences for both Britain and America were catastrophic. British exports to the United States which, in 1810, had been £11,217,685, crashed in 1811 to £1,874,917.[9] The disastrous results for the woollen manufacture of Yorkshire and the cotton trade of Lancashire, both of which were heavily dependent on the United States, would be felt within weeks of the American market's final closure when it came in February 1811.

The effect on mill owners was rapid. Here was yet another reason why William Cartwright hesitated to invest in mechanisation. In a period of only a few weeks the vision he had had of a bright future had evaporated. Rolls of finished cloth were now being piled in his warehouse at a rate far higher than he was able to shift each Tuesday at Huddersfield Cloth Hall. He laid off as many croppers as he needed to steady the business, sold what he could at as low a price as he dared, and sat tight in the hopes that better times would quickly come. They did not. As week followed week and as month followed month it became clear that the industry was in crisis.

Cartwright was far from being alone. By the year's end there was to be scarcely a manufacturer in the whole of the West Riding who was not affected. In the Leeds, Bradford, Wakefield,

Huddersfield and Halifax districts, in the middle of which sat Cartwright's mill, pieces of cloth to the value of £1,000,000 would soon be lying in bulging warehouses with no foreseeable chance of being moved.[10] In the months to come, from a total of 3,200, 1,330 West Riding manufacturers would be forced out of business.

7

A Question of Technology

These troubles and excitements on a national stage with the croppers briefly at its centre had begun just as George Mellor had become an apprentice in John Wood's shop at Longroyd Bridge. Through the years in which he had turned from a boy to a young man he had listened to the talk of journeymen croppers he worked alongside, had followed them to their secret meetings in lonely fields in the Colne valley and in the public houses of the wool villages nearby. He had listened to their stories of how they had travelled to Wiltshire as delegates to meetings of croppers – shearmen these Westcountrymen called themselves – who shared their hopes and fears, and visits to London to appear before great parliamentary committees. He had heard how it had been possible for croppers to organise themselves with such skill that they could gather from all over the country thousands of pounds and use it to buy the time of London lawyers to support their cause.

But there was a great deal else to listen to: talk that stretched beyond the circumscribed world of the cropper which Mellor knew well. The last few decades had been as exciting and turbulent as any in history and although none of the political violence had engulfed Britain, villages of northern England had not been left untouched by events. The American War of Independence, the French Revolution and now Britain's war with France had each of them led to great swings in the cycle of the woollen trade. New nations gave rise to new markets and profits from them rolled into the Cloth Halls of Huddersfield and Halifax. The same rewarding results came as soldiers went off to war. They carried on their backs both uniforms and blankets woven in the West Riding. Then, as battle lines closed ports and communications, so

51

too the Orders in Council closed off the high-volume export trade in finished woollen cloth.

But equally the area had not been left untouched by the momentous changes in the political aspirations of the people who had directly experienced these events – of American revolutionaries who spoke a political language closer to that of the workers than that of the cloth Masters. And the debating chambers of the district where these happenings were discussed – the only covered and tolerably comfortable surroundings outside their cottages and workshops – were the workers' alehouses of the woollen valleys.

Two among many were well known to Mellor. It is highly likely that both were used as meeting places for the Central Committee of cloth workers. The Shears Inn in the Spen valley, overlooking William Cartwright's mill, was, as its name suggests, a meeting place almost exclusively used by croppers. A large room on the first floor above the bar of this old house was set aside for any formal gatherings. Of necessity, as a result of the Combination Acts, these meetings were cautiously, if not secretly, organised.

The other was the St Crispin Inn in the centre of Halifax.[1] Mostly used by shoe-makers (St Crispin was their patron saint) it had a more varied clientele than the Shears. Its most venerable customer was an old hatter called John Baines. White-haired and a little deaf, Baines nevertheless held the Socratic centre whenever he was present. Mellor, when he made the journey with other croppers to Halifax and the Crispin, was known to sit at Baines's feet.

Here in this wider group the wider issues were discussed – the precise issues Parliament feared and which had inspired the Combination Acts. Baines was a 'Tom Painer', familiar with the influence Paine had had on the American Constitution, and was well read in *The Rights of Man*, its defence of the French Revolution and its unrestrained admiration of republicanism. A cheap serialised edition of the work was now having an astonishing circulation. All that Paine stood for, Baines let it be known, he too stood for.

It was precisely the opposite of what the Joseph Radcliffes and the Hammond Robersons represented, united as they were by 'Church and King'. Baines, who was self-educated, intelligent, impressive and tolerant, formed his secret republican club at the Crispin; the younger Mellor, equally intelligent, equally impressive and far less tolerant, came under its influence. There was never any question other than that its dealings needed to be well hidden from the eyes of zealous magistrates such as Radcliffe.

These were heady days for a young working man in a traditional, secure, well-paid job in a nation and in an industry where few jobs were equally secure or well-paid. The melting pot in which he and his young cropper friends were swimming put him – an unusually well-educated worker – into contact with a stimulating flow of ideas: republicanism, dissent, trade unionism, pamphlets, petitions, revolution, the law, parliamentary action. The croppers' place in this pool can only have seemed unusually influential, even powerful, to an apprentice observing the activities of older men.

Then suddenly, the security which both he and they shared had crashed. In 1809, the year in which George Mellor's apprenticeship came to an end, the government repealed all the protective legislation covering apprenticeships, gig-mills and the numbers of looms. Everything that seemed to guarantee the strength of the cropping trade – an industry secured against mechanisation by a platform in law – was now swept away.

Even as things stood, for several years machines of several kinds had appeared in some nearby towns. More Masters, particularly those mill owners who had a stout enough heart for the business had smuggled them into the workplace. Benjamin Gott had openly introduced a few gig-mills into his factory and seen the windows of his house smashed for his trouble. But so long as trade was good and there was plenty of work for the croppers, persistence paid off. During the next few years shearing frames as well as gig-mills were to begin to appear at an astonishing rate. This rise in mechanisation could only have been accommodated without severe repercussions in years of expanding trade. And so these years had been. But with one self-inflicted wound, the British government changed all that with its Orders in Council. The crippling of the export trade had left the manufacturing trades not only not expanding, but now rapidly contracting.

There was no way in which croppers could influence the bold but disastrous strokes of foreign policy dreamed up in Westminster. But past experience made them believe that it was possible to influence the introduction of new technology. By 1811, although several hundred shearing frames had crept into use in cropping sheds, not all parts of the woollen district had succumbed. Such was the fear of violence of the small Masters, that few, if any, of the new machines had appeared in the villages at the heart of the cropping district, the Spen valley.

53

Fear too had kept the machines out of most Colne valley villages. However, it was widely known that at Marsden, Enoch and James Taylor were making a success of their frame-casting foundry and were supplying shearing machines to some of the less timid factory owners. That year, their neighbour William Horsfall had already equipped his father's factory, Ottiwells, on the Colne river banks, with frames from the Taylors. Other manufacturers and small Masters in the same valley cautiously followed suit. It was now rumoured among the croppers that William Cartwright too intended to take the new machines into his factory.

Cartwright, however much he lacked an understanding of the men who worked for him, was an intelligent, well-travelled and well-read man. He was more than passingly familiar with opposition over many years to the attempts to install mechanised processes – particularly the processes to speed up the work he had now decided his factory would specialise in. The strong resistance of the Dutch Guilds to the improved hand-shears had been overcome and was part of history. But opposition to power-driven machines was not only a worrying sign of the times, it was becoming an increasingly bloody affair. He knew well of the details of attacks on machinery which had earlier taken place in Wiltshire. A great deal of national and local newspaper publicity had been given to the violence at Heytesbury when the first gig-mills had been installed there. And he knew, probably from the factory owner himself, of the attacks on Benjamin Gott's home when he had tried to introduce the same machines to his workshop floor eight miles away at Leeds.

England was not the only country where finishing machines had produced the same disturbing reactions. When on the steps of Sedan city hall, Napoleon had raised his hat to the cheers of a wildly adulatory crowd, the mob had screamed, 'Long live the First Consul! Down with the machines!'[2] The machines the citizenry wanted destroyed were those intended for cloth finishing.

Each of these responses was an attempt to suppress a useful technique: in effect to reverse the direction of technological advance by elimination of the process from common practice and even from communal memory. Whether this was possible was never in question by those who proposed it. It was, nevertheless, a question of the utmost importance. Many historic acts have been, and will continue to be, performed in the presumption of the knowledge of its answer.

A Question of Technology

William Cartwright was confident that he could rely on the permanence of technology. The equation it would balance was simple. It would reduce the number of croppers he needed to employ and increase his output. He could therefore sell his product cheap and so lift himself out of the recession. He now began to consider with some care whether or not this was the moment to install the new power-driven shearing frames in his mill. If he did so, he would be required to show great resolve and even bravery. Charlotte Brontë, when she portrayed Cartwright in her novel, invented many qualities that were never his and avoided some that were undesirable for her romantic purposes; these two characteristics, however, she caught well. At some time in early 1811 he made contact with Enoch and James Taylor at Marsden and placed his order for his first cast-iron machines.

8

1811

For those who believed in evil portents the arrival that year of the great comet over the north of England correctly foretold the bad to come. Widely acknowledged to predict pestilence, poverty and famine, this specimen of the heavenly body was not only brightly visible, some claimed that its long tail, said to be 20 to 30 million miles long,[1] was in the shape of a cross, or even a dagger. It hung threateningly over an insecure nation.

The torrential rains which had soaked Patrick Brontë as he travelled across the heights of Hartshead had persisted in some parts of the country throughout the whole summer. By its end, the harvest in much of the country had failed. The scale of the hardship that followed would have been less had it not been that 1810's crop had also been a disaster. Any thoughts to lessen the impact of the tragedy by bringing in cheap imports of wheat quickly subsided. Europe's harvest, besides being mostly under French control, had been as bad as Britain's.

Nature's war was by no means all England had to cope with. The assumed enemy, France, and in particular her leader, were, it seemed, warmed by a benevolent sun rather than threatened by a portentous comet. That year Napoleon's Empire was swelled by a further sixteen departments, his access to the sea was extended by the additions of the mouths of the rivers Rhine, Meuse and Scheldt, his subjects from conquered territories were increased by no less than 5 million and his Empress was safely delivered of a son.

By contrast, Britain's monarchy possessed few characteristics to inspire national sentiments of pride or affection. No breasts could be expected to beat faster in the knowledge that the country had at its head a gabbling, insane king. If George III can be blamed for not keeping better control of his bouts of unpopularity, he cannot be blamed for thoughtlessly failing to regulate his periods of madness. His doctors could neither understand nor influence porphyria. In the previous November the Prince of Wales had assumed authority over the untrusting nation. Loathed by the poor and mocked by the rich, the fat, middle-aged man was required to preside over a country which, like him, was beset by tricky financial problems.

To contain Napoleon by sea cost Britain dear and the cost of containing him by land was becoming dearer. Spencer Perceval's budget for supplies for national security that year was £56 million. From this £20 million went to the navy, £21 million to the army, £5 million to ordnance and £2 million additional subsidies to the war Wellington was fighting in Portugal.[2] It left little for the nation's internal needs. Expenditure on the Home Department, for example, on a policing system and on enforcing law and order was negligible to the point of negligence.

In a stable country in unchanging times this poor provision would have had little consequence. But Britain was far from changeless. What was happening was dramatic and largely out of the control of government. The pivot for the changes was the creation of the wealth the nation needed to live on: the technology of industrial revolution. The land no longer provided the dominant source of income for the British people. That year £4,210,000 was spent on imports of food.[3] In the first decade of the century 1.5 million acres of land had been enclosed.[4] It was the beginning of the destruction of the yeoman farmer. In his place came the worker in the iron industry, in the coal mines and in the burgeoning high-volume production trades of wool and cotton. And, as Adam Smith had seen,[5] the mark of a country of increasing total prosperity was an inevitable, inexplicable increase in population. In the ten years from 1801 the population of Great Britain rose an astonishing 14 per cent from 10,472,048 to 11,911,644.[6] Most of it was added to industrial towns and cities. What was evident, however, was that the newly created industrial wealth was far from being well distributed among this mushrooming industrial population.

This poisonous mixture within the body of the nation inevitably displayed its symptoms. One of the places where a rash of incidents broke out which were to have more than a passing effect on subsequent events in the north, was Nottinghamshire, the centre of the stocking trade.

It had all begun there in February in the village of Arnold. By night a small group of workmen had broken into a workshop and unhooked and removed jack-wires, which were essential pieces of mechanism in the knitting machines in the shop.[7] The wires were hidden in local churches. Throughout February and into March the raids were repeated in different workshops and with increasing violence to the knitting frames.

There had been several reasons for the attacks on the machines. Not least, fashion had turned against the stocking trade. The hose which covered every gentleman's legs like a uniform – to the great advantage of those with shapely calves – suddenly at the end of the eighteenth century had disappeared. To the enormous relief of the thin and the fat-legged – and they were in the majority – the lower parts of the body began to be covered in trousers or boots, or both.

Amusing to the observer of patterns of social behaviour, this fickleness had the makings of tragedy for the framework knitters of the country. Of nearly 30,000 frames, 85 per cent were in the Midlands, most of them in workshops in country districts.[8] With the Orders in Council causing the export trade to plummet, by 1811 thousands of workers who once had made fully fashioned stockings, if they could get the work, were now reduced to making plain hose.

There was one other vital factor which at this depressed time in the hosiery trade had now made its presence felt. The technology of the industry had begun to change. The change was small, but it was critical under the circumstances. The framework knitting machine, invented by the Reverend William Lee, had remained in use in what was virtually its basic design for almost 200 years. Then, in about 1803, in the middle of the inventive upsurge of the Industrial Revolution, it was found possible to widen the machine and for it to remain simple enough in operation to be used by relatively unskilled labour. The larger piece of knitted cloth it produced was of poorer quality and it was used to make cut-up stockings. These, instead of being made and shaped in one piece, were simply made from cloth cut and sewn to the shape of the foot and leg.

The new technology was the trigger for the events which quickly followed. As hosiers took on more cheap labour, usually by employing apprentices, they were able to undercut a dwindling market with a cheaper product. At this point more skilled stocking workers found themselves with the option of either taking less work, requiring less skill and being paid lower wages, or with taking action. Removing the jack-wires from the Arnold workshop had been the first piece of action.

During the rest of February sporadic acts of violence took place at workshops where the new machines were in use. Nobody in government took the riots seriously until March 11th when, in order to disperse a mob of several hundred gathered in Nottingham market place, the local military force had to be called out.[9] That night violence spread to nearby villages when houses as well as workshops were broken into. Not until the Home Office had sent regular cavalry and infantry to the district and after more than 200 frames had been destroyed in the early weeks of April, did the district become quiet again.

A surprisingly quiet summer followed. Then during the first week of November several worrying incidents of frame smashing occurred culminating in the worst of all on the night of the 10th.[10]

It happened at the small town of Bulwell where a greatly disliked hosier, Edward Hollingsworth, kept a large number of frames. Like several employers and frame owners Hollingsworth had been expecting trouble. He had prepared for an attack by laying in guns and barricading his house as best he could. But he had not anticipated the organised and controlled fashion in which the attack was carried out.

A crowd of workers from several villages – some said the number was as high as seventy – gathered in the forest at Bulwell and drew themselves up in an unusually ordered group. At their head was a military-style commander who called himself 'Ned Lud'.[11]

The way in which the attack on Hollingsworth was carried out was unusually controlled. The workers' force moved in formation on the house and guards were placed round it. On command, the leading ranks of men, all of whom carried axes and hammers, moved forward and assaulted the barricaded doors. Shots were fired from Hollingsworth's windows. Surprisingly, the fire was returned from the ranks of the attackers. It was now clear that the weapons the workers were carrying were not limited to those intended to destroy machines.

The first wave of attackers retreated under the gunfire from the house. A justifiably scared Hollingsworth watched as the workers regrouped. One of them was hit and, as was later discovered, killed. Undeterred, the axe and hammer men moved forward again, broke down the door and let the rest of the force move in.

Every man, it was seen, was acting under well-prepared instructions. Some stood over Hollingsworth. Others moved up to the
workshop and set about smashing frames – but selectively. Only
the wide machines which knitted the broader, cheaper cloth came
under the destructive hammer.

The work done, the force withdrew, its retreat covered by well-
placed guards to prevent the rear being surprised by attacks from
the local militia.

In the next weeks, for night after night, the incidents repeated
themselves in different Nottinghamshire villages. Already the
disturbances had spread to parts of Leicestershire and Derbyshire.
The problem for the Lord Lieutenants of these counties, who
were responsible for public order, was that there was no adequate
body of men on which they could call for law enforcement. The
immediate action to be taken on occasions such as these was to get
magistrates to enrol special constables and to call for help from
whatever local militia was at hand. In the Nottinghamshire area at
this time, in spite of the efforts of 400 freshly sworn special
constables,[12] several troops of Yeomanry Cavalry and several
companies of militiamen, frames in workshops were being
destroyed at the rate of fifty a week.

The government inevitably had to be approached for help.
Troops were poured into the area. By the end of January 1812, in
addition to the local regiments of infantry and cavalry, 3,000
regular soldiers had had to be drafted to the Midlands to keep the
peace. In the House of Commons the Home Secretary, Richard
Ryder, described the massing army as 'a larger force than had ever
been found necessary in any period of our history to be employed
in the quelling of a local disturbance.'[13] A *Times* correspondent
looked on it all with an alarmed eye and believed all this marching
of infantry and wheeling of cavalry gave the country every
'appearance of a state of war'.[14]

The Nottingham correspondent to the influential *Leeds
Mercury* – influential over West Yorkshire workers as well as their
employers – had no doubts about the severity of the dangers. He
wrote, 'The insurrectional state to which this country has been
reduced for the last month has no parallel in history, since the
troubled days of Charles the First.'[15]

A whole area of central England was now in an extraordinary
condition. The reason for its turbulence was that large numbers
of working men were not able to keep themselves and their
families fed as a result of a sudden slump in trade, partly brought

on by fashion's change and partly brought on by war and a blockade of exports imposed by Britain herself as much as by her enemies. The workers had chosen to carry out their collective bargaining by riot. But there is no question that, although it was only directly responsible in a small degree for these events, the phenomenon which had triggered the huge reaction in a once peaceful group of workers had been a technological change. The introduction of the wide knitting frame over the previous few years had provided a quantum shift in their work practices. It made it possible for an inexperienced man to produce in a fraction of the time, far more material of lower quality than a skilled craftsman. Insignificant as this technological adaptation of an old machine had seemed, it had released a frightening explosion at the geographical heart of England.

When the troubles had reached their peak the young Lord Byron had appeared on the scene in time to spend Christmas at Newstead Abbey. He had installed three pretty young housemaids there for his amusement. Also he needed a new truss fitted at Nottingham General Hospital. However, in those few weeks he found time for other than distractions of the body. He took in both the riots and their cause. He was quite clear about what he had seen. He wrote to Lord Holland, leader of the Whig opposition in the House:

> By the adoption of a certain kind of frame one man performs ye. work of 7 – 6 are thus thrown out of business. – But it is observed that ye. work thus done is far inferior in quality, hardly marketable at home, and hurried over with a view to exportation.

Byron had discovered technology and its consequences and was in full accord with the workers that the best solution to the problems it created lay in the reversal of the direction of technological advance. 'Surely, my Lord,' he went on,

> ... however we may rejoice in any improvement in ye arts which may be beneficial to mankind; we must not allow mankind to be sacrificed to improvements in Mechanism.[16]

Again, he had also discovered something on which he was specially keen: a cause. He was, as it happened, looking for a subject which might be suitable for his maiden speech to the House of Lords. It needed to be of national importance and to include elements of passion and compassion. Here was a topic that had all these qualities. He had seen the worsening conditions of some of the stocking workers and had seen how their families had been reduced to 'squalid wretchedness'. He genuinely sympathised with their plight and now that he had seen the results of the riots, had no doubts about their gravity. It needed only a touch more drama added to its passion for him to adopt it. He began to consider it seriously enough for him to consult his friends on the matter.

The early signs were, however, that the subject might sink in importance before he had time to draw it to the attention of his fellow peers. As the year drew to a close several hosiers began to give way to the workers' demands, agreeing to pay higher wages and discontinue manufacture of cut-ups. Even more influential, the sheer size of the military force that was now blanketing the area was having its effect. An uneasy calm began to settle over the district, but the embers of revolt were still glowing.

In its last issue of 1811, the *Nottingham Journal* published a proclamation of the Prince of Wales offering £50 reward for information leading to the arrest of any rioter. The newspaper's readership, however, could have looked elsewhere in its advertisement columns for the devil at the root of the troubles. Passmore, Sinkinson, Pearson and Co of Doncaster had just patented their new powered straw-cutting machine, the blades of which 'can be taken off to grind, and fixed on by any one. The smaller machine takes so little power that a stout Boy may work it for hours.'[17]

Even hidden away in the small ads was technology which yet would have a great deal to answer for.

9

Decision

The higher echelon of British society, having endowed itself with every appearance of blithe independence from trade, had already made that word socially unacceptable. In truth, it was as heavily dependent on trade as the rest of the nation.

The insularity of this stratum from the instability of the nation was nothing if not amazing. The brilliant novels of the period brilliantly reflect the calm. The Prince Regent's favourite novelist, Jane Austen, was now assembling her thoughts for *Pride and Prejudice*. Neither here nor elsewhere does she note any privations of any sort affecting the middle classes, which might have resulted from the activities of the ill-bred Napoleon. Nor does she observe any untoward changes as a result of the industrial and technological upheavals beginning to shake the land.

People of her class – Hammond Roberson, for example, who like Jane Austen's father was a parson – had other preoccupations. Early in 1810 Phoebe Roberson had died of a long illness. Local tongues had wagged at the news, in particular those of the non-conformists whom Hammond Roberson so publicly despised. Even Charlotte Brontë repeated the story in *Shirley*, that the Tory vicar's wife had been ill-treated and had died of a broken heart.[1] One of Phoebe's relations, long after her death, told that in spite of her marriage to Hammond, she had kept up her membership of Gildersome Baptist Church and had ridden there on Communion Sundays on a grey pony. To prevent this, the story went, Hammond had deliberately shot the pony before her eyes.[2] The tale is out of character with the horse-loving, pennywise Roberson. More likely, he preferred to shoot the sick animal with his own hand rather than delegate the unpleasant task.

The reason why every incident of this kind should have been so tellingly embroidered by any dissenter with a grudge against Roberson is clear. With Phoebe's death Hammond now inherited the money left her by her mother – Unitarian money. And Roberson's widely advertised ambition was to use every penny he owned to build for the Church of England and to drive out all dissenters from the valley. The Gildersome family members were never to forget that it was their money Roberson was using to fight their religious values.

In 1811 he had crystallised his ambition. He had secured the Act of Parliament allowing him to build the new church on the hillside opposite his home. Roberson had drafted the Act himself.

The same year had been important for the ambitions of that second, eventually more famous, parson of the Spen valley, Patrick Brontë. He was inducted at Hartshead church on July 20th. There was no vicarage and he took rooms nearby with a former lodge-keeper of Sir George Armytage who had the tenancy of Thorn Bush Farm. The level of its owner's hospitality drew no high ratings from the locals who knew it more familiarly as Lousey Thorn Farm.

The parish, which Hammond Roberson had once run with the help of two curates, above all else needed hard, dedicated work if the Church was ever to become a force in the lives of the scattered cloth workers and hill-farming parishioners. It is clear that if Patrick Brontë did work hard, it was neither on the parish nor the parishioners. That year, taking his own writings at face value, he 'spent all his working hours' writing poetry.[3]

Sadly, not even his most charitable biographers claim that the poems had many qualities to justify the time he spent on them or even that they rise above the level of doggerel. They do, nevertheless, reveal aspects in the young man's character which might begin to explain the extraordinary genetic inheritance of his children.

Flimsily disguised as moral parable, present in both his writings and his verse is a passionate interest in and obsession with 'licentious writers' and with illicit sex. One of his *Cottage Poems*, in its moralistic cloak, was able to spell out in unusually frank terms for 1811 the story of a maid named Maria who, after seduction, turns prostitute.

The collection of verse was published at Patrick's expense late in the same year. It included an introduction by the author which was most notable for the fact that, for publication, either he or his printer adopted the diaresis; Bronte became Brontë and remained so. Patrick now settled back and waited for the literary world to beat its way to his doors at Hartshead.

Unlike the clerical class of the county William Cartwright could not so easily detach himself from the affairs which were increasingly creating the wealth upon which society's upper strata lived. 1812, beginning as it did with a period of uncertain industrial calm, was for him a worrying time. The machines he had ordered from the Taylor brothers in Marsden were ready for delivery. He had made what was now a firm decision to install them, irrespective of what the effects of any changes in wool technology were likely to be on those living in the district. One way of deducing the extent of these effects today is to look at the published militia list of 1800 for the Colne valley. It gives 202 names with addresses of all men with not more than one child.[4] One man is listed as a *wright*, one a *mason*, and three as *delvers*. Each of the remaining 197 is described as a clothier – that is to say, as working in the cloth trade. No less than 97 per cent of the younger men of this one valley depended on the trade for their living.

Probably about 5 per cent of these men were croppers. Mellor and Thorpe were the pair at the top of this cream – the acknowledged elite of virtually the whole workers' community of the Colne valley. A good cropper, by his ability to finish a length of superfine cloth could add 20 per cent to its value: put another way, he could lose 20 per cent. The traditional incentive to his skills, therefore, was that he was paid 5 per cent of the value of the finished cloth. When trade was good an unmarried, skilled cropper had no difficulty earning 30 shillings a week,[5] at a time when a labourer could take home as little as 8 shillings to his family. George Mellor was able to lay his hands on £100 of savings if he required to and had ready cash to pay out generously to his companions and their families when the need came.

The actual numbers of croppers in the West Riding in 1806 amounted to more than 3,000, plus a further 2,000 skilled working apprentices. In all they served about 500 Master cloth finishers.[6] Some of these Masters employed as few as three or four croppers, most such as John Wood about ten to fifteen and some, such as Cartwright of Rawfolds, twenty or thirty; Gott of Leeds, had as many as eighty.

The number of families both directly and indirectly affected by a potential radical change in the most critical of the processes was therefore very substantial. Not only did William Cartwright know this to be the case when he decided to install his new machines, he also knew who had led the recent attacks on the Leeds finishing mills. The reason the croppers had done so in the past, and were likely to do so again in the future, was that they believed, like all others in history who had opposed technological change, that their livelihoods were threatened by it.

Those wool workers in the Spen and Colne valleys who opposed the change and who were confident of the affirmative answer to the question of whether technology could be reversed, saw two modes of action at their disposal. The first was the use of the law of the land. Their experience of this during recent years was that it was ineffective and in any case could be shifted to act against their interests.

The second was the use of violence. There is no contemporary written evidence which tells how the workers, in particular the croppers, began the process of organising themselves for action against the new techniques. However, the word of mouth collected chiefly by enthusiastic nineteenth-century historians, in particular the journalist Frank Peel in the Spen valley, makes it possible to build an acceptable picture of what happened in the croppers' community.[7]

During this period the meetings of working men in public houses such as the Shears Inn and the Crispin became more frequent. George Mellor would take with him several young apprentices, from Longroyd Bridge. After seven years, he, William Thorpe, Benjamin Walker, Thomas Smith, William Hall and several others were all on the point of becoming fully qualified journeymen in an industry of uncertain future. The enthusiasts walked, on Friday nights and Saturdays, the several miles from one public house meeting to the next. As they listened over the weeks, the character of the meetings changed. Initially they were passive observers. As months passed and as the recession gripped it dawned that there was now a real threat to their position as the elite among workers should the new machines appear in their valleys to take over their work. Soon it was they, the croppers, who were raising the cry for action. And now that the law had been shifted so that it was no longer on their side, the cry was for action, if necessary outside the law.

It was at this stage that George Mellor began to take a leading part and probably to organise discussions at John Wood's shop. The chief source of political information both here and at other shops was the *Leeds Mercury*. Its editor was Edward Baines (not related to John Baines) who had once been secretary of a Jacobin club in Preston. Baines's radical politics and his paper were regularly watched over by the government and particularly

by the military sent to keep law and order in the area.[8] Charlotte
Brontë consulted the paper's files when she wanted source material for her novel.

Baines's publication, at 6½d a copy – 7d outside Leeds – cost
roughly the same as a labourer would earn in half a day. One copy
a shop was as much as most groups could afford. However, since
the numbers capable of reading it were small, it was inevitable
that many had to listen to it being read by one literate member of
the group. It was also inevitable, therefore, that this man would
be in the position of spokesman, if not leader, of the shop. At
John Wood's that position fell naturally to George Mellor.

The *Mercury* gave a remarkably accurate picture through its
unnamed Nottingham correspondent of the issues involved in the
frame-work knitters' riots and it gave an informed description of
the crucial influence of the new technology that had sparked the
violence. It needed little imagination to make the leap comparing
the position of the frame-work knitters in Nottingham with the
croppers in the West Riding. It also gave a clear indication of how
the rioters had organised themselves into large groups and used
what would now be called para-military methods to attack
selected owners of the new machines.[9] Within these reports, for
those who wanted to find it – and George Mellor was one – was a
prescription for a method of dealing with the factory owners and
Masters who were taking in the new shearing-frames.

But there were other influences at work. The other men with an
even higher standard of living to protect and with most to lose
from technological advance, were the small Masters who had
made the decision not to use the new frames. John Wood was one.
It can now never be resolved what influence Wood himself used to
promote ideas and actions to his own advantage, through Mellor.
Like many small Masters, Wood had realised that the scale of his
operations was too small to compete with mill owners who mechanised on the scale of Gott or even of Horsfall and Cartwright.
Only if finishing machines were kept out of the business could he
hope to survive. The preservation of hand-cropping and of the
way of life of the journeyman cropper was as important to Wood
as to the men who worked for him.

In this conflict involving Masters and men, therefore, the line
was divided well to the right of centre: the Masters' ranks were
split between those who had loyalty to others of their kind and
those who had an allegiance with workers. It is doubtful that the
intensity of the conflict could have developed such extremes of

passion had it not been for the conniving activities of such men as Mellor's stepfather, John Wood.

George Mellor at twenty-one years old was emerging as a leader of a powerful group of working men. There can be no question, he had the presence and powers required of a leader. But there can also be no question that leadership came to him because of the unusual fact that he was educated. This last attribute was one that was soon to be ruthlessly sought out by the authorities; any working man who marked himself by showing both an ability to write and a propensity to lead would in due course find his liberty brutally suppressed.

Not that Mellor and his like were looking hard to be leaders. He had already heard names such as that of Major John Cartwright, brother of the inventor of the weaving loom, and of the romantic radical Sir Francis Burdett, whose activities in favour of parliamentary reform were carefully reported by the *Mercury*. These men, it was rumoured, were the kind to lead the poor in a new society. But besides being impressively titled, they were distant people. What they had to offer was as intangible as a dream: yet Mellor was to cling to the hopes raised by the dream until the day he died. In the meantime he had reached his decision: he was prepared to be an active leader.

10

Trouble

1812 began badly for Viscount Warren Bulkeley. A lover of the good life, having given a great Christmas dinner at his house in Stockport, he had caught a cold there. For several days he felt sufficiently fragile to stay at home. The letter he wrote to the Home Secretary on New Year's Day made sure to give that news.[1] But, although it took second place to his state of health, there was also other disturbing information to reveal. He had just had it confirmed that men from Nottingham had been in the Stockport area and that they had been seen as delegates at secret meetings of cotton trade workers.

It was not the first time that the movements of Midlands workers had been watched in the Lancashire–Cheshire district during the past few weeks. The activity simply confirmed the view of many that this cotton manufacturing area with its distressing conditions was the next likely flashpoint for any violence. However, what interested Bulkeley as much as the news itself was its bearer.

He had recently been introduced to a young lawyer, J S Lloyd, the newly appointed clerk to the Stockport magistrate, the Reverend Mr Prescott. John Lloyd's astuteness in sniffing out information about the secret activities of the working classes and others had astonished Bulkeley. Lloyd told him that he had already been given many rewards by the Bank of England for his work trapping forgers. Now, by using paid spies, and by his own investigations into the affairs of local people, he was able to give what would turn into a stream of information to Bulkeley.

So impressed was the Lord Lieutenant by this 'uncommon clever man' that he explicitly recommended his services to the

Home Secretary and suggested that 'if ever you want a person in London of his description in your police establishment I can safely say he would be uncommonly useful'.[2] Bulkeley's recommendation of Lloyd was not his only activity during the bitter affairs of 1812 but, such were its consequences, it was by far the most significant thing he was to do. Lloyd's work was to be as crucial as it was controversial.

During the next few weeks Lloyd was to keep a sharp eye on the affairs of Stockport and was soon in direct contact with the Home Secretary himself, Richard Ryder, who personally gave him encouragement.[3]

Lloyd, an active horseman, began riding from one Lancashire and Cheshire town to the other to report on the state of the counties. Soon, having established that Nottingham rioters had connections in Manchester, and were attending meetings of disgruntled workers, he was raising Bulkeley's blood pressure by his hints of the violence to come by giving 'your Lordship a sort of prelude to what may (or may not) happen' in the cotton country.[4] Lloyd, it would turn out, was a perceptive young man.

The area in which he worked provided an almost copybook setting for violent social protest. As the new year advanced the conditions of working people wilted as the grip of unemployment tightened. In the cotton weaving trade wages which had been on average about 25 shillings a week, diminished as part-time work spread. The Reverend Mr Prescott, Lloyd's employer, was given a graphic description of the state to which many people had sunk by a weaver who told him,

> I have five children and a wife, the children all under 8 years of age – and I get 12/– per week which is only 9d. clear deducting winding & etc. and I work sixteen hours a day to get that – But there are thousands that do not get 8d. per week – It will take 2d. per week coals, 1d. per week candles. My family live upon potatoes chiefly and we have one pint of milk per day.[5]

It scarcely matters that the writer of this letter probably confused shillings and pence. What is relevant is that during that severe winter of 1811 to 1812, this worker in the cotton trade, after a six-day week of sixteen hours each day at his loom was left with a few pence each day on which to feed and clothe seven people.

Secretly, since he feared being attacked for having passed on the information, the same weaver told Prescott that the likely unemployment as a result of the introduction of the new steam looms to the cotton industry was causing desperate new fears. He said that 45,000 of his fellow cloth workers were suffering, not to mention those in other trades. 'The 45,000,' he told the alarmed magistrate, 'could all rise in one night . . .'

Employers were well aware of the mounting tensions. As one sympathetic Manchester factory owner wrote, when 'an honest, industrious fellow by hard labour cannot get bread much less clothes for himself and children' then the situation was reaching 'the point beyond which human nature cannot bear'.[6]

Yorkshire, however, did not have the same ingredients for uprising as did Lancashire or Cheshire. The *Leeds Mercury* faithfully reported the situation in the country in general. It told of the starvation in Liverpool pushing the working classes to ferment, of the military presence in Manchester necessary to keep the lid on the bubbling pot of revolt, and of the new technology of Nottingham where the mix had spilled over in violence. But the one great industrial town of Yorkshire closest to the rebellious Midland area, Sheffield, the newspaper somewhat opaquely reported as 'being kept quiet by a fictitious trade'.[7] Of Leeds itself, by February 22nd, 1812, it had no reports of starvation or of suffering of any other sort. No places in West Yorkshire were singled out for first-hand experience of distress. The Orders in Council, a huge trade recession and a bad harvest still had some way to go before draining dry the country's richest industry. The complaints of manufacturers of bulging warehouses and bank-ruptcies, and of the cloth workers of part-time work and high food prices, serious as they were, showed that this county at least was not yet on its knees.

Joseph Radcliffe, at Milnsbridge, could see with his own eyes, without taking any detour or travelling far on his weekly journeys up and down the coach road, what, if any, unrest existed in the Colne valley. His route to Huddersfield to fulfil his duties as magistrate at the Crown Inn, took him directly past the best index of the state of health of the woollen industry – the cropping shops. The cluster of these at Longroyd Bridge only a mile or so from Milnsbridge was still providing work for a substantial number of both skilled croppers and apprentices. Both Wood's, where George Mellor worked, and Fisher's, where William Thorpe was employed, were still active. The fact that this final stage in producing cloth was operating testifies that the businesses dependent on the earlier stages were, in the Colne valley at least, also functioning tolerably well.

The Spen valley had more problems. Some finishing shops were failing to survive the chilling economic winds of 1811. One small establishment owned by a Mr Waller,[8] on the hillside above Rawfolds, had had to close. His employees had had to find work elsewhere. But William Cartwright not only was surviving, he had managed to raise or make sufficient capital to implement his plan to invest in new machinery to work himself out of his period of recession.

It was an alarming surprise, therefore, that the first violence in the north came in neither Lancashire nor Cheshire, but in the West Riding of Yorkshire. One Wednesday evening in mid-January local magistrates near Leeds listened to the tale of an informer that a cloth finishing mill was to be attacked. Fortunately for the mill owner they believed what they heard. Acting quickly on the evidence, the magistrates sent a troop of Scots Greys galloping to the mill. There they came across a mob of workmen with blackened faces heading across a bridge outside the town at the appointed hour.[9] At the approach of the law the gang scattered, but not before one of them was arrested. He was immediately escorted by the cavalry to York Castle to await trial.

Four nights later the magistrates had no warning. A nearby mill was attacked and set on fire. It was the signal for a whole series of disturbing events throughout the county which quickly had the middle classes sleeping uneasily in their beds. And far from justifying Joseph Radcliffe's complacency, his district, the Colne valley, began to give the most frightening signals of trouble to come. At first, as in Lancashire, the reports were no more than rumours, but more detailed evidence began to reveal common patterns on both sides of the border.

The first signs were of groups of workmen gathering in unusually large numbers, not just in pubs such as the Shears and the Crispin Inn, but in fields and on common land outside the valley villages. More scaring to those who believed they had something to fear were the reports that the bands of young men, many under twenty and some as young as sixteen,[10] were beginning to take on a military appearance, some of them drilling under leaders, or commanders, and some armed with sticks and other weapons, including guns. One report sent to Lord Fitzwilliam spoke of the units having secret arms depots from which the rebels – if that was what they were – could be supplied as soon as the time came.

Some of the weapons described were pikes which could be dismantled into three parts so that they could be easily hidden, then quickly reassembled with a thorough-pin and nut screw.[11]

Politically more sinister were the descriptions of a national organisation with each area of unrest linked by delegates, usually from Nottinghamshire. There were reported secret systems of passing messages from one group to the other, and members of each organisation administering and taking oaths of loyalty.

Already they had been given, or had taken a name: Luddite – after the title adopted by the leaders of one of the Nottinghamshire attacks. There are several different versions of its origin, though all agree that it was from the Midlands and had been given birth perhaps as early as 1779. The stories go that an apprentice called Ned Lud, Ludd or Ludlam was one day beaten, either by other boys who thought him stupid,[12] by his father,[13] or on the orders of a magistrate.[14] Whatever the details of the irritation, in response the boy took a hammer and beat his stocking frame into a heap. Ned was the first Luddite. All stories are agreed that this upsurge of violence was due to his physical suffering and in no way due to the technology he mangled. But his example in dealing with machines had been well noted. His name was ever after a part of the English language.

The rumours which now flew through the Spen and Colne valleys, and the Huddersfield and Halifax districts as a whole, were considerable and, some felt, exaggerated. Tales of armies on the rise in Britain had been heard before. But certain happenings were more than figments of imagination and could not be discounted as boys' pranks. Joseph Radcliffe was getting reports from serious and sober citizens such as Hammond Roberson describing armed men marching across the hillside tracks at dead of night. And several mill owners – William Cartwright was one – had either heard rumours from their workmen or had had anonymous notes put in their hands telling them that they, their families and their factories would soon be made to suffer. Throughout the early days of February reports of vicious attacks on lonely weaving and finishing sheds and their owners passed from village to village.

The news that pushed Joseph Radcliffe into action came on a Sunday morning, February 24th. There was no question of this being unsubstantiated rumour. The violence was on his doorstep. Moreover, there was no mistaking the fact that it was outrage organised with unusual care closely resembling what had been happening during the Nottingham attacks.

Late the previous night, a mile away in the village of Marsh, a large band of men, their faces blackened, had swooped on Joseph Hirst's mill and broken their way into the finishing shop.[15] Within a few minutes the attackers had smashed every single piece of machinery used for cloth finishing, including shears and shearing-frames.

The scared local inhabitants had watched the impressively calm way in which the masked gang leader had gone about his business. Obviously acting on prearranged orders, his men had divided into two groups. One party, carrying axes and hammers, he had sent into the mill to destroy the machinery whilst the other, which included men armed with pistols, took up defensive positions outside to prevent any resistance.

As soon as the work inside was finished the leader had paraded his men military-style, called the roll to which each man answered with a number rather than a name, then had his gunmen fire off a victory salvo. Immediately they marched off to the other side of the valley to James Balderstone's mill at Crosland Moor and carried out the same manoeuvre. Again all finishing machinery was completely wrecked. One of the mill owners that evening was dragged in front of the leader who, in a lordly fashion, pronounced that not a hair of the man's head should be harmed; but if he gave any reason to require a second visit he could expect no mercy. Neither manufacturer recognised any of the attackers behind their disguises and no local workmen or villagers volunteered any useful information to help in identification.

Radcliffe was now convinced that the scale and the unusual organisation of the violence was unlike anything he had had to deal with in the past. He believed that urgent government action was needed. He wasted little time in recruiting the man who could be relied on to stimulate that action – the county Member of Parliament, William Wilberforce.[16] Within hours Wilberforce was at the Home Office, but had to make do with an interview with the Permanent Under-Secretary, John Beckett, rather than the Home Secretary himself, Richard Ryder.

Ryder's response when he eventually received the news was less than overwhelming. Had the courier not been Wilberforce it is possible he would have done nothing at all. He decided to move in one troop of cavalry – about twenty men – to restore confidence. Also, he advised, another troop could be had from Wakefield if matters truly began to be serious. Ryder's main concern was to persuade Radcliffe to deal firmly with any trouble himself. He languidly recommended to Radcliffe, for your consideration whether it might not be advisable for the magistrates and the most respectable persons in your neighbourhood to adopt immediately some strong resolutions which may shew the persons who are disposed to commit outrages of this sort that there exists a determination not to submit to the system of terror which they are attempting to introduce.[17]

Radcliffe was aghast at the feeble response which his considered assessment of the situation had produced. At eleven o'clock on Monday evening the troop of Scots Greys set off from Leeds to ride the dozen miles to Huddersfield. Replacements were to be sent from Sheffield to Leeds, which was now completely undefended.

All Radcliffe could do to augment his totally inadequate defences was to carry out what Ryder suggested and persuade the worried local manufacturers to gather at the Crown Inn at Huddersfield and hold a public meeting. John Horsfall, whose brother William had just installed great numbers of shearing machines in the family factory at Marsden, took the chair of the newly formed 'Committee for Suppressing the Outrages'. As the Home Secretary had demanded, the air at the Crown rang with resolutions. One set out to raise 100 guineas – two or three years' wages for many workers – for any information leading to a conviction for the acts of violence.[18] It was found, however, that neither at that, nor at any other subsequent meeting, did any worker step forward to claim the cash.

But even before Radcliffe could report to London the local response to the Home Secretary's feeble suggestions, news of fresh attacks was being carried to Milnsbridge House. First to be brought in front of Radcliffe was a very scared cloth dresser, William Hinchcliffe from the neighbouring village of Golcar, who described how the previous night a gun had been pointed through his window and fired off at him. The shot missed, but a gang of men immediately poured into his finishing shop threatening to kill him. He gave a vivid account of the same clear and calm organisation of about fifty men: blackened faces, carefully allotted tasks, swift destruction of shearing machines followed by the threat of worse to come.[19]

Over the next few days and weeks the same pattern of violence repeated itself. John Sykes and his wife of Linthwaite, who worked for a small Master, answered their door at one o'clock in the morning. They were grabbed and held down whilst armed men tied up and stood guard at the bedside of every member of the household, who were made to listen to the sound of ten shearing-frames being shattered by great hammers.[20] Samuel Swallow in the same village, on the same night, was held in his bed, one man with a pistol at his head, another with a pistol at his feet as they took the keys to his barn. When every finishing machine and tool he had stored there had been smashed, his keys were calmly handed back to him.[21]

If Joseph Radcliffe had taken a map and marked the sites of the outrages he could easily have shown how they were distributed in villages in a circle within a few miles' walking distance of his own house – or equally accessible to the finishing shops at Longroyd Bridge, John Wood's shop and the home of George Mellor.

The uneasy peace which had existed in the nearby valleys lasted only a few days longer. William Cartwright had felt secure enough to order a fresh delivery of cropping machines from the Taylor brothers in Marsden. The likelihood is that the cast-iron frames were carried by day by barge down the Ramsden Canal to the end of the River Colne where it joined the Calder. There they were probably loaded on to two carts which then began their journey past Sir George Armytage's estate at Kirklees over the lonely Hartshead Moor past Patrick Brontë's church into the Spen valley.

The February day had turned to dark night by the time the two carters succeeded in getting their heavy load to the head of the valley. Beyond that they had little to tell. They were found with sacks over their heads, trussed like chickens, lying in a ditch alongside the smashed remains of the brittle iron frames. They claimed not to have been able to identify any of the gang which had attacked them and the machinery.

It was at this point that Cartwright, who, like other factory owners, had had threatening notes pushed under his door, began to take the unrest seriously. His mill in the valley bottom was isolated. He decided it might be prudent to prepare to defend it and set about making plans accordingly. He was the first manufacturer to do so.

In the same valley there were others, unconnected with the woollen industry but firmly associated with the Establishment, who were also marked men. Patrick Brontë, for all his later protestations of sympathy for working men's rights, was reported to have had his life threatened.[22] Whoever had gagged and bound the two carters on the moor must have passed within a few hundred yards of his door. Already he regularly carried his shillelagh for protection. Now, in imitation of his hero, Hammond Roberson, he had bought himself a pistol and, as Mrs Gaskell described it, began to put it 'in his pocket, just as regularly as he puts on his watch'.[23] He would frighten his neighbours, as later he would frighten his daughters, by firing it out of the open windows each morning to make sure it was in working order.

Hammond Roberson himself, also threatened with death, was imperturbable. He was in favour of action rather than gestures. On the day the *Leeds Mercury* reported that first wave of Luddite attacks he was offering his own services and petitioning Joseph Radcliffe for a body of cavalry to be sent quickly to the Spen valley. He and other local inhabitants were by now convinced that violence there was a foregone conclusion.[24]

But Radcliffe needed no urging and was beginning to suspect that the rumours which suggested there was a deeper political motive to the outrages might have some foundation. His continuing urgent requests to the Home Secretary for more soldiers had brought one more troop of cavalry to the district of several hundred square miles. Again and again he was to urge John Beckett to try to get his Minister to act. '*Press* my request to Mr Ryder that no time be lost,' he pleaded. He needed a proper military defence for the district before blood was shed.[25] The question was whose blood was likely to drip first. Threatening notes were being pushed through the doors of not only mill owners' houses. One now came through his. It was in a working man's half-educated hand, date-lined Nottingham and signed 'Soliciter to General Ludd'. It told him that, if he were to convict any Luddite, he could expect assassination.[26]

11

The Power of the Law

The Home Department was the great office of State to which Joseph Radcliffe, like most middle-class Englishmen, had to look for the fine-tuning of its continuing peace. Now, for the first time in his experience as a magistrate, the events going on all around had persuaded him that it was no more than his duty to transmit his fears daily directly to government through the Home Secretary rather than through the Lord Lieutenant of the county. But as one feeble response after another followed his request for action, he began to realise, as would many others during the next few months, that the steadying hand which was intended to keep Britain stable, was negligible in its span, and had the firmness not of some serene Britannia, but more that of a trembling old maid.

In modern times a massive network of the forces of law and order of the State touches and, in some way or another, regularly operates on every individual in the land. It is easy to assume, therefore, that a similar, if simpler, system has been in operation for centuries and that the most revolutionary change in the administration of the law has been the introduction of the computer. This is not the case. In 1812 the only regular police force was a handful of Bow Street Runners attached to London magistrates' offices. In the rest of the country local magistrates had to depend on usually unpaid locally recruited constables. These were invariably manufacturers, small Masters or traders, and seldom members of the working class whose misbehaviour they policed. When in difficulties a magistrate could call out detachments of the local militia or yeomanry, and when in great distress, with the permission of government, the regular army. So in times of peace, the only real buttress any small community had to protect itself was the skill of the local magistrate in collecting and applying an irregular, uncertain force.

The man on whom all national responsibility fell for the administration of the system and the maintenance of the peace was the Home Secretary. The balance of the country's stability might not have been so precarious if this had been his only responsibility. But it was not. His other duties included those of 'Grants, Pardons and Regulations in all Civil Matters . . .; Preferments in the Church, Matters of Police, the regular Army, Militia and Volunteers, Dispensations, licences to Trade, Alien Regulations and all Correspondence regarding Ireland, Jersey, Guernsey etc'.[1]

It could easily be imagined, extrapolating from the functions and numbers of today's Civil Service, that a small army of experts and functionaries would have been required as support for the Home Secretary to deal with this massive hotch-potch deriving from the whole of the British Isles. The truth was that all that Richard Ryder had for support besides his Permanent Under-Secretary, John Beckett, were two further Under-Secretaries, a Chief Clerk, four Senior and eight Junior Clerks, joint Chamber Keepers and a person – whose domestic duties have to be imagined – who was warmly categorised as the 'necessary woman'.[2]

Together this little group presided over a wonderfully absorbent system of information storage. However, once that information reached the file of Home Office papers, there was no certainty that it would ever be retrieved again until many years later.

Richard Ryder had been sitting in the House as Member of Parliament for Tiverton for seventeen years and would still be there seventeen years later. As Spencer Perceval's Secretary of State, he had in that undistinguished Ministry managed to achieve a reputation for imperturbability and clear-headedness by exercising a policy of silent inactivity. Ryder's inertia during this critical period of history is unquestionable. It is possible that he and his Permanent Under-Secretary were bowed down by their too numerous, too trivial other activities. John Beckett was certainly conscientious and certainly over-worked, but he showed as little sparkle in response to the excitement of the times as did his Minister.

This is not simply a view made with the benefit of hindsight.

Many contemporaries including journalists were deeply concerned about the way Britain's internal affairs were being run. *The Times* was not over-sensitive in its assessments of the qualities of the people who, at that moment, were responsible for the steadiness of the nation. It thundered,

> The present Ministers, we all know, are weak enough, and but little competent to manage difficult or complicated affairs. There is, too, we believe, less of talent and energy in that office by which our Home concerns are chiefly directed, than in all the rest put together. We say nothing of the head of it; he is a recent appointment, but the subordinate officers are men who, through a long series of years, whatever might be their competence to more arduous stations, have been at least thought sufficiently qualified for a department wherein no difficulty has ever till now occurred, so that it is evident to common reason that the Home Office must have become the sink of all the imbecility attached to every Ministry for the last thirty years; and should therefore, at this period, when occurrences requiring more capable minds have taken place, be instantly and radically reformed.[3]

In confirmation of *The Times'* noun clauses, the department's papers which still remain are a colourful mixture of submissions from parish priests, pleas from disinherited widows, protests from captured French officers, applications from publicans and petitions from the likes of Lady Hamilton. The whole is shuffled without ceremony or classification with letters which might have a more pressing claim as matters of national urgency – such as those from Joseph Radcliffe.

The response on February 26th of John Beckett to Radcliffe's judgement that military help in Yorkshire was urgently needed, drove Radcliffe to disbelief. If Beckett, who was a member of a Leeds woollen family, could not see that a very unusual situation now existed in the north of England, what chance was there that the unimaginative, supine Home Secretary would spring into action? Richard Ryder had not even got to his feet in the House of Commons to mention the matter of the Nottinghamshire frame breaking until twelve days ago. Was he to take the same number of weeks before he thought the violence in Yorkshire deserved the government's consideration?

The Cabinet's neglect of the untidy state of affairs in the north country is nothing short of astonishing. The reason is clear. For months past it had been unalterably obsessed with the Duke of Wellington's campaign in Portugal and Spain, where the best that could be said was that Lisbon had been saved and Napoleon's forces thankfully reduced to a state of inactivity. It was late in January 1812 before any mention of the extraordinary outbreak of outrages in Nottingham was mentioned at the Cabinet table.[4] The result was that on February 14th Ryder addressed the House of Commons on the subject on the first reading of a bill to make frame breaking a capital offence. Three days later the bill had its second, and three days after that its third, reading.

This sudden threat – that those convicted of smashing machines would be put to death – seemed all the more draconian for having been dreamed up by the normally torpid Home Office. It was all Lord Byron, having just celebrated his twenty-fourth birthday, needed to convince himself that at last here was sufficient drama to use as the topic for his maiden speech to the House of Lords. He abandoned some tentative plans he had made to speak on the Catholic Question, put aside the proofs for *Childe Harold* which he was correcting, and launched into prose, strongly under the influence of his political hero, Pitt.

By February 27th, like the actor he was, he had committed the speech to memory, and was ready to perform to the House of Lords. Discounting his worries that his peers might be morbidly more fascinated by his club foot than by his subject-matter, he began his oration in a fever of excitement. Even he admitted that his delivery was 'perhaps a little theatrical'.[5]

Byron's opportunism was blatant. His speech, however, was trenchant. Most of the assembled peers had never before heard such a combination of histrionics and social conscience. He first spelled out the initial cause of the violence at the root of the bill, explaining how the new, improved frames were an advantage to the manufacturer, but were leaving large numbers of men out of work and their families starving.

Warming to his theme, he reminded his listeners that 'bankruptcy, convicted fraud and imputed felony, are in a station not far beneath that of your lordships' and called for compassion for 'the lowest, though once most useful portion of the people'.

He was the first to point out publicly the terrible apathy which government was showing to an explosive situation not all that far from its doorstep.

All this has been transacting within 130 miles of London, and yet we 'good easy men have deemed full sure our greatness was a-ripening', and have sat down to enjoy our foreign triumphs in the midst of domestic calamity. But all the cities you have taken, all the armies that have retreated before your leaders are but paltry subjects of self congratulation if your land divides against itself, and your dragoons and executioners must be let loose against your fellow citizens. You call these men a mob, desperate, dangerous and ignorant. . . . It is the mob that labour in your fields, serve in your houses – that man your navy and recruit your army, that have enabled you to defy all the world, and can also defy you when neglect and calamity have driven them to despair.

Byron demonstrated to his now captivated audience how proposals to emancipate the poor had taken years of deliberation: yet here was a government preparing to pass a death bill with scarcely a thought for what its profound long-term consequences might be.

He had reserved the hottest blast of his rhetoric for his peroration, imagining what would happen to the first man to be arraigned under the bill:

Suppose this man, surrounded by the children for whom he is unable to procure bread at the hazard of his existence, about to be torn for ever from a family which he lately supported in peaceful industry, and which it is not his fault that he can no longer so support, suppose this man, and there are ten thousand such from whom you may select your victim, dragged into court, to be tried for this new offence, by this new law; still there are two things wanting to convict and condemn him; and these are, in my opinion – twelve butchers for a jury, and a Jefferies for a judge.[6]

He sat down to a house of distinguished old men shocked into silence. But his message and its sentiments of sympathy for the suffering poor reached a far wider audience. Newspapers such as the *Leeds Mercury*, the *Nottingham Journal* and the *Manchester Exchange Herald* relayed to the Midland and north country workers that somebody near the seat of governmental power cared about their problems.

Byron basked in the waves of the sensation of his speech, graciously accepting the compliments which flowed from both sides of the House. Within a few days he was sitting on the committee seeking to substitute a fine or imprisonment in place of the death penalty for frame breaking. By March 5th he was flattered to hear the bill, with this amendment, being sent back to the House of Commons.

There, without ceremony, the amendment was thrown out. The bill went its way as though Byron had never existed. And Byron, for his part, went his way as though the bill had never existed. Its passing coincided with the appearance of the publication beside which his performance in the House of Lords paled into insignificance. *Childe Harold* when it appeared in London's bookshops that week was an instant, staggering success. It was devoured by a public which overnight turned Byron into a literary lion.

The young Lord was famous in his time. He could now concentrate on being 'mad – bad – and dangerous to know' and could afford to forget – and did forget – the likely fate of the frame breakers. Lord Byron's contribution to the technological debate of the times was over. The Home Secretary, for his part, had a powerful weapon he could use if he found it necessary.

12

Preparing for the Worst

The intractable problem for Joseph Radcliffe now was, what he should do. Nightly the situation was getting worse. There were many people in the country ready to pooh-pooh the tales of young workmen drilling by moonlight under middle-class leadership and many reasons to doubt the more excited stories. But there was no doubt whatever of the reality of the stream of frightened finishing shop workers who had begun to appear daily at Milnsbridge House to show their bruises and describe the terror they and their families had faced during the previous night.

It might have given Radcliffe more confidence that matters would improve of their own accord and require no vigorous action from him had the punishment to Luddites meted out at the Nottingham Spring Assizes early in March been fierce. However, the accused frame breakers, all of them caught before the new bill became law, were given what many held to be ridiculously light sentences. If committed a few days later the crime could have sent the culprits to the gallows. Of the nine prisoners, Mr Justice Bayley, a thoughtful judge, acquitted two and the remaining seven were transported for periods of up to fourteen years. Mr Bayley's leniency (if fourteen years for smashing a machine can be correctly described as leniency) would not be forgotten by Joseph Radcliffe.

Radcliffe's view that tough military action was an essential first step had been reinforced in several quarters. True to form, first to urge this had been Parson Roberson in the Spen valley. Already he had attached himself to the local Birstall and Batley Militia as military chaplain. But he was equally ready to fight as to pray. In the next few days he visited every one of the few members of the middle class the district could boast, persuaded them to enrol as special constables and sent his list to Radcliffe – his own name at the top, William Cartwright's second.

Roberson had fastened his pair of revolvers back in his belt – the same he had used to win Phoebe's favour – and could scarcely wait for the opportunity to use them:

I have very good reason to think we should have had a visit from these croppers if we had not been prepared – as we are. I almost wish they would make an attempt. I think we should give a good account of them.[1]

Roberson was not the only one to favour the technique of the short, sharp shock. Across the county border Viscount Bulkeley's protégé, the young lawyer John Lloyd, had already decided how he would treat the 'restless and refractory spirit' the workers were showing. Lloyd had seen with his own eyes the threatening gatherings of men on waste ground outside the town, seen them divide into different marching groups, and watched one group led by a man playing a fife parade through the market square in front of nervous Stockport citizens.[2]

The reason why Stockport had begun to simmer with potential violence was precisely that which had turned the Colne valley into a dangerous place in which to live: new technology was suddenly being applied in an unquestionably effective fashion to a traditional industry. Stockport was the first town where factory owners had introduced large numbers of steam-driven looms.

That there might be other reasons why the working classes might have reason to riot – the poverty in industrial Lancashire, the overcrowding, the child labour were all outpacing the workers' conditions in Yorkshire – was too subtle a consideration for the vigorous Mr Lloyd. He had no hesitation in deciding what attitude he should adopt to what he called this 'set of obscure individuals who possess no interest or feeling for their country's honour', who 'dare to dictate to a government or to the proprietor of a manufacture of this sort what they shall do or what machinery they shall use'.[3]

Like Hammond Roberson, J S Lloyd could hardly wait for a showdown with the rioters. He was waiting to pounce on any man foolish enough to step out of line. He told Viscount Bulkeley that on the very first act of violence by any worker he would go into action meeting force with force. Already he had begun to use his own methods of extracting information from unruly workers.

After the firing of a factory at Oxford Road in Manchester early in February he took the prime suspect and interrogated him for several hours. His technique, which he was to refine in a very sinister fashion during the next few months, was to lock away his victim – not always a prisoner, sometimes an informer – and keep him isolated until the information began to flow. The fear he induced by psychological pressures would eventually produce key information. But there is no doubt that much more went on in his interrogation rooms than subtle psychology; henchmen were available for softening up procedures. Lloyd told Bulkeley before he got to work on the Oxford Road suspect: 'Perhaps I may not approve the measures that will be adopted this night and I am well away from taking a part but I beg your Lordship will not notice this expression for I may not be so capable of judging properly as others.'[4]

At the same time as Richard Ryder was sending words of encouragement to Lloyd to increase his flow of information to the Home Office, without inquiring too closely about the methods used to extract the information, he was also encouraging magistrates to use other devious means. The Home Office had a substantial fund set aside for the purpose. One magistrate who used the fund widely was Colonel Ralph Fletcher at Bolton. By the time the first Nottinghamshire rioters had been reported attending workers' meetings in the north, he had three spies in his pay, 'B', 'T' and 'F'.[5]

'B' was a buyer and seller of cotton waste whose actual eponymous name was Mr Bent. He travelled Lancashire extensively and seemed to have the confidence of an unusually wide and an unusually unsettled number of working people. The information Bent was by this time bringing in to Fletcher was sensational, telling as it did of tens of thousands of workers ready to rise in a body.

The problem with paid spies, as all magistrates found who used them during the events of the next months, is their propensity to tell the hearer what he wants to hear. Fletcher would soon be sending in bills, some of them for more than £200, to the Home Office to cover the rewards he paid to these men. The shrillness of the information rose with the price, and the Colonel's gullibility has to be seen as a barrier to a real understanding of the mood of the people in the Lancashire cotton towns in early 1812. Some of Bent's tales, faithfully reported to the Home Office by Fletcher, had to be substantially discounted. But not all could be discarded.

The stories of organised rioting reaching London from Yorkshire were too carefully substantiated by such reliable witnesses as Joseph Radcliffe not to suggest that an unusual ferment of trouble was spreading across the northern counties.

In spite of his age – he was sixty-seven – and his increasing weight, Radcliffe was able and willing to travel about the country to investigate the other troubled areas. With the arrival of the fine spring weather, he was to ride in and out of Lancashire by the short steep Pennine road and learn how men such as Lloyd and Fletcher were acting. Already he had decided to use their system of spies. He had discovered that a few of the troopers under Major Gordon's command at Huddersfield were westcountrymen who had not only worked in the woollen industry before enlisting, but had actually been croppers by trade. He immediately put a plan to Gordon that these men should be used in disguise as Luddite supporters and sent to different villages to try to bring back what information they could about the workers' organisation and their planned attacks. Gordon, however, was extremely unhappy about his soldiers being used as civilian spies. He would only co-operate if Radcliffe first got the Home Office's permission.[6]

Also, faced with a total lack of useful information from workers and local villagers, Radcliffe conceived the idea of offering both rewards and free pardons to any rioters who turned informers. This plan too he put to Richard Ryder.[7]

Lastly he desperately needed more troops. The officer commanding the North-East district in which Radcliffe's territory lay had only just been appointed to this post at York. He was Lieutenant General, the Hon H G Grey: a Grenadier Guardsman, indecisive and insecure as well as unhappy with this uninspiring north country posting. Grey, deposited with his small force in the quiet county town miles away from the bubbling problems of the wool and cotton districts, could scarcely have been less impressed by Radcliffe's demands for infantrymen. It was March 13th before he replied to Radcliffe's urgent letter. He wrote:

> the situation of the forces under my orders is such at this moment that I must regret the impossibility of sending a hundred infantry to Huddersfield, which I should however hope cannot be attended with any bad consequences, as you have not stated any particular cause for alarm.[8]

Faced with what to him seemed to be wilful deafness, all Radcliffe could do was to turn back to the Home Office for help.

He pointed out there was no proper stabling for cavalry in the Huddersfield district. Some troopers were quartered in pubs in one village, their horses in another. He had to have infantrymen in large numbers to begin to give the district the appearance of protection.

On every single one of the issues with which Radcliffe confronted Richard Ryder, the Home Secretary slithered from underneath the necessity of making a firm decision. As far as the soldier-spies went, he felt the matter should be 'one of discretion and arrangement between the Magistrates and the Commanding Officer at Huddersfield'.[9] As for the free pardons for informers, he was worried about 'the prospective nature' of Radcliffe's proposal and was not too sure of the circumstances in which he could put such a tricky proposal to the Prince Regent. And as far as any 'additional Military Force' was concerned, the Home Secretary encouraged Radcliffe to apply again to Lieutenant General Grey.[10] Ryder said this having by now heard Grey's opinion that there was no cause for alarm whatever in the district.[11]

It was on March 13th on the same night that Grey had so contemptuously dismissed Radcliffe's plea for a hundred of his infantry, that the worst series yet of violent attacks took place in West Riding villages: this time in the South Crossland and Lockwood districts. Again Radcliffe listened to the string of frightened witnesses. Again the same story – bands of thirty men or more, well armed, well organised, pistols held to victims' heads, smashed shears.

There was worse to come. Early in the hours of the next morning a large gang swooped on the mill of one of the district's leading manufacturers, Francis Vickerman of Taylor Hill. The doors were quickly hammered in and the attackers set about selectively destroying shearing-frames, but leaving other machinery intact.

The alarm was quickly given to the piquet quartered nearby – a detachment of troopers of the 2nd Dragoon Guards. Ludicrously, they were forced to run the two miles to Huddersfield where their horses were stabled, then saddle and mount them before giving chase to an enemy which had long since vanished up the valley into the night. The only trace left for them was a misspelled, but nevertheless clear note telling Francis Vickerman that unless he now dismantled his spinning machines, he could expect not only to have them smashed, but to be marked for assassination.

Vickerman, knowing the way the rebels were now freely wielding their hammers and pistols, took the threat very seriously. Yet again he and his fellow manufacturers gathered at the George Inn to try to think of some way of forcing action by government. After this meeting they handed a strongly worded resolution intended for Radcliffe to use to put even more pressure on the Home Secretary. If infantry was not available, they asked, then why could not Bow Street Runners be sent?[12]

This gathering at the George Inn was of frightened mill owners in the centre of a district where the last semblances of law and order were disappearing and where the propertied class was defenceless. The degree of violence and organisation now being shown by the workers was of a kind they had never before experienced and – rightly as it happened – they were convinced there was worse to come.

But it would be an inadequate picture which represented this meeting as that of an isolated group of bourgeois businessmen trying to preserve a privileged way of life against the odds. The mood spread far beyond their valley town and into other districts with different preoccupations. Moreover, they were districts where a sizeable fraction of the population of industrial Britain now lived. In Nottinghamshire, Leicestershire, Northamptonshire, Lancashire and Cheshire and particularly in cities such as Manchester, Liverpool, Birmingham and Sheffield a movement of deepening concern for its own safety was infecting the middle classes just as a condition of deepening poverty was beginning to permeate the working classes.

The great recession of 1811 had left the nation desperately vulnerable. The consequence of the most recent violent events was that Britain had smothered itself with a blanket of fear. There was, most obvious and most urgent, fear of the workers. But in this period when the Industrial Revolution was manifesting some of its most profound effects, there was fear of change: change of centuries' old traditional methods and values, change of expectations, change of acceptance of established authority. And with this fear came the frightening possibility of the excesses of a French-style revolution if no grip could be brought to bear on the north country.

The only news to lift the shroud of despair was that from the Peninsula. Wellington, sitting in the middle of his booming artillery, had dispassionately given the order to attack Ciudad Rodrigo. Despatches reported that his columns of troops had successfully swept into the town. What had then followed gave many who heard of it pause for thought. The ranks of disciplined troops quickly transformed themselves into a mob of drunks. Doors were beaten down, houses and shops looted. Bloodstained fingers indiscriminately fired off gunshot, some of which was seen to blast off the heads of the surrendering enemy. Wellington was to report, 'two captains and 47 men were made prisoners, and the remainder of the garrison were put to the sword.'[13] In the Cathedral Square where the bloodiest work went on, Sir Thomas Picton could be heard as a lone voice of protest shouting to the rabble of soldiery to act like 'Men and Englishmen – not savages!'[14]

The *Nottingham Journal* which reported this bloody triumph of the British army also carried an account of the local destruction of yet another hundred new machines by a vicious mob against whose violent methods there had been no resistance.

13

The Enemy Within

The enemy in Europe was easily identifiable. But precisely who was this enemy within? If they were workers, what were the common bonds that seemed to be uniting them across the whole of the Midlands and the north of England? What were their aims? What did they hope to achieve? Increased living standards? Reform? Revolution? From where were they organised? And once decisions had been taken, now that the gangs of apparently well-disciplined men were growing in numbers, where did they meet and train? And – the most perplexing and important question of all – who was organising and leading them?

The problems the worried middle classes had in answering these questions were twofold. The remarkably successful guerrilla tactics of the gangs – sudden attacks by heavily disguised men followed by quick withdrawal – were leaving no clues. And secondly, those who were bodily suffering most from the attacks – the workers who lived on the premises where machinery was stored – if they had any suspicion of the identities of the attackers, were consistently reluctant to pass it on to Establishment figures such as Joseph Radcliffe. Both the fear of brutal reprisals on informants and general sympathies of a solid mass of the population with the rioters' aims were held as the reasons why magistrates were making no progress with their inquiries.

So successful had been the secretive organisation of the gangs that among those who had never seen the aftermath of a Luddite attack were still some who doubted the threat needed to be taken seriously. General Grey, in command at York, was one. Another was the elderly magistrate in the relatively peaceful Birstall district between Leeds and Huddersfield, Richard Walker. He continued to believe that Joseph Radcliffe should not bother himself so; he was sure the troubles could be put down to young boys larking about in the hills with fireworks.[1]

The problem was that few people had actually dared wander into the hillside and look closely at what was going on. However, two men who did so in the next few weeks were J S Lloyd of Stockport and Captain Francis Raynes, an officer of a Scottish militia regiment new to the district. At great personal risk both Lloyd and Raynes would set off alone into the east Lancashire hills. Both gave clear descriptions of the organised bands they came across. Raynes who would both crawl through the wet heather to get a precarious view of the proceedings in secluded copses and valleys, and, even more precariously, dress himself in disguise as a worker attending these meetings, reported the military system of organisation of the Luddites. Around open spaces on commons and moorland he watched sentinels being posted as the body of men paraded in regimental order. Muster rolls were called over, every man being given a number rather than a name.[2] One day in broad daylight he saw a body of rioters the size of a battalion parading on common land near a church where Sunday morning service was in progress.

It was true that many of the men involved were young; the ages of the relatively few later to be identified seldom exceeded twenty-five. And it was true, there were fireworks lighting the sky at night – but with a more sophisticated purpose than Richard Walker guessed. The rockets sent up from hillsides on the nights of Luddite attacks were intended to distract the few available cavalry away from the factories chosen as targets. So successful had this simple manoeuvre been that no troops whatever had yet succeeded in encountering, let alone resisting, an attacking Luddite gang.

Another feature of Luddite meetings which several spies were reporting was an initiation ceremony, held in dark, back rooms with only a few others present, involving a secret oath sworn on the Bible by a new member. Once he had been 'twisted-in' to the organisation to keep its secrets on pain of death, the candidate was expected to

> swear that I will use my utmost endeavour to punish with death any traitor or traitors who may rise up against us, though he should fly to the verge of existence. So help me God to keep this oath inviolable.[3]

The oath, according to papers that fell into the hands of magistrates, was accompanied by a disclosure of the quaint, even unbelievable secret signs that enabled one Luddite to recognise another.

> You must raise your right hand over your right eye. If there be another Luddite in company he will raise his left hand over his left eye, then you must raise the forefinger of your right hand to the right side of your mouth – the other will raise the little finger of his left hand to the left side of his mouth and will say What are you? The answer determined – he will say What for? Your answer, Free Liberty.[4]

If the ritual cannot escape seeming laughable and childish it is worth remembering that behaviour of this sort in Freemasonry and its north country working-class equivalent, the Order of the Buffaloes, persists to the present day. The effect of secret ceremony binding grown men to not always clearly stated aims is none the less inexplicably powerful. It can create what to outside observers of the esoteric procedure appears to be incomprehensible loyalties.

Rumours about the oath were by now passing from village to village. Captain Raynes was to discover that the numbers of men involved far exceeded similar groups known to have existed in Nottingham. In Lancashire and Cheshire he was to find boys of sixteen who had been twisted-in. The very secrecy of the procedure made it almost impossible to identify who was administering the oath. However, it can be said with certainty that one man who was active was George Mellor's mentor, the 66-year-old Halifax shoe-maker, John Baines.

The St Crispin Inn was Baines's catchment area. He would collect or have sent to him from the pub bar, likely candidates: men who knew of the movement and its aims and whom he felt could be trusted. They would arrive at his house at ten o'clock at night, well before the night patrols ordered out by magistrates began their rounds, and sit with one or two witnesses in the candle-lit room while Baines's young son Zachariah guarded the door. Old Baines would then have the candidate stand, put a Bible in his hands and have him repeat the oath, then kiss the book.[5]

Baines's strength, and his danger to established authority, was his ability to attract to his idealism, his republicanism, and to his oath-taking rituals, the most intelligent of the young workers of the nearby valleys. George Mellor was one and William Thorpe another who were undoubtedly twisted-in by the old man in the upper room of the Crispin. Not all were cloth workers, nor were they necessarily from the Methodist strongholds in the valley. Another highly intelligent and well-educated young convert to the cause was John Booth, a nineteen-year-old saddler. Booth's father had once been a cloth cropper, but had had uncommon success in the self-educating tradition of the district. He had been ordained in the Church of England by the same evangelical vicar of Huddersfield who had recruited Hammond Roberson to the district. Booth now had the living of the nearby village of Lowmoor.

His son, John, was remembered in the valleys as a sensitive, effeminate young man, much influenced by utopian socialist ideas. He was also much influenced by the drive and fire of the dominant member of his peer group, George Mellor. But his efforts to interest Mellor in idealism and theory had failed.[6] Vigorous action was Mellor's mainspring. Theory could be safely left to old Baines.

There is no surviving written record of any of the meetings of committed Luddites. Folklore and word-of-mouth descriptions passed on by survivors in the mid-nineteenth century to local historians such as Frank Peel[7] in the Spen valley and D F E Sykes[8] in the Colne valley are all that remain. It is likely that the attack on William Cartwright's new machines as they were being carried over Hartshead Moor was planned and led from the Shears Inn at Liversedge. But as February passed into March, and there followed night after night of successful attacks on cloth finishing shops, the Crispin Inn became the focus for the croppers.

Halifax, where the Crispin stood, was within easy reach of places such as Marsden, Longroyd Bridge and Liversedge. It was away from the centres of the cloth cropping trade, and it was as yet unpatrolled by the troops of cavalry now trickling, at Joseph Radcliffe's insistence, into Huddersfield.

The Crispin, nevertheless, was only one of dozens of public houses in the northern counties where men were meeting to plan, plot and exchange information. This much the authorities knew. What was not known was who these men were. So far none of the magistrates' spies had returned with any worthwhile or believable information to help bring charges. In Lancashire and Cheshire, all Lloyd had succeeded in discovering was that the groups of marching and drilling men were the poor and the out-of-work — colliers, spinners, weavers and foundry workers. In Yorkshire the selective fashion in which machinery was being smashed suggested to magistrates such as Radcliffe that the gangs were chiefly of cloth finishers. Beyond that the efficient pattern of secrecy the Luddites had adopted still kept identities secure.

Even more mysterious and more important for the British government, in particular Richard Ryder, the Home Secretary, was who were the leaders of this swelling movement. It was known from spies that delegates from Nottinghamshire had visited groups in both Yorkshire and Lancashire and addressed meetings. The similarity of the well-organised attacks in Yorkshire to those in Nottinghamshire confirmed the influence. One of those who had come up from Nottingham and who was operating in the West Riding of Yorkshire was a worker from the knitting industry, George Weightman.[9]

But the reason of the upper classes suggested, such was the growing scale and consistent purpose of the attacks, that there had to be individuals of greater standing and experience masterminding the operations. Before the end of March the ill-informed General Grey at York had finally been convinced by his considerably worried commander at Leeds, Colonel Campbell, that the mood of the workers in that town was not just unpleasant but downright dangerous. Now Grey told Richard Ryder, 'I am sure there must be some persons above the common order of people, both in consequence and ability, who direct the operations of the rioters.'[10]

But who? The names of middle-class radicals had been mooted, such as that of Major John Cartwright who believed in a manhood suffrage which seemed capable of spreading democracy towards the working classes. Another name being bandied as a possibility was that of Sir Francis Burdett, who had already been seen at the head of vast politically motivated London mobs. Neither of these gentlemen had yet been suspected of being anywhere near the disaffected northern areas, and had certainly not been seen holding forth at the bars of their pubs.

Just as confusing to the government in Westminster was what it was at this stage the rioters hoped to achieve. The poor of Lancashire and Cheshire needed food. What, if anything, did they have in common with the croppers and the small Masters of Yorkshire who wanted to keep out a technology which might diminish their high earning power? And what did either of these have as a unifying link with the radicals, reformers and democrats who were attempting to introduce some of the results of American and

French revolutions to the governance of England. Were they, like earlier groups who also had secretly twisted-in their members, committed to 'a total change of system'?[11]

Not all of these questions had yet been formulated by those at the seat of power in England. Indeed, there were still many in Government who appear to have been plainly unaware that any questions of any kind needed to be put.

Certainly none had been answered. However, one to whom both questions and answers, as well as issues, were of a considerable simpler nature was George Mellor. His home and workplace were within a night's return walking distance of most of the important attacks yet perpetrated in West Yorkshire and it is certain that he led a shear breaking gang at Linley on February 23rd.[12] The likelihood is that he organised and commanded most of the other raids. He had already discovered the power of a Bible in forcing others to swear allegiance to his methods. He had discovered leadership and he had experienced heady success. The opportunity to use this foundation to raise a far bigger movement with far more potential for power came on a Saturday late in March 1812.[13]

That night, according to stories handed down to Frank Peel, Mellor was called to a secret meeting at the Crispin Inn. It was held in the pub's upstairs meeting room where workers' trade meetings often took place, so that a casual drinker at the bar would think it a routine gathering. Nevertheless, the dark room at the front of the stairs was closely guarded by an apparently innocent and relaxed-looking worker sitting hunched over his pint of beer. The entrance to the room at the top of the stairs was equally well scrutinised by another sentry, this time in a candle-lit booth, through the hatch of which he identified every newcomer. George Mellor had taken William Thorpe with him. Before they were allowed to enter the room they had to give the secret Luddite sign and acknowledge its response from the sentry.

At the long table inside were seated thirty or so delegates. At their head was the white-haired John Baines. But what gave the group its unusually charged air of conspiratorial vibrancy that evening was the presence of the Nottinghamshire Luddite, George Weightman, who had been smuggled into the pub to give words of solidarity and advice.

Baines, an articulate and quietly passionate speaker, was first to address the group. He made clear that his motives for being a Luddite were different from those of most of the croppers present.

Baines's conviction ever since, as he put it, having had his eyes opened to the facts thirty years earlier,[14] was that only the overthrow of the British aristocracy which bled white the nation would bring about 'the glorious triumph of democracy'.[15]

Mellor was next to speak. He was in favour of taking action against not some remote aristocrat, but against the local Masters whose tyranny as a machine-owning class was as effective as any land-owning lord. The aristocrats' turn would come later. Peel suggests that George Weightman tried to persuade Mellor that whatever action was being proposed should be carried out without violence to any factory owners, as in the successful Nottingham attacks. Mellor's view – one which he could support with the results of many nights' work in the last weeks – was that tough, rough action had drawn attention to workers' grievances as had no other methods in living history. He proposed that armed attacks on a far bigger scale than any yet organised should be carried out on selected factories known to be using cropping machines in large numbers. The two he suggested as the first targets were owned by men who, it was now being said, were openly threatening to take whatever strong-arm action was necessary to deal with any Luddite attacks: William Horsfall of Marsden and William Cartwright of Rawfolds. Both mill owners were known to be planning to defend their property with guns and Horsfall had been heard to say at Huddersfield market that, if needs be, he would ride up to his saddle girths in Luddite blood if that was what was required to protect himself.

Mellor's powers of persuasion, as all subsequent evidence showed, were exceptional. Whatever strength of feeling was shown, the issue was clear and in Mellor's favour. The question became not whether to attack, but which factory to choose. The local story goes that a shilling was spun to settle the matter. Mellor picked up the fallen coin, examined it by candlelight where only he could see it, and announced the target to be Cartwright's Rawfolds mill. Whatever the truth of that incident, it is highly likely that Mellor made a deliberate choice of Rawfolds in the Spen valley rather than Marsden nearer his own workshop because of the numbers of cavalry now moving into Huddersfield and the Colne district as a result of Joseph Radcliffe's pressure on the Home Office.

It is probable that a basic agreement on how the attack was to be carried out was reached that evening at the Crispin Inn. Mellor was to be in overall command. The plan he eventually formulated required the assembling, if possible, of a whole regiment of working men – certainly as many as two or three hundred.

Gathering this number undetected and preparing them as a surprise force in an area already nervously bracing itself for the nightly violence of smaller gangs, would be difficult. On the scale he now had in mind Mellor would be well aware that the problems of logistics and communication involved in putting together his working men's army would be substantial. It has to be remembered that neither he nor his associates had yet any of the simplest artefacts that might be required to put itself in fighting order. They had no horses, mules or vehicles; few of their supporters would even have ready access to pen or paper – quite apart from the problems most would face in reading written text – so that the simple act of organising and delivering accurate messages could turn out to be a hazardous business. Yet Mellor's scheme was ambitious and required complex communication over scores of square miles. He planned to recruit men from as far away as Leeds, 15 miles to the east of Longroyd Bridge, as well as from Wakefield, Huddersfield and Halifax and from the scores of villages in between. They needed to be armed with muskets, pistols, pikes and hatchets. They needed instructing in what they were expected to do, and where they were expected to do it. They had to be assembled at dead of night and marched undetected to a place most of them had never heard of and certainly not seen before. When the job was done they would be expected to get back home using their own devices, and as with every other attack in recent weeks in the valleys, remain undetected by magistrates, special constables or troopers.

Before the Saturday evening at the Crispin was out, a probable date for the attack had been fixed – the night of Saturday, April 11th. Also a rallying place where the march on the mill could begin was agreed. It had to be one in a reasonably deserted spot, with good access to the Spen valley, but yet one which strangers from distant villages could find and recognise at night. The site agreed on was a stone obelisk in a field belonging to Sir George Armytage in the shadow of Kirklees. It went by the odd name of the Dumb Steeple. Local people believed this to be a corruption of Doom Steeple. Legend said it was the place where a doomed man, fleeing his pursuers, might seek safety.[16] It was the place to which the dying Robin Hood had fled.

14

Lines of Communication

The slow dawn of recognition that there was a problem of some substantial proportion in its north country now began to break over the Home Office. The great volume of worrying information being carried by every despatch into Whitehall was becoming too oppressive for the Under-Secretaries to acknowledge in their efficient fashion, then equally efficiently file and forget. It was probably the change of tune of the soldier supposedly in command of the situation in Yorkshire, General Grey, which persuaded Richard Ryder that what Joseph Radcliffe had been trying to tell him was actually true.

A few days earlier Grey's message to Ryder had been that the tales of uprising in Yorkshire were the fantasies of panicked magistrates. Now, at last convinced of the reality of the nightly violence, by his reliable garrison commander at Leeds, Colonel Campbell, Grey was beginning to show recognisable signs of unease in his communications to the Home Secretary.

Campbell had seen the situation in both Leeds and Huddersfield and had realised that the mood of a very significant number of workers in and around both towns was on the boil. When the Mayor of Leeds appealed to him to take preventive action, he immediately sent all his available troops out on patrol in the streets and padded out their numbers by arranging for special constables to patrol with them.[1]

In spite of his foresight his small force was nowhere in sight when a large gang – some rumoured it to be more than 100-strong – surrounded Thompson's mill at Rawdon outside the town. They threatened the nearby cottagers with death if they raised the alarm, then systematically smashed all machinery. On the follow-

99

ing night, this time in the town itself, another group poured into a factory, slashed every piece of finished cloth to ribbons and left before any of Campbell's men appeared. In language his commanding officer could not misunderstand Campbell relayed the desperate requests for more troops from villages such as Gildersome and Horbury. The despairing Horbury magistrate had now suggested that the only solution to the violence was for all manufacturers to dismantle all their machinery. 'The state of the country is daily becoming more alarming,' Campbell insisted to Grey.[2]

Seemingly oblivious to the fact that he could better serve the nation in almost any of the troubled places under his North-East command other than the quiet county town in which he now sat, the flustered Grey ordered troops from Sheffield to Leeds and back in the hope that military motion would compensate for lack of personal involvement.

It was a vain hope. The fears of the Horbury magistrate were soon realised. On the night of April 9th a waggoner was moving his horses across the lonely Grange Moor near Huddersfield when he saw a great crowd of men gathering there. He kept well out of their way. That night James Foster's house and mill at Horbury, several miles from Huddersfield, were attacked. Two of Foster's sons were left naked on the floor, tied hand and foot, whilst shears and frames were smashed.

When the masked attackers had finished their work they gathered in a field alongside the mill, a leader called the roll by numbers, and they then marched off.[3] The origin, organisation and style of the raid had the hall-marks of George Mellor clearly attached to it. The fact that it was carried out on an unguarded mill well away from the Colne valley, 11 miles from Grey's closest detachment of troops, suggests that this foray was a dress rehearsal for the more difficult and challenging raid on Rawfolds which Mellor had planned for two nights later. The easy success of raid after raid in the Yorkshire woollen district was now turning heretofore theoretical worker-power into substantial reality.

The news reaching Richard Ryder from the other side of the Pennines was no better. One of the spies in the pay of Colonel Fletcher, the Bolton magistrate, had reported that 823 weavers had been sworn in as Luddites and that 250 of these were armed. The same spy had heard from Manchester Luddites in Stockport that 'upwards of 2,000 including manufacturers, publicans, shop-keepers and others' were all ready to rise against the government when needed.[4]

If Ryder thought Fletcher an unreliable source of information he could take no comfort whatever from the news from Manchester. There the garrison commander, Colonel J G Clay, was deeply concerned about the undercurrents of revolt he knew to be flowing in the cotton towns. And just as Campbell was getting little or no support from his commanding officer, Clay's cries for reinforcements to the commander of the North-West district in Liverpool, General Dirom, were falling on deaf ears. Like Campbell, Clay was in a dilemma. Should he do as Dirom recommended and send his pitifully few troops of cavalry charging off in different directions to the dozens of villages and towns around Manchester? There, magistrates and other perfectly sober citizens such as Hay and Lloyd were assuring him that gangs of men, growing nightly in numbers, were both threatening and succeeding in doing damage to both property and persons. Several prominent citizens in remote country houses had been by now held up and robbed of money and guns. On the other hand, should Clay try to concentrate his troops in one body in this growing poverty-stricken warren of a city and try to face the gangs in action knowing that at least in that situation his men might not be outnumbered?

Clay decided to hold on to them all and billet them within easy reach of the centre of the town. It was as well that he did. The trouble, when it began, had unexpected origins. In the first week of April a meeting had been advertised for the 8th, a Wednesday, to take place in the great dining-room of the Manchester Exchange Building. Its purpose, so the advertisements said, was 'to prepare a dutiful and loyal address to his Royal Highness the Prince Regent expressive of the strongest assurances of our attachment to his Royal Person and of our ardent zeal for the support of his government'.[5]

The political reality behind the flowery expressions of loyalty to the unpopular Regent was an attempt to give a vote of support to the policies of the Tory government of Spencer Perceval which the Prince had kept in office. It had been widely expected that he would bring his Whig friends into power as soon as he had the chance.

However, before the meeting could take place, the manufacturers' Committee responsible for the Exchange Building began to have second thoughts about the wisdom of holding a politically motivated meeting at a time of such obvious social unrest in Manchester. In order to safeguard their famous building, therefore, they hatched the plan of calling in an architect to advise on the safety of the place. On the day before the meeting he duly gave his opinion that the great staircase was of insufficient strength to bear the anticipated crowd. The Committee immediately withdrew its permission for the dining-room to be used.

Before nine o'clock on the morning of the next day hundreds of people, many of them workers from the country districts and towns surrounding Manchester, had gathered in Exchange Street, the market place and St Ann's Square. The mood of the crowd quickly became lively and, since there was no opposition, it began to push its way into the Exchange. The rioting which then began to take place was not of a particularly serious nature. A couple of brave if misguided citizens who tried to pacify the rioters were attacked and several youths began to smash windows. By early afternoon Colonel Clay had gathered the Cumberland Militia together and sent the rioters running. Shortly afterwards a magistrate read the Riot Act and Clay placed the horses of the Scots Greys in position in the streets where they succeeded in keeping good order.

The main reason for the riot as far as could be established was the workers' opposition to recent increases in the price of bread. The Exchange Building was merely a symbol on which to vent anger. The worst harm to come from the day was that a particularly fine painting by the rising star of British portraiture, Sir Thomas Lawrence, had suffered. The mob had mistaken his portrait of their portly local Member of Parliament for that of the Prince Regent and pushed a hole in it.

Later that evening windows were broken in a nearby factory which was thought to be using new machinery. By the end of the day, however, Colonel Clay and his small force had succeeded in subduing Manchester. An uneasy calm settled on the place.

These reports of upheaval in both Yorkshire and Lancashire in the first days of April were not all that the Home Secretary had to face. News now began to reach him that in Birmingham too riots were threatened and that troops were needed.[6] There at least, if matters came to a head, he hoped he had a situation he could contain. General William Dyott had a reserve of several thousand troops sitting nearby in his Midlands encampment. Dyott, however, appeared singularly unconcerned by any event of any proportion of the last few months. Even the Nottingham riots had scarcely disturbed him from his family home in Lichfield.

It was at this point that Richard Ryder realised that both his lines of communication to the military commanders in the troubled areas, and the commanding generals themselves, were not perhaps what they should be. Neither the pusillanimous Grey, in the North-East, nor the retiring Dirom in the North-West, nor the home-loving Dyott in the Midlands were showing the faintest sparks of forceful initiative in moving from the edges of the disturbed districts to the problem at the centre. The views being relayed by them from York, Liverpool or Lichfield were leaving deep uncertainties in the Home Secretary's mind as to whether what was said to be going on was actually going on.

Ryder by now understood that stronger military hands needed to take a grip on the situation if it were to be contained. Finding those hands would be a major task. In the meantime there were short-term measures he could take.

If he were to have a true picture of what conditions were really like in the north country he had best have it from the horse's mouth. He therefore took the unusual step of bypassing the generals in charge. He told both Colonel Campbell in Leeds and Colonel Clay in Manchester to communicate with him direct and not to filter the information through their commanding officers. At the same time he got the message across to the generals themselves to supply their garrison commanders with more men.[7]

However, Richard Ryder's powers to call on the army, now that he was becoming convinced that he needed more support, were strictly limited. As a result of the carryings on in the northern counties, there was hardly even consciousness, let alone tremors of fear, among the nation's leaders. It would not be fair to say that the Prince Regent was entirely out of touch with military matters, but they were scarcely those which touched Richard Ryder. His Royal Highness was in fact at Brighton with his own regiment, the 10th Hussars, entertaining its officers lavishly at the Pavilion. Responding to the Royal pleasure one day, they followed him and his pack of beagles over the Downs and, in spite of all their efforts, failed to find a hare. To prevent boredom setting in, the Prince proposed the cavalrymen should take to their horses and ride a few races over a set of sheep hurdles left lying about the pasture. They obliged, found it pleasurable beyond all expectation, and the sport of hurdle racing was born.[8] It made 1812 a memorable year for the Prince of Wales's Own.

If the nation's hereditary leader was unaware of the army's failure to respond to the brewing civil strife, the elected leaders were no better informed. Their alternative focus of attention, however, was understandable. It was also the main cause of Ryder's problem.

Wellington's campaign in the Peninsula was now consuming even more of both the government and the army command's attention and fears. Allied losses at Ciudad Rodrigo in January had been a bearable 1,100. But at the storming of Badajoz early in April they had risen to 5,000. It was reported that Wellington, seeing the bodies of some of his finest men after the slaughter, had broken down and wept at the sight. He wrote to the War Minister, Lord Liverpool,

> The capture of Badajoz affords as strong an instance of the gallantry of our troops as has ever been displayed. But I greatly hope that I shall never again be the instrument of putting them to such a test. . . .[9]

The preoccupation of Spencer Perceval's ministry, therefore, was at that moment transfixed by the bloody events occurring outside the shores of Britain. It certainly did not occur to the Prime Minister to think of the potential for equally brutal events on his own doorstep.

Ryder nevertheless had begun to respond as best he could under the circumstances to Joseph Radcliffe's constant pressure for troops to be sent to the West Riding. By the middle of March he had managed to get 200 infantry and two more troops of dragoons to Huddersfield.[10] More were on their way before the month was out, by which time also, Grey had moved 100 of his West Kent Militia from Hull to Leeds.

The government's response to the information which the now apprehensive Richard Ryder was feeding them across the Cabinet table was to suggest that the citizens of the northern counties should themselves set about restoring their peace. It was with this in mind that the Watch and Ward Act was introduced on March 20th.[11] This gave magistrates such as Joseph Radcliffe the power to require 'persons to perform the duties of watching by night and warding by day'.

The truth was, however, that those who were concerned enough about their own and their neighbours' safety to take to such duties with both seriousness and energy were already doing so. Hammond Roberson, having demanded that cavalry should be sent to defend his valley, on March 3rd, had ridden over to Milnsbridge to have Joseph Radcliffe swear him in as a special constable; then on March 5th he had sent William Cartwright and six other Liversedge men over and on March 9th four from Heckmondwike.[12]

Sir George Armytage too was taking action. He had assembled his own regiment, the Upper Agbrigg Militia, and marched his men, himself at their head, through Leeds to their training ground. The result was a near disastrous riot. Fights broke out between the militiamen and jeering workers lining the streets. The Mayor of Leeds, a Mr Brown, was appalled and frightened by the spectacle of the 'lower class of people' at their most vicious. When Sir George, undeterred, proposed to repeat the march through the town, Brown protested to both Armytage and the Home Secretary, assuring them that the town is 'v. agitated at present' and suggesting 'the route be elsewhere – through Wakefield perhaps' – anywhere so long as the trouble it caused was not his.[13]

The editor of the *Leeds Mercury*, Edward Baines, was probably better informed about the now precarious state of the nation than most members of government. His view of the prospect for the peace of both the county and the country was extremely troubled.[14] Both Leeds and Huddersfield were suddenly beginning to look more like garrison towns bracing themselves for war than peaceful, profitable centres of the woollen industry.

The other class of people with unequivocal views about the state of unrest were the manufacturers. They knew that if serious violence began, they would be first to sample it. Both William Horsfall and William Cartwright were making substantial preparation.

Horsfall, who had seen just how destructive the attack on Francis Vickerman's factory had been, had already made up his mind how Luddites should be treated and he made sure to advertise his proposed methods. He was a leading member of the Committee for the Suppression of the Outrages, now meeting regularly at the George Inn at Huddersfield; it had raised yet more money to try to entice informers to give any information whatever about the Luddites.

On this Committee and at other times Horsfall used no discretion to hide his loathing of the rioters. His remark that he was ready to ride up to his saddle girths in Luddite blood had now become a catch-phrase in the district. The protection he gave to his family factory at Marsden, Ottiwells, reflected his aggressive style. On an elevation facing the road he had had built a vast castellated stone wall which commanded the whole frontage of the mill. In it were gaps 3 feet high and 10 inches wide, designed to accommodate a wheeled cannon he had bought. In use with small arms it would be bound to inflict bloody injury on any force of men choosing to attack the main gate. He had armed all his workmen, many of whom admired his forthright style, and had started a rota for day and night watch. And as further protection he had arranged to call on the few troopers of regular cavalry who were now being billeted in the town.

In character, William Cartwright, an altogether more private and secretive man than William Horsfall, had more covert defences. They were nevertheless impressive. He had done little to protect the outside of Rawfolds mill, though the whole length of one side had protection enough from the mill dam fed by the Spen beck. He had had a great studded main door fitted, but left the high ground-floor windows unshielded. Inside he had made more lethal preparations. He intended to conduct the defence of his property from the first floor. He had tipped up the flagstones of the floor to form embrasures through which he could safely aim musket fire on to the heads of any force storming the windows below. On the staircase which led to it he had fixed a series of rollers in which were stuck 16-inch-long metal spikes. A Luddite charging up this approach in the half-light would stand a good chance of being impaled there. If not, then Cartwright had placed a large carboy of sulphuric acid at the top of the stairs ready to pour on to any head that came beneath it.[15]

On the roof he had fitted a bell with its rope running to the ground floor. He reckoned it would be heard in any of the three or four villages up the valley from Rawfolds. Troopers from the Bays and 10th Hussars had been billeted there in pubs and disused cropping shops. Cartwright himself, without the permission of any magistrate, had taken over a number of privates from the Cumberland Militia and was using them as an additional night watch.

Unlike the brash Horsfall, there seems to have been little about the introverted Cartwright – the man from outside the valley with foreign blood in his veins – to inspire loyalty. A few workmen who opposed the Luddites were still with him, but he was as uncertain of them as they of him. A handful, no more than half a dozen, was prepared to help him watch and ward. With his large dog, along with the few workers he could persuade, he had been sleeping at the mill every night without exception for the past month. Of his other croppers he was unsure. Two at least he mistrusted: Abraham Pule and Samuel Hartley, even though Hartley was a private in a company of the Halifax Militia of which Cartwright was a captain.

Pule was a sly character. However, on the last Saturday of March he came to Cartwright with news the mill owner could not discount. Pule told him how two nights earlier he had been at Waterhouse's factory in Halifax and had overheard workers saying that Huddersfield men were planning an attack on Rawfolds. The assault would come within four nights unless Cartwright was thought to be too much on his guard. Otherwise it would be delayed for two or three weeks. Pule showed great concern and friendship towards Cartwright and promised that, whatever happened, he would give him a warning of any attack. Pule, and Hartley then left to take new jobs at the Waterhouse Halifax mill.

From the day of that conversation Cartwright, having left soldiers to guard his wife and children, was day and night on the alert in the mill, sleeping on the upper floor with whatever soldiers and workers he could persuade to stay with him.[16]

The four days passed, there was no attack and Pule never returned. Cartwright nevertheless was taking close account of what the worker had said, and of the number of passing days. On April 11th, precisely two weeks after the warning, when darkness fell, he posted two guards with blunderbusses outside the mill and locked himself inside with three workers, five soldiers of the Cumberland Militia, a boy – fourteen-year-old Charles Molyneux – and the dog. Each man was armed and Cartwright had carefully prepared large quantities of gunpowder and ammunition. As midnight passed and all was quiet, he sent them to their beds.[17]

15

Rawfolds

That night is recorded as being bitterly cold. As darkness fell George Mellor walked from Longroyd Bridge. With him were the three men with whom, during the past weeks of violence, he had formed close bonds of solidarity of purpose; William Thorpe, the most ruthless and single-minded, was to share command that night; Benjamin Walker and Thomas Smith were the followers, eager lieutenants, still full of surprise and elation at the easy success of the quick, savage but relatively unbloody attacks they had so far been led into by Mellor and Thorpe.

This night's events were to be not simply more daring than what had gone before, but on a scale and of an organisation which would determine the pattern of any future attack. So far Mellor's organising ability had shown remarkable success. His delegates from the Crispin Inn committee and from Longroyd Bridge had succeeded in contacting and recruiting from widely spread West Riding towns and villages as many as 400 men willing to take part.[1] If half that number turned up at the Dumb Steeple at dead of night, the gathering alone, irrespective of its outcome, would be a triumph.

That morning couriers had visited all the Luddite workshop centres supplying ammunition and, where possible, arms to be carried to the Dumb Steeple. One of these, Joshua Dickinson, had arrived at midday at John Wood's shop and had handed round a pint of gunpowder, ball and ball-cartridge to the men who intended to join the attack.

The plan Mellor had formed was to divide whatever army he could gather into companies of twenty or thirty men, carrying muskets, pistols, axes or hammers. He would clear any exterior defences to the mill with a first wave of a company of musket-men, put in an attack at close quarters with pistol companies, then have his axe-men break through the doors to allow the hammer carriers through to get on with the work of smashing frames. It was a scaled-up version of every successful attack to have taken place throughout the whole of that winter.

But there was still enough uncertainty in the enterprise to inspire anxiety. As he stood in the cold, alone with his three companions, alongside the gaunt obelisk and looked up at the thick dark woods surrounding Kirklees, Mellor could not have been other than aware of the catalogue of unknowns ahead. He was planning to take by storm a large and solid three-storey building, part surrounded by water, in the middle of a valley whose geography was unfamiliar to him. It was known to be defended by guns and had a determined owner supported by an unknown force of both cavalry and infantry whose numbers had been daily increasing in the district. His own force if it assembled at all, was untrained and likely to be only partly armed.

The first few workers who slunk into the field alongside him, some of them carrying only mauls and pikes, must have given pitiful confirmation to his worst fears. By ten o'clock, however, the dribble of men had become a stream. Fifty were already there. Early arrivals were able to tell him that they had overtaken many others. An hour later the obelisk was surrounded by a throng: a whispering crowd of conspirators. The anxiety had given way to apprehension, and, for some, excitement. Ben Walker, looking round, reckoned that there were three or four hundred men there, and all of them armed. Mellor could begin to congratulate himself. The supply of rum he had ordered to bolster any flagging resolve had arrived. Tots were being distributed and drunk.

There were many faces Mellor knew well. From Lockwood village came three members of the Brook family, one of them, the small Master, Thomas Brook, confirming that Masters as well as men were deeply opposed to the new technology whose destruction was the aim of this army. From other Huddersfield villages came a tough core also well known to Mellor; it included James Haigh, Jonathan Dean, John Ogden, John Walker and Joseph Drake. Also present was the effeminate and sensitive John Booth who had tried to educate Mellor with his newly acquired proto-socialist ideals. From Liversedge had come John Hirst; it was Mellor's intention that Hirst, with Samuel Hartley, the cropper who had worked for Cartwright at Rawfolds, should guide him over Hartshead Moor and on to the mill. Other Liversedge men present were William Hall and George Rigg – ordered by Mellor to bring up the rear and hustle on any stragglers.

With Thorpe at his side Mellor could now begin to organise his companies. The men were formed into ranks and given numbers so that they could be re-formed before and after the attack. Mellor insisted on the disguises which had made the guerrilla tactics of previous battles so successful in hiding identities. Those without masks were made to blacken their faces. Those wearing coats or smocks which were too easily distinguishable were made to wear them inside out.

Most particularly, every man had to have and wear a hat. The persisting fashion of the time was that all males wore hats in the open air. A bare-headed man in Regency England drew attention to himself in a way difficult to imagine almost 200 years later. Even in photographs of mass meetings of workers of the 1930s it can be seen how enduring was the habit of the obligatory covered head. That evening in April 1812, the fashion was to be of more than passing significance.

Near eleven o'clock Mellor had organised his force into one company carrying muskets which he was to command, two companies of pistols under Thorpe and a company of axe- and hammer-men, some of them carrying their 'Great Enochs' – the large hammers named after Enoch Taylor. Led by Hirst and Hartley and with Hall and Rigg in the van, the companies formed into pairs and silently began the march over into the Spen valley. Rawfolds lay 3 miles away.[2]

The first part of the journey was the most difficult, up between the fields near Kirklees and then across the pack-horse tracks of Hartshead Moor before reaching the cottages of Hightown perched above the Spen valley. It is inconceivable that this large band of men can have moved unnoticed by villagers. But they operated with the advantage of the sureness of the sympathy of by far the greater proportion of the local inhabitants. If they were heard by Patrick Brontë, whose windows and bed were within yards of their track, then the Ulsterman kept his head down and his pistol's barrel undisturbed.

The descent into the valley took Mellor's force on to the south banks of the Spen beck. There he had to wait for news of the Leeds contingent coming into the valley from the north. It was now shortly after midnight and he was able to re-form his companies, and rest his men, knowing that any distant sounds from the fields would be drowned at Rawfolds by the noise of the rush of water through the mill race.

It was nevertheless the period of greatest anxiety. Discovery now could bring troops of cavalry, each billeted less than a mile away, galloping down the valley road from both east and west. There was a limit to the amount of time he could sit and wait.

Still there was no news from the Leeds men. It was possible that they were hiding themselves, on the north slopes of the common land up the other side of the valley, not making contact from fear of giving the game away. This, as it happened, though never known by Mellor, was the case. He could reason, however, that if they were there, they would surely reinforce him as soon as they heard and saw his guns begin to fire.

The chance was clearly worth taking. Most reassuring was the discovery that the mill's exterior was guarded by only two men who could present no real resistance to the first wave of his attack. He decided he could wait no longer. He ordered his own company to move quietly on to the mill. First sending in Hirst and Hartley, who knew the mill yard well, he was able to jump the blunderbuss-carrying guards without the sound of a shot or a shout. Quickly Cartwright's two workers were gagged and bundled away. Far from seeming impregnable, the silent mill, its high ground-floor windows unshielded, looked to Mellor and his army to be theirs for the taking.

*

It was the furious barking of his dog, left chained on the ground floor, which sent Cartwright tumbling out of the bed he had got into only minutes earlier. At first he was convinced the animal was giving a false alarm since he was expecting an early warning from the guards outside the building. But as he opened the door of his counting-house bedroom, a volley of musket fire smashed through the ground-floor windows. At the same time, the crash of hammers against both the main door and a side door and the yell of charging men from the mill yard produced a frightening cacophony.

Within seconds Cartwright was at the stack of primed guns and was handing them to his workmen and the soldiers. In their nightshirts like him, they took up the positions he had given them behind the embrasured flagstones at the first-floor windows and immediately began to fire down on easy targets.

One of his men reached the bell-rope and began pulling at it for all he was worth. Its first notes clanged out across the valley, drowning the screams of the first workers to be wounded in the yard below. Another of his men, watching Cartwright, saw that the mill owner was using his musket like a man possessed; he had never seen anybody load and fire with such speed.

Cartwright nevertheless, besides keeping the attackers in his gunsights, had to maintain a worried eye on what was happening inside the mill. Three of the Cumberland militiamen were keeping up a good raking fire on the yard. One in particular, a veteran cavalryman discharged from the 11th Dragoons with a broken thigh, was defending the place as though it were his own property. However, the remaining two, as Cartwright saw to his fury, were doing nothing whatever. One of them had retired to the fireplace and refused Cartwright's order to get back in the firing line.

It was not his only worry. He had by this time estimated that the mill was surrounded by as many as 200 attackers. Reinforcement for his puny defences would have to come from without while he fought for time from within. He had no idea how long the two doors would withstand the fearsome battering they were getting and already axes had smashed in not just windows, but some of the window-frames of the ground floor. His main hope, he was convinced, was in the cavalry detachments billeted less than a mile up the valley and well within the sound of the mill. Salvation, therefore, lay in the clanging bell. When, within minutes, the bell-rope broke as a result of panicked tolling, Cartwright had no hesitation in sending two men up to the roof to try to get it pealing again.

With two of his men bound and gagged, two refusing to fight and two on the roof, Cartwright's force was now effectively reduced to four men and a boy. Nevertheless, the small band was able to pour down an almost continuous fire on to the yelling and screaming workers below.

George Mellor, like Cartwright, was under severe pressure. The first wave of musket-men, himself at their head, had succeeded in getting to the mill's windows without opposition. He was able to call in his company of pistol-men and hatchet-men immediately. But the barrage of fire which came down on them from above was a brutal surprise. John Walker, carrying a horse pistol in the second company, found himself quickly at one of the windows and being fired on. As he looked through it he saw a flash and felt a shot pass through the crown of his hat. Fearlessly he lifted his pistol and fired it in the direction of the shot. 'I was

112

determined it should go if my hand went with it,' he later said.[3] Jonathan Dean, wielding his hammer on the mill door, was less fortunate. Part of his hand did go as a musket shot ripped into it. An axe-man at the front with him nevertheless managed to smash a hole in the woodwork of the door. Its studded-metal frame, however, held secure.

Every second the workers spent in front of the windows and the door was time exposed to lethal fire. With the attackers now only a few yards from the flagstone embrasures, Cartwright's muskets were able to wreak terrible damage. As the wounded ran into the darkness of the fields for cover, two workers fell to the ground. One, badly hurt in the chest, was screaming. Others, some not wounded, now began to run.

Mellor, seeing window-frames smashed and the main door holed, already realised how slender was the opposition against him, and how tantalisingly close he was coming to the night's aim. He yelled to those alongside him that the door was open and shouted to the musket-man to fire up at the bell which had once again begun its insistent, threatening pealing. But nothing he could do could now prevent the flight of his men away from the mill's front. Thomas Brook in his panic to move from the line of fire of the guns rushed round the blind side of the mill, tripped, and found himself floundering in the freezing water of the mill dam. Though he quickly hauled himself out, his hat had floated off into the darkness.

By the time Mellor himself withdrew to safety back across the Spen beck, frightened figures were struggling away through the darkness in whatever direction seemed to offer shelter. Some were obviously badly hurt, others were helping the wounded, while yet others were simply scared by the screams of their companions. In vain Mellor looked up in the direction of hills across the other side of the valley, hoping against hope that the Leeds contingent would materialise. But nothing moved there. Hearing the thunder of Cartwright's guns and the clang of his bell amplified by the bowl of the valley, the reinforcement company of workers had assumed that Rawfolds was being defended by a strong military force. Silently its members had melted back into the hills, soon to be overtaken by the first fleeing wave of Mellor's army, already lost in strange country.

All was now disaster. An organised, optimistic gang of young men had suddenly turned into a terrified rabble. Mellor stood unable to check the flow of workers moving past him and heading for the path back to Hightown. He could recognise Thomas Brook, dripping wet and conspicuous without his hat, James Haigh, badly wounded in the shoulder by a musket ball, William Hall, also wet after having splashed through the beck, and Benjamin Walker who told him that at least one wounded man had been left lying outside the mill. As they vanished, Mellor had little alternative but to turn and follow them into the night.

It had lasted no more than twenty minutes. In that period Cartwright's muzzle-loading guns had fired without ceasing. By the time he realised that his enemy had disappeared he had let loose no less than 140 rounds into the mill yard below. From the screams that had come from there he knew he had inflicted some serious damage. The only wound among his own forces was his and had been self-inflicted. Ironically, in his dashes from window to window in the mill, he had forgotten his own defences and spiked himself on one of the rollers intended to trap the croppers. The wound was not serious. The glass carboy of sulphuric acid was still intact.

Not until he heard an identifiable voice outside did Cartwright open the mill's bludgeoned doors. Waiting there in the smoke-filled yard was an open-mouthed neighbour, a wealthy dyer and passionate Tory, Thomas Cockhill, who had run from Littletown when he heard the mill bell tolling. Others were quickly on the scene – Alec Dixon, the manager of a local chemical works, and Billy Clough, one of a persistent breed in the valley: a drunk who had been rolling his way home to Cleckheaton after a night well spent in the public houses of Littletown. A newspaper report of the Rawfolds affair would describe him as *bon vivant*. For ever after history has used this epithet to give the ale-happy Billy elevated status.

Last to arrive was a furious Reverend Hammond Roberson: furious because the news of the Rawfolds attack had taken so long to reach him in his bed at Healds Hall. By the time he had thrown a saddle on his horse and galloped down the valley, all serious action was over. Even so, he arrived ahead of the piquet of dragoons of the Queen's Bays whose quarters close to Cartwright's mill had been chosen to prevent any incident such as this.

Only now did Cartwright pick his way through the mess of broken glass, smashed window-frames and abandoned weapons in the mill yard towards the cries of the abandoned wounded. Two bodies were lying in pools of blood. One of them was John Booth, the gentle nineteen-year-old son of the Lowmoor clergyman, the bones of his leg splintered by a musket ball. The other Cartwright recognised as Samuel Hartley, the 24-year-old cropper he had once employed and who was now a private in the company of Halifax Militia which Cartwright commanded. He had been shot in the chest from a high angle, probably by Cartwright himself. The ball had pierced down into his body and the miracle was that he was still alive and conscious.

The only recollections of the next few minutes in the mill yard are by word of mouth and might well have been embroidered to suit the teller. They suggest that one of the wounded had pleaded for help and that Cartwright refused it, asking first for a full confession of the names of the leaders of the attack. Alec Dixon, moved by the obvious suffering of the pair, in spite of Cartwright, ran to fetch some wine and moistened both men's lips with it. Billy Clough, now a much sobered man, responded to the requests which Cartwright ignored and gave support to each of their heads with a stone. Whether these tales are true or not, they branded Cartwright as the brutal mill owner, dismissive of the sufferings of his workers. The image persists in spite of all Charlotte Brontë's attempts in her novel to paint the hero of Rawfolds in sensitive colours and in spite of her insistence that Cartwright 'is a gentleman: his blood is pure and ancient as mine or thine.'[4]

When none of Cartwright's questions had produced answers, the two men were lifted on to gates which troopers from the Queen's Bays used as litters, and were carried off to a room at The Star, a public house at Roberttown two miles up the Huddersfield road. The reason for choosing such a distant place to take men who can only have been in hideous pain is unclear. It could have been to prevent Rawfolds becoming for the second time in the night the focus of an unsympathetic crowd; more compassionately, it could have been to get them to a surgeon. Whatever the reason, it was in the room at The Star that, with no better anaesthetic than alcohol, heroic surgery was begun to amputate John Booth's leg. When the tormented boy went into convulsions the surgeon had to withdraw. Booth died in the early hours of the morning.

From Samuel Hartley's chest a musket ball was unsatisfactorily removed along with a piece of bone. The terrible cries of the men under the surgeon's knife started rumours that they were being tortured. Later it was even suggested that stains on their mattresses were made by aqua fortis – nitric acid – used in an attempt to extract information.

When Hammond Roberson had appeared at The Star the worst possible motives of the parson were suspected. The story which emerged from the room was that Roberson had stood alongside the dying young Booth's bed and had bent towards him in response to a signal from this son of his brother clergyman. 'Can you keep a secret?' Booth whispered. Roberson eagerly nodded. 'So can I,' Booth replied, and soon breathed his last.[5] Hartley too was silent to the end. He continued to lose blood and was dead by three o'clock on the morning of the next day.

Whether or not the stories of Cartwright and Roberson's cruelty and insensitivity are true or are colourful local inventions, they were circulating throughout the valleys before the echoes from the Rawfolds incident had had time to fade. The inflexible attitudes of an Establishment linked to the manufacturing community were now made manifest. Cartwright and Roberson were marked men.

George Mellor had turned to run with the small group which included the wounded James Haigh. Tending to Haigh, however, was not his first concern; nor was it that Thomas Brook and Benjamin Walker were dripping wet on this freezing night. The fact that in the group was a man without a hat – Brook's had been left floating on the mill dam – occupied Mellor's thoughts to the exclusion of any other factor. If Brook's bare head was seen by a passing patrol of cavalry or by special constables, the chances of their being taken in for questioning was certain. Conviction for taking part in the Rawfolds affray, as they well knew since the passing of the Frame Breaking Act, could lead to death by hanging.

Mellor led the group back out of the dark valley through country still strange to him. Luckily the path he took was close to the one which had brought them there. As soon as he reached the heights of Hightown, therefore, he abandoned caution and knocked on a cottage door. The woman who answered, Sarah Naylor, appeared friendly; she was reputed to be married to a Luddite sympathiser. With few questions asked she lent Thomas Brook her husband's hat so that the group, with a deep sense of relief, could continue its retreat. A mile further on at the village of Clifton, Mellor saw a lighted window and again made contact with an apparently friendly cottager, Mary Brook. In spite of the hour – it was at least 2 a.m. by this time – Mellor persuaded her to sell him muffin bread and a pitcher of water which she passed through the broken pane of glass. Dejected, though less exhausted, they were now able to recross the moor, creep back up the Colne valley, and be back in their beds before dawn.

It is certain, however, that others from Mellor's army did not reach their beds that night and that some besides John Booth and Samuel Hartley never saw their homes again. On the day after the onslaught William Cartwright toured the outskirts of Rawfolds and counted only nine windows out of 300 left intact in the mill's façade. He also counted pools of blood in the outlying fields.

Another who claimed to be a witness to some of the disastrous consequences of the night was the Reverend Patrick Brontë. His ecclesiastical biographers describe Brontë hiding in the dark in Hartshead churchyard to watch a group of Luddites gathering to bury in secret their Rawfolds dead. They give a clear description of him on the following morning examining the freshly turned soil in the south-east corner of the graveyard, and noting on its surface imprint of workers' boots.[6] The fact that the graves were unmarked is attributed to a deliberate decision by the parish priest himself. No source is given for the story, nor any hint whether it might not have been conceived in the fertile mind of Patrick Brontë.

George Mellor was never to know the full tally of deaths from the Rawfolds incident. All that seemed certain to be the consequence of the affair was that it had been a conspicuous failure for working men led by workers. His logistics, his leadership, his aims and some of his companions had come to grief. For the first time in the campaign to fight the new machines, in which he was the rising leader, a machine-owning Master had triumphed over united workers. Even the most liberal minded among the Establishment, Edward Baines of *The Leeds Mercury*, in his next leading article, 'from the regard we feel for the labouring classes', preached the nemesis of Luddism. Baines warned of 'the fatal consequences that await them in the unequal contest which they are now waging with the civil and military powers'.[7]

The effect of the news of the disastrous attack on the working community, however, was quite the opposite of what the newspaper editor, the manufacturers, the received opinion of historical accounts, and George Mellor in the depths of defeat, imagined.

16

The Tide of Sympathy

The inquest on Booth and Hartley was quickly carried out at Roberttown where they lay. A jury of local men returned a verdict of justifiable homicide. In spite of the fact that it was now acknowledged that at least 150 workers had been involved at Rawfolds, and all had passed through this village forty-eight hours earlier, no witness at the inquest gave any hint whatever of the identity of any other attacker. Cartwright's fury at the unwillingness of the people he lived among to give information which might lead to arrests intensified when he looked at the sullen crowd of croppers gathered from many miles around to hear the result of the inquest. Lounging in the village street he could see none other than Abraham Pule, the cropper who had promised to warn him of the date of the Rawfolds attack.[1] He now had no doubts that Pule was a Luddite just as he could have had no doubts that the Rawfolds affair had turned him, Cartwright, into an object of hatred among the workers who now stared at him.

Two days later on April 15th the tide of sympathy of the people could be seen at its full. Samuel Hartley's body was taken to Halifax for burial and huge crowds assembled to accompany it. As the coffin moved through the streets a vast parade of working men, each wearing a white crêpe arm-band, fell in behind and silently followed to the parish churchyard.

That day passed without incident. However, the possibility that the wake would be used as an excuse for an uprising still remained. The funeral of the boy John Booth, planned for the next day for the centre of unrest, Huddersfield, was a potential powder keg.

Troops were poured into the town. In case of trouble, Colonel

Charles Campbell rode from his Leeds headquarters to keep watch on the situation. He was startled even by what he saw on the road before reaching Huddersfield. More great crowds were gathering from every direction and descending on the Calder valley. And on many of the cottage doors he passed he saw scratched the words 'Vengeance for the blood of the innocent'. He told his commanding officer, General Grey, 'The country is in a most perturbed state and the utmost exertions of the military necessary.'[2]

But the worst of his fears were allayed by the sudden decision to move Booth's body secretly by night and bury it in the early morning before most of the crowd had gathered. Huddersfield remained quiet, but only after a firm grip of the place had been taken by the army. Every public house had had billeted on it a detachment of soldiers. 'Huddersfield wears the aspect of a town under military power night and day,' wrote a reporter from the *York Courant* who had travelled over to observe the goings-on in the western districts of the county.[3]

However, the peace which had now been temporarily forced on the area of worst disaffection, the West Riding valleys, belied the destabilising effects of the Rawfolds affair on the rest of the north of England. Within hours the news of the disaster and the deaths of the two workers had spread by word of mouth to villages and towns on both sides of the Pennines. Its consequence was arresting. Insurrection suddenly flared on a wholly unpredictable scale. That the seeds of revolt were already present in fertile soil is evident; it was Rawfolds, however, which pushed these shoots suddenly to the surface.

Sheffield was the town where the first large riot erupted. It began at noon on the day following the inquest. Spontaneously a small crowd had begun to throw potatoes from one of the stalls in the market place. Before long the whole square was in a tumult and magistrates, who by chance were sitting at the Town Hall, had to be called to read the Riot Act. The effect of their prompt action was to incite the crowd to far more serious violence. The rioters began to swell their numbers and move to other parts of the town. Abused and left trailing behind were the magistrates, ineffectually reading the Riot Act in street after street.[4]

Soon the mob had increased its size by many hundreds and after its first wave of window smashing and stone throwing, focused itself on a more substantial target. Lieutenant Colonel Frank Fenton, the officer commanding the Sheffield Militia, had to watch helplessly as the rioters proceeded like a torrent to our Military Depot where the ordinary guard were unable to resist and in a quarter of an hour, before the troops of Hussars arrived, they broke all the windows, burst the door open and broke 222 stand of arms, taking hold of the barrels and dashing them violently against the walls.[5]

It was midnight before Sheffield was again in control and then only after intervention by the 15th Dragoons, the West Riding Yeomanry and the Sheffield Militia, and after a dozen or so workers – women as well as men – had been packed off to the gaols of York Castle. Frank Fenton was particularly worried by the fact that, when at last he was able to parade his regiment of militia, he recognised in their ranks a number of faces he had seen rioting in the market square earlier in the day.[6]

Copycat riots with the same level of violence began in the same week at a number of places: a potato riot at Skipton, another at Carlisle.[7] Most inexplicably, since the city was insulated from the depression in the cloth weaving districts, Birmingham's peace was also being threatened by mobs of marching workers. Birmingham magistrates were beginning to panic and demanded that the Home Secretary should send troops of horse without delay. Richard Ryder, however, succeeded in calming them with the knowledge that General Dyott at Lichfield had now 4,000 troops waiting in the wings should things truly get out of hand.[8]

But in those few days it was soon unmistakably clear to the Home Office where the tinder box had shifted. It was the few miles over the Pennines to Lancashire and Cheshire, already on edge after the Manchester Exchange affair, that the news of the Rawfolds disaster had travelled most quickly and with most dramatic effects. At Stockport the clinically efficient defender of the middle classes, the young solicitor J S Lloyd, was the first to see the danger signals. On the day after Rawfolds he was in Manchester watching the uneasy situation there, poised to stamp on violence wherever he could find it. He was not to be disappointed in his expectations. In the next few days he was to take to his horse and gallop from place to place, scribbling messages to the Home Office – sometimes several a day – describing houses broken into, mills fired, gentlemen dragged from their horses and beaten and the country as a whole terrorised.[9]

On the Monday of that week he was in Chester when a message reached him that a bad riot had broken out in his home town of

Stockport. Immediately he was in his saddle and reached the town at 7 a.m., in time to see smoke rising from the charred remains of the house of a leading manufacturer; the factory next to it had been completely sacked. Several of the local middle-class residents he talked to had been beaten up and robbed.

Lloyd's energy cannot be faulted. He instantly set off and commandeered a troop of inactive regular dragoons and rode out of town with them at top speed. After a few miles he overtook the main body of rioters and sent them scattering. He successfully manoeuvred seven of their number into a corner, arrested them and packed them off, guarded by the dragoons, to Chester Castle.

Without pause he returned to troubled Stockport and there took command of a piquet of Lancashire Militia – the regiment in which he was a captain. That night, about an hour before midnight, he silently led his men to heathland 2 miles outside Stockport. There he put to flight a secret meeting of Luddites, taking one prisoner. It was the opportunity for Lloyd to use the frightening methods he only hinted at in his letters to Ryder. He tersely told the Home Secretary that the wretched man had 'been induced to give important information'. Within a short time of getting to work Lloyd had extracted from him the names of several leading Luddites.[10]

And still, after two nights without sleep, Lloyd had energy to spare to capture four more prisoners. It was little wonder that the Stockport magistrates believed, and told the Home Office, that only John Lloyd stood between this steaming unrest in which their town now simmered and total anarchy. One of these magistrates, the Reverend H D Broughton, fearing that even Lloyd might not sustain them, had ridden to Northwich to try and persuade John Leicester, who had raised a regiment of cavalry, to give aid to Stockport. Broughton failed with this plea, but managed instead to persuade some detachments of the Earl of Chester's Yeomanry Cavalry to return with him to Stockport to try to pacify the place.[11]

Lloyd, when he had ridden out of Manchester, had left behind him the red embers of a revolt which would turn into a worse conflagration than those he set out to douse.

The hard-pressed garrison commander in Manchester, Colonel Clay, realised as soon as rioting began there on the day after Rawfolds that the detachments of Scots Greys and Cumberland Militia he was using to keep control in the teeming city were now totally inadequate for his needs.

No sooner did he succeed in dispersing one window-smashing gang of workers than another would gather and send him and his force dashing to the other side of town. That day, as Clay tried to deal with the situation, he had news that rioting had broken out at Macclesfield, Stockport, Wilmslow and Middleton. Clay flatly refused to send any help in response to the pleas that came from the last two of these towns: 'I could not answer for the safety of Manchester were I to make a further reduction in the force I now have,'[12] he said.

That force was fully stretched in the days which followed and the rioting continued with scarcely a break. By the Saturday of that week mobs of workers from the hill villages were pouring into the Manchester district and causing mayhem. Simultaneously riots and looting were taking place in the Potato Market, the Flour Market, Newton Street, Bank Top and Deansgate.[13] As the centre of the city flared yet again and Clay tried his best to contain the situation with his dragoons, three riders in succession galloped up to him, carrying despatches. The first told him that riots had started at Ashton, the second had the same news of Middleton and the third the same of Eccles. He could spare troops only for Middleton where a large cloth works owned by a Mr Burton was, not for the first time that week, under siege.

Burton's mill was one of the first to use steam looms on a considerable scale. It was an obvious target for Luddite gangs from Saddleworth, a Pennine village notorious for its tough croppers and colliers and for their brutal techniques. Clay had already reinforced the mill with infantry when, at two o'clock in the afternoon of April 18th he read Burton's message that again the factory was besieged by a mob – some said there were as many as 3,000 there.[14] He immediately detached the few troops he could spare – an officer and thirty men of the Scots Greys – and sent them in the direction of Middleton. They arrived at the outskirts of the town too late. Burton's house was already going up in flames.

As soon as the workers saw the troop of grey horses wheel into the centre of the town they withdrew to the high ground around the churchyard. A pitched battle now began. Not before a large detachment of the Cumberland Militia had been sent in to the attack did the crowds withdraw. It was a bloody operation. Five workers were shot and killed, many others seriously wounded. As the cavalry moved in to flush out any remnants, one worker armed with a pistol stood his ground and at close quarters, took aim at the sergeant of the Greys. It was his last act. The sergeant, with a more practised trigger finger, shot him dead. There were no casualties among the soldiers.[15]

The Manchester magistrate, the Reverend Mr Hay, had been in Ashton when the rioting began there and had hurriedly ridden back into Manchester to plead personally with Colonel Clay to release some of his troops. When Clay refused, all Hay could do was send an urgent message to the Home Secretary, begging for more soldiers. If regular infantry was not available then he implored Ryder to send immediately to Lancashire some militia regiments 'of the *Southern* counties, unconnected with manufacturing districts'.[16] Hay, like Frank Fenton, was beginning to worry that north country militiamen, with little prompting, would be prepared to turn their muskets on the very people they were supposed to help.

Richard Ryder was having to note with growing concern the reports now reaching him. Nor could he any longer discount those from people he knew to be prone to exaggerate. For example, Colonel Ralph Fletcher, the Bolton magistrate, was clearly not relying on the whisperings of his spies when he poured out to the Home Office a breathtaking list of atrocities which had taken place that week in his district. Factories had been wrecked, hay ricks set ablaze and private property plundered. Both infantry and cavalry had had to be sent on to the streets and market place of Bolton. Fletcher himself had braved disorderly crowds to read the Riot Act; he had called in troops to disperse the mobs from the centre of the town and special constables to clear the public houses which were so effectively fuelling the mobs.[17]

If the flood of communication from magistrates to the Home Office was not enough, Richard Ryder now found himself at the receiving end of messages directly from troubled citizens who were convinced that local powers of law and order were useless. Graphically one Lancashire factory owner, Thomas Garside, described how a mob, in the act of breaking up his factory, had seen him watching the attack from near his own house. Garside had heard the command ring out, 'Kill him, he is a spy,' then found himself quickly surrounded and being stoned. Bleeding and hatless – Garside emphasised his loss of headgear almost to the exclusion of his wounds – he had picked up a stick and fought his way through to a group of cottages where every door was instantly closed on him except that of an old woman, who gave him temporary shelter. Again Garside tried to dash for safety, but the mob trapped and surrounded him. Helpless, he watched the workers closing in to finish him off when suddenly one man held up his hand. Immediately on this command the crowd halted, parted and mockingly let the bleeding mill owner pass through.

The callous manner in which Garside's life had been threatened, then spared, convinced him of the reality and of the effectiveness of Luddite leadership. He told Richard Ryder, 'this attempt at murder was not the effect of passion – but in obedience to the command of their Leaders.' But Garside went further and repeated what Ryder was now hearing in less graphic phrases day after day from one source or another: that the uprising now under way in the north of England was 'the most desperate and best organised conspiracy that the world has ever witnessed'. Garside pleaded for the government to take action or else, he said, 'the whole nation will be ablaze.'[18]

Ryder could now do no other than raise himself from his torpor and try to face the facts behind these dire warnings. Rawfolds had been the spark that set the fuses of revolt burning across the whole of the north. In the week beginning April 12th, 1812, despatches reached the Home Office telling of riots and violence in, among other places, Ashton, Barnsley, Birmingham, Bolton, Carlisle, Cheadle, Coventry, Doncaster, Eccles, Macclesfield, Manchester, Middleton, Oldham, Rochdale, Saddleworth, Sheffield, Skipton, Stockport, Tintwistle and Wilmslow. The simpler question was not which part of the north of England was rioting but, which was not? The reality sitting squarely in front of Ryder was that these few days had seen the simultaneous insurrection of populations of working class on a scale England had never before experienced.

Information identifying the root of the conspiracy, if conspiracy there was, was still as confusing as ever. Fletcher's spy 'B' had it that Napoleon was ready to supply both men and arms; 10,000 men and 30,000 guns were said to be standing by in Ireland to bolster the coming revolution.[19] But if wild rumours sold as facts could be discounted, the unembroidered reports of a growing number of eye witnesses could not. Larger and larger groups of weavers, croppers, cotton printers, colliers and other workmen, meeting no longer in hidden places, but on open moorland and near towns, some in gangs of several hundreds, were being reported from every one of the northern manufacturing towns.

More uncertain was the co-ordination of each group and the

existence of communication, one to another. The Reverend Henry Broughton in Cheshire insisted that there was 'a complete revolutionary system now pervading the whole part of this country',[20] and several urgent messages to the Home Office had suggested that a date early in May – some suggested the 1st and some the 4th – had been fixed on for a general uprising.[21]

In the middle of all this turmoil, the inactivity of the Home Secretary in the face of the events engulfing him was equalled only by that of one man: the soldier who should have been his most informative source, General H G Grey. The commander of the North-Eastern district, however, still sat immobile in his York seat and, although he conceded the very 'unpleasant temper' of the people of Leeds and Huddersfield, felt the whole business was being much exaggerated. 'The riot at Sheffield,' he told the Home Secretary, 'was not of much consequence,' and he believed the affair at Cartwright's mill to have thoroughly frightened the workers. Nevertheless, for good measure the General proposed to shuffle his pack of soldiers to demonstrate their activity and ready availability. Having moved the Cumberland Militia from Hull to Manchester, he now shifted the Denbigh Militia to Hull and the West Kent Regiment to Leeds – and then returned to his nail-biting inactivity.[22]

Richard Ryder could no longer go on and on doing nothing. In his defence it has to be said that, at the same time as his office was being submerged by this flood of information insisting that the most densely populated areas of the north of England were standing at the threshold of a bloody revolution, his tiny staff was sinking in the morass of its other petty affairs. Preparing audiences for the Prince Regent, managing the time-table of the Privy Council, considering the appointments of Lord Lieutenants and dealing with their complaints once they were in office is only a small sample of the tasks which deluged the Home Office. Passing daily across its few desk tops were numberless trivial requests which daily demanded, and frequently succeeded in getting, instant reply.

By the Tuesday of the second week after Rawfolds Ryder had to respond. By then he had communicated his concern over the state of affairs to the Cabinet. He had asked for and had been given approval to look to the Commander in Chief, the Duke of York, to bring the north country back under control.[23] So long had the situation been allowed to deteriorate and so grave had the threat to England as a whole now become that it was clear that a very substantial army would have to be gathered and moved at high speed. If rumour was to be believed – and considering what had happened so far in this uprising there was no reason why it should not – if the army was to be in position to prevent realisation of the worst fears of a general uprising it would need to be in the north by May 1st. And if it was to continue to be effective it would need to be led by a commanding general of some stature and ability – this at a time when the Duke of Wellington was persistently sucking the most skilful military leaders out of England and into the Peninsula War.

In quick time the army responded that it could comply with Ryder's request. With sighs of relief almost visible on the sentences of the Home Office notepaper, the news could now be sent to the hard-pressed local magistrates that a major military force was heading for the Northern Districts. It was not before Ralph Fletcher had relayed a communication to Whitehall giving in no uncertain terms a local mill owner's views of the inadequacy of central government's response to the reports about the state of the north. 'If more military is not sent into the country,' it said, 'they will not be called upon to protect it, but will be required to reconquer it.'[24]

17

Shots in the Dark

The calm which, in the few days following the funerals of Hartley and Booth, settled on the Spen and Colne valleys, misled neither workers nor manufacturers into believing that a change in attitude of either side had come about. William Cartwright was convinced that it was inevitable that his mill would again be attacked and he now had a permanent detachment of soldiers guarding Rawfolds. However, although he had been deeply impressed by the way in which one private of the Cumberland Militia had stood shoulder to shoulder with him during the worst of the attack, he was determined that the soldier who that night had retired with his back to the fireplace, refusing to fire his musket on 'his brothers', would pay for his act of revolt. Deeply incensed by this derelic-tion of duty, Cartwright had reported it to the militiaman's com-manding officer and agreed to attend the court martial hastily arranged at Huddersfield on April 18th.

Cartwright rode over for the trial which was held early that Saturday afternoon. It was a brief affair and Cartwright's evi-dence was accepted without question. The private was found guilty of neglect of duty. What Cartwright expected as the out-come is not clear. The severity of the punishment, nevertheless, took him by surprise. The soldier was to receive 300 lashes.

The timing of this sentence could scarcely have been more inappropriate for Cartwright. Only three days earlier the parlia-mentary hero of many people in these valleys, Sir Francis Burdett, had addressed the House of Commons as part of his campaign to abolish the evil of flogging. In his speech he gave a clinical account of how each separate whipcord lash of the cat o'nine tails was used with the express purpose of drawing blood from the victim's body. He also told a graphic story of how one soldier from a Yorkshire regiment had recently been ordered to be flogged. The soldier's wife set out from Yorkshire to visit him and arrived at the regimental quarters in time to meet his body being carried to his grave by his comrades. Another example he quoted was that of a Canadian soldier sentenced to 200 lashes who, having received 170, was carried to hospital and after lingering for four days, died.[1]

Cartwright, as he sat in the Huddersfield barracks listening to the verdict of 300 lashes, knew as well as every member of the court martial that the man he accused had been sentenced to almost certain cruel and prolonged death.

The troubled factory owner set out to ride back over the hills to Liversedge at about four o'clock that day. He reached the open countryside at the edge of Huddersfield and headed his horse between the hedgerows bordering the wide road. As he did so, two men simultaneously rising from where they had been hiding behind the hedge at either side, stood and fired pistols. Miraculously, considering the close range, both shots missed. Cartwright put spurs to his horse and was out of range riding fast for home before any second barrels could be used.

Whatever accusation of insensitivity can be levelled against William Cartwright, his manifest characteristics of tenacity and determination to defend to the end what was his, never flagged. The attempt on his life in no way altered his resolve to continue the grim defence of Rawfolds. His spirit was severely tried, however, when three days after the court martial, he saw more great streams of people beginning to converge on the mill. Unknown to him, the commander of the Cumberland Militia had taken the decision to have the punishment inflicted on his private soldier near the spot where he had committed his treachery.

With an escort of mounted dragoons, the militiaman had been force-marched the 7 miles from Huddersfield and taken to a place near the mill dam where the silent crowd now gathered. There, according to military custom, as the line of soldiers chosen to carry out the punishment in relays stood alongside, he was stripped to the waist and tied to a halberd. Nearby stood an army surgeon whose duty, once the lashing had begun, was to assess that sufficient life remained in the victim's body for the punishment to continue.

Whatever the effect of the lash on the soldier Cartwright knew that it would make him an even greater object of loathing to the

workers now gathering round him to take in the scene. Before the
first of the line of militiamen had raised the whip's handle over the
soldier's back, Cartwright pushed through to the officer in command and began to plead with him. Notwithstanding the change
of heart of the chief accuser, the order was given for the punishment to start. Several times in the next few minutes as the whip
tore into the body, Cartwright begged for mercy for the soldier.
Only after it had fallen twenty-five times was the command
shouted for the flogging to stop, and the ropes binding the man
unfastened.[2] A local manufacturer, Abraham Jackson, is then
reputed to have slipped a golden guinea into the hand of the
bleeding victim.[3]

There were several others in the district in addition to Cartwright
who had good reason to believe that they were next in line for
Luddite retribution. The most obvious target was the magistrate
who by now had taken on the main burden of opposition to
Luddism, Joseph Radcliffe. Twice that week within a few
hundred yards of Milnsbridge House attempts were made on the
lives of two men in his pay. The first, a special constable, was
shot at through the window of his house.[4] The second, one of
Radcliffe's gardeners, had the narrowest of escapes when a bullet
passed through his hat as, at dusk, he left a plantation in which he
had been working near the house.[5] There was every reason to
believe that the man had been mistaken for his master.

Other magistrates in the district were beginning to shrink into
inactivity as a result of the threats scrawled in crude handwriting
and signed 'King Lud' now regularly pushed under their door-
jambs. Radcliffe's response was to ask Major Gordon for an
armed guard from Huddersfield and, until it came, begin a life
behind the closed shutters of Milnsbridge House. His activity,
however, far from diminishing, took on new life. He had recognised the first vulnerable point in the unusual armour of anonymity which the Yorkshire Luddites had so far preserved against
all odds: the surviving wounded of Rawfolds.

He had realised that the individuals in the community who
could point to a wounded man's trail – individuals without
commitment to the workers' cause and therefore not bound to the
conspiracy of silence which bedevilled every enquiry so far made
– were the local barber-surgeons. In the days following Rawfolds
Radcliffe's special constables combed the villages and before long
one of them found the information Radcliffe needed. Richard

Tattersall, the surgeon of Lepton, readily volunteered the information that, on the day after the attack, he had treated a gaping wound in the shoulder of the young cropper, James Haigh. The hole in the flesh, Haigh had told him, had been caused by a fall against a stone.

Haigh had consulted Tattersall once more, then gone on the run. Clearly in great pain, he had spent the next twelve days and nights moving from village to village, getting food and shelter wherever he could. Local sympathy for any cropper caught up in the Rawfolds disaster was high; one elderly couple had without question given up their bed to him in the middle of the night. A special constable finally caught up with Haigh on April 23rd. Next day the prisoner, still wearing the shirt in which he was shot, was taken to Milnsbridge House.

Haigh was the first of many that summer to stand in what became known as the 'sweating room' of the mansion. Its owner, avuncular in appearance, but irritable in manner, himself carried out the interrogation, as he was to do in the case of each one of the dozens of suspects soon to be brought in.

Throughout the whole of the questioning that day, the wounded Haigh protested his innocence. Joseph Radcliffe, however, had anticipated his prisoner's story of injury caused by having blundered into a stone. He had taken the precaution of having Major Gordon wait in attendance. When Haigh finished his tale, Radcliffe had the shirt peeled off his back and handed to the cavalry officer. Gordon pronounced that there could be no doubt that the hole in the cloth had been made by a musket ball. But Haigh refused to alter his story and admitted to no Luddite involvement whatever.

Two more suspects brought in with wounds were equally tight-lipped. At this point, however, it seemed that Radcliffe had found another chink in the working-class armour of solidarity and silence. A Huddersfield woman called Betty Armstrong was said to be ready to pass on information which would implicate some of the Rawfolds wounded. On the night before she was due to be interviewed by the magistrate she made the mistake of passing in front of a public house from where she was recognised. Immediately, in spite of the fact that a piquet of cavalry was guarding the pub, she was mobbed, spat at and beaten. A dragoon had to wade into the crowd to drag her away from the brawling workers.

At noon next day, the frightened woman set out with a guard of soldiers for Radcliffe's house. The mob, however, was again waiting, this time less drunk and more effective. The stones which rained down on the troops as they tried to leave the town with their charge were cruelly accurate. Betty Armstrong was hit and fell bleeding. This time when she was at last extracted from the crowd she had to be carried to an inn suffering from severe injuries including a fractured skull.[6] If she had any incriminating evidence it was now never to reach the ear of Joseph Radcliffe.

On every day that Haigh was questioned by Radcliffe he never shifted his story. Throughout the summer the unwavering refusal to admit guilt in the face of overwhelming evidence was to be repeated again and again by men standing in front of interrogating magistrates. Radcliffe, convinced by the evidence of the shirt, decided to send Haigh to York Castle. Under a heavily armed guard of dragoons, a sealed coach and four carried the prisoner east by way of the main coach road. It passed within a half-mile of Rawfolds, stared at, as it was on much of the rest of its journey, by large groups of workers. When the time came for the same workers to watch the return journey Haigh's body would be in a coffin.

18

Awful Times

The key question for the Cabinet after its belated decision to take massive military action against the uprising was, action against whom? Who were the leaders of the marauding gangs increasing in numbers at a rate which, to so many in the north of England, made a revolution seem inevitable? For the government, the inability to answer this question was a misfortune. For the workers who called themselves Luddites, the incapacity to respond to the same question was a tragedy.

Not for almost 200 years had the nation been so perilously close to catastrophic destabilisation, and never before at a time of such anxious involvement in a major European war. If a proletarian revolt was to succeed it would be difficult to imagine a more propitious time. Yet the great swell of violent worker activity which, in April 1812, was poised to become the shifting tide of an army, remained, for the time being at least, immobile. The reason was plain: still no leader had emerged to direct this potentially overwhelming force.

That several workers' leaders existed in a number of areas in the north of England – in Manchester, Bolton and South Yorkshire, for example – is an obvious assumption. It is not possible to orchestrate and repeat mass attacks involving gangs from several hundred to several thousand strong without organisers having recognisable characteristics of leadership. But in only one area – the Calder, Colne and Spen valleys – had an identifiable leader begun to emerge with sufficient stature to focus the present excited energy into a mass movement.

George Mellor's abilities to communicate with workers from a wide variety of trades over a wide area, his mastery of the logistical problems of organised groups, his education – unusual in a working man – his dash, his youth and his unquestionable bravery had already made him widely respected and acknowledged as a man men followed. Had Rawfolds succeeded he might immediately have extended his organising abilities over county borders, instead of over valley borders, where they now reached. But for all its incendiary effects on the attitudes of workers in other parts of the north, to the people in the valleys most concerned, Rawfolds, with its dead and wounded, had been a bitter failure.

Mellor and William Thorpe, who with him had planned most of the district's attacks of the past few weeks,[1] had to look to other methods. The responsibility for the deaths of the two known Rawfolds victims had deeply affected Mellor. Rather than scale up the size of his army, which would have been the obvious step had Cartwright's mill been destroyed, he now took the decision to scale down the numbers involved, but to make the attacks more deadly for the mill owners. In the plain words of a cropper who worked alongside him and who was present at Mellor's meetings, 'Mellor said, the method of breaking the shears must be given up, and instead of it the Masters must be shot.'[2] It was to be a watershed decision in his brief career as a leader of working men. His judgements on both the size and the nature of the violence to be adopted, it would turn out, were to be serious misreadings of the wishes of the mass of people hoping to be led.

Mellor's new policy was intended to have maximum terrorising effect on the middle classes of the district: this effect at least he did not misjudge. On April 27th – a Monday – a letter was delivered to Joseph Radcliffe whilst the wounded James Haigh was still in his custody. This note, probably written by Mellor himself, was explicit in its aims of offering to trade an end to the violence in the valleys for the removal of the new cropping machines. Addressed to Radcliffe in his capacity as principal magistrate of the district, its contents were taken with seriousness and quickly made known to every leading mill owner in the district. It was a simply expressed document and said among other things,

> If this machinery is suffer'd to go on it will probably terminate with Civil War, which I could wish to be avoided, therefore as you are not interested by machinery and the spirit of the people appears so resolute in the cause that if some measures are not adopted and immediately, it will be

attended with great distruction, and particular those who are our greatest persecutors ... Mr Thos Atkinson, and Mr Wm. Horsfall, who will soon be numbered with the dead.[3]

The letter, its grim warnings mixed with touchingly naive grammatical errors, is in a self-educated hand and does not leave the impression of a world-wise man. Its weakness lay in its failure to understand the irreversibility of the technology sweeping over the district. Its strength was in the understanding of the power of the popular movement as well as its understanding of the fears of the middle class. The man least likely to flinch under its threats, however, the owner of the largest number of cropping machines in the district and the man still loudly threatening to ride up to his saddle girths in Luddite blood, was the last named in the letter, William Horsfall.

The next morning was the day of Huddersfield cloth market. That day, as he did every Tuesday at the same time, Horsfall left his Marsden mill and took the old Manchester coach road high in the hills past scattered weavers' cottages and farmsteads. His route was near Joseph Radcliffe's mansion, over Longroyd Bridge and past the most dense cluster of small Master cropping shops. Taken on that particular Tuesday, it seems to have been a conspicuous display of his determination not to change even the most provocative of his habits as a result of workers' threats. As he passed over the bridge astride his Yeomanry cavalry horse, he could be seen from any of the cropping shops on the Colne river's banks. John Wood's shop windows had as easy a view as any.

Soon after Horsfall had passed by, George Mellor took his bed-mate William Hall aside in John Wood's shop and asked him to fetch the long-barrelled pistol which he had brought back from Russia. It was a formidable weapon, studded with brass screws and with an iron end to its foot-long barrel. Hall watched intrigued as Mellor loaded it with two pipe-heads of powder.[4] This was followed by two or three pistol balls which Mellor hammered into slugs before ramming them into the barrel. The effect on the balls, as Hall well knew, would be to turn them into what would today be called dum-dum bullets; rather than pierce their victim they would blast out large areas of flesh and bone in a crippling wound. Worried by what he was watching Hall pointed out to Mellor that, irrespective of the devastating effect it was likely to have on any intended victim, the pistol was so tightly loaded that its recoil would be dangerous to whoever fired it. Mellor responded, 'I mean to give Mr Horsfall that.'[5]

The same afternoon Hall watched William Thorpe load a second pistol in the same way. Shortly afterwards Mellor and Thorpe, along with two other veterans from the Rawfolds mill attack, Benjamin Walker and Thomas Smith, also armed with pistols, left the workshop. Hall himself declined when Mellor asked him to join the party.

As he always did after the close of the Cloth Hall, William Horsfall rode back over Longroyd Bridge in the early evening, heading for Marsden. At Milnsbridge within sight of Joseph Radcliffe's house he rode up the turnpike hill and stopped his horse outside an inn – the Warrener House. Without dismounting he called for the landlord to bring him a glass of rum and water, and to bring two more for a couple of cloth hawkers he recognised sitting at the pub door. He paid for all three and rode on.

Henry Parr was another manufacturer riding home to Marsden the same evening. He reached the Warrener House in time to see Horsfall not much more than 100 yards ahead passing next to one of Joseph Radcliffe's plantations. As Horsfall reached the nearest corner of the plantation Parr heard the formidable explosions of guns and saw Horsfall slump in the saddle then pull himself upright. A dark-coated figure carrying a pistol now jumped to the top of the plantation's four foot wall as though about to finish the victim off, but seeing Parr galloping up, the man turned and ran off through the plantation with three others.

When Parr reached Horsfall he was still upright in the saddle. He turned to Parr, then in a clear voice, said, 'Good man, I am shot,' before collapsing from the horse's back, his boots dragging in the stirrups. By the time Parr had freed his feet and the victim had been got back to the Warrener House, Horsfall was covered in blood from a mass of wounds to the lower part of his body; one of the wounds, according to Parr, was several inches long.

It was two hours before any competent medical man reached Horsfall at the Warrener. The scenes which followed were a near repetition of what had occurred two weeks earlier at the Star Inn when the two Luddites had been the victims. Perhaps it was what Mellor had intended.

First to arrive was the young assistant cavalry surgeon of the Queen's Bays, Mason Stanhope Kenny. A civilian surgeon from Huddersfield came shortly afterwards. The wounds they found appalled even the two doctors: two in the left thigh, one in the lower part of the abdomen, one in the scrotum and two more on the right side. Kenny extracted one deformed bullet from the right thigh, the Huddersfield surgeon took out a second and handed it to Horsfall's clergyman brother, Abraham.

The blood was unstaunchable. Horsfall's pulse became weaker. Conscious for much of the time, he lingered on for a day and a half. He eventually died in the arms of Mason Kenny. Before he did so he turned to the surgeon and said, 'These are awful times, doctor.'[6]

Even before Mellor, with the three other croppers, left the hiding place in the wood, he saw the possibility of dangerous consequences as a result of what had happened in the last few minutes. First, what William Hall had predicted had come about. The overloaded Russian pistol had recoiled and badly injured his index finger which was bleeding and probably broken. More worrying, only he and Thorpe had actually fired at Horsfall in spite of his orders that all four should simultaneously share the act of killing. The other pair had simply stood and watched as he and Thorpe had fired. Smith and Walker were now scared and uncooperative. When Thorpe tried to make Benjamin Walker take one of the murder weapons, Walker threw it to the ground in panic and Mellor was forced to pick it up himself. Even at this stage it seems to have crossed Mellor's mind that Smith and Walker were potential informers against him and Thorpe.

Although he cursed them for their disobedience, he nevertheless supplied them with money, told them to make for a public house in a village in the direction opposite to the one he and Thorpe intended to take, and ordered them to be back at the workshop early the following morning.

All four reached places where, before the evening was out, the tales of the shooting and the injuries suffered by William Horsfall were being told and retold. Not all these tales, however, were antagonistic to Horsfall, who at this time was still clinging to life. The way in which the injuries had been calculated to maim was turning paranoiac hatred of the factory owner, if not into support, then into a surprising attitude of tolerance. By the time, several hours later, Horsfall had died and the news had reached the cropping shop, Mellor was worried enough to take steps which, until then, he and Thorpe never considered necessary in a community of workers united in common purpose.

All the croppers in John Wood's shop knew of Mellor and

Thorpe's activities, most had been involved in the Rawfolds fight and two, besides Mellor – Thorpe worked in a neighbouring shop – had been at Horsfall's killing. And all by now knew that Mellor and Thorpe had fired the murder weapons. Only one cropper – his name was Joseph Sowden – had shown sufficient lack of sympathy with the Luddite aims to refuse to take part in any of their activities.

On the morning following Horsfall's death Sowden, working alone in his shop, was surprised to see William Thorpe come through the door carrying a Bible. He had every reason to be apprehensive of Thorpe; he knew that, in addition to the Bible, the burly young cropper carried, as he always did, a loaded gun. When Thorpe now faced him and told him that he must swear an oath on the Bible, Sowden's worst fears were realised. After having so far successfully distanced himself from all Luddite involvement he was being made to take an illegal oath, for which the well-advertised punishment was seven years' transportation. Thorpe's threat to shoot him dead if he refused helped him reach a quick decision. 'I submitted,' Sowden later said, 'and he administered the oath: the substance of which was to keep the murder of Horsfall secret in all its circumstances on pain of death, and being finally put out of existence by the first brother I should meet.'[7]

It was a typical Luddite oath and one which magistrates had made clear would, if discovered, be rewarded with the swingeing sentence reserved for it. But the worst for Sowden was yet to come. Thorpe now handed him the Bible and told him to prepare himself for administering the same oath to the rest of the workers. The punishment a parliamentary Act would soon lay down for the administration of an illegal oath was death by hanging. Faced again with the muzzle of Thorpe's pistol the terrified Sowden prepared to comply. Within minutes George Mellor appeared leading the co-conspirators, Thomas Smith and Benjamin Walker. They were made to swear on Sowden's Bible.

By twos and threes the rest of the croppers were brought in and lined up before him until Sowden had implicated the whole workshop of young men. The situation had been designed by Mellor and Thorpe to prevent the loss of the anonymity which had been their most precious possession of the past months and which had kept them from the gallows. If there was to be a Judas, he now stood in front of them.

*

The effect of William Horsfall's death on the manufacturing middle classes of the surrounding valleys was every bit as dramatic as George Mellor had hoped it would be. Within hours the Huddersfield Committee for Preventing Unlawful Depredations on Machinery and Shearing Frames – which was the name the frightened group of West Riding mill owners had now adopted – was meeting in secret session at the George Inn and was composing a 1,000-word memorandum to the Home Secretary.[8] This described in some detail the most recent set of outrages, drew attention to the fact that Luddite meetings held in nearby villages were being attended by whole populations, and called for martial law to be imposed immediately.

The man who was to deliver this paper in person to Richard Ryder was Thomas Atkinson. The choice of William Cartwright's brother-in-law served two purposes. First, he would be able to give to government a graphic first-hand account of the tumultuous state of affairs in the north of England, but also it would remove him for the time being at least from his position as next named in line for assassination.

Atkinson slipped quietly out of Huddersfield and aimed his horse for the south. Next day was the last day of April 1812. The character of the gentle valley he could look back on was changing rapidly from that which had existed when his sister married William Cartwright so few years before – or even since the year had begun. Even then, the main features of the unusually settled community Daniel Defoe had seen were still intact: peaceful places with easy social gradations within a society where wealth was reasonably well distributed among people who subscribed willingly enough to a vigorous work ethic.

Now an upheaval was taking place. As George Mellor's letter to Joseph Radcliffe had pointed out, their house, once so uniquely united, was now divided against itself.[9] The use of the word 'house' was significant; it was a literal reality as well as a meaningful metaphor. Once the community had been such that the worker and the Master were linked by a common purpose often under a common roof. The new technology was removing the shared aim and its benefits, as well as the shared dwelling and all the advantages that too bestowed. Now two communities were evolving: manufacturer and worker. Aligned with the manufacturer was an establishment which subscribed to Church and King; bound to the worker were the poor and the failing small Master. The divide in the house was deep. For the first time in their history the valleys were stratified by class barriers; from here on these were to be permanent structures in the community. The class division based on wealth and poverty that had now established itself would never disappear.

Edward Baines, the editor of the *Leeds Mercury*, for the first time since the beginning of the troubles, was also beginning to look on this north country which he loved, with deep despair. The present revolutionary mood, he predicted, 'points to the destruction of society itself'. A people on whom the sun had once shone was now, he felt, bent on self-destruction. The attempted assassination of Cartwright, and now the assassination of Horsfall, was to him a 'crime so cowardly, so foreign to the feelings of Englishmen'.[10]

But if assassination was to be a prelude to Civil War, whose life was next in line and where would it all end? Thomas Atkinson, Joseph Radcliffe and William Cartwright were taking the threats to their lives with justifiable seriousness. But there were others in far higher echelons of English society whose lives were also being threatened by the same hands. How much sleep need they lose over the posturings of a band of north country workmen? Joseph Radcliffe had yet another letter placed in his hands, this one naming the 'rascally' Prince Regent and 'that damned set of rogues, Perceval and Co.'. It was addressed to 'all croppers, weavers etc. and the public at large' and encouraged the workers of England to take up arms: 'Come let us follow the noble example of the brave citizens of Paris who in the sight of 3000 tyrannical Red Coats brought tyranny to the ground by so doing.'[11]

Joseph Radcliffe was having to reconsider his beliefs that England could consider herself safe from a French-style bloody revolution, just as he had had to reconsider his belief that men of his standing could walk in the streets without fear of a pistol bullet aimed at their breasts. But was it really conceivable that the assassin's arm could stretch as high as the Prince Regent or the Prime Minister?

Dutifully Radcliffe sent the letter off to the Home Secretary, and equally dutifully Richard Ryder read it. It was of course an impossible consideration: that the nation's appointed leader might be assassinated could not be a serious question for a Home Secretary in 1812 to have to ponder. Kings, it was true, had been done to death, but Prime Ministers – never.

He placed the paper for posterity in the Home Office files along with the dozens of other letters from magistrates, ministers, peers and parsons which he had received that day.

19

Radical Reformers

In spite of the licence it had given its magistrates to use virtually whatever methods and whichever spies they chose, the Home Office had still come to no conclusion whether or not it was conceivable that a member of the lower classes might rise and assume the cloak of revolutionary leader. It now remained for members of government to consider whether, from among their own class, there might emerge a man capable of and concerned to lead a British Revolution of what would become known as the proletariat.

The workers themselves, it was known, were already parading likely thoroughbred starters in their minds. The card of possible runners, however, was forbiddingly short. The names of some – William Cobbett, Samuel Whitbread and William Wilberforce, for example – were occasionally dragged into workers' pamphlets because they were known to be reformers and therefore were *de facto* working-class heroes. But in Westminster, such as these were never seriously considered as a threat to the stability of the nation.

In the past months, however, the two remaining favoured candidates had begun to be mentioned with some regularity in both the testimonies and the captured documents of arrested workers. Both were radicals and the activities of both were being monitored by the Home Office.

Of the first, any frank assessment of his failing physical powers should have dismissed him early; the working classes, who had never seen him, were probably unaware of his age. In 1812 Major John Cartwright, the brother of Dr Edmund Cartwright, the inventor of the power loom, was seventy-two years old. After a life of political campaigning, and unsuccessful attempts to enter Parliament, he was beginning to show his age.

It had been in the year of the American Declaration of Independence, thirty-six years earlier, that he had published his pamphlet *Take Your Choice*, and advocated annual parliaments and manhood suffrage. Since then, one ponderous tract had followed another. But at least, for the lower classes, his name and what they thought it stood for, offered a political alternative both to the Tories, who believed in the divine right of kings, and to the Whigs, who believed in the same right of gentlemen.

Cartwright, however, had seldom been seen north of Nottingham and in 1812 was little more than a name to the workers of the north country. Long before this date he had had to acknowledge his own burdensome shortcomings, easily recognisable to any realist who knew him. He admitted he was no orator, had little charisma and no capacity to lead. Even ten years earlier he had confessed to his wife that he was 'too old to pursue politics for popularity'.[1]

The same cannot be said of the other likely candidate. In 1812 Sir Francis Burdett, at forty-two, was at the peak of his powers and his charisma was overflowing his tall, slim, patrician body. His abilities to lead were well recognised by those in, as well as those out of, political power. Already his few years in politics had made him a familiar figure to both the crowds and the mobs of London.

The origins and experiences of the handsome baronet could not have been more alien to the workers of England who saw in him the qualities of a potential saviour. Educated at Westminster and Oxford, Burdett had been sent on a European tour and had found himself in France in the later stages of the Revolution. There he appears to have seen neither extraordinary nor distressing scenes. However, he returned to England with qualified approval of the results of the Revolution as well as a certain sympathy for the lower orders of whom, until this tourist trip abroad, he had known nothing.

He had also returned to England to marry Sophia, daughter of the banker Thomas Coutts, reputedly the richest man in England. Coutts gave an immediate dowry of £25,000 to the bride-to-be. By the age of twenty-six, rich, with estates in Derbyshire and Wiltshire, from where he could indulge his deep passion for fox-hunting, Burdett was able to find a seat in Parliament and launch himself at that institution with a view to reforming it. This was to be his other all-consuming interest and, as with fox-hunting, it was to be a lifetime's pursuit.

Before he was thirty his single-minded political goal of parliamentary reform had already marked him out as a popular champion of liberty. By the time he had espoused campaigns against political corruption, flogging and the muzzling of the press, he had been elevated by those who had no representation in Parliament, to be one of their natural leaders. That he was prematurely placed in this position *by* the people, led some to think he was also *of* the people. No such blurring of the edges of class structure occurred, however, in Sir Francis's mind; he had every intention of supporting the continuing security of the landed gentry of England for as long as he was in Parliament – which was to be most of his life.

By 1807, Burdett had lost his seat in the Commons. Then, as a result of a farcical misunderstanding, he was drawn into a duel with the parliamentary candidate for the City of Westminster, John Paull. The confrontation, early one morning on Wimbledon Common, spoke little for the marksmanship of either man. After each had missed with his first shot, the second rounds found targets: Paull was shot through the leg and Burdett through the thigh.

The curious upshot of this eccentric and dangerous affair was that Burdett was raised in popular eyes to heroic stature. On the following Monday he was adopted as candidate in place of Paull and, in the poll that followed, triumphantly elected for Westminster.

As soon as he was able to walk on crutches, an ecstatic crowd prepared to chair Burdett in an extraordinary procession.[2] A huge ornamented 'Triumphal Car', drawn by four milk-white caparisoned horses decorated with purple ribbon had been got ready. At its front was a figure of Britannia. At its rear was a great pedestal on which the hero was to be placed, his patrician head uncovered, his wounded limb resting on a purple footstool.

Led by buglers and riders carrying flags, the car, supported by 200 more horsemen wearing dark blue favours, and followed by a vast London crowd, was conducted from Covent Garden to the baronet's London house in Piccadilly. There, wearing a blue coat, nankeen breeches, white stockings and with a white beaver hat in his hand with which to acknowledge the crowd, Sir Francis was carried by two gentlemen and placed in the car. The popular response exceeded belief. Half a million people were estimated to have enthusiastically crowded the streets. No politician in living memory had ever excited such a response.

This display of his theatrical personality so carefully stage managed, Burdett was led off to a celebratory dinner as dark blue banners inscribed 'Burdett the Choice of the People' and 'Burdett For Ever' were waved. The epithets, once started on their rounds, were to echo from many other plebeian crowds in the few years to come.

Early in 1810 Burdett's fame as the banner carrier for liberty came to a peak. In February the little surgeon, and political agitator, John Gale Jones had been imprisoned in Newgate prison at the behest of the Speaker of the House of Commons. Gale Jones, a Radical like Burdett and also, like him, an impressive orator and crowd stirrer, had overstepped the bounds of caution by questioning the freedom of speech in proceedings in Parliament. He had published a placard denouncing the recent enforcement of standing orders which excluded strangers from the House of Commons.[3] What this exclusion meant in practice was that press reporters could be kept out of the House of Commons. Gale Jones had attacked the exclusion as an insidious curb on the freedom of the press. The price for his outspokenness was the sobering spell in Newgate.

On March 24th, Burdett published in *Cobbett's Weekly Register* a 'Letter to his Constituents' describing the committal of Gale Jones as a gross breach of privilege. He later had it reprinted as a shilling pamphlet which sold in huge numbers. This action was a serious miscalculation on Burdett's part and its consequence was severe. On April 5th, after a long debate in the House, a motion was passed committing him to the Tower of London.

The Prime Minister, Spencer Perceval, speaking in the debate, expressed his full approval of the intended punishment when he said that he considered that Burdett had made one of the worst attacks ever made upon the character and privileges of the House of Commons. A warrant was now issued for the arrest of the startled baronet.

From the vantage point of the next century this wordy affair has the appearance of a storm of modest proportions especially created in its own teacup. Nevertheless, the reality was that there was every intention of locking Sir Francis Burdett away in the Tower of London. And Burdett, after his initial surprise, had every intention of making the most of the unfortunate situation he had created for himself.

He first of all let it be known that he considered the measure threatened against him illegal. He therefore refused to accompany the Sergeant at Arms, who had been sent to arrest him, to the specially prepared cell in the Tower.

Sensing that Burdett was yet again preparing to embellish his parliamentary career with a *coup de théâtre*, the crowds of London had already begun to gather outside the doors of the baronet's house in Piccadilly. So vast were the numbers to which the throng grew that as a precautionary measure, the military magazine in Hyde Park was given a guard of 350 men and some of the guns at the Tower were loaded with grapeshot.

By the afternoon of Saturday, April 7th, the huge mob in Piccadilly had become so threatening that a magistrate was forced to read the Riot Act. For good measure, a militia regiment and three detachments of cavalry were rushed from Windsor and sixteen pieces of artillery stationed in St James's Park. During a night of rioting two men were badly injured.

Next day, after a spate of window smashing, it took the Life Guards and a sharp shower of rain to keep the mob in reasonable control. It had by now taken up what was fast becoming the ubiquitous cry of the people, 'Burdett For Ever!' Whoever refused to take off his hat and repeat the slogan was plastered with mud. Nearby, Lord Castlereagh's windows, chandeliers and furniture were demolished and the Earl of Chatham's house was 'hideously disfigured'; so too was that of the Prime Minister, Spencer Perceval.

It was not until Monday morning that the Sergeant at Arms dared to make an attempt to gain entry to Sir Francis's house – through a kitchen window forced by two Bow Street Runners armed with a crowbar. Eventually, with the arresting party holding him by each arm, Sir Francis accepted the inevitable. 'As force is used', he said, 'I must go.' He then kissed his wife and 'parted with his family as if he was only leaving town for his country seat'.[4]

By the time the huge military cavalcade sent to surround Burdett and accompany him to the Tower had reached the city, the crowds in the streets were so dense that all business was brought to a halt. Several thousand troops were required to keep order until Sir Francis was locked away in the place where so many romantic figures of British history had spent their last days. When the soldiers withdrew, however, serious rioting broke out and several people were killed. With what now seemed like most of the population of London ready to support Burdett's cause, serious insurrection seemed likely. The sudden outbreak of torrential rain, which continued for most of the night, finally cleared the crowds off the street, rather than effective action by the military.

Burdett stayed in the Tower for several weeks – far longer than he had bargained for. And although he brought a legal action against the Speaker of the House of Commons he was not able to reverse the verdict against him.

When the time finally came for him to be released from the Tower another huge crowd was assembled in the hope of seeing him lead it triumphantly through the streets of London raised on a victor's chariot. The disappointment, when it was found he had slipped away quietly by boat to avoid any such display, was intense. His popularity with the working classes which made up the mob sank instantly. Their yearnings for a visible leader had been summarily ignored. What they had failed to realise was Burdett's commitment to the law of the land and his disapproval of any move that could be interpreted as attempting to overthrow a government by unconstitutional means.

His concern had been from the start, and now remained, the reform of Parliament. Every act of his theatrical behaviour was designed to bring this about. That vast plebeian crowds had seen in him the image of a powerful revolutionary leader quite failed to touch his patrician consciousness. That the cry 'Burdett For Ever' was beginning to inspire thousands of the country's workers who felt their cause hopeless because until now they had been leaderless, did not budge by the smallest fraction from its path, nor urge it beyond his single-minded aim.

In 1812 there existed a remarkable characteristic concerning those English radical movements desperate for a change in the social structure. On the one hand was the vast uncoordinated workers' movement, predominantly in the north. On the other, the small orderly middle- and upper-class movement, predominantly in the south. But they had no points of contact. There was no dialogue which could give the potential leader the groundswell of support he needed if he were to be taken seriously, or which could give the potentially overwhelming masses the captain they needed to make them an effective force in the land.

For those such as Sir Francis Burdett and Major John Cartwright, the lack of understanding and of dialogue were setbacks to aspirations and to careers, but nothing more. For those such as the northern workers, whose actions were by now taking them outside the law, this absence would eventually lead to disaster. In the meantime, however, Burdett's performances at the head of the mob had been so conspicuously successful that the lower classes would not discount him. And, as a result of more immediate evidence, there were reasons why the government could not discount him.

On April 29th, a gaoler, making a routine search of prisoners thrown into the cells of Lancaster Castle after the rioting at Bolton, found in the pocket of a cloth worker a letter written in a well-educated hand. Signed William James Burdett, Piccadilly, April 16th, 1812, it mentioned the name of the writer's brother, Sir Francis Burdett, and linked him with the cause of a Bolton workers' committee. The gaol's governor reported with speed to the Home Office the discovery that the Burdett family was in direct contact with the rioters.[5]

More unsettling information was to come. On the same day a prisoner being interrogated in Chester gaol spoke of a nationwide plot in which the Royal Family was to be deposed, and of a New Commonwealth over which Sir Francis Burdett would preside. This news too was quickly transmitted to the Home Office.[6]

The day after these revelations the Home Secretary sat in the House of Commons to listen to a speech made by Burdett himself. His subject was the riots which appeared to be engulfing the nation's manufacturing districts. The main thrust of Burdett's speech was to point out that the Riot Act gave the government no power whatever to use the army to put down a civilian population.[7]

Richard Ryder, both on hearing Burdett's speech and on reading the incriminating evidence of treasonable intent now adding to the file mounting against the people's champion, behaved in character. He stored the information and did nothing. He had, however, taken a firm decision in another area which arguably justified this inactivity. Burdett was not only unaware of how deeply suspect his connections with the leadership of the northern uprisings had become, he was also unaware of the critical orders Ryder had passed to the army. Indeed the troops to be used to flood the north of England were already on the move.

20

Maitland

The mobilisation was impressive, the more so considering that the trained core of the British Army was unreachable, overseas with Wellington in the Peninsula. The number of men involved was extraordinary. During the next few days artillery, infantry, horse guards and dragoons were to be collected and shifted, together with as many regular militia regiments as could be made available, from all parts of England, Scotland and Wales. Eventually, as soon as sufficient horses could be mustered, no less than five full cavalry regiments were to be added to the vast army now on the road.

Before the summer was out Wellington was to be forced to send four regiments home because of the serious shortage of horses brought about by the mobilisation of cavalry as a result of the industrial unrest of Yorkshire, Lancashire and Cheshire.[1]

At the head of this northward marching force was an unquestionably unusual soldier. Given the time needed for decision, the government's choice of commander had been severely restricted. It was not more than lucky chance that Lieutenant General the Hon Thomas Maitland was on British soil at a time when the nation's best military brains were being stretched by Napoleon's commanders in Spain and Portugal. Few men of stature were available to take on the simultaneously delicate and brutal political and military task that had, at such short notice, been handed to him. At fifty-two and very much at the height of his powers, he was set to play the most influential role of his career – not that he would ever recognise it as such.

Maitland was the second son of the seventh Earl of Lauderdale. But he had neither the inclination nor had had the career which

matched the stereotype of the upper-class Regency military man.
He had a suave exterior with fleshy and effeminate good looks.
They hid a complex character. His aristocratic origins notwithstanding, wherever he travelled, he left a trail of sensitivities
bruised by his abruptness. Many who came face to face with him
were made nervous by his manner and his methods. Some called
these coarse.[2] Far from disguising his Scots accent he used it like a
stick on the back of any of his subordinates, and others when
necessary.

His habits were irregular – startlingly so to some of the young
men who served under him. He slept at unusual hours, enjoyed
drink, was often the worse for it, but was unconcerned if seen by
junior officers in that condition; in any case it did not seem to
weaken his judgement.

Finesse in human relations was not one of his strong points.
The style of the man can well be judged by the reports of his
behaviour in Corfu, shortly after he left the north of England. His
method of dealing with letters of introduction was to throw them
into the fire unread. Once, when he was High Commissioner and
displeased with the ruling body of Corfu, he walked from his
bedroom to the saloon of the palace where the island's senators
had been gathered. Standing in the middle of the room with his
hands behind his back, he addressed the secretary of the senate.
He was wearing at the time only a short night-shirt, slippers and a
red night-cap. 'Damn them!' he said. 'Tell them all to go to hell!'
and walked back to his room with a grunt.[3] He had by this time
earned the nickname 'King Tom'.

Alcohol was not Maitland's only pleasure. Bawdy certainly, and
with what appears to be a strong interest in both male and female
sexual matters, his indulgences and singular sense of humour
attracted speculation. On one occasion, in order to inflate the
importance of minor Cephalonian officials, he invented a blue and
yellow 'Ionian uniform' with conspicuously tight breeches. One of
Maitland's newly arrived and surprised officials, Charles Napier,
described the result as 'a taste which, for a time, infringed upon
the laws of decency, for many an *"ambitieux"* whose inexpress-
ibles had passed their grand climacteric'.[4] On another occasion a
travelling British official insisted on seeing Maitland at short
notice. He found King Tom still in bed with his back towards the
door, his bedclothes awry and his backside exposed. The traveller
made his bow to the only part of the Governor he could see. From
under the clothes a gruff voice asked, 'Wha's that?' On being told,

Maitland went on, 'Wha the de'il do ye want, mun?' 'I have brought a good many letters of introduction, Sir,' was the reply. 'Have you, by [God]?' came from beneath the blankets. 'Then just cover up [my arse]!'[5]

If men were a weakness of Maitland's, they were simultaneously a strength. He took care to surround himself with a court of young, able supporters, always encouraging wherever he went a group of intelligent officers to join his staff and support his methods. The admiration of those who joined him frequently bordered on idolisation. He had an easy knack of winning them over to his rough ways. Charles Napier, when he was first ushered into Maitland's room, had scarcely finished his bow before King Tom said 'Who the devil are you?' On being told, the response then was, 'I hope you are not such a damned scoundrel as your predecessor.' It was said with a twinkle in the eye, and followed by, 'Well, now go away, and if you will dine with me, I shall be glad to see you.'[6]

Not all observers of Maitland's manners and habits were charitable. Some mistakenly believed he surrounded himself with sycophants because he craved flattery for his obvious intelligence. One critic remarked that there were some good men among these, and that Lord Sydney Osborne was one of them; his only fault, the critic said, was 'that he thought the sun rose and set in Sir Thomas Maitland's hinder disk!'[7]

Whatever criticisms could be levelled at Maitland's idiosyncrasies and at his entourage, there could be no questioning the results his methods had achieved in every part of the world in which he had travelled. He had had as active, as brilliant and as varied a career as any officer in the army, let alone those accompanying him on the road to Manchester. He had seen successful battle in both India and the West Indies and had served in San Domingo as a Brigadier General. During the terror of 1789 he had been sent to Paris to help royalists – so he was no newcomer to civil violence. Four years later he had transferred to the army reserve, but since then had acquired political and administrational skills unusual for an army officer. He had twice sat as Member of Parliament for the Scottish Haddington Burghs and had been made Governor of Ceylon in 1806 at a time of low British fortunes. Following the Madras mutinies he had completely reorganised the East India Company.

Now he was expected to apply his methods in the north of England. His first step would be to build his customary court from young men attracted by his rough charm and by the essential shrewdness – some called it genius – behind the coarseness.

There were disadvantages to becoming part of Maitland's favoured group. The delegation of powers he freely handed out to his young men was given only in return for dedication to the task in hand. When he was indulging either in military matters or in pleasure, his subordinates were expected to keep in close touch wherever he might be and, when necessary, move any mountainous problem to Mahomet.

His second-in-command was well chosen. An experienced young professional officer, a Coldstream Guard, Wroth Acland had been promoted to major general at the age of forty, two years earlier. He had commanded a brigade under Wellington in Portugal and had been invalided home after having been struck down by a fever. He was to be alongside Maitland during the whole of the Luddite campaign.

Another soon to join the tight little group was Captain Francis Raynes. He was typical of many of the officers suddenly finding themselves required for duty during those few days early in May. Many were seasoned campaigners having already seen battle not only in Europe, but in India and Africa. Negligibly few had been involved in putting down civilian populations.

Raynes had served an exciting tour as a subaltern in a light dragoon regiment in Egypt where he had distinguished himself by chasing his mounted patrol across the desert in a rout of the French. As with Wroth Acland, a bout of fever had forced him to return to England and now, at thirty-five, he was a captain on half pay in a Scottish militia regiment.[8] Raynes was on leave in London with his sick young wife and small children when he read that the great mobilisation was under way. His regiment, the Stirlingshire Militia, had already set off from its headquarters in Kent in a series of rapid forced marches to the north. Having absorbed the news he enthusiastically abandoned both his leave and his wife; however, the regiment had reached Leicester before the eager captain caught up. He was immediately given command of two companies.

On the morning of May 4th Maitland led the van of his impressive force into riot-torn Manchester. No potential revolutionary could fail to have been impressed by the force which during the next three days, could be seen rolling through the surrounding country and on to the city streets. The approach of the massed red jackets of the infantry, the flashing brass of newly designed cavalry helmets, the jangling harness of mounted artillery and the waggons of the rocket detachment, not to mention the streams of supply carts stretching back for several miles, was choreographed to plant caution if not terror in the minds of those who witnessed it. Maitland listed the bulk of his force:[9]

	Troops
Royal Horse Artillery	1
Rocket Corps	1
Royal Horse Guards	8
2nd (Royal North British) Dragoons	11

	Companies
Cumberland Militia	8
Buckinghamshire Militia	10
Louth Militia	9
West Suffolk Militia	8
West Lincolnshire Militia	8
Berkshire Militia	8
Wiltshire Militia	10
Stirlingshire Militia	8
West Norfolk Militia	10

But sizeable as this army was – about 7,000 men of which 1,400 were mounted – it by no means represented the whole of the force under Maitland's command. The Midland District troops of General Dyott – another 4,000 men – also now fell under his control, while in the West Riding he could call on the support of General Grey's 1,000 infantry and 800 cavalry. The total regular troops available, therefore, approached 13,000. Certainly many generals had fought major campaigns on foreign soil with less and that number is far more than the force Wellington sailed with to the Peninsula in 1808.[10] To appreciate the significance of this number in terms of the newly discovered deep anxieties of the British government and of its newly adopted policies, it has to be seen in the context of Richard Ryder's speech to the House of Commons three months earlier. Then the Home Secretary had described the regular force of 3,000 acting in the Midlands as being larger than ever before in history to be used in a local disturbance. Maitland now had under his command more than four times that number. But even these figures do not fully represent the immense force of arms at his disposal. At meetings shortly to be convened by him in Yorkshire, he was to assess that he had access to 12,000 soldiers of local militia regiments; a similar number was also available to him in Lancashire and Cheshire.

The purpose to be achieved by this grand total of upwards of 35,000 men was, as Maitland saw it, quite clear: the subjugation of the north of England.

21

In Manchester

Maitland's first act on arrival was to put 2,000 troops from the Stirlingshire, the Louth and the Buckinghamshire Militias – one Church of Scotland, one Catholic and one Church of England regiment – into a camp on the site of Manchester race course at Kersal Moor.[1] His policy, in contrast to that of Dirom, the general he was replacing, was not to disperse his force into small detachments about the countryside, but to cluster them into large groups prepared to move quickly as a body. The force at Kersal Moor was ready to pounce on Manchester at the first sign of local inhabitants turning to violence. This, Maitland's first simple manoeuvre, combined with the panoply of his arrival in the city, was a predictable success. Both Manchester and the surrounding district fell into a calm they had not experienced for several weeks.

Arriving early in the morning after an overnight march, Maitland spent his first day riding the city streets, talking to Manchester citizens. As was expected of him he spoke to the manufacturers who were bearing the brunt of the rioting, and to the local professionals and volunteers who had been providing temporary defences – men such as the magistrate, Reverend William Hay, the Deputy Constable, Joseph Nadin, and the hyperactive young solicitor J S Lloyd.

That night Maitland reported to Richard Ryder the result of his first few hours' inquiry. At this stage he was prepared to reflect the alarms and the concerns of the manufacturers and magistrates who told him that the violence they were living with had little or nothing to do with the conditions under which the people of the cotton towns lived and worked. Their belief, and the one they pressed on Maitland, was that a well-designed conspiracy had spread through the whole of the working community of the north and would soon endanger the nation. But, as in many of his affairs, and as in all his letters to Ryder, Maitland in his first response took care not to be seen backing one horse in a crowd of runners. He was the master of equivocation. He told the Home Secretary that his initial conclusions were:

> I cannot help believing on the whole that the existence of a Combination to overcome all Legal Authority is the real groundwork of the existing state of things. At the same time however I say this, I am far from believing this Combination either to have gone the length or to be in the state of organization supposed by many.[2]

Before the next two days were out Maitland had briefed all his Commanding Officers in the simple holding policy he planned to adopt: he told each one to keep his regiment 'as much as possible together and not fritter it away in small or unnecessary parties'[3] and he insisted that local populations should be made to protect themselves by organising effective Watch and Ward patrols.

Meantime he began to look more carefully and more critically at his sources of information. 'Mr Hay of this place and Mr Loyd', he told Ryder, 'both in their ways appear to be intelligent men.'[4] The sentence damned with faint praise. He had already formed a less than satisfactory opinion of the chicken-heartedness of local magistrates in facing local riots. If Lloyd had more spirit than the magistrates he served, Maitland nevertheless developed an instant dislike and distrust of the young solicitor who had just announced his intention of riding up to London to report personally to Ryder. Maitland already saw that Lloyd's ambitions ran high and suspected them; he told the Home Secretary he believed Lloyd would do more good by staying at home and added, 'I must however submit that when you see this Gentleman, or hear from others in the neighbourhood, you would be good enough to signify your wish that they should communicate with me on all topics they state to you in writing.'[5] Maitland was in command, intended it to be understood by all that he was in command, and was to remain impressively so for every minute he remained in the north.

He now began to look at sources of information, not reporting daily, nor with any other frequency, to the Home Secretary. He made contact with the workers themselves, saw where they worked, how they worked, the conditions under which they lived, and what they ate. In forty-eight hours he took more trouble to try to identify the social roots of the problem he had come to solve than many who had been living there for years. He was not the first nor the last to observe the great gulf between worker and manufacturer. Canon Parkinson writing *On the Present Condition of the Labouring Poor in Manchester*, would later state,

> There is no town in the world where the distance between the rich and the poor is so great, or the barrier between them so difficult to be crossed.... There is far less *personal* communication between the master cotton spinner and his workmen, between the calico printer and his blue handed boys, between the master tailor and his apprentices, than there is between the Duke of Wellington and the humblest labourer on his estate, or than there *was* between good old George the Third and the meanest errand-boy about his palace. I mention this not as a matter of blame, but I state it simply as a *fact*.[6]

Before the end of his second day in Manchester Maitland was telling Ryder that the high price of food in relation to wages required very serious consideration. He gave some precise examples. Potatoes, now the most frequent food of the cotton worker, had risen from 7/6d to 18s a wholesale load. This had caused an increase in retail price to the worker such that, where once his penny would buy him 3lbs of potatoes, now it bought only 1lb. Maitland went on,

> Had prices of wages kept up, the distress would have been by no means considerable. These however have unfortunately fallen nearly in the same ratio to that in which provisions have risen, so that where the common weaver used to receive a guinea and a half or thirty shillings a week, ten shillings I am well informed is the outside they now earn and for that they work six days in the week and hard.

Maitland also noticed a shortage of silver currency in the markets and shrewdly identified this as an easily soluble economic problem contributing to the unrest. 'I am convinced it is of the greatest importance,' he told Ryder. Nevertheless, he also saw that many of the weavers in work and earning good wages were causing as much trouble as the genuinely distressed. They were, it appeared, being organised and manipulated. He confirmed, therefore, all Ryder's worst fears.

155

22

Death of a Minister

One day that week, a regular visitor to the House of Commons gallery, W G Bowling, was nudged by the occupant of the next seat. The man was carrying a pair of opera glasses. His name was John Bellingham and he asked Bowling to point out to him the figure of Richard Ryder below them on the government benches. Bowling did so, and when Ryder rose to speak Bellingham raised his glasses and looked through them intently. When the Home Secretary sat down Bellingham again turned to Bowling and asked him to confirm that this was indeed Ryder. Bellingham now used what to Bowling subsequently seemed deliberately chosen words: 'I think I shall know him. I could not mistake him if I saw him in another place.'[1]

One afternoon a few days later the lobby of the House was crowded with Members of Parliament awaiting the start of the next session. Several members of the Cabinet had already pushed their way through, including the Earl of Liverpool and Lord Mulgrave. Richard Ryder had yet to put in an appearance and so too had the Prime Minister, Spencer Perceval.

Whatever else can be said of Perceval, it cannot be said that his leadership of the nation up until this portentous point in his career impressed iridescent memories on posterity; indeed he is most remembered for the fact that he left few memories of any description. It is true that he had a liquid tongue and a reputation as an accomplished debater, particularly when expressing his prejudices against Catholics. It is also true that his sincerity was palpable and his honesty unimpeachable: although he had been Attorney General, legal adviser to the Princess of Wales, Chancellor of the Exchequer and first Minister in the land, he was to die a relatively poor man. In spite of these honourable qualities, Perceval lived to suffer such epithets as 'a third-rate politician, scarcely fit to carry Lord Chatham's crutch',[2] and in the main seems to have deserved them.

Although he commanded the English language with ease, few of his sentences have passed into history. One which did, showed singularly unfortunate prescience. Composed when he was Attorney General it was on the subject of assassination. Perceval said of it, 'there is something so base and disgraceful – there is something so contrary to everything that belongs to the character of an Englishman – there is something so immoral in the idea of assassination.'[3]

Confident in this idea characteristic of Englishmen, therefore, at about 5.15 on that afternoon of May 11th, late for a meeting with Henry Brougham, Perceval stepped hurriedly into the entrance of the lobby of the House of Commons. As he did so, John Bellingham, having tired of waiting for Richard Ryder, pushed forward from where he had been waiting in an alcove, aimed a pistol at chest height, and pulled the trigger.

Those who were watching near the entrance from where the sound of the shot came, saw the figure of a man, his right hand clutching at his chest, rush from the crowd and stagger towards the door of the House before falling face down. Nobody now moved, except the Member of Parliament for Norwich, William Smith. Thinking the man had thrown a fit, Smith gingerly walked in a circle around the body, then eventually took courage and bent to lift the head. He saw instantly it was Spencer Perceval. Blood was oozing from the mouth. He was immediately carried by Smith and other bystanders and placed on a table in the room of the Speaker's secretary. Within minutes he was dead. Bellingham meanwhile, making no attempt to escape, sat on a bench near the lobby fireplace. General Isaac Gascoyne, the member for Liverpool, nevertheless took prompt military action; he grabbed Bellingham by the neck, removed the smoking pistol from his hand and held him until he was taken away.

A hackney coach was called to Lower Palace yard and a crowd gathered as the prisoner was loaded into it. Before it could be driven off, Members of Parliament who were present were astonished to hear the cry 'Burdett For Ever' being shouted from what had now become a pushing mob. One man tried to open the coach door as though to let the prisoner escape and Life Guards had to be called in to clear a path for the coach to begin its journey to Newgate.[4]

The Prime Minister had been assassinated. When the hubbub had died down somewhat, a file of grave and silent men moved in and peered at the body, laid out waiting to be moved from the Speaker's drawing room. They shared the grief of all loyalists. However, the overwhelming emotion which swept through the establishment, rather than sorrow at the senseless killing of an honest if unspectacular politician, was one of fear. The conviction was that Perceval was the unfortunate first in a long line. The news, which had so caught and battered the imaginations of the upper middle class, was that Bellingham was a Lancashire merchant with a Luddite involvement. The possibilities of dreadful things yet to come seemed limitless.

This fear spread through every rank of the upper stratum. The Prince Regent's name had already been linked with that of Perceval as a target for assassination in captured Luddite documents. So too had the names of Lord Castlereagh and the Home Secretary; Richard Ryder now knew from Bowling how close he had been to becoming Bellingham's target.

Only the madness of George III protected the King from the fear of an extant hit list. When told of the assassination, he had some difficulty in calling up the identity of the Prime Minister from the interstices of his deluded mind. When it came he murmured, 'Oh, yes, I know now, I ordered him to be hanged for keeping me in confinement.'[5]

Any conviction that the army at least was an unshakeable bulwark against a revolutionary movement was rudely shaken within hours of Perceval's death. The following morning Grenadiers mounting guard in Pall Mall on being told of the assassination, to the horror of elderly, affluent spectators, burst into spontaneous applause.[6] This behaviour in times of war was deeply worrying, and made even more so by simultaneous reports that privates in militia regiments had been heard saying that if ordered to fire at rioters they would shoot over their heads.[7]

News of the reaction in other parts of the country, when it reached the leaderless Cabinet, was of a consistently unnerving character. In Nottingham the announcement of the assassination was received with greatest joy by frame knitters who built a huge bonfire in celebration. Violence quickly spread in the town and magistrates had to be called to read the Riot Act.[8] In Bolton Colonel Ralph Fletcher watched crowds of rioters gathering yet again, this time chanting their approval of the murder.[9] In Macclesfield the colonel of the West Norfolk Militia took particular trouble to sound out his soldiers, now billeted in the town, about their conversations with local workers. The response, which he reported with distaste, was unequivocal. 'The lower orders of people here', he said, 'have expressed their approbation of the horrid assassination of Mr Perceval.'[10]

There was little consolation to be found even in more educated opinion. The *Leicester Chronicle* went so far as to publish an article justifying the assassination.[11] In Liverpool, the vicar of St Mark's, the church standing in the street in which the assassin lived, felt it no more than his duty to preach a sermon on the 'melancholy event which deprived the country of one of its best and brightest ornaments'. The response to this from one of his parishioners came by penny post through his letterbox. Signed 'Julius – Lt. de Luddites', the letter not only ridiculed the vicar's sermon, its writer added that, 'had it been in any other place than the church, my pistol would have silenced thy blasphemy'. It went on to speak of the 'brave and patriotic Bellingham' and threatened death to the 'depraved George the Prince'.[12]

In the hours immediately following the killing of Spencer Perceval the link between the murderer and the Luddite revolt in the north appeared unquestionable. This was the view being forced on Richard Ryder by magistrates in the most troubled districts who were convinced that Bellingham's motives were revolutionary.[13] With his Prime Minister dead and his own life having been preserved only by the whim of a capricious assassin, with the north country in turmoil and the loyalty of the army suspect, with every sign pointing to organised revolution and with an aristocratic leader apparently waiting opportunely to be called to its head, Ryder would have been understood had he now encouraged the Cabinet to drastic measures.

But for all its lack of stability Britain again failed to descend into the chaos advertising itself as an inevitability. There were good reasons why this was so. The most significant of these was that the right force under the right man had been – fortuitously – positioned at the right time. In the seven days in which Thomas Maitland had been at his command, with no shots fired in anger, the north-west of England had already been reduced to quiescence.

The second reason was that the great mass of people who had already shown themselves as potential revolutionaries remained without a leader. The chief contender from the upper classes for this role remained Sir Francis Burdett, MP. He, however, as verbose as ever in and out of Parliament, was behaving with the utmost circumspection and showing no signs of wanting to trail his coat tails in any action which might lead to another spell in the Tower of London. The leader from the workers' own ranks who had raised his head sufficiently to be identified, George Mellor, had had to let it sink back out of sight. He was by now preoccupied with the likely consequences of the bloody murder in which, only a fortnight earlier, he had been involved. Inadequately experienced or equipped to judge the depths of the undercurrents of sympathy which were moving nationally through the lower classes, Mellor had even misread the local symptoms of grief at the consequences of the Rawfolds incident as acceptance of its failure. The chance to turn himself into a general was passing. Instead of mobilising an army, to achieve his aims and what he believed should be the aims of the poor in general, he was adopting the tactics of a small-time gangster. His failure to capitalise on a movement to which he had given critical impetus was palpable. The epigram that the tragedy of the poor lies in the poverty of their aspiration is exemplified in nobody better than in George Mellor. If there were others capable of doing what he had attempted, they had not shown their heads above the parapet, alongside his.

The last but far from insignificant reason why the revolution, against which so many in the nation were bracing themselves, never burst forth at this juncture, lay in the irreducible laconic character of Richard Ryder. With the passing of Spencer Perceval, Ryder alone in the Cabinet was in touch with the true seriousness of events. Had he quickly forced any of the draconian measures which were available to government after the murder – arrest, hangings, martial law – the inevitable reaction of a seething population could have been critical. But Ryder at this juncture was well aware that, with his Prime Minister dead, the possibility of a new government being formed without his own talents being called on, was high. He therefore followed the course his nature most frequently recommended and did nothing. Yet again events justified this his universal policy, and fortune smiled. As the days passed more detailed inquiries into John Bellingham's connections, his past and his motivation, revealed that the worst fears were not to be realised. Bellingham, it emerged, had few, if any, connections with Luddism.

General Gascoyne who, immediately after the shocking business in the House of Commons lobby, had held the intruder by
the scruff of the neck, had also declared that he recognised the
prisoner. Bellingham had visited him only a few weeks earlier. As
the Member of Parliament for Liverpool, Gascoyne's help had
been sought by Bellingham to press his claims on Parliament for
redress for what he claimed was unjust imprisonment in Russia.

Under questioning in his cell Bellingham had more than willingly told his story.[14] In 1804 he had been roughly arrested and
thrown into gaol on the orders of the governor of Archangel
because of his connection with an unsettled marine insurance
claim at Lloyds. In spite of Bellingham's impassioned pleas for
help from the British Ambassador, Lord Leveson Gower, he had
spent three years in Russian prisons as a common felon under
appalling conditions, sometimes on bread and water. Since his
return his petitions to the Prince Regent, to the Privy Council and
to members of government, including one petition to Richard
Ryder on April 13th,[15] for compensation, for loss of health, reputation and business, had come to nothing.

On further questioning Bellingham made it abundantly clear
that he was not part of a conspiracy nor of a confederacy, Luddite
or otherwise. He had acted entirely alone and on behalf of himself
and he was driven by no political motive whatever.[16]

On May 15th, six days after the death of Spencer Perceval,
Bellingham was tried for murder at the Old Bailey. His counsel's
application for postponement on grounds of insanity being rejected, he pleaded Not Guilty. With the prisoner simultaneously
resolutely reaffirming his sanity and admitting the shooting, the
case was virtually indefensible. After an eight-hour trial the jury
returned within ten minutes of retiring carrying a verdict of
guilty.

Shortly before eight o'clock on the morning of May 18th,
Bellingham's hands were bound and pinioned to his sides as he
waited near the Newgate scaffold. After a minute or two he
complained that he was not sufficiently tightly bound. 'I wish not
to have the power of offering any resistance,' he said.[17]

At four minutes to eight he hurriedly stepped on to the platform
and into the centre of the drop. Watching the scene from the
window of a house he had specially rented for the occasion was
Lord Byron, his interest in the affairs of the manufacturing industry and its workers having diminished in favour of more dramatic events.

When Bellingham was finally ready, a cry of 'God bless you' was heard to come from the back of the crowd.

A clergyman removed Bellingham's cravat, adjusted the rope around his neck and pulled a night-cap over his face as the clock began to strike eight. On the seventh stroke the bolt of the platform on which he stood was withdrawn.

Lord Byron wrote, 'On Monday, after sitting up all night I saw Bellingham launched into eternity, and at three the same day I saw [Lady Caroline Lamb] launched into the country.[18] He had sat as close as he ever would to the weighty matters disturbing the nation's balance.

23

Officer in Command

The effect of Maitland's force had been salutary. Manchester, for the first time for weeks, was a peaceful place to live in. Only days earlier, middle-class citizens had had visions of the city streets running red with their blood. Now, in spite of his congenital pessimism, the chairman of the magistrates, the Reverend Mr Hay,[1] who had spent so many recent days virtually besieged in the Police Office with Joseph Nadin, the Deputy Constable, conceded that Maitland's methods had transformed the town.

Maitland himself had no illusions that his control over the north was either permanent or widespread. He was more firmly convinced than ever that although there was no single cause of the revolutionary spirit shaking the country, social problems were critical. The effects of the long-drawn out war in the Peninsula, the series of bad harvests throughout Europe, the introduction of new machinery – particularly steam looms in Lancashire – he acknowledged had all played their part in the present unrest; but he saw that the harsh working environment and the appalling living conditions of so many of the poor were among the main factors dictating the present state of the North-West.

It was not a soldier's job to provide solutions to social inequalities. He had already decided what his most important task should be once he had found a way of controlling the violence throughout the whole of the north. He told Richard Ryder,

the only real difficulty in our way, is to ascertain completely how far, the designs of these disaffected against government ... proceed from a head of more or less consequence, and what is the real state of the strength of this body whatever it may be. That it exists I have no doubt, but I do not believe either to the extent or combination credited by many. To find out its true nature and character must be the first object of government.[2]

This object – to find out who was running the revolt and how powerful they were – Maitland had now spelled out as desirable Cabinet policy for Ryder to press on his colleagues. Maitland intended to achieve it, if necessary by ruthless means. He would use military force as soon as that became appropriate. He was a pragmatic man. His unusual career had liberated him from military dogma. He would continue his present policy of concentrating his forces in a show of pomp and strength for as long as the method worked, but no longer.

However, he had methods other than strictly military ones in mind. He was less than impressed by local officials, particularly Mr Lloyd, who had been searching frenetically for workers' secret organisations and committees. 'Their great zeal leads them to think they have done a most meritorious act,' he complained of the magistrates, 'if they can prove the existence of these committees.'

Maitland now conceived a policy of infiltration of working-class groups in co-operation with the civil power. He proposed that the Home Office should find a suitable London police officer who would select a dozen 'men of the lower orders of the community who are thoroughly to be relied on, and to send them unknown to each other to this neighbourhood for the direct purpose of getting into their committees' in order to discover who was at their head. His plan was that these men should report to his commanding officers in Manchester who would arrange for him to meet the spies secretly.

Now that Manchester was under his thumb Maitland quickly realised that the more urgent and more durable problem lay not in Lancashire but in Yorkshire. Already he had sent one of his young officers over the Pennines to Huddersfield who had reported back that the situation there was 'by no means comfortable'. There were also disturbing reports of mutinous behaviour among soldiers in Yorkshire militia regiments.[3]

He lost no time in riding over himself to observe what he described to the Home Office as 'the Yorkshire Border'. But the truth was Maitland had no intention whatever in limiting his sphere of operation to the country which bordered the North-

West and the North-East Commands. He had come to the north country with troops sufficient in number to subdue the whole of it, and he intended to do no less. Whether his opposite number, Lt Gen the Hon H G Grey, would be an aid or an obstacle to his plans remained to be seen.

On May 13th the two generals met by arrangement in Huddersfield. It was, it seems, one of the few occasions on which Grey could bring himself to visit this, the most unruly town under his command. Neither man left any record of what was said there. The outcome, however, was clear. Grey was weak, insecure and obsessed by irrelevancies and suspicions. He was not in favour of yet deeper involvement by his force. He now believed that local magistrates were complaining to the government of both his inability and his unwillingness to come to their aid during the worst days and nights of the past weeks. He was, events would show, pitifully inadequate opposition to the crudely spoken and disturbingly confident ex-Governor of Ceylon. Grey had to suffer the indignity of hearing from Maitland the news that he had already arranged, for the following day, a full meeting of the Lieutenancy of the West Riding, the county which supposedly lay in Grey's command. More humiliating still, Grey was pointedly not invited to the meeting and was left in no doubt that it was of little consequence whether he attended or not.[4] Whatever else he learned that day, Maitland was able to conclude that Grey was unlikely to prove a serious brake to the implementation of any plans he might conceive for the north as a whole.

Maitland, in the short time available to him, began to assess the problem in Yorkshire. Since Horsfall's murder, there had been no pause in the nightly outbursts of violence. Whilst he was in Huddersfield he was able to meet the man who, more than any other, he discovered, had taken on the burden of meeting the rioters face on. Joseph Radcliffe was now bringing in and interrogating every possible suspect, so focusing the hatred of the whole community of which his mansion house was the dominant centrepiece. He told Maitland that so long as the disturbances lasted, come what may, he would stay at Milnsbridge.[5]

As to what might come needed no imagination. In the most recent threatening letter opened by Radcliffe, the writer promised that 'I most assuredly will make myself another Bellingham and I have the pellit made that shall be sent in your hart's blood if I should do it in the house of God.'[6]

Maitland found that Radcliffe's house now had a permanen̂t detachment of ten soldiers from Major Gordon's force in Huddersfield. Radcliffe had provided comfortable rooms for them next to the stables and a fire in the servants' room to encourage them to stay at their task.[7] In case they did not he had commissioned his clerk, on a visit to London, to return with a good pair of blunderbusses which he intended to keep by his side night and day.[8]

The strain of it all, however, was beginning to tell on both the mind and the too corpulent body. The man Maitland met that day in Huddersfield was losing some of the imperturbable autocratic qualities that had first made him the scourge of the lower classes of this district. A tremble had appeared in his right hand and his irritability was beginning to increase. Fearful for his life and that of his wife, they were now having to live like prisoners in Milnsbridge. Also, Maitland found, Radcliffe was becoming jealous of the activities of the Lancashire magistrates, and particularly those of young Mr Lloyd, who was beginning to chase his suspects into Radcliffe's territory. He was also to complain bitterly that, until Maitland's appearance, he was getting less than inspired support either from the inadequate General Grey, or the inactive Richard Ryder.

The reports Maitland heard from Grey's officers at first seemed to confirm that Radcliffe tended to wear his worries on his sleeve. Colonel Campbell, who had been sent from Leeds by General Grey to report on the state of Huddersfield, had pointed out that the current talk of Huddersfield being taken over by a revolutionary force seemed unlikely. All the heavily populated villages in the surrounding hills were crawling with rebels. Why should they choose to gather in vulnerable Huddersfield?

Nevertheless, Campbell's report did contain enough additional information to suggest that Radcliffe's view of the dangers of life in Yorkshire was far from being the gross exaggerations of a frightened old man. Almost as an afterthought to his report, in the throwaway style of a seasoned cavalry colonel, Campbell revealed what had happened on the previous evening as he returned to his Leeds home from Huddersfield. When he approached the house two men hiding in the darkness 20 yards from him sprang out and loosed off revolvers. Both shots were stopped by a tree alongside him. Then, from behind a low wall, a third shot was fired into the window of the sitting-room usually occupied by his wife and family. 'I feel it prudent to remain in Leeds today,' Campbell concluded.[9]

The meeting of the West Riding Lieutenancy[10] which took place in the Wakefield court house was crowded to the doors with magistrates and military in spite of the fact that it had been called at not much more than a few hours' notice to coincide with Maitland's visit to the county. Every leading justice of the peace was present, including Joseph Radcliffe; so too was the High Sheriff, Sir Thomas Turner Slingsby, and the Deputy Lieutenants, including Sir Francis Wood who, for several weeks now, had been sending near hysterical messages demanding strong governmental action to prevent Yorkshire falling under mob rule. Lt Gen Grey, swallowing his pride, was also in attendance.

Opening the proceedings was the man whose meeting this nominally was: the Lord Lieutenant, the gentle and gentlemanly Wentworth Fitzwilliam. His introduction, however, simply served to present the platform to the true begetter of the assembly: the less gentle but infinitely more regal Thomas Maitland. 'King Tom's' performance was once more masterful. Treating earl, baronets, generals and justices as he would his junior subalterns on parade, he delivered a detailed lecture on the state of the military under his command, mapped out the position and the numbers of troops stationed in the north and gave as little indication as he thought fit of how he intended to use them at this stage. Forcefully he made the point that he did not believe that the local population under threat was doing enough to defend itself. Rather, it was running for military help at the mere mention of the word Luddite. Almost threateningly, he announced that he intended to put the regular army into action only in exceptional circumstances.

Maitland now called on Lord Fitzwilliam to give a description of the volunteer corps and local militia which were available to the Lieutenancy. Obligingly, Fitzwilliam stood and gave details of the 12,000 men, some of whose loyalty had so recently been in question. Maitland immediately asked for them to be formed into four divisions of 3,000 each, ready to be called out a division at a time as the case required. When this was agreed, without further ado he asked Fitzwilliam to put the whole of this force immediately under his, Maitland's, command. Again Fitzwilliam obliged. And so within the space of an hour or so Maitland had nominally doubled the initial force under his orders and spread his new empire, still only a few days old, into England's biggest county.

Maitland left the meeting having imprinted his authority on

every man in the hall. And, as a consequence, two of those present left it more clearly conscious of their own approaching redundancy. General Grey returned to York undecided whether he had any military force he could call his own left in the county. Lord Wentworth Fitzwilliam thought it best if he himself left Yorkshire entirely. The Wakefield meeting, he told the Home Secretary unconvincingly, had convinced him that any violence now likely to break out would be strictly limited, probably to attacks against individuals, and that these should be dealt with 'by those who happen to be on the spot – my presence in the Riding therefore I conceive to be no longer usefull, and shall on that presumption return to town to receive your further instructions, and to attend to other publick duties'.[11] Any possible hindrance to the way Maitland chose to run the north was fast disappearing.

Two government-inspired events were yet to take place that month which were too far advanced for Maitland to influence. Special Commissions had been arranged for Chester and Lancaster Assizes to try the workers arrested by Mr Lloyd and others during the riots in April. The subject of what was probably Spencer Perceval's last communication with Richard Ryder before his assassination had been the appointment of the judges for the Lancaster trial.[12] Several magistrates – Joseph Radcliffe was one – had made it their business to pass on their displeasure at the leniency with which Mr Justice Bayley had dealt with the Nottinghamshire rioters in March, and wanted him to have nothing more to do with Luddite cases in the northern counties. The pressure was effective. Bayley did not appear in any of the four judges' seats available at Chester and Lancaster.

The Chester trial was set to begin in the last week of May. Local interest was intense and a large detachment of troops was despatched to Chester Castle yard to forestall any Luddite attempt to free the forty-four prisoners awaiting trial. The Cabinet was kept in close touch with the events leading up to the Commission and with the trial itself, by the Treasury Solicitor, Henry Hobhouse, who had been sent to handle the prosecution's case. Educated at Eton and Oxford but with the pressing need to find a career for himself, Hobhouse had the view of a permanent post in the Home Office in his sights. He was appointed to his Treasury post and was most keen and eager to impress with his astute legal brain. He soon acquired for himself an obsessive commitment to achieving maximum sentences in the maximum number of cases. During the next few months Hobhouse's influence over the lives and deaths of captured Luddites was to be critical.

On this, his first important mission for government, Hobhouse soon discovered a soul-mate. He found bustling around Cheshire the young solicitor J S Lloyd. Hobhouse was instantly impressed by his qualities and by the discovery that, besides acting for the magistrates in a legal capacity, Lloyd had clearly been the district's chief of police and captain general of militia when the panicked middle classes had seemed on the point of being submerged by rioting cotton workers. Lloyd shared Hobhouse's obsessions. He himself had interrogated prisoners and produced for Hobhouse evidence in minute detail including corroborative accounts from accomplices. These last were vital if the Treasury Solicitor was to get convictions.

As the trial approached Lloyd had even persuaded one of the cotton workers, 44-year-old Thomas Whittaker, to make a written statement. Hobhouse was greatly interested by this news since it was one of the few coherent written statements made by any Luddite prisoner. What Whittaker had to say was scarcely the ranting of a rabid revolutionary: more the apologia of a naïve idealist.

A poor weaver getting poorer, Whittaker told that he had been drawn into the workers' committees simply to try to raise wages 'to a standard which would make life tolerably comfortable' for his wife and five children. 'I wished for nothing to take place but what could be honourable to both employer and workman', he said. He told how, against his will, a secret committee had been formed in Stockport with the initial aim of using force against machinery, but soon its object had become 'riot, plunder, assassination and everything subversive to the law of civilised nations'.[13]

However, what truly excited Hobhouse, rather than the content of Whittaker's innocuous confession, was the simple act of the man himself putting pen to paper. Whittaker was revealed as having had, no matter how basic, an education. It made him, for Hobhouse, as it had for Lloyd, a marked man – as indeed it made every articulate or literate Luddite discovered in the next weeks.

The news of results of the Chester Special Commission when it spread across the northern manufacturing towns was seen at first, as being of stunning savagery. Those who had feared for the leniency of the judges, Sir Alexander Thomson and Sir Simon

Le Blanc, could put their minds at rest. Fourteen men, most of them brought in by John Lloyd, had been given the death sentence. In the end, however, only two were to be hanged, both of them weavers: their crimes, even by the standards of 1812, appeared pathetic and to fall well outside the capacity of the brutal sentences reserved for them. One had been involved in robbing a house and setting fire to it, and another had stolen some clothes and some silver spoons.

The Lancaster Special Commission, which ended a week later in early June, took an even more drastic toll with equally little apparent justification. Seven men and one woman were sentenced to death by hanging. Three of the men had stolen bread, cheese and potatoes in the Manchester riots, and four were convicted of arson in an attack on a West Houghton mill. The woman, 54-year-old Hannah Smith, had stolen potatoes and was condemned to hanging for having jumped on a butter cart, having harangued the crowd following in her wake and having sold to its cheering members 20lbs of butter worth 36 shillings for a shilling a pound.[14] Sir Alexander Thomson had this to say to her when he delivered his sentence of death: 'Sex is not entitled to any mitigation of punishment when the crime is of such a nature to deserve it.'[15] Seventeen others, including teenaged boys and girls, were each sentenced to seven years' transportation.

The case which most aggravated the thoughts of Henry Hobhouse, however, was that of the literate Thomas Whittaker who, at Chester, had also been sent for transportation. Hobhouse, when he reported the results of the trials to the Home Office, demonstrated how little he adhered to the legal maxim of letting the punishment fit the crime. He wrote,

> The case on which I have had the greatest anxiety is that of Whittaker, whom it appeared to me very important to convict, not merely on account of his crime, but because he is a man of superior ability and education and of proportionate importance among his confederates.[16]

Throughout the trial Hobhouse had been alert to any loophole which might mitigate the sentence of a rioter. He was well aware that the operation to round up the Yorkshire Luddites had already begun. He was determined that if and when they came to trial, the law would be in a state which would prevent any escaping the most crushing power of British justice if it were deemed proper to apply it. Some of the judges' questions at the Chester trial had not been to his liking. For example, when considering the cases of machine smashing, they had asked whether a shearing machine,

(which is adapted to *finishing* the cloth which is made) be a *tool* used for the *making* of the cloth within the first section of the statute 22 Geo. 3.c.40; and secondly, whether such a frame being fixed to a building and turned by a shaft worked by a water-wheel, be a part of the works of a mill within the meaning of the 9 Geo. 3.c.19.[17]

These were fine technological lines of definition. They could mean that a rioter who had used his hammer to smash a loom might hang, and one who smashed a shearing machine might not – just as one who attacked a shearing-frame attached to the belt of a water mill might hang, and one who attacked the same machine being transported to the mill might not. These, as Henry Hobhouse knew, would be important questions whenever the question of the orgy of machine breaking in the Colne and Spen valleys came to a court of law. He immediately made a note to recommend to Richard Ryder that an Act of Parliament extending capital punishment to the destruction of *all* machinery should be introduced so that in future the sentence would not be, as it still was, dependent on the nature of the machinery destroyed.

A second series of questions concerned the Luddite oath; it was equally pertinent in determining whether or not a rope would end up round a Luddite's neck. There was some doubt in the judges' minds as to whether a man who administered an oath should be punished more severely than one who simply swore it. Hobhouse, however, had no doubts. He drew Richard Ryder's attention to the differentiation and suggested that the Bill which was at the very moment before Parliament should 'leave the latter offence to be punishable by transportation (extended perhaps to 14 years)' and the former by death.[18] Hobhouse's mind, a model of clarity, allowed for no half-hearted measures. Indeed, he allowed for no measures of the heart whatever.

24

The Doctor

On May 21st, J Stuart-Wortley, one of the Members of Parliament for Yorkshire, acutely conscious of the parlous state of the county he represented and far from sure that anything was being done about it, rose to move a motion in the House of Commons. It begged the Prince Regent 'to take measures forming a strong and efficient administration'.[1] In the division that followed the debate, defeated by four votes, the government fell. The episode brought to an end, not without sighs of relief, the far from distinguished ministries of Richard Ryder and his colleagues.

Finding a new leader for the nation, however, was not without difficulties. After a good deal of vacillation the Prince Regent eventually turned to the stolid rather than strong Lord Liverpool. When the new Prime Minister returned from his audience with the Regent and entered the room in which the nervous members of the embryonic Cabinet were waiting, his first words to the surprised, mild-mannered man alongside him were, '*You* must take the Home Department, Lord Sidmouth – it will be every thing to me.'[2]

And so pitched into the hub of the political maelstrom which the north of England had become was yet another newcomer. Sidmouth was an unfashionable politician. Born Henry Addington, he was the son of a doctor who had run a private lunatic asylum next to his home in Reading and then successfully moved his practice to London. Not being an aristocrat was a considerable disadvantage to Addington in the rough and tumble of Regency politics. So too was not being an orator. Worst of all, however, was not being William Pitt. As the brilliant Pitt's close friend and admirer, Addington had himself succeeded to the post of Prime Minister in 1801. The shadow of Pitt had been too long. For the short time Addington filled the post his lack of distinction as leader had only been exceeded by his lack of popularity. The few attempts he had made to leave his imprint on the nation had been singularly unwelcome. Once he had been laughed off the floor of the House when he quoted his father's notes advocating the value of bran in the diet. It would take more than a century and a half for the medical profession to catch up with 'the Doctor', as he was now mockingly called, and endorse the virtues of roughage. However, in one of his budgets he left a permanent mark on national life. Some might regard it as a scar. It was nevertheless a brilliant concept: the principle of Income Tax deduction at source was a brainchild of Addington's efficient but cold scientific thought.

Ennobled as Viscount Sidmouth in 1805, he had recently re-joined government under Spencer Perceval as President of Council. Shortly after Perceval's murder two members of the House of Lords, leaning on a writing table, felt the piece of furniture begin to collapse underneath them. It was Lord Sidmouth who caught it, but not before the ink pot had spilled on him. 'Well,' he said as, in a reasonably well-timed jest, he wiped his fingers, 'I did hope to have gone out of office with clean hands.'[3] It is unlikely, had he made the joke a few months later, that the remark would have won the laughter it did on that occasion.

Soon after this incident, the essentially kindly and unspectacu-lar man moved into what under normal circumstances was an unimportant Cabinet post. These, however, were not normal circumstances. The events of 1812 had already turned the role of Home Secretary into a keystone of government: its importance would grow beyond recognition during the turbulent term of domestic politics Sidmouth had now inherited.

His period of office, apparently running to form, began un-spectacularly enough. He found the crowded conditions of the tiny Home Department greatly to his distaste and he took to doing much of his work in the peace of his Richmond Park home. He made an unfortunate choice by appointing his younger brother, Hiley Addington, as his Parliamentary Under-Secretary. Hiley was inadequate and hypochondriacal, likely to take to his bed at the mere suggestion of an ailment. The result was to throw an even greater burden of work on the conscientious elder brother.

Sidmouth soon saw that much of his time was to be taken up by the problems of the working class who lived far north of London.

He was familiar with neither the class nor the area of the disturbances. He did, however, make a gracious gesture when a deputation of Nottingham stockingers visited the capital in an attempt to publicise their grievances. He ordered stockings and a shawl for his daughters. However, none of his experience of life, spent almost wholly either in Westminster or in the agricultural southwest of England, persuaded him that there was any necessity to look carefully beneath him. There, out of sight, were many people living in near disastrous conditions trying to attract his attention. Sidmouth's reaction to their state, when it was drawn to his attention, also ran to form. He saw his first duty as being that of maintaining public order, no matter what the cost in human suffering. He therefore set about crushing the rebellion of the lower orders by the best mechanical means available.

These means were now in place and of a quite different order from those existing such a few weeks earlier. He, Sidmouth, with his chilling efficiency, would be the anvil on which the hot iron of the north could be laid. Maitland's was the muscular arm already raised to wield the hammers. The tools themselves would be important. Henry Hobhouse, the Treasury Solicitor, clever and hard, would be one. Francis Raynes, the captain of militia, keen and unswerving in his devotion to duty, would be another. Manipulating them together, Sidmouth and Maitland would turn England into a repressive state which would last through Sidmouth's term of office, the like of which the nation has never since needed to experience.

It could well have been that the worst violence which had spread across the north during the past weeks could have been headed off by the repeal of some of the most disastrous parliamentary legislation of the early nineteenth century. Indeed Spencer Perceval was hurrying to consider the matter at the very moment he was gunned down in the House of Commons lobby. An inquiry into the Orders in Council had been that day in progress. Henry Brougham, the man most bitterly opposed to these barriers to Britain's trade with America and Europe, now involved in examining witnesses, had had a tart note sent to Perceval reminding him that he was due to give evidence. Perceval had failed entirely to attend the previous day and he knew he was already late for that day's session as he pushed in front of John Bellingham.[4]

All attempts by government to delay his inquiry because of the matter of the assassination of the Prime Minister were rejected by

Brougham who, with a certain political dispassion, realised that his most effective opponent had now departed permanently from the scene. One day's mourning for Perceval was all the delay he would brook those taking part in his proceedings.

At thirty-four, Henry Brougham was one of the most restlessly active and ambitious of politicians. Even the greatest admirers of this tall, gawky, bulbous-nosed young barrister conceded his ugliness as much as they did his brilliance. He had a talent for publicity and a genius for attaching himself to popular causes. Already he had taken up most of the best espoused by Sir Francis Burdett. Against slavery, flogging and the muzzling of the press, his fervent opposition to the Orders in Council won him the universal admiration of every class in the north of England. For weeks now petitions had been pouring in to the House of Commons from manufacturing counties trying to persuade government to get rid of the Orders which had so effectively undermined so much of the nation's export market. Even if the war with Napoleon meant that parts of Europe would still be inaccessible, the potential American market was so important that, at a stroke, large sections of the woollen, cotton and silk districts could begin turning their looms again.

The presence of Lord Sidmouth in government meant that Brougham now had well-placed support, and by June 23rd the Orders in Council were repealed. Tragically, it was too late. Five days earlier the United States had declared war on Britain and her ports would remain closed to British goods. The effects on the state of the north of England of what Brougham for ever after considered to be the greatest achievement of his life were, in the first instance, negligible. However, it was not by any means to be the last attempt the up-and-coming barrister would make to influence conditions affecting the Luddites whose behaviour he was watching closely, and not unsympathetically.

During these days of continuous upheaval to their lives no single piece of government legislation could have succeeded in convincing leading citizens of the north country that an end to their justifiable fears was in sight. Maitland, it is true, had gripped the Manchester districts, but mobs of workers were still rampaging whenever and wherever they fancied over the countryside, particularly that near the Yorkshire–Lancashire border. The Chester magistrate, the Reverend Henry Broughton, told Lord Sidmouth how,

Not a night in the last week passed without some house being attacked and plundered of firearms it contained. And on Sunday last during divine service some hundreds assembled on a hill near Ashton-under-Lyne, hoisted a flag, went through the manouvers of a regiment, and before any military could arrive, dispersed.[5]

Not only the middle classes believed that the smell of the French Revolution was hanging heavily in the air; every indication from the lower strata seemed to lead to the conclusion that a vast number of workers also fervently believed in and hoped for the same possibility. One of the prisoners pounced on by J S Lloyd had passed on the information, probably under the influence of Mr Lloyd's frightening techniques of interrogation, that the manufacturing area had been divided into districts, organised by Luddite delegates, in preparation for a revolution. A day for a general uprising had been fixed. All stage coaches would be stopped to prevent communication. All manufacturers would be put to death, and the Royal Family deposed in preparation for the establishment of a Commonwealth.[6] How much of this was invented to forestall more of Lloyd's brutality and how much wishful thinking is impossible to know. However, other sources were producing similar evidence.

The Chaplain of Chester Gaol, irrespective of any priestly vows of confidentiality, reported the conversations of prisoners describing vast armament depots prepared in readiness for a general uprising.[7] A letter found on one man spoke of a force of 100,000-strong being mustered in Yorkshire, and another 40,000 in Lancashire. It described London as the great objective where another 40,000 were ready to join the force.[8]

The identity of the leadership of any organisation such as this remained as conjectural as ever. One report of a meeting of Luddites near Stockport had spoken of a 'genteel stranger' haranguing the crowd with his revolutionary doctrine.[9] The name of only one man occurred with any frequency who might answer this description: that of Sir Francis Burdett. Lloyd's prisoner had spoken of him as destined to become the first president of the Commonwealth when George III and the Prince Regent had been dispatched. Police spies had also reported Burdett's name being used in Manchester public house meetings aimed at a reform of Parliament.[10]

Thomas Maitland was watching these events and absorbing the

intelligence he was receiving with a mixture of sensitivity and boredom. Boredom because, after having spent so many of his early years in warm countries, dealing with powerful personages and influential administrations, he was not now well disposed to his new role in a northern English climate among untidy manufacturing towns and frightened manufacturers. Riding about these cold, wet hills with a posse of dragoons was a tedious way of passing his evenings, achieved little and was bad for his health: he was beginning to suffer from rheumatism.

Nevertheless, in spite of these physical irritants he was still greatly intrigued by 'the seeds of great mischief' he could see threatening the nation. He, probably more than any other close to government, was still most responsive to the social and economic roots of Britain's current explosive condition. He believed that if the repeal of the Orders in Council could be made to take effect, if the export trade could be rebuilt and if the harvest did not fail, the government would be able to see out the present unrest.[11] He was also one of the first to notice that the towns in which financial relief had been given to the poor were also those where rioting most quickly abated.[12]

As far as the Luddite leadership was concerned, Maitland remained unconvinced by the 'genteel stranger' hypothesis adopted by magistrates and manufacturers alike. They believed, so enormous had the spread of the signals of popular revolt now become, that the whole revolutionary enterprise could not be led by anybody with less stature, experience and education than a Sir Francis Burdett figure. Maitland's assessment was quite different: 'Were I to give a distinct opinion in regard to their heads,' he told Lord Sidmouth, 'I feel certainly inclined most decidedly to say, that tho' some of them may possess considerable talent, they are still of the lowest orders – men of desparate fortunes.'[13]

Maitland had now begun to understand the perplexing mechanism which had sustained this great Luddite movement. He was receiving and examining letters captured from conspiratory sympathisers in London, and had begun to compare them with those taken from groups in Yorkshire and Lancashire. He saw that the plotters in London were looking for links with the north, where they believed lay strength, support, leadership and an organisation poised for action, whilst similarly those in Yorkshire and Lancashire were looking for precisely the same characteristics from the south and making the same assumptions as to the energy which would be generated there.[14]

This undirected activity, Maitland realised, had been responsible for charging the whole of this vast and dangerous Luddite
movement with its present destructive momentum. There were
no leaders in the true sense of the word, neither was there a
central organisation. In Maitland's words, there was no 'solid
bottom' to the movement.[15]

His was the first correct simple solution to the complex riddle
of the powerful natural mechanism which sustained the Luddite
revolt. Luddism, Maitland realised, was built on nothing more
tangible than hope. No politician had been capable of making the
same analysis which, once made, showed both the size and the
limits of the problem facing the establishment.

Nevertheless, Maitland's answer to the riddle, as he well knew,
was not a solution to the violence which continued to threaten the
stability of the nation. Within days of Sidmouth's appointment to
the Home Office, Maitland was in London to discuss face to face
with him precisely what could be done.

The signals were poor that these two men would see eye to eye:
Maitland, the aristocrat, the imperious, coarse intriguer and
traveller, with half a life of vigorous excitement behind him;
Sidmouth, the doctor's son, straightforward to the point of dull-
ness, with a visit to Berkshire or Hampshire as the height of
any one week's titillation. Yet the chemistry worked. Sympathy
flowed between the two and together they were able to sit down
and agree with the greatest ease and friendliness under what
precise terms they would grip their countrymen and return their
land to the peace it deserved. In the weeks to come Sidmouth and
Maitland would develop their friendship in an intimate, not to say
long-winded, correspondence.

Both men were in agreement that they were vigorously opposed
to 'the Great Remedies in everbodies Mouth'[16] – those instruments of undemocratic society, the imposition of martial law and
the suspension of the Habeas Corpus Act. Having paid lip-service
to constitutional rights, therefore, they now together set about
devising methods by which these most effective weapons of the
military and the police state could be applied in England without
governmental decree.

One of Maitland's problems was that his troops of soldiers
raiding Pennine villages in the hope of finding Luddite supporters were unable to make arrests unless they had an accompanying
magistrate or a special constable. The solution devised by Sidmouth
and Maitland, with the Solicitor General's connivance, was blind-

ingly simple. It was agreed that an army officer could be sworn in as special constable by a magistrate. Thus, henceforth, any of Maitland's patrols could act as though it were the civil power whenever and wherever it chose. The first stage of martial law was in place in fact if not in name.[17]

Maitland had a further suggestion. Would it not be possible to consider an Act of Parliament whereby magistrates would have the powers to force into the army or navy for a limited period 'persons of a bad character'?[18]

The suggestion was not taken up, but it was clearly well within the tolerance of Sidmouth's consideration that Maitland could clear from the streets for a length of time equivalent to a prison sentence anybody who looked like being a nuisance.

In the matter of supplying instruments of the police state Sidmouth was instantly supportive. The plan Maitland had put to Richard Ryder of sending police spies from London to the north to infiltrate workers' committees had suffered from Ryder's customary inactivity. Sidmouth, unlike his predecessor, responded with alacrity when Maitland raised the possibility.[19] However, Maitland's suggestion that Wiltshire croppers would be ideal recruits for his secret service was easier said than done. Sidmouth had to turn to rural Gloucestershire to try to find a few men desperate enough to want to earn a few pounds by risking their necks with Luddite committees. But in any case, there were other problems. As Sidmouth said,

> the inhabitants of those parts have not the sharpness of understanding nor the determination of character which belongs to those of the north and it is very difficult to find amongst them persons fit for the purpose.[20]

Maitland, a north countryman, would have found it difficult to agree other than wholeheartedly with the premise. Nevertheless, the police spy system and all it entailed was established. Maitland himself was driven to adopting a pseudonym (Benjamin Harris) when he met and interviewed the spies he intended to place in Huddersfield, Halifax, Bradford, Saddleworth and Leeds.[21] Some of his officers went to more cloak and dagger extremes. The colonel of the West Norfolk Militia quartered in Stockport wrote a cautionary note: 'Should you meet me riding about Newton pray don't speak to me. I shall probably be in coloured clothes, be so good as to mention this to Captn Thornhill.'[22]

This behaviour, which on the surface seems harmless enough

Boy's Own adventure stuff, nevertheless had very real repressive political implications. Many men's lives would eventually dangle on the successful application of these methods.

Maitland had assessed the situation across the whole of the north and had judged his support from within the Cabinet. And now that he could begin to see more clearly how to deal with the problem he could look for a suitable place from which to direct his operation. He had no intention of wasting either time or energy carrying out reconnaissances in hill villages and valley towns with all the accompanying discomfort of horseback, rain and late nights. These could safely be left to his selected junior officers. Nor did he intend to set up a permanent headquarters in any of the – socially at least – stiflingly dull manufacturing centres such as Manchester, Leeds or Huddersfield. For Maitland had discovered a new delight to compensate for the geographical misfortune of his present posting. He casually rationalised his indulgence in it in the postscript of a letter from Manchester to Sidmouth: 'I am going to Buxton for a few days which is equally near the scene of disturbances as this, to try the waters for the rheumatism where I request I may be directed to.'[23]

Buxton – a haven safely insulated by the Derbyshire hills from the recent terrible disturbances – was all the rage. The hotels and spas built a few years earlier by an astute Duke of Devonshire to exploit the much-vaunted healing properties of the hot springs were doing excellent business. A good deal else had grown up besides. John Carr, the best architect in the north, had turned the town into a Palladian gem and much of fashionable England had responded to the jewel's attraction. During the summer season, which had now begun, hot vapour and shower baths at the Great Hotel provided the motivation for attendance.

However, the other pleasures were not discountable and certainly embraced Maitland's interests: coffee houses (6 shillings for the season with different London papers), candle-lit balls in the Crescent Ball Room (punctually at seven o'clock, subscription one guinea), 'Card Assemblies' (subscription 3 shillings for what had become the most compulsive pastime of the age) and shops taken by London retail traders for the season.[24] London apothecaries were also in residence for the summer and available for consultation; their customary habit was to prescribe a box of pills and a comforting hot bath before dinner and dancing.[25] So successful had the whole enterprise become that Carr had had to build his magnificent circular Great Stables to house the 300 horses of the spa's visitors, with rooms above for coaches and grooms ringing the enormous interior exercise yard.

It was all much closer to the style of Thomas Maitland than the conditions he had tolerated during the past two months. The company too was more to his liking than that provided by the Manchester barracks. When he arrived at Buxton, Maitland found that Earl O'Neill, Sir Oswald and Lady Mosley, Sir John and the two Miss Edens, Sir John Heathcote, the Hon Mr and Mrs Erskine, Lady Fleming etc., etc., had all arrived just ahead of him.[26] It all promised a most worthwhile season. Moreover, Maitland would find it a most suitable place to consider at appropriate leisure the problems facing him. Indeed one might be forgiven for making the assumption that many of the prolix pages of the letters which from hereon he began to send to Sidmouth were dictated to his military secretary from the comfort of his bath.

25

Raynes

Maitland's style in all matters was distinctive. With those serving under him it was to note the individualist, accept him into the small circle of favourites, then exploit the talent to its limits. If the young man was attractive, so much the better.

Buxton was as convenient a place as any from which he could monitor the activities of the many junior officers serving in a huge area of northern England. One of these had been brought to his attention by his second in command, General Acland. He told Maitland that the dragoon captain, Francis Raynes, now serving with the 28th Foot Regiment, the Stirlingshire Militia, was one of the few to have recorded successes in Luddite-dominated areas.

Raynes's first assignment had been to one of the toughest and most troublesome areas in Cheshire: the hill country and its mining villages above Stockport. There, local special constables were being miserably ineffective against marauding Luddite bands. One Tuesday in May before Raynes's arrival, one Luddite had at last been headed off and chased to the top of a nearby coal pit shaft. As the officers closed in, the man quickly went to earth by sliding with practised ease down a rope inside the shaft. For three days and nights a patrol of forty men guarded the entrance intent on starving out their victim. Then on the Friday a large band of armed Luddites suddenly swept on to the pithead, drove off the guard with no real difficulty and gave a loud whistle. In seconds the collier was up the rope and running off with his gang.[1] It was in response to the bitter complaints of local residents who were nightly being attacked by fearless and virtually un-opposed groups such as this that Raynes, with a company of his Highlanders, was sent into the district. His orders were explicit. He was neither to divide nor detach his men in any circumstances.[2]

On his arrival near Mottram, Raynes found himself besieged by some frightened and some furious mill and property owners demanding any sort of protection from the unchecked raids on their factories, machines and houses. Raynes spent several days verifying that the tales he was hearing were not those of panicked imaginations. Initially he had difficulty getting any first-hand experience of the Luddites' activities. They had, he found, a very efficient system of scouts reporting on military movements. However, eventually he was able to persuade the curate of Mottram, a Mr Lightfoot, who knew the moorland tracks well, to take him with two of his soldiers secretly into the hills. There, at midnight, they suddenly came across a great crowd of marching Luddites. Almost immediately, however, Raynes's little party was sighted and his militiamen's uniforms recognised. Rather than turning to run, Raynes stood his ground; his Highlanders took aim with their muskets and as they did so began calling into the darkness for reinforcements from an imaginary piquet.

To Raynes's immense surprise the childish trick worked. The Luddites turned tail and fled as though attacked by a full battalion. Better still, a second gang, so far unnoticed by Raynes, seeing the retreat, rose from the heather and also began to flee, overrunning Raynes's position in the process. Raynes, the party of Highlanders and the shaking curate simply stayed where they were, hidden in a ditch.

Raynes, who soon was to see many similar groups of upwards of 100 Luddites armed with guns and bludgeons, was to learn a good deal from this incident. It taught him how a leaderless rabble was seldom a match for a few disciplined troops. Within days, with no battalion commander within miles for consultation, he was deliberately disobeying orders, sending small groups of his best men at dead of night in quick pursuit of any attacking gang. Moving quickly and silently, learning the geography of the Pennine foothills by walking their paths, Raynes and his men quickly discovered how to harass the enemy and how consistently to put it to rout. Soon he began to collect prisoners. It was not long before rumours spread of the treatment a worker who fell into the hands of Raynes and his tough soldiers could expect. Until now brutality had been the hallmark of Luddite behaviour: Raynes set about discovering its advantages for himself.

The news of the zealous young captain's behaviour in defiance of explicit orders was relayed upwards by the Stirlingshire's nervous commanding officer, Lt Col Russell, to General Acland, thence to Maitland. Far from a reprimand rebounding down the line, Raynes found a message of congratulation being passed back. And after several more incidents in which he and small groups of his men put the fear of God into Luddite gangs whose numbers far exceeded those of his soldiers, Raynes was himself summoned to Maitland. It was the signal to become one of the small group from whom the commanding general expected personal reports by mouth. 'King Tom' was not in the habit, Raynes found, of accepting written reports from junior officers and he soon had to accustom himself to travelling at a moment's notice, night or day, to wherever the general happened to be.

As Raynes's successes increased, so Maitland recognised his unusual qualities and kept up a flattering interest in his unique methods. Soon Maitland was sending Wroth Acland to tell Raynes to divide his force as he, Raynes, felt appropriate and to keep it moving rapidly by night across the hills from village to village 'like a body in constant motion, fixed no where'. 'Write to me daily', Maitland told Acland, 'and watch Raine [sic] closely.' He insisted, however, not yet having had Sidmouth's approval of his plan to swear in army officers as special constables, that no troops should act on civilians without a magistrate or at least a constable being present.[3] Raynes's temporary solution to this problem was to use a constable disguised as his servant.

Maitland soon recognised that Raynes's methods were extra-ordinary in their consistent success. No other group from Maitland's force had produced such results in relation to its size in such a vast country. He realised that he could use Raynes and his techniques as a model to implement his policy over the whole of the northern country districts. Eventually, this policy was to be based on only one human emotion: fear. The instrument to instil it would be the highly mobile autonomous army patrol. It was to be the first explicitly devised commando unit of the British Army. Maitland gave clear written instructions through Acland how Raynes's force would operate. Raynes kept them to his dying day.[4]

He was told to choose personally the best men of his regiment and to include one lieutenant, two sergeants, two corporals and forty privates. He was to quarter himself wherever he chose, to keep his troops constantly on the move and to move by night, never to stay more than one night in the same place, never disclose his destination and divide the party as he felt fit.

He was given permission to get rid of any officer who questioned his plans and demands, and to make replacements of his own choice. Senior officers were given equally clear instructions to allow Raynes to operate freely and independently in the areas they commanded. The Stirlingshire captain, they were told, answered only to Maitland.[5]

Raynes was enchanted not only by this return to active soldiering, but equally by the heady feeling of power and autonomy so unreservedly handed to him. The power, however, generated burdens. The news of his new unit produced a sensation among the officers of both his own and other regiments; also, inevitably, there was jealousy. By senior officers – on whom he could make demands for any reason he chose, without in return putting them in his confidence – he was quickly resented. As for junior officers – 'It became a most unpleasant part of my duty', Raynes wrote, 'to be obliged to decline the services of officers under me, and to request that they should be exchanged for others.'[6]

A second difficulty grew as he moved further into his assignment. He was mounted and needed forage for his horses. Also he had to pay the special constables who came and went with his detachments. But now no longer on the forage return of a regiment, and resented by the officers who might have helped him, he was forced to pay for forage for himself and his men, and keep the constables, all from his own pocket. It was a consideration well beneath Maitland's attention. Raynes had, in any case, no intention of troubling the man he by now admired fervently, with this domestic problem. Maitland's ADC, Captain Thornhill, promised to do something about it, but the matter eventually slipped his memory. With only a small income in addition to his pay on which to keep himself, his young wife and family, the problem for Raynes was to grow.

The physical demands of the commando were also a burden but, the matter of money apart, Raynes revelled in the activity. Moving by night, sleeping by day, never in the same place from one night to the next was an exhausting experience. It nevertheless was bringing the rewards of manifest success and with it, the constant monitoring, feedback and, above all, approval of Maitland.

Leadership of the group frequently made heavy demands on his personal courage. One night he rode into a village where workers, banned by law from being part of a union or Combination, were holding what their spokesman, Solomon Law, claimed was a

'Friendly Society' or sick club meeting. Whatever other symptom most of the crowd of more than 300 men spilling out of the public house into the village streets showed, it was not sickness. The best part of them were drunk, or armed, or both. Solomon Law's mocking insistence that his men had gathered 'for charitable purposes' persuaded Raynes that he had the makings of yet another full-scale riot on his hands. When all his softly, softly attempts to influence the crowd failed, he faced it with his small patrol behind him and threatened to fire unless they dispersed. Far from retreating, the mob began to close in. Raynes now had to take the enormous risk of ordering his men to prime and load, knowing that at best their bullets would bring down only half a dozen of the massed bodies slowly encircling them. His order had no effect whatever on the movement of men towards him. Finally Raynes gave the order to his Highlanders to raise their muskets and take aim. In his own words, 'they absolutely presented.'[7] In the seconds before the command, 'Fire!', his bluff succeeded. A worker turned tail and ran; others followed. Yet again Raynes found himself dividing a small force into even smaller groups to chase off potentially overwhelming numbers of Luddites. He himself hared after Solomon Law and arrested him. It was midnight before he restored order in the village.

It was the evening of the following day, having spent the whole night interrogating prisoners in his own way, and having moved his force on, before he had time to write his report for General Acland. Exhausted and exhilarated, he ended it with an apology: 'From having been up all last night, and engaged with persons of one description or other the whole of the day, I do not feel myself so clear as I could wish.'[8]

And so it went on for night after night – Raynes sweeping in to village or community, delivering a short, sharp shock, then moving on. Before long, the technique of instilling fear was being successfully applied by other commandos set up by Maitland and modelled on Raynes's group. And before the summer was out every village of East Lancashire and Cheshire was to ring with the sounds of the hoofs of cantering cavalry or the footsteps of fast-moving, lightly armed infantry.

26

Goodbye, Grey

Maitland had by now made completely clear to the Home Secretary that, whereas the army was beginning to get the upper hand in the north-western counties, and the situation there was controllable, that in Yorkshire was dangerous and getting worse.[1] Not only were the nightly gatherings of Luddite gangs across the county becoming more frequent and more barefaced, marauding mobs of considerable size had begun a series of raids stealing arms and committing common robberies.

In the Spen valley eight houses in Sir George Armytage's village of Clifton, a mile from Kirklees House, had been violently robbed in one evening.[2] Nearby at Rawfolds William Cartwright was still constantly under threat. John Cartwright had paid a visit there and had been horrified not only by the life of constant vigilance and fear his brother and his family had to lead, but by the brazen behaviour of the Luddites. During his visit he watched helpless as at ten o'clock in the morning, nine or ten of them, all armed, gathered within 200 yards of Cartwright's home, put up a practice target, and fired at it for a time. Then, when the family inside the house was thoroughly scared, the men casually walked off up the valley.[3]

For three months now Cartwright had slept every night in the mill waiting for the next attack. The cost of manning the new set of defences he had built, together with the cost of repairing the damage after the April raid, had long ago used up any profits from the cloth finishing business. The strain was beginning to tell. But although daily becoming more bitter at the government's apparent refusal to intervene with financial or other assistance, he was nevertheless prepared to see the affair out, if necessary to its violent end.

Sir Francis Wood, the thoroughly panicked Vice Lieutenant of the county, had used Cartwright's case, as he had dozens of other cases of violence, to demonstrate to the Lord Lieutenant and anybody else who would listen the vicious level to which life in the West Riding had now sunk. Wood, suffering badly from gout, was under constant pressure, with which he was not well equipped to deal. Magistrates and manufacturers repeatedly demanded of him, as the Lord Lieutenant's representative, more effective action. He was convinced that neither Lord Fitzwilliam, sitting at his safe, comfortable and beautiful seat on the Yorkshire borders, nor Lord Sidmouth, insulated 200 miles away in the Home Office, had any perception of the truly awful state of the county. Daily he was bombarding Fitzwilliam with graphic descriptions of roaming banditti spreading terror across the countryside and predicting the assassination of magistrates and others. 'The country', he wrote, is 'virtually in possession of the lawless'.[4] Every attempt he had made to persuade General Grey – still in York – to intervene had met with Grey's nervous reluctance to move into action any but the most minute part of his force from fear of weakening it.[5]

Wood's predictions for the future, however, were not based on improbable speculations:

> Should the harvest be only moderately good and no outlet be opened to the manufacturers of the West Riding there is no doubt but that every species of outrage will increase on the approach of winter when the long nights and bad weather will render the prevention impossible and their detection more difficult.[6]

Wood need not have feared that this sort of consideration had not occurred to others. Maitland was well attuned to the critical nature of both the harvest and the state of the wool trade. Already he had emphasised to the government his belief in the necessity of strong legal and military action before the summer ended. Sidmouth, in return, had begun to consider setting up secret parliamentary committees of inquiry into the situation in the north, with a brief to recommend the steps that should be taken to return it to permanent stability.

But before these even began their work, the worst riot yet erupted in Sheffield on 19th June. Lord Fitzwilliam, still at his mansion, Wentworth Woodhouse, was not neglectful of his duty.

He rode for the town and plunged into the middle of the scene at its most threatening.

It had started in the morning with a mob of women rushing into shops where flour was being sold at 7 shillings a stone, and forcing the owners to sell it at 3 shillings. It was the beginning of a whole day of frightening violence. The East Devon Militia was quickly called in to try to restore order. The regiment's commanding officer, after a night without sleep, described the scenes that followed:

> The 15th Hussars and ourselves have been constantly on duty since yesterday morning. I am sorry to say these lawless proceedings continue today; and parties are gone into the country to attack the mills; but are followed by dragoons. Not a mechanic has been at work yesterday or today, though there is no want of employment. The Riot Act has just been read to at least 5000, and Lord Fitzwilliam gave them five minutes to disperse, when, as they did not obey, the hussars charged down the street and cleared it immediately. We now have orders to fire if we meet the least resistance. Thousands were added today to their numbers from the country. . . .
>
> Nine o'clock – Lord Fitzwilliam, who appears very determined, left this place an hour ago; and I hope this troublesome business may end without our having recourse to fire. No lives have, as yet, been lost.[7]

The possibility of yet another catastrophic chain reaction of rioting spreading across the country as it had two months earlier, spurred Sidmouth's Secret Committees into action in both Houses of Parliament. Both heard detailed reports of the Rawfolds affair, the Horsfall murder and other outrages and deaths in the northern riots and both reported their findings in late June. Neither, however, revealed much more than a well-informed citizen could have gathered by reading selected local newspapers. Nevertheless, their reports were used as the basis of the Preservation of the Public Peace Bill to give magistrates in Yorkshire and Lancashire the wider powers they had been clamouring for for weeks: the powers to search for and seize arms wherever they chose, to make arrests of any suspects at riots without first having read the Riot Act and to act in areas adjoining their own where a shortage of magistrates occurred. Unedifying as the Secret Committees had been, they presented the opportunity for the fingers of what was becoming an effective police state to take a tighter grip.[8]

In the debate on the Bill in the House of Commons on July 10th a whole battery of speeches approving the measures recommended by its Secret Committee was heard. William Wilberforce, notwithstanding the evangelical Christian principles that had driven him to oppose slavery, gave the most reactionary speech of the session, expressing dissatisfaction only in the fact that the proposed measures were not sufficiently swingeing.

Among the very few opponents of the Bill, Sir Francis Burdett, as was his uncontrollable habit, spoke at length. Compassionately he reminded the House of the pitiful convictions at the recent Lancaster Special Commission: 'Women executed for stealing potatoes, and children as I might call those of 16 years old.'[9] Again and again he repeated the cry that the only way to bring peace was by reform of Parliament.

Free of the burdens of office and listening to Burdett's speech was Richard Ryder. He celebrated his new-found liberty by making fun of Burdett's declamatory style of oratory, defending the execution of the potato-stealing Hannah Smith, and hinting to the House that Burdett had darker motives inspiring him than simple compassion for his fellow men.

Ryder could afford to feel satisfied with the legislation being enacted that month. The Unlawful Oaths Bill, whose path he had smoothed, was now law and incorporated Henry Hobhouse's suggested amendments. The penalty for giving an oath was to be death, and taking it, transportation for life. As with that Bill, the Public Peace Bill swept through its third reading in the Commons with an overwhelming majority. Such was the belief in the foregone conclusion of it passing through the upper house without worthwhile opposition that only seventeen members of the Lords put in an appearance for its third reading.

Maitland, his rheumatism much relieved, was maintaining from the comfort of his Buxton bath a close watch on the political events which would affect the way he could operate in his territory. Wroth Acland was keeping him fully briefed on his force's military activities. Though in case the subordinate general might think his commanding general was spending an inordinately extended time in the spa town, Maitland assured him that 'communications from London' had kept him at Buxton. Nevertheless, Maitland was not averse to sharing the pleasures of the Crescent hotels. 'I think a day or two at this place would do you a great deal of good,' he told Acland.[10]

The news Acland had to tell when they met was interesting. The clever Mr Lloyd of Stockport had joined forces with Raynes. As he had with Hobhouse, the Treasury Solicitor, Lloyd found a kindred spirit in Raynes: in particular they shared the same view that the interrogation of a prisoner was effective only if it extracted a maximum quantity of information and that the method of extracting that information did not much matter.

A spy had just reported to Lloyd that a sergeant serving in Sir George Armytage's Militia regiment was believed to be a secret Luddite leader and to have key information about the murder of William Horsfall. Maitland immediately sent Lloyd galloping across the Yorkshire border to the Colne valley, accompanied by his ADC, Captain Thornhill, and a party of dragoons to arrest the soldier – a corporal as it turned out – named Barrowclough.[11]

From under the nose of Joseph Radcliffe, Lloyd swept his prisoner at top speed back into Lancashire, arraigned him before the Manchester magistrate, Mr Hay, and spent two days questioning him in a closed room where, Hay wrote, 'I have thought it best not to be present myself.'[12] Lloyd emerged from the interrogation room carrying a signed confession which he admitted had been 'troublesome to take'.[13] Its contents were sensational.

Not only had Barrowclough positively identified William Horsfall's murderer as a Luddite named Samuel Haigh, he told how escaped French prisoners – officers in Napoleon's army – were organising and drilling squads of Luddites. In addition he identified fifteen sites where large quantities of small arms had been stored in readiness for the imminent uprising of the north. He made many other startling revelations.[14]

Maitland had his officers check Barrowclough's leads one by one, including making, across a vast acreage of Yorkshire, searches for the supposed hidden arms stores. Not a single gun was discovered. Every other piece of information also turned out to be an invention of Barrowclough's mind, clearly driven to desperate fertility by the frightful techniques Lloyd had used in the closed interrogation room.

Maitland, though not too fussed about the way the information had been got, was furious at the time-wasting distraction which diverted hundreds of his men in fruitless searches. It was not to be the last false trail that summer. However, almost equally annoying, the incident trapped Maitland in the petty quarrels of local magistrates.

Joseph Radcliffe, hearing that John Lloyd had been acting in the Colne valley and had taken a prisoner from there to be put in front of the Manchester magistrate, was apoplectic with fury. Maitland had little time for Radcliffe's temper and less for his jealousy. He pointed out that, since a regular arrest warrant had been issued, Lloyd had been acting well within the law. Equally, however, Maitland found both Lloyd's ambitions and his methods distasteful; he told Lord Sidmouth: 'I did not admire the hands [Barrowclough] was in.'[15]

Mr Lloyd, meantime, was well aware of the jealousies his activities were arousing in Yorkshire and that rumours of his ambitions were spreading. The speed with which he now wrote to the Permanent Under-Secretary at the Home Office to assure all concerned that his motives were pure, and that he was not angling for the job of Agent-Solicitor in the inevitable forthcoming prosecutions of the Yorkshire Luddite prisoners, suggests that this was precisely what John Lloyd had in mind.[16]

However, Maitland's annoyance at the outcome of the Barrowclough affair was tempered by signs of much more certain success as a result of one of his own initiatives. He had persisted in his idea of using police spies to identify the Luddite organisers and leaders. Now at last what seemed to be evidence from a reliable source, unattenuated by brutal methods of interrogation, had arrived.[17]

Maitland had arranged for the deputy constable of Manchester, Joseph Nadin, to send a pair of locally recruited spies into Yorkshire to see what they could ferret out. Maitland was not concerned with the background of the two spies – John M'Donald and John Gossling – only that they should be men of the people who would be able to mix freely with workers in the Yorkshire woollen trade. It was evident that they were both sharp characters. M'Donald's report of their visit across the border fulfilled all expectations.

They had arrived in Halifax on July 8th. That afternoon they had both paid a visit to the Crispin Inn and had managed to strike up a conversation there with a worker, Charles Milnes. As the three men drank together Milnes began to talk of the attack on Cartwright's Rawfolds mill. Soon he revealed that he knew one of the Luddite officers present at the attack. M'Donald then primed Milnes by saying that if he, M'Donald, were sworn as a Luddite, he too could be active in the cause.

Milnes, after a few hours' drinking, was ready to take the bait. At ten o'clock that night he led M'Donald alone to a house where the grizzle-haired John Baines with his nephew, John, and his fifteen-year-old son, Zachariah, as well as several others, were waiting. Baines produced a Bible, gave it to M'Donald to hold, asked him his name – to which M'Donald replied 'John Smith' – and had him repeat a Luddite oath and kiss the Bible.

Baines now welcomed M'Donald as a brother. M'Donald in response offered to buy drinks for all those present. Baines, however, firmly refused. He said he knew very well that local magistrates suspected him and he did not want to risk a visit from the Watch and Ward patrol. Leaving old Baines and his young son together, M'Donald and the rest returned to the Crispin to celebrate 'John Smith's' inauguration as a Luddite.

M'Donald was wily. He knew that, to be useful in a court of law, any evidence against Baines and the rest would have to be corroborated. Two days later, therefore, this time with Gossling, he visited the old man at his hatter's workshop and persuaded him to drink with them and other workers Baines trusted, in a private room of a nearby public house. As they drank, M'Donald, pointing at Baines, said casually to Gossling, 'This is the old man that twisted me in.' Baines, annoyed, agreed that he had, but warned M'Donald in future to be very careful about revealing that sort of information, particularly at the present time; Baines had heard, he told the pair, that two Bow Street police spies were operating in Halifax.[18]

Unlike so many spies' tales, M'Donald's was simple and had the ring of truth. Maitland, for the first time, was convinced that here was incontrovertible evidence against the first key Luddite figure.

Baines, so long suspected by Joseph Radcliffe and other magistrates as the malign intelligence directing local violence, could be brought in for questioning at Milnsbridge House whenever the time was opportune. The chances of that arrest leading to other arrests was exceedingly high.

Meantime fortune again dealt an ace into Maitland's hand. And again he did not have to move far from the card tables of Buxton to exploit it.

The opportunity Maitland was looking for was inadvertently presented to him by an officer in his own force. During the weeks around early July, Major J H Seale, who was in command of the South Devon Militia serving alongside the East Devons in Yorkshire, had sent several letters direct to Lord Sidmouth. Why the Home Secretary chose to encourage a correspondence with a serving mid-ranking army officer is not clear. It seems likely, however, that the major and Sidmouth had some personal or family relationship which made Seale's letters acceptable outside normal military channels.

On the last day of June Seale sent to Sidmouth evidence which suggested that the situation in Yorkshire was under worrying lack of control. He had, he said, discovered how the Luddite system of organisation now stretched 'all the way from Glasgow to London'. He described how the basic strategy of the revolutionary movement was to draw away from southern England as many troops as possible by starting riots such as the one which had just taken place in Sheffield, and that then a great rising would take place in London.[19]

Two weeks later Seale was again writing about the alarming state of the county and asking for police help in detecting Luddites.[20] And in yet another letter he appears to have written to draw attention to the lack of any military action in the area from General Grey.[21]

This was not the only uninvited reference to General Grey which the Home Secretary had received. One correspondent from the Spen valley describing the most recent armed attacks, complained bitterly how the speeches of radical Members of Parliament, such as Sir Francis Burdett and Samuel Whitbread, were actively encouraging the rioters. General Grey, the letter pointed out, was Whitbread's brother-in-law — so implying that Grey's reluctance to send troops into the area was politically motivated.[22] That Grey was still being unbelievably inactive in West Yorkshire is at least unquestionable. Hammond Roberson had yet again demanded more troops to protect Cartwright's mill, and yet again been refused.[23]

The situation, when he heard of it from Lord Sidmouth, was ripe for Maitland to manipulate in his most calculating and brutal fashion. First, knowing full well that the damage to Grey's reputation had already been done, Maitland wrote to Seale to reprimand him for not having sent his communications to government through General Grey himself.[24]

Next he wrote to Sidmouth. The unctuous letter, marked 'Secret and Confidential', has been preserved in the Home Office files. It began by reminding Sidmouth that when Maitland had been sent to the north ten weeks ago, he had been given command of the Inland and North-West Districts; that Yorkshire was left under Grey; and that the two generals were to communicate with each other. In oiled phrases Maitland protested how the subject was a most unpleasant one for him to have to deal with, how he had no wish whatever to extend his own command or interfere with that of his friend Grey, but added, 'I think it right you should be privately informed, particularly after the application relative to Major Seale, of my feelings.'

Maitland's feelings were simple to express. The country would be better provided for if the whole of the disturbed part of it were under one command – his. He described the problem of interfering in another general's district without running the risk of 'disturbing that harmony, so congenial to my own feelings, and so necessary for the good of the Service'. As for Grey personally, he said, 'I am certainly the last man that would wish to propose anything that would in the smallest degree affect his situation.' And after this last piece of blatant hypocrisy, he went on, 'We have been and I trust ever will be, on the most friendly terms.'[25]

Within twenty-four hours Sidmouth had had Grey relieved of his post. Maitland was immediately informed by the Adjutant General. Lt General the Hon H G Grey, Maitland was told, had asked for three months' leave – because of his impending marriage. The whole of Yorkshire was henceforth to be added to his, Maitland's, command.[26]

27

On Oath

As July ended Sir Francis Burdett yet again stood in the House of Commons and yet again began to speak at enormous length. After what one newspaper reporter described as 'a copious prefatory speech'[1] he began his attack proper: an address to the Prince Regent exhorting him to return the country to safety and content,

> by restoring to the people their undoubted rights 'claimed, demanded and insisted on' but unfortunately not established at the Revolution; amongst which the chief and paramount is, the free choice of Representation in the Commons House of Parliament.

The motion was not seconded. Burdett sat down and the House, deaf to any hints of the advantages to be gained by a revolution, got on with what it thought to be better business.

Shortly afterwards yet another Luddite prisoner was taken in, this time at Barnsley, who under questioning confessed that his Luddite Committee believed in the early possibility of the overthrow of the government and that Sir Francis Burdett and Major John Cartwright were ready to join them.[2]

Words and deeds, however, were still as far removed from each other as ever. The truth was that neither Burdett nor Cartwright had yet shown the least sign of leading the workers to their salvation. It was still further confirmation of Maitland's theory of the self-fuelling nature of Luddite philosophy and hope.

Maitland was more convinced than ever of the essentially leaderless quality of the Luddite revolt, particularly in Lancashire and Cheshire. As his communiqués to government had repeatedly made clear, he was astutely aware of the social and economic steps that could be taken to help solve the present crisis. Meantime his only reponsibility was to provide a military solution, and this he was doing.

Raynes and the other young officers leading the commandos which Maitland had modelled on the original, were having an effectiveness in the countryside west of the Pennines beyond all expectation. Their rapid, rough and tough methods of instilling fear were already beginning to reduce the frequency of Luddite attacks.

When Raynes had first moved to the district he had had some problems when local people had tried, occasionally successfully, to turn his men to the Luddite cause. Now, however, his domination of the villages and small towns was such that in several of them he had begun to find men who were willing to act as informers – at a price. Naïvely he told Maitland, 'I find nothing will provide information but money.'[3]

Those villagers who did accept his golden guineas did so at substantial risks to their own lives. At Newtown in Cheshire, one man who had provided him with information, William Cooper, needed protection for both himself and his family, from Luddite supporters who were furious at his treachery. When one day Raynes was told that a body lay behind Cooper's house, he rode there fully prepared for the news that Cooper had been murdered. On the ground he found a terribly burned, disfigured and at first unrecognisable corpse. After he had examined it closely, however, Raynes found it to be not Cooper, but Samuel Crabtree, a young Luddite. Crabtree had over-loaded a pistol, presumably intended for Cooper, and put it in his pocket, where it had exploded. Several bullets had entered Crabtree's back. The exploding gunpowder had set fire to his clothes, cauterising most of his flesh.[4]

Raynes was later to recall[5] that during these days early in August 1812, he believed the potential for revolt was reaching crisis point. His informants had convinced him that there was now a real possibility that, before the month was out, the Luddites would rise as a body. From the experience he had so far had of this campaign, he also believed that only harsh uncompromising military action – at which he had discovered he was particularly adept – could prevent this rising.

Maitland was prepared to accept Raynes's summary of the situation. He agreed that this was the juncture at which decisive and highly visible measures should be taken. He was in any case particularly worried about the effect that news of any defeats in the war with America might have on the military situation in the north of England.[6] However, with his customary finely tuned equivocation he made the decision to use the iron fingers of Raynes on the one hand, with the velvet glove of newly introduced legislation covering those of the other.

Already in mid-July he had asked the Home Secretary to persuade government to avoid the use of harsh measures where they were unnecessary.[7] He particularly had in mind the possible use of the third section of the Unlawful Oaths Act, which provided immunity from prosecution for those confessing to having taken illegal oaths. It was at Maitland's suggestion that a Royal Proclamation had been issued which offered a pardon to any Luddite who, at the same time as he confessed, took an oath of allegiance to the Crown.[8]

Maitland used the new proclamation with the psychological insight of a twentieth-century ad-man. He ordered handbills to be printed with very simple text – in noticeable contrast to the crowded information on customary official notices – and headed each in huge type resembling the modern banner headline with the words PARDON OF ILLEGAL OATHS. These he had distributed in vast numbers across the countryside and had them posted in every village. Simultaneously he took advertising space in local newspapers printing the same message in banner type three times in each edition.

With the Regency advertising media stretched to their limit and with fresh orders to Raynes's commandos and those of his brother officers to move forcefully into action, the result was a triumph of astute judgement on Maitland's part.

Magistrates were primed and ready to receive the furtive knocks on their doors. It was not long before a trickle of workers began to come down from the villages and into towns such as Stockport, Ashton, Bolton and Bury. As one worker watched another giving himself protection from the law, the numbers began to swell.

Raynes, knowing that the Royal pardon expired at the month's end, urged the process along. He rode over to Newtown, the place he believed to be 'the very hot bed of sedition'.[9] There he showed the constable, James Lees, a long list of names of Luddite supporters he planned to arrest. He had extracted these from interrogees and from informants. But Lees was scared and at first refused to co-operate in the identification of the men. His brother, who had done local duty in the Watch and Ward patrol, had just been beaten up, and had nearly died. Eventually, after smooth talking by Raynes and the promise of more protection for himself and his family, the constable set off round the town with the patrol.

Raynes had chosen his time carefully. It was Sunday and it was raining. Most of the workers were at home. Even so, news of the military's approach ran ahead. But although three out of every four got wind of his coming and fled, Raynes was well pleased with the numbers he took into custody. Using his intimidatory methods he was able to make several men 'tolerably communicative', as he put it. That day's work gave Raynes a comprehensive picture of Luddite supporters throughout the whole area, and he was able to move rapidly through it, making more arrests.

The next day, a Monday, 300 men from the Newton area poured into Stockport to swear the oath of allegiance. What was a trickle was now a flood. In the last week of August one magistrate alone, the Reverend Charles Prescott, opened his door to hear the confessions of 500 men and to administer to each of them the oath of allegiance.[10] Even the *Leeds Mercury* – that 'very mischievous paper universally read among them', as Maitland described it[11] – reported 1,000 Luddites flocking to magistrates in the Stockport area.

John Lloyd, the solicitor, had now joined forces with Raynes and, as the militia captain galloped from village to village to apply his rough methods, Lloyd moved from town to town to capitalise on them. At Chester when men came in from the countryside to swear allegiance he made them do so in open court. It had, he reported, 'an admirable effect' on the townsfolk.[12] The evidence was now clear that whole districts of Lancashire and Cheshire had been fully committed to Luddism. 'It is painful to reflect on the number', the sententious Mr Lloyd said, that had 'been misled'.[13]

By the end of that week Maitland could assess the result of his policy and could rub his hands in satisfaction. He reported to the Home Secretary that, at least as far as Cheshire went, 'they are completely beat'.[14] The measure of the confidence of the magistrates in the likely permanent effect of what he had achieved was manifest; for the first time since the troubles began, they allowed public houses to stay open until 11 p.m.

In these last days of August, however, there were two distractions which could have persuaded Maitland that the revolutionary tide in the country as a whole was still not ready to ebb. The first was caused by an informer. Maitland was immediately sceptical of the value of the man's information since, if it were true, he would need to reverse all the theories he held contrary to local belief concerning the absence of a credible Luddite leadership. However, the conviction of his second-in-command, Wroth Acland, that the informer was genuine, carried Maitland against his better judgement.

The man, who gave his name as Sergeant James Lawson, a deserter from the 1st Royal Surrey Militia – an easily verified fact – had turned up in Liverpool and had succeeded in getting access to Acland. In his interview he had told a convincing story of how Lord Lovat was organising a Catholic force in Dublin which would join with the Luddites in a major rising to establish a British Republic. Lawson himself had been Lord Lovat's secretary in Dublin, before moving to Lancashire, where he had taken the Luddite Oath. He had been elected to a Luddite Grand Council of twenty-five which was planning the assassination of Lord Castlereagh as a prelude to the uprising. Lawson carried with him convincing samples of forged notes, printed, he said, in vast quantities which would finance Lovat's army.

Acland fell for Lawson's story hook, line and sinker. He sent samples of the notes to Maitland should his commanding officer doubt that rapid action was necessary. Before Maitland could himself interview the man, Acland had packed him off – with a reward for his troubles – by stage coach to London to make direct contact with the Home Secretary, Lord Sidmouth. As a result of Lawson's visit to the Home Office more than twenty arrest warrants were issued, including one for Lord Lovat.

Before the affair ended weeks later with the slow realisation that Lawson was a skilled confidence trickster operating consummately well at the highest social levels, he had taken in the Home Secretary, the Parliamentary Under-Secretary, the staff of the Adjutant General, as well as Major General Acland and others of lower governmental and military rank. From each one he had taken a £10 or £20 tip before disappearing for ever, once more benefiting from the comfort of a north-bound stage coach, into the mists of the Pennines.[15]

The diversion of part of his force up the con-man's blind alley, the abortive attempts to execute warrants on non-existent or totally innocent citizens, the forces sent to root out imaginary Luddite Grand Council concourses, all these were time-wasting and infuriating activities for Maitland at a crucial period. But like previous distractions of a similar kind, he could bestride this one with ease. What he could not discount, however, was the news which reached him on August 29th. Maitland had travelled to Yorkshire where he knew he must now concentrate all his efforts. That evening he sat down in Wakefield to write his report to the Home Office.

He kept his letter open until the arrival of a special dispatch from Lancaster for which he had been most anxiously waiting. He believed its contents to be vital to the momentum of the campaign facing him in Yorkshire.

They were the outcome of an important incident which had taken place ten weeks earlier when Joseph Nadin, the Deputy Constable, had surrounded the Prince Regent Arms in Ancoats Lane, Manchester, with a group of special constables bolstered by soldiers from Maitland's force. Inside the pub, a meeting attended by thirty-nine workers was taking place. Nadin had arrested thirty-eight of those present and had charged them with administering an illegal oath.

It was the verdict of the Lancaster assizes jury on these thirty-eight men which Maitland so eagerly awaited. Harsh sentences for the guilty – death penalties or transportation for life – could only have had a most sobering effect on the problematical Yorkshire areas at just the time Maitland planned to inflict himself on them.

The contents of the dispatch which he now tore open were beyond belief. He scribbled a furious postscript to his report to the Home Office: 'I have just heard of the miserable acquittal of the 30 [sic] at Lancaster.'[16] The thirty-ninth man, who had hidden under the stairs of the pub, had evaded arrest and given evidence in favour of the other thirty-eight. A brilliant defence led by Henry Brougham had won for the astonished prisoners the right to walk from the courtroom as free men.

Maitland would have to move on to his most difficult and unpredictable task – without the psychological advantage he had so confidently assumed would be his.

He had wasted no time in getting across the border. Within hours of Grey's ignominious departure to his fiancée and their wedding, Maitland had moved into Yorkshire ahead of the official announcement of his appointment and taken command of the north.

After two days seeing for himself, he was able to confirm for the

Home Secretary both the scale and the viciousness of the Luddite rioting still plaguing the West Riding. Scarcely any worker from any town or village in the county, he discovered, had come forward to magistrates to swear the oath of allegiance.[17] He told Lord Sidmouth,

> I believe that a system of terror prevails and that we are shutting our eyes to an evil, small in amount, but serious in its nature, from the dread of trying totally to extirpate it.[18]

He had reached the decision to extirpate it by one method alone: harsh military exertion. He now planned to deploy large numbers of high-ranking officers throughout the country, with a full general, Acland, in charge of Huddersfield, which he believed to be the centre of revolt.[19]

But who would be the touchstone as to the best military techniques to apply? The answer was never in doubt. Raynes, even though still in Cheshire must be consulted. Acland was already kowtowing to Maitland's favourite young soldier. 'Pray give me your opinion on this,' Acland wrote in a note to Raynes about one scheme, 'you have so much local knowledge of what is going on, that you can best judge which plan is likely to have the most beneficial effect.'[20]

And when Maitland needed advice, although Raynes was out of contact riding between Pennine towns, the general unhesitatingly ordered Acland to send his ADC, Captain Thornhill, to find the oracle wherever he might be. 'Raynes's opinion is what I want most,' Maitland cried.[21]

Raynes, in his turn, unhesitatingly confirmed what his master wanted to hear. *Fear*, replied Raynes, should be Maitland's policy for Yorkshire.[22]

And so it was that Maitland went into his new command having abandoned the velvet glove. 'Fear, and Fear alone', he told Beckett, had produced the best results in the past.[23] 'Fear, and Fear only', he told Acland, was the effect he wanted to induce in the future.[24] 'I am convinced we can by this means', he told Lord Sidmouth, 'terrify them into a sense of their own weakness.'[25]

28

An Anonymous Letter

Maitland had already discovered where the pressure points were and where, as an example for the rest of the turbulent county, he would apply the tourniquet. The Calder valley, and in particular the little valleys leading from it, the Colne and the Spen, were the centres from which the bloody violence of the last six months had spread and from where it still continued to flow unchecked.

It was to Huddersfield that Maitland now sent General Acland with orders to base himself there and get the town in a firm grip. Acland wasted no time. By the last day of August, as *The Times* reported with some concern, Huddersfield had been swamped with 1,000 troops.[1] Every public house in the place was bursting at the seams with southern regiments of infantry and cavalry. Whole detachments had been forced on truculent publicans who were reluctant to be intimidated by any soldiery, let alone by well-bred young subalterns from the South. As one perhaps chinless and certainly open-mouthed infantry lieutenant, Alfred Cooper, discovered, after having been kept waiting in the wind and rain for half an hour outside a bar-room door, the pub's owner was capable of rounding on him with 'the most violent and haughty language'.[2]

Maitland himself made his headquarters, not as Grey had done so ineffectively at York, but at Wakefield. This was not only the administrative capital of the West Riding, it had good communication by road with South Yorkshire where worryingly large-scale revolt still sporadically occurred, as well as being within easy reach of the Huddersfield–Halifax districts.

Maitland now considered the time to be ripe for bringing the commando groups which had operated so effectively in

Lancashire and Cheshire, across the border to Yorkshire. Raynes was the first to be called. With orders to move his force to the Spen valley, marching his men by night across the Pennines and resting by day, he was told to appear in Huddersfield before taking up his new sphere of command.

On his arrival, much to the surprise of the young soldier, a party of welcome was waiting for him. He was greeted not only by Major General Acland, but also by Lieutenant General Maitland himself who had ridden over from Wakefield especially to brief this highly favoured captain. There Raynes was given 'a most flattering reception'. Maitland, exerting the personal touch which had made him such a successful leader, made it abundantly clear that the privations and the unpleasant soldiering of the past weeks which had brought so many striking successes, would not be forgotten when the affair was over. In Raynes's words Maitland assured him 'that it should be made up to me'.[3]

Meantime his knowledge that his methods had been approved at the highest level was reinforced by what Maitland now told him. He was to be given immediate personal command of three companies of the West Suffolk Militia along with a detachment of dragoons – in other words, virtually a regiment of his own with cavalry support. He was to base himself at Millbridge, near the scene of the Rawfolds attack, where more trouble was daily expected, and operate freely over the whole of the area bounded by Bradford, Halifax, Huddersfield, Leeds and Wakefield. Other commando groups would support him. The aim was to instil fear, to make arrests and, finally, to make possible harsh exemplary punishment.

Both generals also used the occasion of this meeting in Huddersfield to familiarise themselves with the rancorous old man who, almost single-handedly, throughout that year had kept up an offensive posture towards the Luddites. Joseph Radcliffe, in spite of the death threats, the shots in the dark that had whistled past his head, the smashed windows and the unremitting hatred of every worker in the district, continued his aggressive stance. When every other magistrate in Yorkshire, intimidated by the threats to themselves and their families, had shrunk from the consequences of hunting down suspected Luddites, Radcliffe had forced his special constables into making arrests.

Daily he was still personally interrogating every worker brought into Milnsbridge House. He had succeeded in committing one or two suspects to York Castle but on what he knew too well to be inadequate evidence. He was fully aware that he had failed to penetrate the Luddite organisation and still knew nothing of its leaders. Loyalty among the lower classes was solid. The only evidence he had managed to gather that might point to the murderers of Horsfall or to the Rawfolds attackers had come from several paid informers and was probably worthless. No evidence had been satisfactorily corroborated and Radcliffe did not need reminding that it would not bring conviction in a court of law.

The strain on the elderly justice of the peace was considerable. Not a single man or woman in the whole of the Colne valley had appeared before him to swear the oath of allegiance to the Crown.[4] He told Lord Sidmouth, 'People are so terrified, no one will voluntarily come forwards, nor dare they, when brought speak the truth; what is got from them is with the utmost difficulty.'[5] He also told the Home Secretary that 'the odium of the disaffected' put a 'terrific' burden on the members of his family. Their sufferings, as a result of the abuse and threats flung at them, he insisted, were greater than his own.[6] However, the severe tremble in his right hand had continued to worsen during the past week.

Maitland, for all that he realised that Radcliffe had been the bulwark which had prevented the district from crumbling into Luddite anarchy, disliked the man as much as he did most of the magistrates and attorneys he had seen failing to rise above the chaos. He made it plain that his tolerance of the jealousies which existed between the magistrate, Mr Radcliffe, and the solicitor, Mr Lloyd, was now burning on a short fuse.

Acland, though, was prepared to listen with less annoyance to the worried old man's abuse of the pushy Mr Lloyd. 'I walked him into another room,' Acland told Maitland, 'talked to him about managing and clearing the country in the way proposed, in which he properly coincided and I found him ready to do anything that can be wished and I have no doubt we shall get on most cordially and quietly together.'[7]

Whatever else was in doubt, 'the way proposed' was clear. Both military and civil authorities were now in agreement about the manner in which Yorkshire was to be treated.

*

The arrival of a new military force in the county precipitated a sudden surge in Luddite activity. No certain evidence exists as to who was leading the raids, but most bore the unmistakable stamp

of George Mellor. Joseph Radcliffe listened one morning to
the tale of a typical attack from a householder at Sheepridge.
Forty men armed with 'guns, mattocks, malls, swords and other
weapons' had suddenly descended on David Hepworth's farm
shortly after midnight. As they held the terrified man down they
asked him the price of his milk. When he replied, they invited him
with a gun at his head, to lower it to 2 pence a quart. They
promised to 'shoot him to atoms' if he refused. Before they left
they smashed the whole of his furniture and crockery.[8]

The raids were now on a smaller scale than George Mellor had
tried with his Rawfolds army and were becoming recriminatory as
well as involving petty robbery and gratuitous violence. Nevertheless there still remained a strong primitive socially motivated
force behind many of these and they were frequently aimed at
bettering the lot of the poor. However, the blundering decision
which had led to the murder of Horsfall had cost Mellor dear.
Too many others had been involved in that gory and unpopular
business and too many others had been drawn into the aftermath.
He realised full well that only a slender thread held his name from
tripping from an informer's tongue. For him to carry on working
by day as a cropper at John Wood's shop – long suspected as a
dissidents' cell – and to continue to lead violence by night inevitably would become a more hazardous way of life now that the
surge of military activity had begun.

However, by the end of the first week of September, Maitland
had to admit that the nightly raids and the plunder for arms had
continued as bad as ever.[9] In his report to the Home Office
he confessed that the destruction of machinery was still 'truly
alarming' and that the evil spirit abroad had not been 'broke in
upon in the smallest degree'.[10]

One of the gig-mills destroyed that week, in spite of intensive
military patrols, had been Waterhouse's at Halifax.[11] William
Cartwright was quick to point out to Acland that the likely
attackers were Waterhouse's own employees. The blatantly
untrustworthy Abraham Pule, who had once worked at Rawfolds,
and George Hartley, brother of the man shot during the Rawfolds
attack, were both croppers there.[12] But there was no evidence
against them and Acland was as powerless as the magistrates to act
on hearsay.

Cartwright himself was taking no chances. Nightly he continued to expect an attack on his mill. Hammond Roberson that
week had already reported that at nearby Gildersome, the scene

of his courtship with his beloved Phoebe, an undefended property had had its shearing-frames and dressing machines totally destroyed.[13] Also close by at Elland one sentry on guard had had his fingers cleavered off by a broad sword, before retreating to let a gang do its worst.[14]

But Cartwright had no intention of being either undefended or taken by surprise. Whoever took on Rawfolds a second time would be made to suffer. Raynes, as soon as he arrived at Millbridge, rode up the valley to meet the mill owner. What he saw made his eyes shine with admiration. Sixteen soldiers were now quartered there.[15] Cartwright, he found, had raised the technology of his defences to the same level as the technology of the wool finishing which had caused him his problems in the first place.

He had cleared a space on the second floor of the mill and placed there a specially designed gun on a swivel which was capable of rapidly discharging sixty musket balls. It was mounted on what Raynes described as 'an ingeniously constructed carriage and could be moved from one window to the other'. He had also improved the *chevaux de frise*, the roller with 16-inch spikes which defended his staircase, and had devised a set of reflecting search lights which he could beam at any night attacker and by which 'the features of any person could be seen at a considerable distance'.[16]

Cartwright's methods, like his machines, were products of the Industrial Revolution. Nevertheless, there existed a powerful motive for caution to accompany his technological innovation. He had been told in threatening letters that when the second attack came, its success would be ensured by his wife and children being placed in front of the mill to take the full blast of any defending musket shot. Such was the level to which the viciousness in the valley had now sunk, there was no reason why he should not take the threat seriously.

Raynes, as soon as he arrived, began to look for ways to apply the methods that had been so successful on the other side of the Pennines. He also soon recognised the uncompromising toughness of the people ranged against him. 'They are a very turbulent set here and speak their sentiments freely, even before the soldiers,' he told Acland.[17] With the few exceptions of men such as William Cartwright and Hammond Roberson, any citizen who supported the establishment had long ago been intimidated into keeping the fact to himself. Watch and Ward, and Voluntary Defence

Associations were non-existent in the valley. 'I fear Sir, it will be some time before we can break up this lawless band,' Raynes reported.[18]

Nevertheless, he had complete faith in the eventual effectiveness of a thorough dose of brutality – particularly of the kind handed out by his more thug-like men. 'Strapper has been with me this morning,' he told Acland. 'He thinks he shall get a number of Ludds to attend his dancing school.'[19]

Immediately he set foot in the valley Raynes looked for the informer who could be moved to talk for a few guineas' surreptitious payment. That the information the money produced might be either wrong or invented was neither here nor there. The sensation it could be made to produce under well-engineered circumstances was all Raynes needed in order to put a wedge in an apparently solid front.

Within days he had bought information from two men who told him that at Millbridge a young Luddite, James Starkey, had revealed to them a plan to blow up Cartwright's mill and had also indicated to them where arms were hidden. Instantly Raynes had the youth taken to Joseph Radcliffe for arraignment, then bundled away to the dungeons of York Castle 'for endeavouring to incite two persons to felonious outrage'.[20] Then, having discovered at Healds Hall the enthusiastic Luddite-hunter, the Reverend Hammond Roberson,[21] Raynes set off with the clergyman as his guide to begin the search of the properties named by the informers. No arms of any description were found as firm evidence. The hatred of the Spen valley workers against Roberson and the informers was nevertheless intense. But the first seeds of fear in the valley had been sown.

Soon Raynes discovered that the Colne valley magistrate, Joseph Radcliffe, strongly approved of his methods and, as in the case of Starkey, was prepared to capitalise on their results. It was probably Raynes who effected a reconciliation between Radcliffe and Raynes's friend from the Cheshire campaign, John Lloyd. The ubiquitous attorney had followed troops into Yorkshire in order to stay at the centre of the action. Whatever the reason, a grudging *modus vivendi* appears to have been arranged between the magistrate and the young Lloyd. Now that they were together, these administrators of the law, utilising the military muscle of Raynes, were to be a powerful combination.

The three men were able to pool much information and many resources. The account book of the paid informers and spies used in Yorkshire now began to mount in numbers; before the end of September it included dozens of names of local men who had fallen to the temptation of a little hard cash.[22] From these and other sources it was possible to form a dossier of Luddite delegates, sympathisers and suspects operating in the West Yorkshire area. It still exists as a neatly kept, cloth-bound and alphabetically indexed book.[23] Joseph Radcliffe used it as the source of the names of those he wanted brought in to Milnsbridge House for interrogation by his constables during the first days of September.

Those listed in the book were men from areas covering many square miles of Yorkshire. Several of the more interesting were from villages and towns on Radcliffe's own doorstep: 'Jops. Mellor, a draper living under Dungeon Wood ... Mellor's brother, who lives at Huddersfield, a cropper ... John Kinder, an apprentice of Mellor ... Benjamin Walker ... John Wood'. And during these days George Mellor was one of several of the young croppers of Longroyd Bridge who were routinely brought in to stand in front of Joseph Radcliffe's bench.

Mellor, tall and handsome – and if on this occasion he behaved as he did on others, proud – gave nothing away that could be used to cast suspicion on himself or any other conspirator. Like others brought before the magistrate he was released without charge. Yet the confidence of the Luddite-hunters that a breakthrough must come can be seen by the now rapidly increasing activity of Raynes and Lloyd and the increasing numbers of suspects they were beginning to push in front of the already mentally and physically overstretched Joseph Radcliffe.

Lloyd was still privately deeply scathing about Radcliffe's abilities. He considered him a pompous old man who talked too much and who still used inappropriate and ineffective techniques of interrogation on these tough young croppers. Whenever he felt it necessary he would pump a suspect dry before handing him over to the old magistrate. Lloyd used his methods indiscriminately on both the Luddites and the Luddites' victims. One such victim was John Hinchcliffe.

Early one morning in July this cloth worker had been forced from his house by two masked men. One of them he recognised as John Schofield, who, some weeks earlier, had attempted to swear him into the Luddite cause. Hinchcliffe had refused to be sworn. The cause of the early morning violence was that Schofield suspected that Hinchcliffe had told the authorities of the incident. Had it been the case, it could have meant a death penalty for Schofield.

The affray that summer morning ended when Schofield's companion pulled a pistol from his coat and shot Hinchcliffe in the
head. Both attackers fled. The trigger-happy accomplice was
never found, but two weeks later Schofield was arrested on board
a ship waiting to sail for America.[24] Mr Lloyd had discovered all
these facts and, whilst the victim was still in great pain from
his appalling injuries and unquestionably suffering from severe
shock, had him examined by local magistrates. Hinchcliffe,
scarcely surprisingly, was so terrified of further Luddite punishment that he claimed he recognised neither of his attackers.

J S Lloyd had none of Mr Justice Radcliffe's restraining sensitivities. He told the Home Office how he had used his customary
uncompromising technique of spiriting the injured man away.
'Hinchcliffe', he reported from Huddersfield, 'is now safe at a
gentleman's house in this neighbourhood, not to be seen by any
except myself . . .' He then told how, by his 'particular mode
of examination', he had 'prevailed over Hinchcliffe to identify
Schofield as one of the two men concerned in the outrage.'[25]

Much as Maitland viewed Lloyd's pragmatic methods with
distaste, it seemed highly likely that Schofield was the leader of
a Luddite cell. Provided Hinchcliffe, once free from Lloyd's
sinister influence, did not change his evidence in court, the
chances of conviction were high. But Maitland was deeply concerned that some of the workers now being committed to York
Castle on slender evidence by Radcliffe, might be acquitted.
If proceedings were brought against Yorkshiremen and the
result was as at Lancaster, where every single prisoner had
been acquitted, it would, Maitland said, be 'a triumph for the
disaffected'.[26]

Conviction and the ultimate sentence which the law allowed –
and nothing short of that sentence – was what Maitland believed
alone could bring the Luddite crisis to an end. Lloyd's methods,
therefore, provided they brought about the result, were not to be
discouraged. With this in mind, Lloyd was now let loose in the
district to use the information which Maitland's military patrols
and the more reliable of his spies had provided.

The first breakthrough was pure chance – chance augmented
by the not inconsiderable intuition of Mr Lloyd. One night in the
second week in September an army patrol operating at Flockton
near Huddersfield, brought in a man for no better reason than he
was out of his house 'at an unreasonable hour'.[27] Lloyd, hearing

that the man had been known to associate with a Luddite suspect, immediately set off with Maitland's ADC, Captain Thornhill, to examine him.

In remarkably short time Lloyd had got the name of, and had arrested this suspect, an illiterate mill worker turned coal miner, Earl Parkin. Lloyd then somehow extracted a confession from Parkin, along with the names of the rest of the gang. The total evidence Lloyd was able to gather showed there had been nothing much worse than a common robbery of £3 or £4, along with a little food and clothing taken from the family of an old man. In the course of the raid, however, guns had been fired, and the old man had clearly heard the word 'Luddite' used.

But although the crime amounted to very little, for the first time since the disturbances had begun, the evidence relating to it was supported by the confession of a worker. Armed with this confession Lloyd was able to parade the gang in front of Joseph Radcliffe knowing that he had put his fingers into the first crack of the heretofore solid wall of silence from Luddite members.

Radcliffe spent the whole of September 13th interrogating the prisoners.[28] By the day's end he had committed what he described as a 'desperate gang' – John Swallow, John Bentley, Joseph Fisher, John Lumb and Thomas Green – to York Castle on the basis of the information supplied by Earl Parkin.

Lloyd had more than successfully transmitted to the squealer the fear of being hanged as a Luddite conspirator. In the end, Parkin had agreed to turn King's Evidence against the rest. It would be no more than a matter of time before this confession could be used to persuade witnesses to provide corroborative evidence. Fear, as Lloyd was demonstrating, was an infinitely adaptable weapon.

Maitland now judged the time to be ripe to put the information from the spies M'Donald and Gossling to good use. Lloyd and Thornhill,[29] therefore, fresh from their success at Flockton, were sent off with a party of soldiers to Halifax to arrest the hatter, John Baines, and his accomplices on a charge of having administered a Luddite oath to M'Donald. There can scarcely have been much resistance to Thornhill's military force. John Baines was sixty-four years old and rather deaf. Zachariah, the son of his late years in marriage taken into custody with him, was fifteen. Four others arrested at the same time, including John Baines the younger, were workers who had neither a past history of violence, nor a present tendency to it. They had simply been present when

M'Donald had tricked old Baines into administering the Luddite Oath.

Joseph Radcliffe spent the whole of September 14th, without a break, questioning the five men and the boy. At the end of the day he wrote an order committing each one, including young Zachariah, to the cells of York Castle.

For the first time since the riots had begun in February, Radcliffe felt that the result of his work was likely to end in convictions and, just as reassuring, that he was getting the support he needed from the army command. As if some release valve had been opened on his high blood pressure, the next few days were spent in a frenzy of arrests, interrogation and committal. He committed one worker for having shouted his wish that 'King George and the Royal Family were in Hell'. Another he sent down for the words, 'Damn the soldiers, they are damned scamps, damn the General, he's a rogue and a rascal for bringing you here.'[30]

Maitland, however, remained as sceptical of Radcliffe as ever. Having been given the news of the magistrate's unbridled activity, in an aside to Acland he wrote, 'As far as relates to myself, and I think I may venture to say for you, and I am sure I may say it for the military at large, we are all equally indifferent to what may be said in ale houses with regard to us.'[31] But never for a minute did he waver from the cold, studied plan, involving Radcliffe, which would sacrifice human beings if that was necessary. He instructed Wroth Acland to keep the magistrate in good temper, and active, at all costs. For Maitland knew full well and freely admitted that Earl Parkin's gang were simple vagabonds rather than plotting revolutionaries.[32] Nevertheless, he had chosen to make the first example of them. If they were convicted – and he believed they would be – they would die. Meantime he gave Acland the task of humouring Radcliffe into more committals, the outcome of which was also likely to be fearsome and final.

Radcliffe himself was not going unpunished for his mental exertions. After three days of unceasing activity in Milnsbridge House, interrogating prisoners, threatened and vilified by them and their relatives waiting outside, the tremble in his right hand had reached an uncontrollable climax. He was no longer able to hold his pen. Jonas Allison, his clerk, was forced that night to take hold of it to complete Radcliffe's report to the Home Secretary. Lloyd stood over him to give advice should it be needed.[33]

No such stress as affected the old magistrate troubled the young solicitor. Nevertheless, a worrisome shadow of doubt momentarily crossed the confident John Lloyd's consciousness. Knowing he needed good corroborative evidence to be sure of convictions, he decided to reinterview the two spies who had trapped John Baines. Lloyd did not like the look of either M'Donald or Gossling. He felt a judge in a court of law might see them as he did – a couple of shady characters who sold their unsavoury services to whoever required them for a few guineas a time. M'Donald in particular troubled him. 'I dislike . . . his character,' Lloyd wrote. 'He has done too much in the like sort of manner. But I hope to God he has not been base enough to swear a lie.'[34]

But the fleeting shadow passed. If he had doubts about M'Donald, he quelled them with ease. Next day he resumed his rounding up and interrogation of Luddite suspects with unclouded enthusiasm. Serendipitous help had been provided which dispelled conscientious distractions. Probably within hours, most certainly within days of John Baines's arrest, an undated and unsigned note in an educated hand was pushed through a letter box and reached its intended reader, Joseph Radcliffe.

The contents of the letter were not dissimilar to several others Radcliffe had received that summer. They included the names of a number of public houses where Luddites were believed to meet secretly and listed croppers who were known to object to the new machines. But most interestingly they gave a version of the Horsfall murder whose source was said to be a 'Mr V'. The facts the story contained and the names it named, brought together several previously unrelated elements already noted in the cloth-bound dossier which Radcliffe had at his disposal. Mr V's nephew was said to work for a cloth dresser named Mellor whose young apprentice, Thomas Kinder, had been somehow involved with two of the murderers shortly after the shooting. A master cropper named Wood was mentioned. 'The report and belief is', the letter went on, 'that 2 of the persons who shot Horsfall are Jos. Mellor's brother who lives at Huddersfield, cropper or draper, and a young man who lives [with the] said Wood whose wife is the young man's mother.'[35]

It can have taken little time to discover that an apprentice named Varley, possibly V's nephew, had indeed worked for Joseph Mellor of Dungeon Wood, as also did Thomas Kinder. In the brief period that followed, these and several other apprentices, most of them young boys, were taken, some not for the first time, into Milnsbridge House and to other places, for questioning. Mr Lloyd's influence over them was decisive. Some he 'spirited away' from purported 'fear of their being tampered with.' After they had spent a short spell in his custody he was able to report that 'compensation or the influence of friends or both have produced a disposition in some of the witnesses to come forward and declare what they before concealed of their knowledge.'[36]

Knowing that more than a dozen men were now in York Castle facing capital charges for their Luddite associations, the birds had begun to sing.

Two of the apprentices had turned their tune to the theme of George Mellor. John Lloyd's ear was listening for it when it burst out. On October 10th he had a warrant issued for the arrest of Mellor. It produced what Lloyd described as a 'sensation' in the district. Within hours he had the cropper in Milnsbridge House standing in front of Joseph Radcliffe.[37]

The evidence against Mellor was, as yet, feeble. He himself still admitted nothing whatever. Nevertheless there was already enough for Radcliffe to issue a committal order.

Bound in chains and sitting between armed guards on a stage coach's exterior seats, George Mellor was driven down the Leeds road on the start of the 35-mile journey to York. Folk memory of the occasion recalls that, as the coach horses began to move off, he tried to raise a cheer from the watching crowd. None responded. The large group of workers he passed on the road to York remained equally and prophetically strangely silent.[38]

29

King's Evidence

The two boys Lloyd had put in front of Joseph Radcliffe that day were thoroughly scared. The magistrate had had to examine them only briefly to extract as much as he needed to agree to put George Mellor in irons with speed.

The young pair, Joseph Oldham and Thomas Kinder, both apprentices, worked for Joseph Mellor, George's cousin, a cloth dresser. Joseph's house and workshop were at the bottom of the steep slope of Dungeon Wood, less than a mile from where William Horsfall had been murdered.

They had told how,[1] on the night of the killing, two croppers – one they recognised as George Mellor – had come into the finishing shop. The men were anxious to change their dark topcoats. Mellor had a wounded hand.

The names that under further examination poured from the boys' mouths, instantly activated Joseph Radcliffe into a further round-up of possible suspects and witnesses. Within twenty-four hours those he had brought into Milnsbridge House included the owner of the Dungeon Wood workshop, Joe Mellor, his wife Martha, one of his apprentices, Thomas Durrance, and an apprentice from John Wood's shop who appeared to fit the description of 'Mr V's' nephew, James Varley.

The stories told by Joe Mellor, his wife and his apprentices[2] coincided in all essential facts. Martha Mellor, without incriminating her husband's cousin, George, made no attempt to hide his identity as one of the visitors on the night in question. Joe Mellor told how, on returning from Huddersfield market, he was shown a pair of brass inlaid pistols left behind by the croppers. He and Durrance had hidden them in a pile of straw under a lathe. John

Kinder, somewhat pathetically, described how Martha had taken his treasured black silk handkerchief – undoubtedly one of the boy's few possessions – to give to George Mellor to bind his wounded hand.

James Varley,[3] however, whose evidence that day did not coincide with that of the others questioned, succeeded thereby in loading the evidence with even more certainty against George Mellor. Varley, at four in the morning after the night of the murder, according to Joe Mellor, had called Joe out of bed in order to retrieve the hidden pistols. Varley at first denied the workshop owner's story. Then, when Radcliffe began to reveal his hand of evidence, in a desperate attempt to counter each of the cards put in front of him, Varley adjusted the explanation of his movements that night.

The magistrate now told Varley that unless he told the truth about what he knew of the murder, he would be prosecuted as a principal – and with this threat left him to stew overnight. Joseph Radcliffe thus brought his triumphant day of examination to its close.

Maitland, told of this sudden turn of events, asked to be fed with communiqués of the magistrate's progress. Wroth Acland waited near Radcliffe's examination room reporting on the statement of each new witness as it emerged. However, as he emphasised to Maitland, the evidence, revelatory as it was, was circumstantial and far from sufficient to ensure conviction of Mellor or any other Luddite connected with either Rawfolds or Horsfall's murder. 'You are well aware', he told Maitland, 'how extremely difficult it is to extract anything like good evidence from the people who are brought forward as informers.'[4]

But Mr Lloyd admitted no such difficulties. As Joseph Radcliffe paused for breath, in the end Lloyd's inimical and devious methods again produced the crucial evidence which was to break the back of the Luddite resistance in Yorkshire.

His perceptive antennae were tuned to a casual sentence he had heard in a conversation with a Huddersfield wool merchant.[5] The man had recently met a Colne valley woman, whose son was one of many croppers routinely examined by Radcliffe in the past weeks. She had visited the merchant several times for advice. She was concerned that some of the prisoners now in York Castle, to save their own skins, might impeach some of those under suspicion. Lloyd's informant, the manufacturer, had firmly refused to give the name of this woman; she had spoken in confidence.

This was no deterrent to Lloyd. He simply put a watch on the man and noted any stranger who visited his house. Before the week was out he had pinpointed the identity of the secret visitor, a Mrs Walker. Her son, Benjamin, he soon discovered, was none other than Ben O'Bucks, the cropper who worked alongside George Mellor. Lloyd took her into custody.

At first, Mrs Walker told nothing. Nor, when questioned by Lloyd, did one of her women friends, who reputedly knew the identity of the murderers, give any fresh information. But Lloyd applied his usual technique. It was with considerable self-satisfaction that he could now tell Hiley Addington, the Home Secretary's brother, 'I have run away with one of the witnesses to prevent her being tampered with and have placed her in my own house where she will more fully and freely give her examination.'

But Mrs Walker held firm. In spite of whatever pressure Lloyd put on her and in spite of the fact that in the middle of the night he told her he had taken her son into custody, she gave away no evidence whatever to incriminate the young cropper.[6] She did, however, name William Thorpe as being involved in the Horsfall affair.

Thorpe was immediately brought into custody. He too told nothing,[7] although Radcliffe revealed that one of the topcoats left at Joseph Mellor's had been identified as Thorpe's.

Walker also at first succeeded in keeping his mouth closed. Lloyd, however, had sensed the weak link. For four days and certainly some of the nights from October 17th to 21 gated his prisoner. On the 22nd Walker broke. Joseph Radcliffe took down his confession.[8]

The facts flowed freely and fully: a complete description of the planning of the Rawfolds attack, and of its leaders; George Mellor named with Thorpe as the organiser of all the neighbourhood's Luddite disturbances, as well as being responsible for several murder attempts; many of the rank and file involved in several attacks named; and finally a full admission by Walker to being an accomplice, along with Mellor, Thorpe and Smith, to the killing of William Horsfall. All this was given by Walker on the assurance that if he gave King's Evidence in court against the rest, he would not be prosecuted for any Luddite offence. In addition reward money was mentioned: he claimed as much as £2,000 – a substantial fortune in 1812.[9]

By the end of a further forty-eight hours Radcliffe had pulled into Milnsbridge House most of the ringleaders of the Luddite organisation in West Yorkshire. Some, in the hope of saving their skins, had crept in of their own accord. And at least one other who had been involved at Rawfolds had begun to show signs of seeking the uncertain safety of King's evidence. William Hall, Mellor's bedmate, who had been alongside him in the April attack, was beginning to recognise that there was now only one way by which he could with certainty avoid a noose round his neck.[10]

John Lloyd, as ever one jump ahead of the rest, as soon as the incontrovertible evidence began to flow, saw what aggressive prophylactic measures needed to be taken. Although it was late in the night of October 23rd before Radcliffe had finished examining witnesses, Lloyd collected military and police help, and rushed to John Wood's finishing shop at Longroyd Bridge. There, so that they had no time for collusion, he separated Mellor's workmates, one from the other. Now certain that they had had no opportunity to cook up fresh alibis, he there and then individually interrogated each man in the shop.[11]

Again the technique worked like an oiled trap. By next day Joseph Sowden, the nervous young cloth dresser who had been forced at gunpoint by Mellor and Thorpe to kiss the Bible and swear-in other Luddites, was ready to tell his tale in full.[12] No clearer evidence for the capital crime of swearing an illegal oath could be wished for. Now, apart from collecting a mass of information from a whole string of minor witnesses, thoroughly scared by the rumours of confessions, a case for prosecution was almost complete.

The despair among the workers' community was profound: its secret organisation, never more secure than a gossamer web of worker intercommunication, was not only laid open wide, it was seen to have few strands left untorn; its leaders too were not only revealed, they stood accused of bloody and unpopular murder.

By contrast, the euphoria among the once hard-pressed establishment was unbounded. Radcliffe and Lloyd were for the first time able to give each other metaphorical hugs of admiration. Lloyd looked on approvingly[13] as Radcliffe, his nervous tic quite forgotten, 'cheerfully' got on with the business of examination and committal. Wroth Acland was instantly mindful to press praise and flattery where they were due; that is, to the man whose skills with both the military force and the civil power under him, had led to this now indubitable breakthrough. He wrote to Maitland, 'I sincerely congratulate you on the development of this business.'[14]

During that week Radcliffe had had so many men put in the overflowing Huddersfield gaol, or placed on the stage coach for the journey to the cells of York Castle, that the Home Office was beginning to lose track of both the committals and the offences these prisoners were supposed to have committed. In a state of some anxiety Hiley Addington urgently implored Joseph Radcliffe, in order to avoid confusion in Whitehall, to write out for the Attorney and the Solicitor General a comprehensive list of those he had sent for trial.[15]

What Radcliffe produced could not fail to be other than an awe-inspiring document. The numbers were already approaching forty[16] and in the days to follow, with queues of witnesses still to be arraigned, could well rise to double that number. Each one of these was to be on a charge, which, if proved, could carry the death sentence.

30

The Turning Tide

The middle – particularly the merchant – classes of Lancashire, Cheshire and other northern counties were experiencing uncontainable relief at their escape from the rigours and the fears of the past months. The manufacturers of Stockport, astonished by how the extraordinary activity, not to mention the unconventional methods, of young Mr Lloyd had removed Luddite violence from their towns and villages, composed a long memorial to the Home Secretary asking that he should be suitably recompensed in cash.[1] Other citizens had clubbed together to buy 100 guineas' worth of silver plate to present to Captain Raynes in recognition of the success of his commando groups.[2] Joseph Nadin, the dour Deputy Constable of Manchester, could even afford to make a joke: 'I think General Ludd has left this neighbourhood. We are very quiet only I often get a delightful letter threatening to blow out my brains.'[3]

In Yorkshire there was no joking. On the last night of the previous month another gunshot assassination attempt on Joseph Radcliffe had been made.[4] Then a few days later and shortly before the arrest of George Mellor, Captain Raynes had unearthed plans for a group of 400 Luddites to attack Milnsbridge House and kill its owner.[5] How close he had come to death was revealed to Radcliffe in a further interrogation of Ben Walker, now being kept for his own safety in Chester Castle. Walker claimed that the bullet which in April had drilled the window-frame next to the head of one of Radcliffe's special constables, had in fact been fired by George Mellor. It had been intended, Walker said, for the magistrate.[6]

Joseph Radcliffe, however, had every intention that his psychological sufferings no less than his successes in hounding the Yorkshire Luddites should go neither unremarked nor unrewarded. Moreover, he had in mind much more than a few guineas' worth of cash or silver plate to be sought as compensation for his trouble. Here at last was the plainly signposted path to the ennoblement which the man born plain Joe Pickford had been searching for.

He had prepared the ground well. Throughout the whole of that summer he had kept the Lord Lieutenant of his county, that gentlemanly straw in the wind, Lord Fitzwilliam, fully versed in the efforts he had made in preventing West Yorkshire falling to the rule of the mob. Radcliffe was now sending regular accounts of the numbers he was daily committing to the cells of York Castle, much as he might have recorded a bag of game.[7] As Radcliffe intended, Fitzwilliam was responding with fulsome praise for the magistrates 'laudable activity and perseverance' for which 'the county is indebted'.[8]

When Radcliffe attempted similar jostling for recognition by the Home Secretary, however, he found Lord Sidmouth as coldly uninterested as he was in the domestic aspirations of the working class. 'His Lordship is disposed to consider [it] as of no great moment,' Radcliffe was told after he sent to the Home Office the latest of a series of Luddite letters threatening his life.[9]

Radcliffe, however, was not prepared to see sacrifices dismissed easily. He wrote to Sidmouth direct to describe how he had converted one of his own outhouses into a prison to accommodate the overflowing shoal of Luddites he was arresting, and made sure to add how he had 'for the last 8 months shut myself off from all society, devoting my whole time to the disturbances existing in this part of the West Riding, and also been at considerable expence'.[10]

Joseph Radcliffe was not the only man looking to see how he could make the present situation work for his future well-being. Mr Lloyd had by now begun to write letters marked 'private' to the Permanent Under-Secretary at the Home Office, John Beckett. In these he not only flatly contradicted some of the opinions of Joseph Radcliffe, he offered his own services in place of those of the Treasury Solicitor who was to deal with the Luddite offences.[11]

Maitland was well aware of the manoeuvring going on around him and watched it with a mixture of amusement and contempt. Among the myriads of reports being despatched to the Home

Office during these anxious weeks, Maitland's alone rose above the immediate problems and made a serious attempt to understand both the causes and likely social consequences of the situation which the government had asked him to control. Whatever sybaritic delights he indulged himself in at Buxton and however much he expected those beneath him to dance attendance, it cannot be said that he was unfamiliar with, or untouched by, the conditions of the industrial poor of Britain. His years spent as a world traveller with considerable political experience made him a unique observer of the upheavals of 1812. No local worthy – manufacturer or magistrate – nor any member of Lord Liverpool's government analysed the social unrest unsettling the nation better than this soldier.

When he left Yorkshire for a few days he gave instructions to Wroth Acland, his second-in-command. These show how keenly he had observed that although the great mass of people were not involved in Luddite activity in any way, and indeed feared the Luddites, nevertheless, the first crack of what was to become a great social divide had appeared in the north. He told Acland,

> Let us have no quarrel with the country, which will be infallibly the case without the utmost caution is observed, as the general disposition here is a feeling of fear, that renders the military necessary, but at the same time there exists a feeling of detestation against us that makes its appearance ever in the middle of the fears.[12]

Yet again he spelled out simply for the Home Secretary the economic roots of the unrest and the likely consequences unless appropriate action was taken. He told Lord Sidmouth, 'So long as the price of manufacturing labour is so low, and that of provisions so high, we must still contemplate with a considerable degree of anxiety the result of the present winter.'[13]

Again and again he emphasised the importance of reopening the ports of America in order to revive the north's most important export market.[14] Without it, the woollen and cotton trade would never get back on a sound economic footing.

During the weeks that had just passed, Maitland had not sat still. He had travelled to London to report in person to the Home Secretary and had also been as far north as Dunbar where once more he was considering standing as parliamentary candidate. As soon as he returned from Scotland he was made aware of the most recent machinations of Radcliffe and Lloyd. He was furious to discover that not only had Lloyd attempted to sell his services to government, he was now making suggestions to the Home Office as to how and where the Luddite prisoners should be tried. By this time Maitland had had enough of both the magistrate and the solicitor. In his customary deadly equivocal style he made his opinion and his wishes crystally clear to the Lord Lieutenant of the county, Lord Fitzwilliam. This opinion, he said,

> is very much formed from a perfect knowledge of the parties who have been principally employed in bringing forward those cases and though I certainly do not mean to mention them with disrespect, still I much fear their over zeal unless it be corrected by the calm and considerate judgement of some disinterested person may lead to numerous acquittals which I think your Lordship will agree with me is a thing extremely to be avoided.[15]

Maitland left no doubts as to how the prisoners should be dealt with. He wanted a Special Commission established to try the cases quickly at York under conditions which would lead to no ambiguity of outcome. Under no circumstances did he want to see a repeat performance of the disastrous trial of the thirty-eight at Lancaster.

He emphasised to the Home Secretary that in all the cases to be tried, capital punishment should be an achievable goal. Moreover, he was prepared to forecast the consequences if his advice was taken. He told Lord Sidmouth, 'If we make good our cases at the ensuing York Assizes and do not attempt too much, I think the spirit of the late combinations will be completely broken.'[16]

Within three days Sidmouth had agreed to recommend to the Prime Minister that a show trial should take place, the ground rules of which were those outlined by Maitland.

The manner in which this peculiarly inhuman Home Secretary responded to the suggestion which would bring swingeing punishment to bear on the lower classes is in stark contrast to that in which he responded to Maitland's suggestion for positive economic aid for the poor. A few days later, the Member of Parliament for Leicester wrote to Lord Sidmouth describing the suffering of unemployed local workmen and their families as a result of the now unprecedented price to which corn had risen. Sidmouth's response was not only wantonly insensitive to the conditions in the worst affected manufacturing areas, it also showed how little he had absorbed of Maitland's lesson in economics. He replied,

Corn must be expected to continue dear; a painful consideration after the hopes which had been raised. The foreign demand for some branches of our manufactures is also likely, I fear, to remain very limited, and under these circumstances, there must unhappily be a considerable degree of suffering, and, consequently, of irritation amongst the people.

The best friends of the poor, Sidmouth assured the MP, were those who mercilessly put down the rioters. Others might choose, he added, to provide relief and sympathy. He was prepared to provide neither.[17]

For the workers who had been at the centre of the revolt there was to be no relief of any kind. In the face of the presumed guilt of the arrested men and particularly the one man of their kind who had at any time begun to look like a leader, George Mellor, a sense of the doom of their cause began to spread among those still at liberty.

As for Mellor's guilt, there was no doubt in the eyes of those who administered the law that it was beyond question. Mr Radcliffe's clerk, Jonas Allison, was keeping in close touch with what was happening at York. As he packed off eight more rioters to the gaols, he told Acland, 'I have not heard of Mellors having made any confession of guilt, nor do I think it at all likely as I believe he will die as hardened a villain as ever disgraced a gallows.'[18]

The authorities were taking no chances. Outside York Castle was a ring of troops. Inside, every attempt was being made to trap Mellor into a confession of guilt. There was an air of triumph when a visitor to his cell was caught smuggling out a letter in Mellor's hand addressed to his friend, Thomas Eddie. When it had been torn open its contents were considered of such importance that it was immediately rushed to the Treasury Solicitor, who had just arrived in York.[19]

The letter is in a confident hand in confident grammar. When it reached Lord Sidmouth it told him nothing he did not already know. It merely confirmed his prejudices: the putative leader of the Yorkshire Luddites was educated, and it was precisely because he was educated that he was dangerous.

The contents of the letter, however, are not confident. They are touching in their expression, in their naïvety, and in their forlorn hope. Mellor asks Thomas Eddie to reassure his cousin

Joe and make sure that he and his apprentices will not change the first stories they had told at Joseph Radcliffe's interrogation. The letter apprehensively continues, 'Tell him and his wife, I hope they will befriend me and never mind their work for if I come home I will do for them. Remember a soul is of more value than work or gould.'

Mellor then adds, 'I have heard you are a pettitionary for a parliamentary reform and I wish these names to be given as follows . . .'[20]

He then lists thirty-nine of his fellow prisoners, most of whom had been deeply involved with him in his Luddite activities.

The hope that some legitimate parliamentary activity might at the eleventh hour benefit the workers and release him from the awful predicament he now found himself in, was all that was left.

How little the Luddites knew of the true state of the parliamentary reform movement, and of the attitudes of the man Mellor believed to be the leader of that movement, is revealed in these sentences. In the very week in which George Mellor had been arrested, Sir Francis Burdett had addressed a great crowd on this very subject in his constituency at Westminster. He had, as usual, spoken with great oratorical passion and, as usual, at enormous length. But nowhere in his diatribe did he see fit to mention the terrible events taking place in the north of England, the Luddites, the croppers, the worsening state of the manufacturing poor, or for that matter the poor of any description.[21]

Thomas Maitland's divination was manifestly displayed: the radical movement of the north had no sense of the motivations and the preoccupations of those in the south. The one was simply fuelled by the hot air of the other.

Maitland returned to the wool towns, rode through the streets and observed the surly, chastened faces there. He was now sure that the structure on which a near revolution had been built was exposed as nothing much better than an illusion. Confidently, he could tell Lord Fitzwilliam, 'The supposed magic charm of illegal oaths is at an end and the essence of Luddism seems to be fast falling to the ground.'[22]

Raynes, that unfailing barometer of the mood of the local people, confirmed the conclusion of his superior officer. For the first time since he arrived in Yorkshire his soldiers, as they moved in and out of local villages, were no longer spat at. Even the public houses, he reported, 'are becoming tolerably orderly and the inhabitants are more inclined to be civil'.[23] The whole atmosphere of the place, he found, had changed; an aggressive hatred was transformed to an acceptance of the inevitable. People were preparing for the worst.

31

Retreat and Retrenchment

After nine months of siege conditions it was now time for the middle classes of the Yorkshire valleys running into the Calder to pick up the torn threads of their lives and see which they could rejoin.

Characteristically, one of the few who could step with vigour and purpose back into the role from which he had been forced earlier that year was the Reverend Hammond Roberson. During the whole of the period of rioting he had relentlessly pushed forward his plans to build a church in the 'godless' Spen valley. The fact that it required him to secure an Act of Parliament to achieve this, his greatest ambition, had been no barrier. Symbolically, as soon as he knew the Luddites to be crushed, he planned to lay the foundation stone. On December 9th, 1812, under the protective eye of Captain Raynes standing alertly by with a troop of his men, he had the stone tapped into its place on the knoll across the river in sight of the front windows of Healds Hall. Every farthing of the £7,474.11s. 10¾d[1] it would cost to build was to come from his own pocket — very near the total of his own savings and Phoebe's inheritance. 'There will still be a shilling left for the sexton to level up my grave,' he said after he had completed his accounts.[2] He had achieved his dream and he was content.

The same cannot be said of William Cartwright. The fictional hero Charlotte Brontë was to create was based on a man who, for all his bravery against overwhelming Luddite odds, privately displayed less than wholly admirable characteristics. It has to be conceded that this was not without provocation. Throughout these terrible months, much more so than Joseph Radcliffe, Cartwright had been under severe mental and physical strain. To

227

add to his sufferings caused by the violence of the workers and the hatred of the community, one of his children had died. During this period he had grovelled before whomever he thought had influence and had moaned to whomever he thought would listen – Sidmouth, Fitzwilliam, Maitland, Acland, his brother. The government, he maintained, had given him insubstantial support in what to him had become almost a religious crusade against the forces of evil operating in the valley. In a self-pitying plea to the Home Secretary, he spoke of

> the bitterness of my feelings as a father of my remaining children, aggravated by the miserable prospect of ruin, in consequence of the desertion of those whose best interests had been promoted by my successful stand against a lawless and bloodthirsty banditti . . . my health or reason would have been sunk, under the load, had I not tenaciously adhered, to the consciousness, that thought what I had done had been to me so very fruitful in calamity alone, I still had acted on it.[3]

Touched, at least, by this outpouring, Sidmouth released more Treasury cash. Maitland himself rode over to Rawfolds with it. It made what was clearly a very acceptable Christmas present to Cartwright who still, night after night, sat guarding his mill.

The other person in the valley, Patrick Brontë, had been spending as much time away from his troubled Hartshead parish as he decently could. He had been courting Maria Branwell, taking her for lingering walks among the ruins of Kirkstall Abbey. When they were apart during 1812 the couple continued their courtship by correspondence – in which she soon came to call him 'my saucy Pat'. If Brontë's replies to Maria are to be judged by the contents of her long, devoted letters, he spent no time whatever concerning himself with the social turmoil that had bubbled all about him.

Two days before 1812 ended he had married Maria and taken her to live at Hightown in a house on the road to what had been the Luddites' path to Rawfolds. Here, within what can only have been days, the first of the Brontës' daughters was conceived.

In the Calder valley itself the embers left in the wake of Luddism were still occasionally flickering back to life. Joseph Radcliffe, quickly back to rubicund good health and basking in the admiration of the factory owners he had protected, was able to quench the flames with ease. The last of the Luddite gangs to attempt a pathetic robbery of a poor collier's house, taking an old gun and a pound note, was quickly rounded up.[4] No longer could a Luddite assume that his behaviour was a secret known only in the community in which he lived. Within hours of an offence having been committed, it was now possible to find some frightened man or woman who, with Lloyd's particular form of encouragement, could be persuaded to give evidence.

Radcliffe sent the last gang of three men – James Hey, Joseph Crowther and Nathan Hoyle – down to the York Castle cells on December 18th. It brought his tally to a total of more than a hundred. Sixty-four of these were to be charged with offences committed in the West Riding. Only three of them had not been brought in by Radcliffe.

If he was to receive the reward he felt he deserved for his pains and his unquestionable successes, it would clearly need to be specifically urged. And who better to urge it than his own clerk? It is difficult to believe that the letter Jonas Allison now concocted with what he stated to be the support of 'the principal inhabitants of the town of Huddersfield and its vicinity' was entirely uninfluenced by his master. With still more than a month even before any possibility of a trial, let alone a conviction, Allison proposed to Lord Fitzwilliam that he should persuade the Prince Regent to create Radcliffe a baronet.[5]

For a time it seemed as though Fitzwilliam, on this occasion, might avoid his habitual tendency to be all things to all men and duck this very presumptuous request. For a few days he dithered. But by this time Allison had provided a list of names of Huddersfield merchants, including those of the murdered William Horsfall's brothers, who supported this claim on the nation's gratitude. Predictably the result was that the Lord Lieutenant bent affably with the breeze. He told the magistrate that he had reason to believe that 'the most respectable gentlemen' wished 'that a honourable mark of the Royal approbation should be conferred upon you: such an one as is suitable to the independent fortune you possess. . . . Allow me to ask', Fitzwilliam said with congenital politeness, 'would a baronetage be acceptable?'[6]

Radcliffe could scarcely contain his joy in his rapid affirmatory response. The title to match his station was in his grasp.[7]

In his premature welcome of this regal benefaction, however, Radcliffe had made no reckoning for the blessing of 'King Tom'. When the news reached Maitland at his Wakefield headquarters the soldier's intolerance of the magistrate, never well concealed, finally burst out.

Abandoning the equivocal style he customarily maintained for even his most brutal decisions, he rapidly acquainted the Home Office with his displeasure at the proposal.[8]

The Home Secretary fell into line with Maitland's wishes immediately and without demur. At his desk on Christmas day, as on every day, the lonely, inwardly as well as actually cold Lord Sidmouth composed a letter to Lord Fitzwilliam regretting that the suggestion of a baronetcy for Radcliffe was 'inconvenient and embarrassing' and that he could not make it to the Prince Regent. The reason he gave had been spelled out for him by Thomas Maitland: it might create an unfortunate precedent.[9]

In a flutter of uncertainty, Fitzwilliam was forced to retract the honour that had never properly been within his gift.[10] Radcliffe, as a result, had ignominiously to forgo the nomenclature of gentry he had by now incautiously assumed to be his of right.

Having dealt with the tedious business of overweening magistrates, Maitland could observe the altered conditions in these valleys, at peace for the first time since he set foot in them more than half a year earlier. Another far distant event had suddenly stimulated unexpected optimism. The news of Napoleon's retreat from Moscow, which had caused as much patriotic stir in the Yorkshire valleys as it had in London, was beginning to swing the balance of the local economy.

As the cloth export trade reopened and as Luddism's twitches became more feeble, Maitland watched a 'tremendous change' taking place in the mills. Cotton was the first to be affected; wool quickly followed. Thus, as soon as the market for the products of innovatory technology was beginning to open wide, the evils believed to be inseparable from the technology were suddenly of no consequence. Maitland was able to report to the government the outcome which justified both his policies and his fundamental belief in economic solutions. He told the Home Office,

> everything is up and I understand that in some of the cotton parts of the country they are even working long days. ... Here the people from having nothing to do are full of business. If this continues all will go well notwithstanding the high price of provisions.[11]

The crisis was over. He could now concentrate on the retribution which would dissuade any worker in the valleys causing it to happen again.

The first step to be taken was to ensure that there was no chance of recurrence of the Lancaster acquittals. If the outcome of the York Special Commission – the mass trial – was to be what was intended, it was vital that the Lancaster judge should be excluded. But any views Maitland might have wanted to express on the lenient Mr Justice Bayley, had already been pre-empted by Radcliffe and Lloyd, both of whom had made their opinions known to the Home Secretary. Lloyd had not only suggested that York prisoners should be kept out of Bayley's court, he had advised they be kept safe in their cells 'till we can make ourselves more certain of fixing them'.[12] No action was necessary from Maitland. Bayley was never considered for the York bench. That administrative hurdle passed, Maitland could look now at the trial's likely side effects. As for its outcome, as far as he was concerned, that was no longer in doubt. There was no need to question, in particular, whether George Mellor and his fellow prisoners would be found guilty, nor even whether they would die for their crimes, but rather how their executed bodies should subsequently be dealt with.

Henry Hobhouse, the Treasury Solicitor, had already visited Yorkshire and reviewed the evidence. In order that he could prepare for any possibility of a violent public reaction to verdicts of guilty, Maitland had his second-in-command seek out Hobhouse's views on the subject. The Solicitor was frank. He agreed it was most important to consider how the bodies of the Luddites were to be disposed of. A triumphant and potentially explosive Luddite burial procession was the last thing the government could afford to be the consequence of the Commission. Hobhouse considered all the possibilities. He said,

> I lay gibbeting out of the question. The alternative is order-
> ing the bodies to be anatomised. But is there any surgeon at
> or near Huddersfield who would dare to dissect the bodies?
> If not I am very much disposed to think that an execution at
> York should be preferred.[13]

Acland told Maitland he thought he could persuade a Leeds surgeon to travel to York and collect the bodies by pack-horse then carry them away for dissection.[14]

And so, a full week before the trial was due to begin, not only had a baronetcy come within a hair's-breadth of being offered on the certainty of its outcome, the place of execution of the accused men, where their bodies should be afterwards cut up, and by whom, had been agreed.

231

32

Defence

Being a county town, York was not unused to trials which culminated in one or even several death sentences. But this occasion was unprecedented. The extraordinary numbers of workers now in the castle's cells ensured that the Commission would dominate the life of the city and its citizens for many days to come. So great was the number of witnesses to be called – in what was likely to be more than a dozen cases, some involving six or eight accused men – that inns and lodging houses had been quickly filled. What had not been anticipated, however, were the great crowds of workers moving on the city; each of the travellers expected to be a spectator at the trial. They had come by stage coach and in carriage and cartloads. But many had walked, some as much as 30 and 40 miles. Most had come in from the west. The Huddersfield–Leeds–York road had seen a stream of traffic beginning to swell even before the end of the week of Christmas. Captain Raynes, from his quarters at Millbridge, watched an 'immense number of people going from this part of the country to York, even from out of Saddleworth' up in the hills on the Lancashire border. The keeper of the toll-bar at the bridge told him that he had never seen the road so thronged.[1]

Henry Hobhouse, now in York, had been worried since he arrived. This influx on one old walled town, he saw, was potentially dangerous. Lord Fitzwilliam shared this opinion. He had already asked the castle gaoler if he was confident he could prevent either a rescue or a breakout. The gaoler had replied he was not in the least confident and was in constant fear of 'a disagreeable occurrence'.[2]

As news came in of yet another great crowd arriving from the

Lancashire–Yorkshire border, Hobhouse urged the Home Office to make sure that Lord Sidmouth realised that firm precautionary measures were necessary.[3] Maitland, however, had already moved. Several regiments, both cavalry and infantry, were standing close by.

Hobhouse had selected the sixty-four men who eventually were to go to trial. In the hours before it was due to begin, he walked the cold corridors of the gaol to prepare the cases for the prosecution. He was astonished to discover on this brief tour that the county town had only one condemned cell.[4] He could say with some certainty, having reviewed the evidence, that before the trial had run its course, it would prove wholly inadequate.

The fracas resulting from Mr Justice Bayley's judgement at Lancaster had caused the Lord Chancellor some embarrassment.[5] The judges he had chosen to sit at York had no similar reputation for lenity. Sir Alexander Thomson and Sir Simon Le Blanc, who were to share what promised to be a lengthy and arduous task, had previously sat together on the Chester Special Commission in May when several Luddites, along with the potato-stealing Hannah Smith, had been sentenced to death. It was an ominous coupling.

The prosecution's case was to be led by J A Park, a barrister whose aggressive energy in court had already won him a considerable reputation. The attorneys for the prosecution employed by Hobhouse were John Lloyd and Jonas Allison. Both solicitors had successfully placed themselves in useful employment as reward for their work as Luddite-hunters. Together with Hobhouse, they were to make a formidable team.

By contrast the prisoners' attorney was of doubtful quality. They had managed to gather together a few pounds to employ a Mr Blackburn of Huddersfield. In the end the paucity of his work matched his pay.

The appointment of the leading counsel for the defence, however, was considered a triumph by the radical supporters of the Luddites. Several of these had persuaded Henry Brougham to take on the case, though whether he needed much persuasion is doubtful.

Brougham was ascending the high peaks of the career which would lead to Lord Chancellorship. It was true that only days earlier he had lost a case which had excited enormous public interest. The Prince Regent had sued Leigh and John Hunt for libel for their careless but delicious description of him as 'a fat

Adonis of fifty'. Brougham's vigorous defence had failed, the Hunts had been sentenced to two years' imprisonment, but the offensive phrase had carried itself a permanent place in history, and Brougham's fame, in spite of the outcome, had soared to new heights.

As a result of his success in securing the repeal of the Orders in Council, in October he had been invited by grateful Liverpool manufacturers to stand for Parliament in their constituency. He had accepted, knowing he had little hope of winning the seat. His defeat simply strengthened his radical reputation. He pointed out that of 100,000 people in Liverpool only 3,000 had votes. His advocacy of a reform of Parliament, therefore, made him a natural sympathiser with the few articulate Luddites such as George Mellor.

The strikingly ugly and notably successful young Brougham was not, however, without critics. Many found him maddening and unreliable, and his naked ambition – in the search for a higher income from his legal practice as well as in the search for high government office – was not beyond reproach. Too often he took on too much work and the Yorkshire Luddites' brief was accepted at a time when he was laden with other commitments.

A good example of how he stretched his immense energies across thirty hours is that of part of his campaign subsequently spent as parliamentary candidate for Yorkshire. After an assizes at York, he left the city at 5 a.m., refreshed himself at Leeds, went to Bradford, spoke at a public breakfast, went on to a second public meeting there, went to Elland, spoke there, then again at Honley, New Mill, Pontefract and Sheffield, and then on to Barnsley to deliver a long address by torchlight to a crowd in the market place. He was in Wakefield at six o'clock next morning and addressing a crowd by nine before getting back to York to be in time for a sitting of the court.[6]

A man who could generate this theatrical display of talent, who had a sure touch on the pulse of popular radical sentiment and who had a genuine concern for the poor and the needy – one of his commitments was to a charitable committee which raised funds for the distressed manufacturing areas – made him the natural advocate for those in conflict with the oppressive laws of this Tory government. Much more of a recommendation to the workers in the York cells, however, was the fact that it was Brougham's defence that had secured the acquittal of the Lancaster thirty-eight.

There was every reason, therefore, why some at least of the accused men could move into the York courtroom with boosted confidence.

The Commission opened on January 2nd, 1813, a Saturday. It then met early on the following Monday to swear in its grand jury. The court was filled to the doors and was to remain so every day of the trial. Large crowds were left locked outside. Prosecuting and defending counsel had to push their way to their seats through relatives of the accused men hoping for the leniency of the Lancaster judgement, through manufacturers expecting and demanding retribution for the perpetrators of the most calamitous year of their lives, and through those others who had considerable professional interest in the outcome of the proceedings. Maitland, who had both designed this set piece and engineered the participation of the chief characters in it, had found a seat. So too had Acland who had sought and been given special permission by his general to leave Huddersfield for the trial's duration. Also in the well of the court was Edward Baines, editor of the *Leeds Mercury*; he was to leave at least as accurate and certainly as human an account of the trial as that subsequently produced by official court reporters.

A grand jury of twenty-three was sworn. Among them was Joseph Radcliffe who had to settle for a low rank in the order of those chosen; many nobility including no less than five baronets preceded him.

From the start of the proceedings[7] it was clear to those near him that Mr Justice Le Blanc was seriously unwell that day. His appearance worried Henry Hobhouse[8] sufficiently to concern himself that a substitute – a less severe substitute, such as Bayley – might have to be found.

Under the circumstances Sir Alexander Thomson, Baron of the Exchequer, addressed the grand jury.[9] What he had to say was unusually lengthy, admirably clear, and spelled out to those listening to him that he intended to support the purpose the government had designed for the Commission. Its outcome would be, he emphasised, that those found guilty at these proceedings would suffer the full severity of the several penalties made available by the law.

He spoke of the 'tumultuous outrage, violence and rapine' which had shattered the public tranquillity of the West Riding for almost a whole year, and pointed to the origins of the riots as the destruction of machinery specifically invented to save manual labour.

He put it to the grand jury that 'evil designing persons' had persuaded workers to commit crimes by persuading them 'that the use of machinery occasions a decrease of the demand for personal labour, and a consequent decrease of wages, or total want of work'. That kind of reasoning, he maintained, was fallacious. Adam Smith's well-reasoned market economic argument in favour of machinery was clear; he went on,

> Whatever diminishes expense increases consumption and the demand for the article both in the home and foreign market; and were the use of machinery entirely to be abolished, the cessation of the manufacture itself would soon follow, inasmuch as other countries, to which the machinery would be banished, would be enabled to undersell us.

The bitter dispute concerning men and machines, of which Thomson had put only one side, would still be heard in ten years' time, as it would in 100 and more years' time.

The judge left no doubt in the mind of any worker present what the consequences would be of furthering alternative arguments by violent means. He listed the statutes which could be referred to in this case. 'Persons being riotously and tumultuously assembled, to pull down or demolish, or to begin to pull down or demolish any wind saw-mill or other windmill or any watermill or other mill', could suffer capital punishment. Any person administering an oath which bound an individual to 'any association, society or confederacy', formed to engage in seditious purposes, could be transported for seven years; the person taking the oath could suffer the same consequence.

These and others were all relatively new statutes. However, Thomson took care to remind the court of the statute which had been in effect only since July 9th, 1812, in which Mr Hobhouse had had a considerable hand. This was, that any person administering an oath, or assisting in the process, which was intended to bind the oath-taker to commit any act punishable by death, should themselves be condemned to death. Every person taking the oath should be transported for life.

Thomson brought his address to a close by pointedly urging, though without naming names, those men in front of him such as Joseph Radcliffe, to continue their efforts to restore the comforts of a civil society.

Defence

Soon afterwards, J A Park and Henry Hobhouse, as they expected, learned that the grand jury had concluded that there was a case to answer in the Horsfall affair, for which George Mellor, William Thorpe and Thomas Smith were to be arraigned. On Maitland's behalf, Park and Hobhouse wanted to stage-manage the whole series of trials around this case and give it maximum dramatic impact. Being confident of convictions of these three men, they thought it vital that this case should be tried first. They reckoned that the display of a major incident in which Luddites had been shown to behave with brutality and without real provocation would unquestionably influence the conduct and no doubt the outcome of the rest of the cases to be heard.

However, what they feared might happen when they applied to have that case tried on the following day, did happen. Henry Brougham, recognising the prosecution's tactic, submitted an affidavit stating that the three prisoners' defence needed more preparation. Since Brougham had only just arrived in York, and had therefore only just discovered how little the prisoners' solicitor, Blackburn, had prepared on behalf of his clients, it is highly likely that this was no invention. 'The consequence is', Hobhouse told John Beckett, 'we must fill up tomorrow with some other case. We shall take care to select one in which the murderers are not implicated.'[10]

Brougham did his utmost to have the trial of Mellor, Thorpe and Smith delayed until the following Friday, but in the end the judges fixed it for the Wednesday, in two days' time. Hobhouse, therefore, brought forward a minor case, but one in which he had exceptionally high hopes of a conviction.

At nine o'clock the next day, the trials proper began before a newly sworn petty jury of twelve.

33

Trial

The manacled men led from the gaols to the York Castle court-room that Tuesday morning were John Swallow, John Batley, Joseph Fisher and John Lumb.[1] They had been the first Luddite prisoners taken in for questioning by John Lloyd to have made damning admissions and so given him his first breakthrough. The man on whom he had used his techniques, and who had told all, Earl Parkin, was also in the court and ready to turn King's Evidence on what Radcliffe had described as a 'desperate gang'; it was the gang to which Parkin had once belonged.

Since Mr Justice Le Blanc was still far from well – in Hobhouse's words looking very 'knocked up' – this first day of the Commission was taken by Mr Baron Thomson sitting alone. The prosecution's case, put by Mr Park, was in essence a very simple one. An old man, Samuel Moxon, too infirm now to appear to give evidence, on July 4th of the previous year had had his house broken into by a group of men, three of them coal miners with blacked-up faces. They had been en route to a Luddite meeting. At first they had demanded fire-arms from Moxon and his son, William, but when none could be produced, they had put a gun to William's head and relieved him of two pound notes, a few pounds' weight of hung beef and tongues, seven or eight pounds of butter and some linen. In explaining the detailed tally, Mr Park had had some difficulty with the Yorkshire dialect. What is still called in that part of the world a 'wintredge' he eventually had discovered to be a 'winter hedge' – a wooden clothes-horse on which the linen was drying. Having removed the cloth, the men had then left and divided their spoils, though it appeared that John Lumb had stayed outside the house when the robbery was committed.

Trial

There was not much more to the case than that – one of common burglary with nobody hurt and scarcely more damage than a few panes of glass. Mr Park, however, addressed the jury on the details of the events of that July night at inordinate length. His speech took up most of the morning. As he intended and, unquestionably, as Henry Hobhouse strongly advised, no doubt of the enormity of the crime was left in the minds of the jury. When he finally concluded his opening address, he apologised to them for the time he had taken, but added, 'I thought it my bounden duty, at least in the first of these cases, to enter largely into it, that you may be fully aware of the manner in which I hope to conduct these prosecutions.' He was, in the days that followed, to be as good as his word.

But there was one other aspect of Park's long speech which was considerably worrying to some of the legal observers in the court.[2] Park made more than full use of his opening statement to the jury by including references to matters which his witnesses, when they gave evidence, subsequently failed to support. It should have been the judge's duty to draw the jury's attention to the discrepancies between Park's opening and the actual evidence, and to tell them clearly that they should reach their decision on the evidence alone. Without strong judicial guidance, untrained minds – and the minds of this jury were palpably untrained – could easily be persuaded by a tendentious and prejudiced opening to overlook the fact that the actual evidence bore little relationship to the statement which preceded it. Throughout the string of trials yet to be heard in that courtroom, this unscrupulous technique was to be widely used by Park.

The chief witness he now called, Earl Parkin, was clearly something of a ruffian. But both he and his coal miner brother, Samuel, who did not take part in the robbery, but witnessed the share-out of the loot, gave convincing stories. These were corroborated by others.

It has to be recalled that, at this time in British legal history, accused persons could not speak in court on their own behalf. The defence, therefore, were it to make its case, needed to do so at this juncture in its cross-examination of the witnesses for the prosecution. Brougham, however, is not recorded as having spoken a single word in this case in which he was leading counsel. Nor did he produce witnesses for the defence. Three of the accused men had nothing better to offer than statements taken by Joseph Radcliffe at their examination which were read to the court. Only one of them, John Lumb, managed to raise a witness to speak of his character. And the last weapon remaining to a modern defence counsel – his address to the jury – was not available in 1812. In cases of felony, counsel could not speak on behalf of his clients. The prisoners, therefore, were left almost naked in a cut and dried case.

The court had sat all day. As darkness had fallen lamps had to be brought into the court. At twenty minutes to seven Sir Alexander Thomson sent the jury to consider its verdict.

In less than ten minutes, according to Hobhouse's watch, they had returned. The charge, as all in the well of the court knew, carried a maximum sentence of death. When the foreman pronounced the word, 'Guilty', Hobhouse looked round at the courtroom full of workers 'of a very ill complexion' expecting some sort of reaction, or violent demonstration. But none came. 'The verdict', he said, 'was received with perfect silence.'[3]

John Lumb was recommended to mercy. Mr Baron Thomson heard this news with evident astonishment and he asked the jury to state the grounds on which they made their recommendation. The foreman told him it was because Lumb 'had no firearms and had not his face blacked'.

Thomson then turned to the anxious and expectant faces in the courtroom. Expectations, however, were not to be fulfilled. He had decided, he said, to reserve sentencing the four until all other cases had been heard.

Edward Baines recorded that in the early hours of the morning, long before the next day's case was due to be heard, the courtroom was crowded beyond reasonable bounds. This was to be the trial of the three accused of the murder of William Horsfall – the first high point in the Commission's sitting. Baines had never witnessed a scene like this before and felt certain enough to write that the excitement generated could have 'seldom been equalled in a court of justice'. Only with the greatest difficulty could officers of the court get to their seats.[4]

Mr Justice Le Blanc, now apparently recovered from his illness of the previous day, was at the bench with Mr Baron Thomson. Mr Park, for the prosecution, was supported by two junior counsel, as was Henry Brougham for the defence.

The appearance of the three prisoners, when they were led in, took Edward Baines, seeing them for the first time, by surprise.

Rather than the three vicious-looking villains he had expected, George Mellor, William Thorpe and Thomas Smith were all tall, good-looking and instantly gave a favourable impression: 'all young men, the eldest of them not more than three and twenty years of age, and their appearance was very respectable'.

From the first sentence of his address to the jury, Park launched himself into an impassioned attack on the emotions. 'You have been sworn', he told them, 'to inquire into a matter of blood. I need not tell you that the offence with which the prisoners stand charged is the greatest crime that can be committed in society.'

He reminded them how the origin of the dreadful outrages that year had been the breaking of stocking frames in Nottingham and how the movement to destroy new manufacturing machinery had spread to other parts of the country.

He painted a picture of William Horsfall, the murdered manufacturer, as a family man, much loved by the 400 workers in his mills. Horsfall, as he put it, had promoted the installation of new cropping machinery in his factories, 'because he was sure it was advantageous to the country'. Looking round at the grey faces packed into the room behind him, Mr Park continued his technological theme. He believed, he said, there was a prevalent delusion in the country:

Amongst the lower orders . . . it has been supposed that the increase of the machinery, by which manufactures are rendered more easy, abridges the quantity of labour wanted in the country. It is a fallacious argument, that no man who understands the subject at all, will seriously maintain. I mention this, not so much for the sake of you, or of these unfortunate prisoners, as for the sake of the vast number of persons who are assembled in this place.

Irrespective of examples of history to the contrary, he persisted with this argument throughout the trial.

Park described the act of the killing in terms which missed none of the bloody death nor its drama: how Horsfall was shot, how Henry Parr had ridden up when he heard the scream of 'Murder!' from the wounded man and how Horsfall, bleeding profusely, had been supported until he could be carried back to the Warrener House, 'where he languished thirty-eight hours, and then died'.

The first witness to be called was the publican of the Warrener House, who under precise questioning from Park, established the time of Horsfall's departure from the inn as shortly after 6 p.m. on April 28th. His shooting, after he had ridden the 400 yards to Joseph Radcliffe's plantation, therefore took place at about 6.10 p.m.

The witnesses who followed – Henry Parr, the surgeon Rowland Houghton who tried to staunch the flow of Horsfall's blood, the Reverend Abraham Horsfall, and John Horsfall, each of whom produced in court the dum-dum bullets the surgeon had cut from their brother's body – added gore to the picture Park had already painted. All that Henry Brougham's cross-examination of the surgeon succeeded in doing was to add more medical details to the now bloody canvas.

Clinical details of the killing had already been given several times before Park called his chief witness, Ben Walker, the man who claimed to have been with Mellor, Thorpe and Smith on the fateful day. Park used Walker to describe the fear Mellor had engendered: the fear which had driven him and Smith, armed with their gun, to the plantation. Walker told how minutes after the murder, Mellor had damned them both for their failure to use the gun on Horsfall. He described how he had hidden his pistol and then gone with Smith to a Honley public house where they had each drunk seven or eight pints of ale. When the news of Horsfall's death had been brought in by some Huddersfield market traders, Smith, a skilled whistler, had quickly struck up a tune to distract the attention of the rest of the house. A drunken collier had unwittingly helped the diversion by getting up to give a clog dance to Smith's tune.

Henry Brougham cannot have been other than aware that the witness in the box, Walker, was not only vulnerable because, giving King's Evidence, he was the focus of hatred of every worker in the court; he was also suspected of having been offered or having been given money by John Lloyd or Joseph Radcliffe in return for his evidence. If this were the case, as Hobhouse had pointed out to the Home Secretary, the fact could invalidate his testimony.

Brougham, however, failed to rise from his seat to face Walker and left the cross-examination of this key figure to his junior, Mr Hullock. In a long examination, all that Hullock managed to extract from Walker on the question of money was, that being illiterate he therefore could not have read in the newspapers of any reward. He admitted, however, that before he had gone in for questioning by Joseph Radcliffe, he had heard a rumour that £2,000 was being offered for information.

The next witness was also turning King's Evidence: William Hall, the Liversedge cropper who shared Mellor's bed on the night of the murder. He described how Mellor had shown him his hand, wounded by the firing of a pistol. The day after the killing, Hall had been made to swear on the Bible and then kiss it. Next to the book had been a piece of paper on which was written the threat that if anybody taking the oath revealed any detail of the shooting incident 'they were to be shot by the first brother'.

Next in the dock was Joseph Sowden, the cropper at John Wood's shop who had been forced by Mellor and Thorpe, so he maintained, to administer the oath. There was no reason to doubt Sowden's story. He had offered it to John Lloyd voluntarily and had never been suspected by Joseph Radcliffe or any other magistrate of being an active Luddite. Yet it was Sowden whom Brougham chose for his own detailed questioning.

It was a half-hearted cross-examination. Brougham asked why, in the knowledge that it was punishable by seven years' transportation, he had taken the oath in the first place. Sowden's response was that he had not taken the oath voluntarily; a pistol had been at his head. Other evidence confirmed his story.

Brougham, if Edward Baines's diligent record of the events is to be believed, appears to have taken little part in the defence during the remainder of the morning and even less during the rest of the day. He took no share in the cross-examination of any of the remaining prosecution witnesses – George Mellor's cousin, Joseph, and his wife, Martha, or of the apprentices Thomas Durrance and John Kinder. The ineradicable impression of the trial transcripts is that, from the outset, Brougham had decided that the case against the three young men was so strong and the defence prepared for him was so weak, that he had best save his eloquence for another day and for other prisoners.

Mellor, Thorpe and Smith, however, had no inkling of any such attitude in the man whom they had been led to believe, more than any other in England, could sway a jury in their favour. When Mr Justice Le Blanc asked them if they wished to say anything for themselves, they replied, 'We leave it to our counsel.'

Counsel, however, had not much to offer. The defence's decision had been to rely entirely on alibi, and this is what had been prepared on behalf of all three of the accused. Such had been the publicity, two years earlier, in the case championed by Patrick Brontë, that consistency in an alibi was now widely believed among the working classes to be unchallengeable. Then, it will be recalled, William Nowell had produced fifteen friends who, one after the other, testified in court to his having been at the funeral, conducted by Brontë, of the unfortunate Samuel Jackson, rather than at Lee Fair where he had been charged with taking the King's Shilling. Nowell's triumphant acquittal, even though – or perhaps, because – Brontë had had no recollection of having seen him at the funeral, had never been forgotten in the woollen valleys.

The strength of George Mellor's alibi and the consistency of his witnesses were shortly to be apparent. In comparison, the weakness of those provided by the other two defendants, suggest that it was Mellor himself who, before his arrest, or from his York Castle cell, learning from what had happened two years ago, had prepared the ground for his counsel to tread.

One witness after another appeared at the stand with a clear statement of when and where they had seen Mellor in and around Huddersfield on the evening of April 28th. All evidence had now fixed the murder as having taken place at 6.10 p.m. almost to the minute.

John Womersley, a clock- and watch-maker no less, said on oath that at 6.15 that same evening he had met Mellor in Huddersfield. They had gone into a public house near the Cloth Hall where Mellor had paid him 7 shillings he owed. The clock-maker could produce the bill to show the settlement of the debt and so fix the date of the meeting. Under cross-examination by Park, Womersley maintained that Mellor could not have walked the distance from the site of the murder to the Cloth Hall in the five minutes which had passed since the supposed time of the murder.

William Battersby, who had drunk with Mellor and Womersley at the White Hart, confirmed the story. He had still been there with Mellor when news came of the murder of Horsfall.

Next, John Thorpe said he had seen Mellor outside the George Inn in Huddersfield at ten to six. He claimed to remember the time clearly since he was carrying a watch which he tried unsuccessfully to sell to Mellor for £3.13s. He remembered the time well since he took out the watch to display it to Mellor.

A shoe-maker, a blacksmith and a shopkeeper all now appeared in turn to echo that they had clear recall of Mellor walking towards Huddersfield, or being in the town shortly before the time of the murder.

Of the other two prisoners, William Thorpe had succeeded in raising only two witnesses to testify to his having been in Fisher's workshop at the crucial hour: a girl fetching cans of water from the shop in preparation for her washing next day and a shoe-maker who delivered shoes and stayed to talk to Thorpe.

Smith had managed far worse. His alibi was provided by John Bower, a seventeen-year-old apprentice from John Wood's workshop.

If the boy's hesitancy under examination was a blow to Smith, the full implication of what he had to say was, for Mellor as well as Smith, a disaster. Bower, in his innocence of what other witnesses had said before him, claimed that up to seven o'clock on the evening of the murder, not only had this pair been pressing cloth in John Wood's shop, their shirt-sleeves stripped, but among the other croppers present was Ben Walker. Bower's tale, therefore, was not only at variance with the witnesses who had spoken on Mellor's behalf, who claimed to have met him in Huddersfield at that time, it was in direct contradiction to Walker's evidence given from the same stand a few hours earlier that day. Walker had freely admitted that, not only was he not in John Wood's workshop in the hour preceding seven, he was actually running away from it accompanied by Smith in the direction of the Honley public house. The publican's wife, also in court, had earlier recalled the incident of Smith's whistling for the drunken collier's dance, and had thus confirmed Walker's tale.

The remaining few witnesses had little to add which could re-order the state of confusion into which the defence had now been so unwittingly thrown by young Bower. In any event Mr Justice Le Blanc, in his summary of the evidence, attached little importance to anything any further witnesses could add.

This summing up, when it began late that Wednesday evening, considering that Le Blanc had been too ill to be in court on the previous day, was admirable for its clarity, and suggests itself as the utterings of a perfectly healthy man.[5]

He began by restating the indictment for the jury. It had been formulated in such a way, said Le Blanc, that it was immaterial which, or whether one or two of the three men facing them actually fired the pistol. If any of them had used the weapon that killed William Horsfall, then each of the three was a principal in the murder; in such a case, there was no doubt in law that, as Le Blanc put it, 'it is murder in all of them'.

If any of the three young men had doubts, they were now dispelled. One hang, all hang.

When he reached the crucial matter of the disparities in the various alibis, Le Blanc was equally clear. The key issue to be resolved was that at the precise time of the murder, radically different events had been described involving the same person at different places.

For example, John Thorpe had claimed to have met George Mellor in Huddersfield outside the George Inn, from where Mellor was to proceed to drink at the White Hart. It was then 5.50 p.m. precisely by the watch he was trying to sell Mellor. Yet Martha Mellor maintained that her cousin had come into her husband's workshop at Dungeon Wood at 6.15 p.m. These accounts were only reconcilable, said Le Blanc, by supposing that clocks or watches vary very much or, he said after a meaningful pause, that the memories of people vary very much.

Similarly, George Armitage, the blacksmith had claimed that, as he shod a horse, he had seen Mellor heading towards Huddersfield between 5 and 6 p.m., whereas Martha Mellor had said that he did not leave the workshop until 6.30 p.m. 'To be sure, either Joseph Mellor's wife, or this man, must have erred very much in the time. ... Or,' added Le Blanc after another pause, 'they were not aware of each other's evidence.'

Le Blanc continued that, even if the witnesses had not come under improper influence (he did not need to tell the jury that the clock-maker's and the watch-seller's stories in defence of George Mellor smacked of tall tales) they were speaking of events that had taken place months earlier. The murder had occurred in April; magistrates' inquiries had not begun until October. How was it that so many good people of Yorkshire could remember so accurately the time of these most ordinary events in the street and in the workshop after an interval of six months?

And so he remorselessly proceeded to expose the all too patent weaknesses in an ill-prepared defence. Brougham, having spent most of the day in silence, had by now abandoned the last opportunity to construct a case of any solidity for his clients.

Le Blanc, so that there was no chance of misunderstanding on the part of the jury, reminded them that the prosecution's evidence did not rest solely on the testimony of the man who had turned King's Evidence, and who had been tempted to give it, and therefore invalidate it by the smell of money: Benjamin Walker. It also rested on the evidence of several croppers from John Wood's workshop who were not accomplices.

He ended his summary for the jury by asking them to lay the

facts together in their minds in a way that 'will do justice between the country and the prisoners'.

The twelve men retired that evening at five minutes to eight. After twenty-five minutes, as again precisely timed by the watch of Henry Hobhouse,[6] they filed back into their seats. Edward Baines faithfully recorded the silence that gripped the court. He was planning a special edition of the *Leeds Mercury* to be on sale, if possible, within hours, devoted entirely to this one trial. Every element of drama he could capture, therefore – and there was much of it – stood to boost his sales.

When the foreman pronounced the word 'Guilty', Baines registered the unbroken stillness and the conspicuous degree of self-composure shown by the three men.

Mr Justice Le Blanc, in spite of the fact that on the previous evening Mr Baron Thomson had made a specific point of delaying sentence on those found guilty, until the end of the Commission, now immediately turned to the three croppers and asked if they had anything to say why sentence of death should not be passed on them. In a clear voice Mellor said, 'I have nothing to say, but that I am not guilty.' Thorpe said, 'I am not guilty. False evidence has been given against me.' And Smith simply added, 'Not guilty.'

Neither here, nor at any other point during Le Blanc's haste to see the prisoners on the gallows, did Henry Brougham suggest that the three men should be given both the right and the time to appeal to the Crown for clemency.

Le Blanc proceeded to don the black cap and address the prisoners on what he called 'an offence of the deepest malignity'. He went on,

> The only kindness I can offer is in the advice to prepare, as speedily as you can, for that execution of this sentence, which must shortly await you; to make the best use you can of the period still allotted to you in this world – longer far than was allowed to the unfortunate person who was the object of your revenge.

The judge's exhortation that they should prepare for the afterlife with speed was not lightly meant. It was then 9 o'clock on Wednesday evening. Their execution, he pronounced, would take place on the Friday morning – long before the Commission had completed its work.

They were, Le Blanc told them, to be 'severally hanged by the neck' until they were dead. And, as Maitland had arranged, their 'bodies afterwards delivered to the surgeons to be dissected and anatomised'.

34

Retribution

Either late that night or early the following morning the jury had some second thoughts concerning the absoluteness of the sentence their verdict had imposed on the three young men and the speed with which it was intended it should be carried out. As soon as the court opened that Thursday, the foreman communicated to the surprised judges that Thomas Smith should be recommended to mercy.

But Mr Justice Le Blanc had already made himself painfully clear. He had earlier said it made no difference in law that Smith did not actually fire the murder weapon. Murder in one of the three, he had said, 'is murder in all of them'. The jury's recommendation was rejected.

As if to compensate for this perhaps over-generous act of compassion towards Smith, the foreman now went on to recommend that the jury believed the murderers deserved to be hanged, not at the usual place of execution, but on the spot where they committed their crime – alongside Joseph Radcliffe's plantation in the Colne valley.

But the possibly dangerous consequences of this dramatic gesture had already been well considered by Maitland and Hobhouse. Any focal point for an uprising deep in Luddite country had to be avoided at all costs. This request too was rejected. Le Blanc and Thomson moved rapidly on to the next case.[1]

In the dock was John Schofield, the young cloth worker who, in August of 1812, had been found by a Whitechapel constable on board an outward-bound American ship, *The Independent*, just before she set sail from London Dock. He was now accused of being involved in the incident which had taken place near Huddersfield at midnight on July 22nd where John Hinchcliffe had been dragged by two masked Luddites from his house and had been left bleeding profusely from a gunshot wound to the head.

. The chief witness was Hinchcliffe himself. He stood a pathetic figure who had miraculously survived the assault. A patch was over the socket from which the eye had been completely shot away by one of the gunmen, after the other, whom he believed to be Schofield, had run off. Schofield, the young man now opposite him in the dock, whose voice he had recognised, had been his neighbour and his singing pupil.

Again the trial lasted all day and again the defence rested almost solely on a string of witnesses who gave a consistent alibi maintaining that Schofield was at home in bed at the time of the attack.

This alibi was neither more nor less believable than that of George Mellor on the previous day, nor was the prisoner's involvement in the shooting, if Hinchcliffe was to be believed, more nor less than that of Thomas Smith in the Horsfall murder. In spite of the fact that Hinchcliffe's testimony was uncorroborated, Schofield can therefore only have had the most terrible forebodings when the jury, having again retired for about half an hour, returned with its verdict.

It was one of not guilty. Henry Brougham was no doubt as astonished by this inconsistency as his client was relieved by it.

Throughout that night, as preparations for the execution were made, warders in York Castle gaol stood by waiting for George Mellor and his accomplices to make their confession. The chaplain of the castle too, believing them unquestionably guilty, also listened. The priest was nevertheless to leave a careful record that at no time in the few hours left to them did any of the three men make any admissions whatever.[2] At some time during the night George Mellor fainted, but recovered himself before dawn.

The day broke cold and fine. Again, a scene such as this had never before been experienced by the people of York. A new scaffold had been built behind the castle. The size of the crowd which had massed in front of it was extraordinary. It was what Maitland had planned. The greater the number of onlookers, provided their mood could be controlled as he wished, the greater the intimidatory effect the hanging would engender. He had taken stringent security precautions. He had ordered every avenue to the castle to be guarded by ranks of infantry. Cavalry regiments were waiting nearby in case of any serious disturbance from the crowd. Two full troops of dragoons had been drawn up in front of the gallows to discourage any last-minute rescue attempt.

Although the crowd was kept at bay, the hangman had been given instructions that the complete act of the punishment should be fully displayed to this massed gathering of Luddite sympathisers. The customary form of drop was one which, at execution, hid from view all except the feet and head. This new construction was designed to show the whole body of each dangling man.

Shortly before 9 o'clock, judges, jury and all those who had taken part in the trial lined themselves in the shadow of the castle's wall. Present also were those who had chiefly been responsible for achieving this climax in the year of violence in the north country: General the Hon Thomas Maitland for the army, Joseph Radcliffe JP and J S Lloyd for the law enforcement officers, and Henry Hobhouse for the government, had joined the spectators.

Then, still in their irons, George Mellor, William Thorpe and Thomas Smith were led from the castle and up to the scaffold. Invited to pray by the castle chaplain, they went down on their knees. Mellor stayed there, longer than his companions, for a full ten minutes. His words were audible and were passionately spoken. He openly confessed his sins – but not that one for which he was preparing to die. The pathos of his prayer had a profound, melancholic effect on the crowd.

The three were then led to the front of the drop and asked to make their final words. His public composure still unbroken, Mellor was Christ-like. He expressed no bitterness towards those responsible for sending him to this Calvary. In a clear voice, he spoke: 'Some of my enemies may be here,' he said. 'If there be, I freely forgive them, and all the world, and I hope the world will forgive me.'

Thorpe too added a few words. Then the drop fell. The bodies hung, still in irons. Baines again recorded the cowed silence of the crowd which never broke. 'And thus have perished in the very bloom of life', he wrote, 'three young men ... on whose countenances nature had not imprinted the features of assassins.'

Almost immediately after the hanging, the bodies, accompanied by a strong military escort, were taken to York County Hospital and the building surrounded by troops. The anatomical dissection planned by Maitland now began.

In the two hours before the court was due to reassemble, Hobhouse walked the streets of York looking into the faces of ordinary people. There, as when he returned to the courtroom, he could see written the tremendous impact of the executions. A defeated and dispirited air had everywhere infected what he called the 'adherents of the prisoners now at York'.[3]

There was still, however, much unfinished legal business to be performed, and in spite of the depressed spirits of the Luddites' supporters, the crowds had again flooded back into the court. By eleven o'clock it was back in motion.

The first two indictments involved prisoners who had administered the Luddite oath.[4] However, since the supposed offences had taken place in the early summer of the year, before the introduction of the new parliamentary Act, the death penalty could not be invoked. Mr Justice Le Blanc and Mr Baron Thomson, therefore, proceeded quickly through the first case which involved a weaver, John Eaden. The evidence against him was provided by two informers, one of whom appeared to have been as much or as little involved in Luddite recruitment as Eaden himself. Responding to the tempo now being set by the judges, the jury, when the time came to retire, did not even bother to leave the box, but gave their verdict of guilty after having put their heads together. Le Blanc directed that a second worker, along with Eaden on a second charge, be found not guilty.

Scarcely pausing to draw breath, the judges moved on to the next case.[5] Even though, again, the indictment did not carry the death penalty, the fame of one of the prisoners nevertheless raised the Commission to another high point of interest and attention. Leading the six prisoners to the bar of the court was 66-year-old John Baines – the articulate republican whose hatred of the aristocracy had so impressed George Mellor when he first sat at Baines's feet.

Maitland had never had any doubts as to the power of the political ideas which Baines had spread from his seat in the Crispin Inn. Mellor was only one of several young men to appear in the court that week who had been influenced by them. It had been in order to put an end to this influence that, in the previous July, Maitland had arranged for the police spies, John M'Donald and John Gossling, to infiltrate Baines's group in Halifax in order to try to trick him into administering the Luddite oath. The hour at which he had sprung his trap, had been carefully chosen by M'Donald. But it was perhaps not the timing Thomas Maitland might have wished – two days before the crime became a capital offence. But although there was no chance Baines would hang, it was important, if Maitland's grand design for the Commission were to have its most salutary effect on both county and country, that Baines should be seen to suffer the maximum sentence.

Following the old man to the bar of the court were Charles Milnes, who had led M'Donald from the Crispin Inn to Baines's house, and the four others who had been present at the secret swearing ceremony: John Baines the younger, William Blakeborough, George Duckworth and Baines's son of his later years, fifteen-year-old Zachariah, who had guarded the door while M'Donald swore his soul to the Luddites.

Mr Park, fittingly for Baines's importance, rose to give a long address to the jury on behalf of the prosecution. His first concern was to attempt to neutralise the acid taste which the detail of this case was bound to stimulate in the mouths of the jury. M'Donald, who had applied the simple and unashamed methods of *agent provocateur*, was in court and soon would be revealed as an unsavoury character. So patently untrustworthy had he seemed that even John Lloyd had once had doubts about using his testimony. M'Donald was known to have a criminal record. To be in the York courtroom at all that day it had been necessary to extricate him from Manchester police cells where he was being held on a charge of assault.

Mr Park at once addressed what he called 'the moral question' on behalf of the jury.

> If a man goes to incite another to commit a crime which he had no intention to commit, if he seduces his neighbour from the paths of innocence to those of guilt, he is, without exception, one of the most infamous of mankind. But if you get at information that certain practices are carrying on by individuals most destructive to the state, and to the individuals composing the country, and you can arrive at the conviction of those who are so engaged by no other means so well as by employing someone to see whether they are the persons of that description or not; it is most highly laudible to bring such offenders to justice.

Old Baines, so that he missed as few of Park's words as possible, cupped his hand to his ear at that point. Instantly, Park seeing this, rounded on him. 'I am very glad', he hissed, 'that the prisoner John Baines the elder, who appears to be a little deaf, hears what I say ... for perhaps the preservation of the country has been effected by such means having been resorted to.'

In the eyes of the Crown, therefore, Baines was one of those chiefly responsible for having taken England to the brink of revolution those few months earlier. Whether the jury would accept the charge, however, as Mr Park well knew, depended on how his chief prosecution witnesses performed under examination and cross-examination.

When their time came, both M'Donald and Gossling, unsavoury though they might have been, gave reasonably mutually consistent evidence. M'Donald described how, that night at Baines's Halifax house, the old man had bidden him kiss the Bible and swear the Luddite oath. The others in the room – the three remaining prisoners at the bar, along with young Zachariah – had stood whilst it was administered. And any doubts the jury might have had about the propriety of trying a youth of fifteen in this case, had already been dispelled by Mr Park. He had, at the same time as reassuring them of 'the humanity of the law of England', introduced them to the phrase *malitia supplet aetatem* – malice supplies age.

The end of M'Donald's examination by Park brought an air of expectancy to the court. Here now had arrived the point at which Henry Brougham could justify his reputation for brilliance. In front of him preparing to be cross-examined was a down-at-heel police informer, a shifty character with his own criminal record, brought from gaol to give evidence. Moreover, the man was standing in the well of a court in which the hostility and disbelief of the crowded spectators was almost tangible.

All Brougham needed to do that day to make his case was expose M'Donald as a known liar and burnish the fact that there was no prosecution witness to the crucial act of oath-swearing by Baines other than this paid spy. The barrister's performance, however, was so noticeably inept as to startle the cognoscenti in court. In no single sentence, at what should have been a turning point in the defence's case, was the brilliance of the rising star of jurisprudence displayed. Brougham's cross-examination was halting and badly prepared. M'Donald, sensing the incompetence facing him, instantly began to use the occasion for his own purposes. In a succession of quick-witted responses he succeeded in building a firmer base under his initially insecure testimony.

Hobhouse, who had feared that this was to be by far the most vulnerable spot in the case he had prepared for the Crown, could scarcely believe the good fortune his ears could hear.[6] The Manchester magistrate, the Reverend Mr Hay, was also over-joyed. 'It is quite delightful', he wrote, 'for us who witnessed the triumphant ground on which M'Donald stood. ... He certainly rose powerful in proportion as he found how weak Mr Brougham was ...'[7]

There then followed a string of predictable defence witnesses – family and friends – who, as in every other case heard in that courtroom that week, provided evidence which suggested that each one of the accused men was elsewhere at the time of the alleged offence. Hollow and repetitive as these alibis were fast becoming, Mr Baron Thomson, in his summing up, repeated them fully and faithfully as was his duty. Nevertheless, in his final words to the jury Thomson emphasised that the believability of these witnesses was where the nub of the case lay, rather than with the credibility of the police spy, M'Donald.

The jury took five minutes to reach their verdict. John Baines the elder, John Baines the younger and their three Luddite supporters were found guilty as charged. The twelve in the jury box, however, in spite of Park's didactic Latin tag, rejected the possibility of malice in the boy, Zachariah. He was acquitted.

35

This Deluded County

It was by now Saturday. The Commission had completed its
first full week of work.

The stage that day which had been reserved for the largest
number of the mass trials, if it fell short of mounting the dramatic
climax of the whole session, only did so because three of its chief
actors had already been expunged. In the trial of the attackers of
Cartwright's Rawfolds mill,[1] the man Mr Park described as the
commander-in-chief, George Mellor, could no longer play a part.
Nor could his lieutenants William Thorpe and Thomas Smith.
Eight other men – a tiny proportion from the brigade of workers
which had swept down into the Spen valley on the night of April
11th – were facing trial. Mr Park paraded them before the jury
and before William Cartwright, the manufacturer whose defences
that night, Park told an attentive court, 'seemed almost impossible for any, but a most active military force, to destroy.'

They were, in the face of the sentences already pronounced, a
frightened group. James Haigh had been the first to have been
arrested; he had been taken after spending days nursing his
wounded shoulder, struggling from one Pennine cottage to another, then finally and fatally seeking help from Richard Tattersall,
the local surgeon who betrayed him.

Jonathan Dean, Park said, had been at the front of the wave
which attacked Cartwright's main entrance and had been shot in
the hand in which he was raising the hatchet to smash down the
door. Dean had been one of the first prisoners taken by Joseph
Radcliffe to have confessed to having been at Rawfolds.

John Ogden's sword had broken off in its scabbard before he
could use it; Park had the scabbard itself ready as evidence.

James Brook had returned from Rawfolds in a sobered state; Park could produce the woman who heard him say, 'Before I will be engaged in anything of this sort again, I will suffer myself to be clammed to death; it was one of the most dreadful things I ever saw, and one might hear them screaming for half a mile.'

John Brook, the jury would hear, had been responsible for hiding weapons left at John Wood's shop after the attack in which he took part.

Thomas Brook was the man who had fallen into the mill dam that freezing cold night and lost his hat; Park would be able to make the hat Brook's undoing; witnesses could trace the path of both the lost hat and the hat borrowed for Brook by Mellor, back to their original owners.

John Walker, according to the prosecution, had felt a bullet pass through his hat; he later boasted how he put his pistol arm through a broken window at the mill and was determined to take aim even if his hand was shot off. He had subsequently enlisted in the Royal Artillery at Woolwich and had only been plucked from the security of the army by the disclosures of William Hall.

Last of the eight was John Hirst who, it was said, had had the misfortune of retreating from Rawfolds with William Hall; Hirst and Hall, both Liversedge men, had worked together at Cartwright's mill. Now Hall was waiting to turn King's Evidence against his former Luddite friends.

There was one other man walking free in York that day whose name was already familiar to the jury and who many believed must have been involved in the affair on April 11th, and probably in many other Luddite activities. Mr Park had no hesitation in mentioning John Wood, George Mellor's stepfather and employer, in a context that suggested he should have been the ninth prisoner at the bar. 'Mr Wood's name', said Park, 'has unfortunately been too often mentioned, and whether he knew more than has been discovered, God and his own conscience only know: but at Mr Wood's house it seems wonderful that all these transactions should be going on and the master of these men knew nothing about them.'

The first witness was William Cartwright himself. As the only manufacturer, unaided by large numbers of troops, to have successfully stood up to a major Luddite attack, Cartwright was by now a national celebrity. The court showed him due deference and listened at length to his description of his defence – his pride in it was near boastful – of Rawfolds. He produced a great sack from which he drew samples of the hatchets, mauls, hammers, masks and musket butts which he had collected the morning after the raid. Mr Justice Le Blanc questioned him carefully about the nature of the damage to his mill, in particular the window-frames. Cartwright replied that these had been so badly splintered that he had been forced to remove every one of them.

The chief witnesses for the prosecution, Benjamin Walker and William Hall, were the same pair whose testimony had been responsible for sending Mellor, Thorpe and Smith to the gallows. One other Rawfolds raider, Joseph Drake, had also been persuaded to appear at the witness stand to turn King's Evidence.

These three, all of them giving evidence to save their own skins, were vulnerable. Mr Williams, one of Henry Brougham's junior counsel, recognised this and pressed William Hall to explain how he succeeded in recognising so many of the accused men with such accuracy on such a dark night. Brougham, apparently at last trying to salvage some of his reputation, briefly stood up to take over the same theme in his cross-examination of Joseph Drake. These, however, were not much more than pinpricks at the prosecution's sword, its case prepared so meticulously for Mr Park, by Henry Hobhouse from the testimonies collected by Joseph Radcliffe and John Lloyd.

As prosecution witness followed prosecution witness, Brougham lapsed into the silence into which he had slumped during most of the week. His witnesses for the defence hardly made up for his shortcomings. They produced not only the same stereotyped alibis which had now been heard on every day of the trial, some were being spoken by the same voices. The blacksmith, George Armitage, described how, at the exact time of the Rawfolds attack he had sat by the fire with the defendant, James Brook. He told the tale with the same ring of conviction as that with which, three days earlier, he had described seeing Mellor heading for Huddersfield on the evening of William Horsfall's murder.

Mr Park, however, had already prepared the jury for these utterances from the prisoners' friends and family. 'I know persons, unaccustomed to these matters, are often induced to say, "How can people make up such a train of circumstances?"' he had said to them. 'Why, the circumstances, gentlemen, are generally true; only give another date, and then the story is all true. And their maxim is ... that it is no harm to tell one lie to save a brother.' All these witnesses, Park was saying, were perjurers.

Again, darkness had fallen by the time Mr Justice Le Blanc

began his summing up. Before beginning to touch on the evidence, he made certain that the jury understood the nature of the indictment. It was this which would determine whether or not the alleged offence was punishable by hanging. Le Blanc twice emphasised for them that these eight men were charged not with having demolished Cartwright's mill but having *begun* to demolish it. The Act under which the prisoners were charged referred to 'wind-saw-mill or other wind-mill, or any water-mill or other mill'. It had been passed in 1769. Such had been the technological changes in the past forty years of Industrial Revolution that the terms sounded decidedly old-fashioned. Le Blanc hastened to assure the jury that there was no doubt that the Act was meant to include 'all mills by which a power is used for the purpose of working machinery', and most certainly the factory at Rawfolds fell within this category. The only question, he told them again, was whether they 'did assemble in a tumultuous manner, and whether they began to demolish this mill'. The breaking of glass windows, he explained, would not be a beginning to demolish, though the breaking of the frames of the windows would – as unquestionably, he had established for them, was the case at Rawfolds.

And should there be any doubt as to his feelings on the part played by Mr Cartwright in this affair, he added, 'It was not, in fact, demolished, in consequence of the spirit displayed by the owner of it, and which one wishes the possessor of every house, and of every description of property in this country, that may happen to be attacked, would display.'

In the end, then, Le Blanc had framed the proposition that for the jury to decide whether any of the eight might hang, it needed the answer to a simple question. Was the worker in question at Rawfolds on the night of April 11th?

They retired for exactly an hour – far longer than any other retirement that week. James Haigh, Jonathan Dean, John Ogden, Thomas Brook and John Walker were all found guilty. James Brook, John Brook and John Hirst were found not guilty. Whatever had been unacceptable to the jury in blacksmith George Armitage's alibi on behalf of George Mellor, had clearly not been present in his evidence that day. The smith's was one of the alibis that gave James Brook his freedom.

After its second Sunday of rest, the court continued with its momentum unchecked. Equally unrestrained were Mr Park's energy and enthusiasm. The first of the week's cases which he now took up was another of common robbery.[2] The only one arrested of a group of Luddites who, at dead of night, had brought off a robbery at Kirk Heaton in October, was Joseph Brooke. He was accused of demanding a gun and stealing 15 shillings from the house of a farmer.

The main evidence against him was provided by a young girl, Ann Armitage, the farmer's niece. She claimed that, as she lay in bed that night in her unlit room, in order to frighten her, Brooke had struck a sword on the stone floor. From the single flash of light caused by the blow, not only had she been able to see, she claimed, that his forehead and cheeks were streaked with black and that he had on a dark-coloured top-coat and wore a dark-coloured handkerchief, she also insisted she had recognised his face. Later, when she had been sent for by Joseph Radcliffe at Milnsbridge House, and the prisoner had been made to speak, she had identified his voice.

The jury, after a five-minute retirement, found Brooke not guilty. The evidence against him, they felt sure enough to conclude, had been tenuous. Nevertheless, having guaranteed him his freedom, the foreman completed a paradoxical performance by telling the judges that the jury had not believed a word of Brooke's alibi.

The case, the result of which could have cost Brooke his life, had lasted much of the morning and afternoon. Immediately the next trial[3] for a similar offence began, Mr Park had this to say to the jury: 'This case, I hope, will not occupy so much time as the last did, for we have been employed three hours, I think very unnecessarily.' The case he wanted tried at speed was one in which three were accused of the robbery of a gun and a pistol; they were Job Hey, John Hill and William Hartley. They admitted being present with a group of Luddites on the night in question but denied having used or taken any guns. Another member of the same pathetic gang appeared to give evidence against them.

Hey and Hill's only defence was from character witnesses: employers who spoke of them as honest, sober men. Hartley, desperately poor, a widower and the father of seven children, one of whom was in court, had failed even to find a witness to speak to his character.

The jury, taking Park's strictures to heart, had no intention of letting the case drag on beyond the end of the afternoon. Without bothering to retire, they found all three guilty.

Next day's case[4] was that of the robbery which had taken place at Far Town, near Huddersfield, only six weeks earlier. Again three prisoners accused of the same capital offence, were at the bar, James Hey, Joseph Crowther and Nathan Hoyle. The same Luddite informer who had made his appearance in court the previous day was used to give evidence for the prosecution.

Before luncheon, after a five-minute retirement, the jury returned with a verdict which found all three guilty. All six men they had just pronounced on with such speed, stood to lose their lives.

During the adjournment Park decided to consider what he had achieved during the past few days. It had been considerable. He had now succeeded in securing the convictions of eighteen men for crimes which carried the death sentence. Three of these had already been executed. One only had been recommended to mercy. Six others had been found guilty of offences for which the punishment was transportation. All these remaining were yet to be sentenced.

Would the sentences to be passed give results which would measure up to the design of the architect of the Home Office's policy, Thomas Maitland? Would the experience of so much punishment be enough to instil into the workers of the north of England the fear which alone, 'King Tom' considered, could kill off Luddism?

Astonishingly, Park had already conferred in private on this matter with Mr Justice Le Blanc. The judge had told him that when all cases had been considered, a decision would be made as to who was 'the fittest for execution'. The orders for the hanging would then be given quickly so as to allow the prisoners no time to make an application for mercy.[5]

Park still had on his calendar no less than twenty prisoners who were capitally indicted and who, if he chose, could be brought instantly to trial. Maitland's view had been that enough force should be used, but no more. Could Park risk that eighteen executions would achieve what double that number more surely might? It was a brutal decision of delicate psychology that had nothing to do with the law. He concluded that he had done enough to create the required traumatic example. It would make at least as massive an impression as the executions of Mellor, Thorpe and Smith. It was, he decided, all that was required to win the victory he had in mind.

When the afternoon session began Park placed himself before the judges and told the jury that in the case of the two men now in front of them at the bar, he intended to offer no evidence.[6] Le Blanc would therefore be obliged to acquit them.

But Park had also a prepared speech to deliver. He told the jury,

> I hope and trust what has been done here will restore peace and comfort to this deluded county; and that those within these walls, and all, in every part of the Kingdom, to whom the account of what has passed here may come, will be induced to abstain from the commission of the like offences; and will be satisfied, that lives of honest industry are far preferable (considered even in a temporal view) to lives of rapine, violence and outrage against their neighbours, and to the assassination of honest and innocent individuals.

It was clear that the words now being spoken by Park would direct whether the majority of prisoners still waiting in the York Castle cells would live rather than die. They included some who had been deeply involved in the terror of that year and some who had been brought to the edge of trial for a capital crime by casual words rather than by militant deeds. James Starkey was one of the latter.[7]

He was the Millbridge cloth worker tricked by two of Captain Raynes's men into mentioning a half-baked plot to blow up Cartwright's mill.

Hammond Roberson had recognised the injustice of the case against Starkey, just as he recognised the young man's foolishness. Roberson had taken some trouble to intercede on Starkey's behalf. It was the only one of the generous gestures by the militant Liversedge parson which workers in the Spen valley chose to remember in the years that followed the trial.

James Varley[8] was one of those waiting down below who undoubtedly had been far closer than Starkey to violent action in the spring of 1812. He was known to have tried to rescue the murder weapons from where they were hidden in the straw in Joseph Mellor's workshop after the death of William Horsfall. The prosecution had a second indictment waiting if he escaped the first.

As it happened, neither was needed. Starkey, Varley and the sixteen remaining prisoners were recommended by Park for bail – to be recalled at the discretion of the Crown. 'I trust that this lenity and forbearance,' said Park, '... will have a powerful effect on their minds.'

All that was left was for the law to have its effect on the bodies of the remaining convicted prisoners. It had been a crowded day. Sir Alexander Thomson, nevertheless, did not intend to waste what was left of it.

He immediately had the twenty-one men got ready for sentencing. In the first group at the bar were John Baines the elder, John Baines the younger, the three other workers who had been present at the Crispin Inn and John Eaden.[9]

Thomson looked at John Baines and told him,

You have made it your boast that your eyes have been opened for three and twenty years; and you also declared your sentiments with respect to government, and with respect to no government, plainly ... preferring anarchy and confusion to order and subordination in society.

He assured the remainder, as well as Baines, that the sentence they were about to receive – the result of having sworn an oath on the Bible –

is certainly not a severe one, if we consider only what a profanation of religion it is, to make such a daring appeal to the Almighty to witness your desperate engagements and what are the horrid consequences that follow from it.

And finally, he reminded John Baines that had his offence been committed two days later, he would now be facing the gallows.

In the event, the sentence for each prisoner was the same: 'to be severally transported beyond the seas for the term of seven years'.

Baines, who knew he was unlikely ever to see his beloved north country or his family again, was faced with an irony of no small cruelty. Had Zachariah not been acquitted, he might have had the consolation that his last years exiled from England would have been eased by the company of his young son.

Thomson now had the remaining fifteen prisoners brought up to the bar.[10] Large as it was, it was too small to hold them all. A bench in front of it had to be cleared of spectators so that both judges could simultaneously view all prisoners – five of them from the Rawfolds attack, the remainder from three separate cases.

As the Clerk of the Arraigns stood to ask why sentence of death should not be carried out on them, Edward Baines was again struck by the simple respectability of these two rows of young workers – 'in the prime of life . . . many of them particularly good looking men'. Henry Hobhouse at this point noted with satisfaction that not one prisoner attempted to deny his guilt.[11] Each in turn spoke simply asking that his life be spared. Thomson and Le Blanc now both donned black caps.

Thomson read out the names of each of the fifteen. They had been 'part of that desperate association of men', he told them, who suffered from 'a strange delusion . . . that the use of machinery in the woollen manufacture was a detriment to the hands that were employed in another way in it. A grosser delusion,' he went on, 'never could be entertained.'

He turned first to the ten burglars who had gone 'armed and disguised in the night'. The evidence against them, he said, was too clear to admit any doubt. What Thomson did not, but might have said, however, was that the sum total value of goods stolen in the three bungled robberies which between them they had committed, was almost negligible, the arms they had taken were few and insubstantial and no victim had suffered bodily harm of any consequence whatever.

Turning to the Rawfolds five, Thomson described their crime as 'one of the greatest outrages that ever was committed in a civilised country'. He went on, 'It was but the defect of you and other wicked confederates that afterwards occasioned that fatal attack upon the person of another gentleman, by which he was assassinated and murdered.' In other words, he was fixing blame for the murder of Horsfall on them as he had on their already hanged confederates.

The five were made to understand, even before the moment of sentencing, that no leniency would be shown. He told them, 'The persons immediately concerned in that murder have suffered the punishment which the law inflicts, and a similar fate is about to await you, prisoners at the bar.'

However, he was able to turn with the benefit of leniency to the one man who, alone throughout the days of the trial, had been recommended to mercy. He told John Lumb that an application for mercy might spare his life.

As for the fate of the rest, Thomson made plain that, in fixing it, he had, above all, the well-being of the country in mind. 'It is of infinite importance', he said, 'that no mercy should be shewn to any of you.' And he would require his sentence (as Le Blanc, days ago, had assured Park would be the case) to be 'very speedily executed'. The sentence was death by hanging for all fourteen.

During his closing words one of the prisoners fell on the floor in a fit. Several of the others let out anguished groans. 'The scene', wrote Baines, 'was inexpressibly painful.'

36

The Last of the Luddites

Immediately the trial of the remnants of the Rawfolds army had been concluded, a note was handed to William Cartwright. It had been sent by the prisoners' solicitor, Mr Blackburn of Huddersfield. It was a petition protesting the innocence of the convicted prisoners and asked for mercy for them. Blackburn proposed that Cartwright should add his signature to it.

This desperate request made Cartwright purple with rage. It disturbed him more than any of the malicious and threatening letters he had received during the past year. He saw it as a cheap attempt to bring odium on him for his inevitable refusal to sign.[1]

His reply to Blackburn was precious, and in character. 'A sense of duty only having guided me up to the present moment,' he said, 'I cannot step out of that line by interfering with the course of justice until after the most satisfactory disclosure – you will then find me ready to aid you in the best manner I am able'.

Cartwright wrote this, however, after the clear private assurance from J A Park three days earlier, that nobody in York would hold out the slightest hope of leniency to any prisoner, even one who sought to make a last-minute confession.[2] The fourteen would swing, the Rawfolds attackers among them, and Cartwright knew it.

The hanging had been set for the following Saturday. A cold-eyed recollection – something resembling a jest – remains of how the arrangements for the execution were planned. Park was reported to have asked the judge if the fourteen men should all be hanged on one beam. To this his Lordship replied, 'Well, no, sir, I consider they would hang more comfortably on two.'[3] And so it was to be: the first batch at 11 a.m.

The editor of the *York Herald*, seeing the success Edward Baines had made of his *Leeds Mercury* special edition of the trial report, was planning a rival special second edition devoted entirely to the mass hangings. He had noted that the number to be executed on that one day was higher than any 'that stands upon any record within our knowledge'. The nearest number he had found was that at the Tyburn in York, on November 1st, 1746, when ten rebels were put to death.[4]

Maitland was taking no chances in spite of the chilling success of the hanging of Mellor and his two confederates. The crowd that morning was even more immense. It was watched over by still larger bodies of Maitland's infantry and cavalry than had been present at the execution in the previous week. Maitland had had his force paraded in such a way, both in front of the gallows and along the avenues approaching the castle, that they cast what Edward Baines saw was 'a peculiar degree of terror' over those watching. The result, he said, 'exhibited the appearance of a military execution'.[5]

The Under Sheriff who had gone to the cells to collect the men – John Ogden, Nathan Hoyle, Joseph Crowther, John Hill, John Walker, Jonathan Dean and Thomas Brook – had found one of them repeating aloud to the rest the words of the Methodist hymn, 'Behold the Saviour of Mankind, Nail'd to the shameful tree'. They sang it as they walked manacled to the scaffold and continued to do so as they stood on the platform. Baines described the scene as 'inexpressibly awful'. Prayers were then said by the castle chaplain. Each man fervently joined in. One or two plaintively shouted their farewells to friends below them. As they waited for the eleventh hour to strike, only one, John Ogden, showed signs of distress.

When the executioner released the drop and simultaneously the seven bodies fell, a great involuntary shriek was let out by many in the vast crowd. The *York Herald* reporter wrote that he never recollected seeing more pity depicted upon the human countenance than he saw in the instantaneous reaction of this great gathering of spectators.

The bodies were allowed to hang for an hour. They were still warm when taken down. The drop was immediately prepared for the seven who were to follow. Before the advertised time, however, the crowd had thinned considerably. Many, sickened by what they had seen, had shuffled silently away.

In the cells, William Hartley, the father of seven young children, had refused all visitors and had even turned a deaf ear to a plea from his eldest daughter for a final word. Shortly before his turn came to be led out, however, he relented and agreed to see the girl.

At half-past two he walked to the scaffold with John Swallow, John Batley, Joseph Fisher, James Haigh, James Hey and Job Hey, all of them singing 'Behold the Saviour of Mankind'.

Placed in front of the drop, one of them, James Haigh, spoke of his guilt and of his deep contrition for his offences. Another, John Swallow, gave a short prepared speech in which he spoke of 'that dreadful crime' for which he had now been convinced he deserved his fate. He prayed that those present would 'live a life of sobriety and uprightness, in order to prevent your being brought to that situation in which I am now placed'.[6] It was a sentiment to which, as he listened to the voices of the kneeling prisoners earnestly making their last prayer, Thomas Maitland could most readily add, 'Amen!'

At half-past two precisely, the boards were cut from beneath the seven men's feet. There was, it was noticed after the drop, practically no twitching of the bodies.

No matter what the mood of the workers after this signal day of mass execution, the manufacturers were still on edge. Some had reason to be. Joseph Mellor, the small Master who had been subpoenaed to appear at York to give evidence against his nephew, had had his considerable nervousness regenerated by new experiences. On New Year's Eve, while walking through his yard, a shot had been fired and had struck the wall behind his head. Then again, on the night of his return from the trial, the cloth he had left outside hooked to his tenter, had had the letters BFBSGL – Blood for Blood says General Ludd – chalked on it.[7]

Sceptical and bitter as ever, William Cartwright believed Mellor had done the deed himself.[8]

Maitland, however, was not to be deviated from his plan by the shaken nerves of the middle classes. Even before the last day's hangings he had made the decision to withdraw the more visible detachments of his troops from the most disaffected areas and then watch the result of allowing people to recover quietly from the inevitable shock of the executions.

Moreover, he intended to put a strict curb on the activities of his most unfavourite member of the legal profession. Mr Lloyd's methods – his admitted use of beatings up and of extended solitary confinement of suspects, along with the suspicion of more

268

inhuman treatment – had been the spearhead of Maitland's breaking of the Luddite wall of secrecy in the north of England. Maitland had turned a blind eye to all of this when it suited him. Now, however, he had no intention of watching Lloyd's continuing techniques undermine his new policy of passive domination of the workers. Immediately the York trial ended, Maitland told Hobhouse, in his capacity of Treasury Solicitor, to terminate Lloyd's employment and instruct him 'to take no step whatever on the part of government without express orders'.[9]

Lloyd was to leave York immediately without reward and without the esteem of the man who had used the results of his methods to the full. Joseph Radcliffe's clerk, Jonas Allison, was given the same instruction. He also left the city immediately and returned home without rancour. On his way past Huddersfield he took the trouble to ride past the houses of the convicted Luddites. His main reason for doing so was to see how the most rebellious people in the north were reacting to the savage sentences inflicted on their kinfolk. He saw nothing worth remarking on other than to report on the feelings of the stunned families and friends which, using an unfortunate metaphor, he described as having 'subsided into a dead calm'. What did strike him forcefully, however, as he looked through the doorways into their pitifully inadequate living quarters, was the abject poverty of these people; so much so that he doubted whether they could possibly afford to bring back the bodies of the victims from York.[10]

Maitland's latest assessment of the situation was that the Commission had 'succeeded in every point beyond my most sanguine expectations'. His instruction to his commanders through his second-in-command was to leave the worst parts of the country 'distinctly to themselves' and then see what happened.[11]

Nevertheless, he intended to monitor the burials and the inevitable funeral processions that would accompany them. Maitland handed the direct responsibility of watching over the carts carrying the fourteen bodies from York, to his still favourite funnel of information, Captain Raynes. He instructed Raynes to ride at a discreet distance from the procession along the whole of its two-day journey to Huddersfield and to remain constantly on the alert until every burial was complete.[12]

General Acland was told to place patrols of cavalry at each burial site under a senior officer who would ensure there were no demonstrations and see people quietly on their way home after each funeral.[13] Near Huddersfield, where the route was through potentially the most explosive areas, soldiers in disguise were to infiltrate the procession.[14]

Raynes joined the line of carts on the York road near Leeds. Before it reached Birstall crowds had attached themselves in some numbers. By the time it was moving down the hill into the Spen valley, passing near Hammond Roberson's house and Cartwright's mill, the total had become large and worrying.

Raynes quickly had a sergeant intervene and arrest a man at Millbridge, who as the bodies passed, called for revenge. 'Blood should have blood,' he had shouted. But no others took up the cry. Raynes himself kept his distance as Maitland had ordered, careful not to irritate the grieving people.[15]

By the time the procession reached the head of the valley, the carts had begun to disperse to the different towns and villages that had once been the homes of the dead men – Huddersfield, Halifax, Sowerby, Elland, Lockwood and Longroyd Bridge. This dilution of the crowd stilled the mounting nervous apprehension of Maitland's watching cavalry commanders. One of them, Major R Lacey, was able to report with relief that the large numbers of people he saw through Huddersfield were now 'perfectly quiet and orderly'.[16]

At Halifax, Major Bruce of the Stirling Militia was considerably moved as he watched two of the corpses being off-loaded at a warehouse. Friends came with carts and quietly took the bodies away to their respective villages. 'Both parties were accompanied by a fine people very much affected,' he said.[17]

Captain Raynes, still at a distance, watched over another of the funerals. A severe, ambitious young soldier who had had more than a little part in directing the course of the drama at which he was now a spectator, Raynes was not insensitive to what had, and what had not been achieved by it all. He wrote,

> After this awfully impressive finishing scene, little remained to be done, but to silently observe the effect produced on the minds and conduct of the *Luddites*, by the wretched fate of their companions in guilt. A sullen silence prevailed, occasionally interrupted by acknowledgements of having done wrong; not, it appeared, from a sense of the enormity of their crimes; but because they had failed in accomplishing their object.[18]

Maitland also kept his distance as he took from Acland the reports of each of his commanders. He was now certain that he had got all he needed to know: 'a fair knowledge of the real feelings of the people'.[19]

Within two days he had called in most of his military force.

37

The Law of Technology

The tally of York was complete. There had been no equal in English history. In the space of two weeks, of more than 100 men imprisoned in the castle's cells, sixty-six had been charged to appear before the Commission; seventeen of these had been hanged and seven transported. In the unlikely event that the Commission had not achieved its purpose, seventeen had been kept in reserve to be discharged on bail. A further fifteen had been discharged by proclamation and one indicted for misdemeanour to be tried at the next assizes. Seven only had been acquitted.

Irrespective of the methods by which convictions had been arrived at, and in spite of protestations of the innocence of Mellor, Thorpe and Smith which have persisted to the present day,[1] all detailed contemporary evidence points to their guilt as the murderers of William Horsfall. Mellor, potentially so attractive as a working-class leader, had sunk to using the methods of a thug. With his companions he died as the law dictated he should. But he died with dignity. The dream of what his revolt had stood for, and which he had only partially articulated, died with him.

However, even taking into account the legal standards of the times in which the trial took place, the outcome – the conviction of capital offences of fourteen other men, and the transportation of the rest, chiefly on the evidence of paid spies – must remain highly questionable.

In no important instance, even that involving those from the Rawfolds brigade, were crimes committed which resulted in the permanent injury of any individual under attack. The only serious wound displayed in court was that of John Hinchcliffe, whose eye had been shot out, and of the likely perpetrators of this deed, one had been let off scot free and the other had never been identified.

Those who had been convicted of robbery, with the exception of the few who had stolen arms, had got away with cash and goods which in total had an almost derisory value. There are few arguments of substance to suggest that the punishment fitted the crimes.

From the moment that each Luddite had entered the courtroom to the moment he breathed his last gasp in York Castle yard, the reality was that a united establishment had prepared a setting of great dramatic influence in which fairness was never a consideration. A verdict of guilty in the key cases had been a foregone conclusion from the instant the Special Commission sat. So too had been the multiple sentences of death.

The Commission had watched over a flagrant political manipulation of the judiciary. Sanctified by the law of the land, the outcome had been one of the severest acts of brutality ever engineered by a British government against a section of its citizenry. The reason why it was considered necessary was because the governing class was convinced that the workers put to death or banished had, as their prime aim, the overthrow of the government, that the aim might be achieved, and that therefore the threat was real and dangerous. Yet no evidence was produced on any of the many days that the court sat to show that this was indeed the case.

It was true that there had been within the Luddite groups across the north country, considerable organisation. Communication from one group to another by a system of delegates was good, and they were strengthened by an effective system of oath-taking. It needed, however, somebody with greater than Mellor's experience and abilities to make the organisation cohere into an effective revolutionary national force. Captured documents show that it was also true that the Luddites looked to France and to Ireland for support, and to men such as Sir Francis Burdett and Major John Cartwright for leadership. These, however, as Thomas Maitland had seen, were expressions of hope rather than descriptions of reality.

What, then, did Luddism – the movement that has been described as 'the purest of English working-class ideologies'[2] – achieve for the workers? By the spring of 1813 it was clear to the people of the valley towns of the Calder, Colne and Spen, as it had earlier become clear to the people of Lancashire, Cheshire

273

and Nottinghamshire, that the immediate gains they could count after a full year of violence and upheaval in their lives, was the wounds on their arms and the bodies in their graveyards. In the short term, the rising of the Yorkshire Luddites had been a great and terrible failure. The blow to the workers – to those who were now beginning to think of themselves as a class of people – was one of the most terrible ever inflicted on them.

Sidmouth and Maitland had entered into an exchange of mutual self-congratulation at the satisfactory outcome of the campaign. Maitland would soon be confident enough to announce with great sureness that 'the spirit of Luddism is completely extinguished.'[3] Raynes and others were reporting back that, not only was the sense of hostility disappearing from the places he now most frequently used as information sources – the public houses – there was an increasing optimism about trade and job prospects.

The tragedy was that this optimism, which seemed well founded, would have arrived with or without Luddism. Napoleon's defeat in Russia and the end of the Orders in Council were now having a sweeping effect on the prospects for trade. Even before the end of the trial, in the depths of January, one local manufacturer was telling General Acland how the price of wool was beginning to rise, orders for not just coarse military material but for luxury fine cloths had suddenly greatly improved, and remittances as well as orders from overseas were flooding in.[4]

Pay was up across the whole of the woollen and cotton industries. To add to the prospects, the early summer weather was announcing the possibility of a record harvest. And forecasts were to be fulfilled. The Annual Register for 1813 would be able to announce that 'few years had passed in which more internal public tranquillity has been enjoyed by the people of these islands'.[5]

It all appeared to confirm what the manufacturers had claimed and what the tyros of the new industrial order had forecast. The way ahead was to grasp the new technology firmly and make it yield its wealth for the nation. Henry Hobhouse was one of the keen young breed who saw the road forward most clearly. During the York trials he had had dinner with the Grand Jury. He beat the table as he expounded to them the value of new inventions in the manufacturing industries to Britain as a trading nation. He believed it was vital that the government should use the publicity value of the York convictions to spread the message across the land. He was prepared to push his beliefs even further. Soon he was telling the Home Office that he recommended the government should publish a proclamation explaining at the level of 'the capacity of the meanest artisan the absolute necessity of our manufacturers availing themselves of every new piece of machinery for the purpose of preventing their being undersold in the market and the consequent decay and total loss of their trade'.[6]

The government took him at his word. Immediately the trial ended a pardon was offered to all confessing rioters who were prepared to swear an oath of allegiance to the Prince Regent. Ten days later on February 1st a second proclamation, distributed widely across the north of England, exhorted the working classes to observe 'the extent and progress of the trade and manufactures of this country, which have been continually advanced by the invention and improvement of machinery'.[7]

The brightly shining progress of 1813 patently vindicated the foresight of every middle-class merchant and manufacturer. With barns full of wheat, an export market sucking up all the cloth the woollen district could supply, whether finished by machine or by hand, and with a home market now able to afford the cheap cottons churned out by the new steam-powered looms, the troubles of manufacturing England were at an end.

It was all, of course, illusory. If, for those most deeply involved, the croppers, the short-term results of Luddism were a sad failure, the middle-term consequences were a ghastly disaster. In 1806, there had been at work in the whole of Yorkshire only five gig-mills. Within five years of the collapse of the Luddite revolt, however, that number had risen to seventy-two. In the same period the number of shears worked by machinery had increased even more dramatically – from less than 100 to 1,462. As a result, by October 1817, with the job market flooded with soldiers returning from the war in Europe and with mechanisation surging through the industry, 3,625 croppers were forced to petition Parliament with a plea for help of any sort. Only 860 of these had full employment; the rest were either partially or totally out of work.[8]

By this time the only solution most could see to finding some sort of employment was to emigrate. This, however, they were forbidden to do. Laws existed to prevent woollen workers travelling abroad and taking their trade skills with them. Eventually a moving appeal was made from Yorkshire to the Home Secretary by Lord Lascelles asking for help for those who were destitute.

Perhaps fresh laws to protect their dying trade could be insti-
tuted; possibly some financial assistance for them to look for a
new life in North America could be given.

But Lord Sidmouth, forever incapable of risking the exposure
to warmth of his frigid front, never wavered. Consultation with
the Prime Minister merely served to stiffen his resolve. Lord
Liverpool and he, he said, were agreed that no restraints should
be put on the machinery of the woollen trade; moreover, he had
no intention of helping croppers, starving or otherwise, to leave
the country with their specialist knowledge.[9]

As power from water, coal, steam, iron and eventually steel
spread to every industry and as mechanisation began to take over
each part of it, it became clear that the technological forecasters of
the day had been correct. The machines were capable of creating
great wealth. It was wealth capable of sustaining a population
which, at the beginning of the nineteenth century, was rising to
a rate of 15 per cent each decade. It was also to be the wealth on
which the British Empire could be founded. However, it was
clear too that the wealth was not being widely distributed. Within
a small fraction of their lifetimes many observers of the industrial
scene saw the appearance of frightening disparities.

By the early 1830s Peter Gaskell had taken to waiting at the
street corners of the towns of northern England, looking into the
places where the steam engine had 'drawn together the population
in dense masses'.[10] What he saw written on the bodies of factory
workers was disconcerting.

> Any man who has stood at twelve o'clock at the single narrow
> doorway, which serves as the place of exit for the hands
> employed in the great cotton-mills, must acknowledge that
> an uglier set of men and women, of boys and girls, taken
> them in the mass, it would be impossible to congregate in a
> smaller compass. Their complexion is sallow and pallid –
> with a peculiar flatness of feature, caused by the want of
> proper quantity of adipose substance to cushion out the
> cheeks . . . A spiritless and dejected air, a sprawling and wide
> action of the legs, and an appearance, taken as a whole,
> giving the world but 'little assurance of a man,' or if so, 'most
> sadly cheated of his fair proportion.'[11]

Conditions in some mills, long before those who took part in
the riots had grown into middle-aged men, deteriorated at a speed

beyond belief. In the *Leeds Mercury* of October 16th, 1830, Richard Oastler gave a description of the infants who now kept the woollen industry profitable:

> who are compelled (not by the car-whip of the negro slave driver) but the dread of the equally appalling thong or strap of the overlooker, to hasten half-dressed, but not half-fed, to those magazines of British Infantile Slavery – the Worsted Mills in the town and neighbourhood of Bradford!!!

One boy employed in a Bradford factory gave evidence to a Commissioner who contributed to the official *Reports on the Employment of Children in Factories*. The boy, who was fifteen, was 3 feet 9 inches tall and had dreadfully bent knees. He said,

> I first began to work before I was five years of age. It was a worsted mill. We used to begin at six o'clock in the morning and go on till eight o'clock; sometimes nine. My legs are now bent as you see. Got my knees bent with standing so long. Have asked my mother and father to let me stop away; they said they could not do with me laiking at home, there was so many of us laiking from not being old enough.[12]

Just a few years later Friedrich Engels, like Daniel Defoe before him, crossed Blackstone Edge into Yorkshire. What he saw there was very different from Defoe's pre-Industrial Revolution vision of perfect marriage of man and industry. The water that ran into the Calder and Aire valleys, he discovered, was now carried in stinking streams. In one part of Leeds in 1839, the sewers had become so choked and had led to such disease, that there had been three deaths to every two births.

In places like Halifax, Huddersfield and Bradford he could see the remains of great natural beauty being swamped as factory upon factory was being built up on the hill slopes to accommodate the new machines. Even in Huddersfield, 'by far the handsomest of all the factory towns of Yorkshire and Lancashire, by reason of its charming situation,' he now saw streets

> neither paved nor supplied with sewers nor other drains; that in them refuse, *debris*, and filth of every sort lies accumulating, festers and rots, and that, nearly everywhere, stagnant water accumulates in pools, in consequence of which the adjoining dwellings must inevitably be bad and filthy, so that

in such places diseases arise and threaten the health of the whole town.[13]

A seemingly settled and widely envied way of life had been replaced, in not much more than a single generation, by an industrial hell.

The frightening paradox of the age was that the cause of this substantial disaster was identical to that which had been responsible for the now steadily rising total wealth of the nation: industrial technology.

Many plausible reasons have been put forward as the key factors which caused Luddism to erupt when it did, and as it did in different forms in different places. They include the market forces which made Luddism the function of a trade cycle,[14] and they include the absence of free trade[15] as well as its opposite – the *laissez-faire* which caused an eruption of working-class feeling against unrestrained industrial capitalism.[16]

There are good grounds for looking at all these propositions seriously. Is it possible, however, to single out one predominant force which embraces all these reasons for revolt: one which could be said to be the fundamental cause of the swings in the trade cycle of Regency England, the international battle to control export markets, the evils of *laissez-faire*, the simultaneous attempts to impose trade restrictions and the destabilising effects of a growing population?

Only one factor – technology – offers itself as being ultimately responsible for the simultaneous convergence of the events which had descended on the nation with such socially catastrophic results. Not, however, the individual pieces of technology which have played their part in this story – the cropping machine, the spinning jenny, the steam loom and the stocking machine. These were important. They were triggers to individual acts of violence. But no one of these, not even the cropping machine, was responsible for the great events of 1812. These were all part of a much greater movement.

The Leviathan which had swamped Britain, pushing across it a great wave still rising towards a crest in 1812, was the inventive mechanical age which had begun in the middle of the eighteenth century. It had been a phenomenal event in world history. The tide would sweep the nation into the nineteenth century and still continue to surge through the whole of the twentieth.

All civilisations throughout history until that age had been sustained by the discoveries that made it possible to raise temperatures, to harness power and to work the land; in other words by those techniques which gave control over the chemistry, the physics and the biology of the environment. It was not necessary to understand how these technologies worked. All that was required to benefit from them was to know that they *did* work. The scale of the economy, the power of the politics the ability to wage war – all these aggrandising achievements of successive civilisations – were each determined by the success of progressive technologies.

But the changes which each of these civilisations had imposed on itself had in every case taken place over many hundreds, sometimes thousands, of years. What made the Industrial Revolution in Britain so different from any other technological revolution was that it took place over such a few years. The crucial difference between the technology of the Industrial Revolution and that of Egypt, Greece or Rome was that it now had found a new rational scientific base. Not only was it possible to see that the techniques worked, the newly established foundations of modern science showed why they worked. The progress in discovery as a result was astounding. So rapidly were these changes to be felt by the ordinary citizen that the English civilisation could not adjust with sufficient speed to cope with the destabilising effects shaking its base.

It was this that had been at the root cause of the revolt. The violence of Luddism had been the only way in which one group believed itself able to oppose the changes which technological advance was imposing on its way of life.

But no group can afford to pay lip-service to one unalterable characteristic of technology. This quality can be written as a strictly applicable rule – even as an iron law. That is that technology is irreversible. The croppers had believed that by destroying the shearing machine there was a real possibility that this tiny piece of technology could be eliminated. They were not the first skilled manual workers to hold this belief, nor the last. But technology, they confirmed, cannot be wiped from the memory. Invention, once made, is as permanent a part of civilisation as the DNA of a gene of a human embryo which becomes a permanent part of the individual. Once the characteristic it represents has been encoded, it is inevitable that eventually it will be expressed.

The arrow of time moves in one direction only – from the handshears to the water-powered cropping machine to the steam-driven finishing mill, from the printing press to movable type to computerised type-setting, from the coal pick to the revolving wheel coal-cutter to the continuous mining machine. New stages can be added to the progress of invention. But it is not possible to uninvent.[17]

The Luddites set themselves squarely in the path of a corollary of the law of technology. That is that, although legislation or violence might delay it, they cannot prevent the introduction of a new technique. The croppers fell victim to the inevitable consequences as had many before them.

Queen Elizabeth I, if she is to be believed, had the well-being of the poorer classes in mind when she chose to oppose technological advance. She did so after examining a pair of worsted stockings made by the Reverend William Lee on his newly invented stocking loom. When Lee's patron, Lord Hunsdon, asked her to grant a patent she replied with the ringing words:

> My Lord, I have too much love for my poor people who obtain their bread by the employment of knitting to give my money to forward an invention that will tend to their ruin by depriving them of employment, and thus make them beggars. Had Mr Lee made a machine that made *silk* stockings, I should, I think have been somewhat justified in granting him a patent for the monopoly, which would have affected only a small number of my subjects.[18]

Lee was hounded out of England and died disillusioned in France, not however before examples of his machine had begun to creep into use in his native country. By the eighteenth century his invention had become in Nottingham the basis of a major English industry.[19]

The gig-mill had been specifically forbidden in England by a statute of Edward VI. Yorkshire croppers were still struggling to have the law upheld as the Luddite riots began. This was at the beginning of a decade in which gig-mills were to increase by a factor of fifteen. But disbelief in technology's irreversibility did not end with the Luddites. Modern times continue to provide their own examples. In 1979 a lawsuit was filed on behalf of Californian farm-workers to prevent the use of public funds on mechanisation research which, it was alleged, would eliminate jobs in the harvesting of grapes, oranges, peaches, lettuce and tomatoes. The lawsuit cited as evidence the statistic that the mechanical harvester developed by the University of California had reduced the number of tomato harvest workers from 50,000 in 1963 to 18,000 in 1970.[20]

And just as the legal restraint consistently showed itself to be an inadequate obstacle to technology's forward momentum, so too violence has never been better than a temporary brake. The Municipal Council of Danzig, which, in the sixteenth century, attempted to prevent the spread of the newly invented ribbon weaving treadle mill, by drowning its inventor, committed an error of judgement besides a crime.[21] Less than fifty years later it was in use in London in the workshops of Danzig's industrial competitors.

The Yorkshire Luddites too were to achieve notoriety and a permanent place in history because they used spectacular violence as a means of attempting to influence technological advance and because, equally spectacularly, they failed. They were not to be the last to use force in a test of technology's law. Miners who, in Yorkshire in 1984, attacked and destroyed the pithead machines of their own industry were nominally protesting the closure of pits they had been told were uneconomic. The most significant origins of their problem, however, lay in the changed techniques of an industry in which, in the 1920s, the quantity of coal produced by each man was essentially determined by what he could hew in a day. By 1950 machines were being installed in underground collieries which could each produce more than ten tons of coal a minute. By 1983, as a result of new technologies which had produced cheap oil and natural gas, the demand for coal had fallen to half its peak figure; but the number of men required to produce that coal had fallen to less than one-fifth of those employed in the 1920s.

A further almost invariable consequence of a new technique is that once it has been applied in industry its effects are quicker and greater than anticipated. This result is widely demonstrated in history, but nowhere more tragically illustrated than in the case of the workers who took part in the Luddite revolt. By 1820 machines which could be operated by unskilled hands and weak arms had annihilated this complete section of a major industry. The cropping trade had wholly, not partially, ceased to exist. Croppers who failed to find employment elsewhere, and there were many, and who were forbidden to emigrate, were now unable to feed their families as their work became the property of young children.

The speed with which applied technology's influence is felt

increases with every age. It was only in 1959 that a single electronic component could be fitted on to a single silicon chip. In 1964 it was forecast[22] that the number of components that could be fitted would double every year. At the time this prophecy of a geometrical increase seemed outrageous. But it proved remarkably accurate. By 1979 it was possible to manufacture a single chip on which were 250,000 components. In those twenty years computer technology had swept into every manufacturing industry of substance with immense consequences. Its full effects on both production and employment are still to be felt.

There are certain other consequences of technology's irreversibility. One is that the longer the delay in the introduction of a new technique, the greater is likely to be the social consequence when it finally is introduced. The unemployment, hunger and misery – the lot of the workers caught by the thrashing limbs of the dying cropping trade – were substantially worsened by the delays caused by the attempts to eliminate machines already introduced. An uninterrupted introduction of the new technique would have softened the force of the blow which eventually came with cruel effects.

By far the most frequent reason for the introduction of an innovatory manufacturing technique is that it increases the volume of the product and decreases the amount of labour required to produce the same volume. Because it generally does this in advance of a market having been created to absorb the product, it is inevitable that even in the short term, a loss of jobs will result. A further consequence of technology's law, therefore, is that if suffering takes place as a result of the introduction of a new technique, the first to suffer are invariably the working class.

After the aberrations produced by the shock of the early years of the Industrial Revolution, the material wealth of workers in the manufacturing industries slowly began to rise. Eventually, even before the end of the nineteenth century, in a population which continued to increase at a rate which made Malthus's predictions of disaster-to-come seem highly likely to be fulfilled, material possessions reached a level which, in pre-Industrial Revolution times, would have been inconceivable.

Acts of government intervention were necessary to create more acceptable social conditions in a more just society after the turmoil of that revolution. These acts, continuous through the next century of industrialisation – the Factory Acts, the Education Acts, the Trade-Union Act – were measures which were humanitarian, liberal and overdue. But they were only possible in a society rich enough to be able to make them effective. The source for these riches, for this wealth, was technology. And the embittering and paradoxical by-product in this process of wealth generation continued to be the unemployment and suffering which accompanied it.

The traumas associated with the introduction of the machines of modern times have been as overwhelming to the communities affected as were those produced by the previous century. In the very same valleys of the Calder, Colne and Spen in which Mellor and the Luddites fought, the 1950s saw the failure of the woollen and cotton industries to invest with sufficient speed in new technologies. The collapse of these industries and the resulting unemployment were entirely predictable as new machines were applied abroad to capture world markets. Many of the great stone and brick factories which had once seemed immovable growths on the face of the valleys were soon to become benign abandoned hulks. By the 1970s from makeshift stalls on their now silent shopfloors, the bobbins and shuttles of an outmoded industrial age were being sold off to souvenir hunters.

In the same period the British steel, shipbuilding and newsprint industries faced collapse or turmoil for similar reasons. And just as in these cases the irreversibility of each industry's new technology was displayed, so too was it possible to forecast the outcome of the violent coal strike of 1984. It was as inevitable that miners' union leaders' attempts to prevent the closure of pits would fail as comprehensively as did George Mellor's battle to destroy Rawfolds.

The wealth of a society is the chief product of its technology. Its by-products are not always so welcome. The decrease in size of the workforce of the manufacturing industries is as surely one of its by-products as are potential pollutants and other environmental hazards. One other such certainty is Luddism. In 1813 Thomas Maitland rode out of the valleys believing that not only he, but those remaining there had seen the last of the Luddites. But they had not seen the last of Luddism. Even within four years yet more individuals who believed they could escape the consequences of technology by destroying its machines were being hanged in order to discourage imitators.

Luddism is a human behavioural response of fear. It is not, as Henry Hobhouse persuaded Lord Sidmouth and the rest of British government, an irrational response. George Mellor and his army of croppers were correct in their belief that the new machinery would destroy their livelihood. Equally, in 1984, Yorkshire miners were correct in their conviction that a modernised coal industry would destroy traditional mining communities.

Whereas the irreversibility of technology is certain and its consequences predictable, the timing of the manifestation of these consequences is not. The effects on industries, on towns and valleys and on other groups of people living and working together can be as calamitous as those which in other circumstances would be called Acts of God. It is not unreasonable, therefore, that communities smitten by catastrophe as a result of technological change should look to intervention – whether from government or from some other source – on the scale of that which dealt with the worst of the turmoil left by the Industrial Revolution. The nature of the intervention must depend on the nature of the problem. Most of the examples in history of the suffering produced by technological change could have been ameliorated by the introduction of new technology and of new industry. Still today, the most realistic solutions to problems created by technology are likely themselves to be technological, irrespective of whether they are imposed by political or social means.

It would be a mistake to believe that any modern industry has its own special safety line to eternity. The computer industry today involves thousands of men and women whose nineteenth-century equivalents were employed in the woollen and cotton manufacturing trades of northern England. Not to recognise that current computer techniques will one day become as outmoded as the hand-cropping industry is to deny the law of technology and risk the possibility of upheavals which have faced all Luddite attitudes.

38

Ever After

It is more difficult to recognise individual faces among the crowd of working people who survived the Luddite affair of 1812 than it is to identify those who destroyed themselves in it. Even these, in the end, went to unmarked graves.

So successfully had fear been carved on the minds of those who escaped the Commission and who saw the lines of hanging bodies at York, that they clung to their secrets to the end of their lives. Shortly after the trials one young cloth worker, John Mitchell, who had fled from Millbridge to Manchester, was momentarily tempted by a letter which suggested that he and his father should meet back in their Yorkshire village. There were, it was being said, promises of freedom from prosecution in return for information. Young Mitchell, however, took the precaution of consulting his new employer. 'Master desired me not to be too hasty,' Mitchell wrote. Before he reappeared anywhere near the scene of his former activities, the worldly-wise employer suggested he should seek legal advice. The attorney's counsel was that the pardon then being offered the confessing Luddites 'only reached such as had not been charged and if I came I must sufer as the others had done. Therefore, I am going to leave the country as soon as posable so I return you all thanks for your love to me and my father so no more at present from yours John Mitchell. farewell.'[1] And he was never seen in England again.

Frank Peel, the local journalist, talked in their old age to some of those reputed to have been Luddites still left in the valleys. None, however, was willing to discuss any of the incidents which might incriminate him. The fear of the death penalty persisted to the end. Peel had to rely on the tales of relatives, some second-hand, and some richly embroidered.

A few of the men who were last seen in their home villages on the night of April 11th, 1812 – the night of Rawfolds – were said to have emerged briefly from the mists of time and were recognised at trade union meetings and Chartist gatherings in other parts of England in the 1830s and 1840s. If it was so, none of these left any record of their involvement in the events that drove them out of their native valley for ever.

Of the croppers who fought in the Spen valley that night, notes of only one – the villain of the piece in local eyes, Benjamin Walker – remain to tell something of the life he led in the now bitterly divided community.[2] Having confessed to being involved in Horsfall's murder and having turned King's Evidence against not only the Luddite leaders, but also the Rawfolds attackers, Walker was reviled throughout the Colne valley. His claim on the £2,000 which had been offered by the Committee of Huddersfield Manufacturers for information leading to the arrest of the murderers, was rebuffed by the mill owners who now believed he should have swung with the rest on the scaffold. It was said of him that at one point he tried, but failed, to escape from where he was hated by emigrating to America. In the end he was reduced to begging on the streets of Huddersfield. It was reported that, after Walker's death as a pauper, his body was immediately exhumed by those with long memories and sold for dissection.[3]

Of the other informers – William Hall, Joseph Drake and the rest who were promised and given freedom for their free flow of information – only a little more is recorded. When, in June 1813, cases for damages were heard in which some of these men were required to give evidence, J A Park once more indulged in insider dealings to protect them in return for their services. Again, what he did was with the intimate knowledge of the judge concerned. He told the Home Secretary that he had prevented certain cases from being introduced at the last Assizes at York, since he did not wish to have the witnesses who had given evidence to the Special Commission, particularly the accomplices, again submitted unnecessarily to 'public inspection'. He made his wishes known to Sir Alexander Thomson who strongly approved of his motives.

Beyond these few facts a fog of anonymity now descends on the workers left to live out the rest of their lives in the uncontrolled backwash of the Industrial Revolution. However, of the upper middle classes whom they vainly believed would lead them back to some ill-defined Jerusalem, there is more than enough to tell.

Of the two candidates most favoured by rumour to have been

prepared to stand in front of ranks of workers and aim them towards a reformed society, one – astonishingly so, being in reality most unsuited for the task – had actually appeared in Luddite country during the York trials. Major Cartwright, in the evening of his life, had decided to tour northern towns to try to gather signatures for his petition for a reform of Parliament.

During the uncertain period in the few hours after the burial of the hanged Rawfolds raiders, the landlord of the George Inn at Huddersfield discovered the true identity of the elderly gentleman who had hired one of his back rooms for a meeting. Panicking at the thought of the possible consequences, his house so recently linked with the name of George Mellor, the publican had immediately sent for one of Maitland's local commanders, Major Hankin of the Scots Greys.[4]

Hankin, along with three special constables, a posse of the Huddersfield Watch and Ward and men of his own regiment, rushed to the George and burst into the meeting room. The anticlimax, when the door was flung open, was substantial. Hankin found an elderly man and a few strangers – 'all tippling'. One of the drinkers told him – and there was little reason for disbelief – 'that they had come to pay their respects to the good old gentleman Major Cartwright and to talk about parliamentary reform'.[5]

In the corner was a bundle of innocuous petitions waiting hopefully for signatures.

Highly agitated that his high but innocent purpose should have been misinterpreted, Cartwright at first refused to be searched. Before he was calmed down, it was, as his niece recorded, 'about half past three in the morning; a most unseasonable hour for one who seldom sat up later than ten at night'.[6]

But of the other, potential leader of the poor, Sir Francis Burdett, there was and never would be any sign in the north. Still, however, his name was being everywhere used by the underprivileged as the touchstone to a radical new life. Just as captured, hardly literate Luddite documents had done throughout 1812, so too did pathetic letters smuggled from gaols throughout England continue to mention him with reverence and hope.[7]

Those who died in the Luddite revolt were never to know that Burdett had not the slightest interest in leading a revolution. He continued his histrionic but peaceful path through life until at last, twenty years later, the first inadequate Reform Bill was carried. He was then able to devote more time to his other passion, fox-hunting, and to a defence of the land-owners of

England, of whom he believed 'there is no set of people in the world more liberal, just and honourable,'[8] and among whom he was one. The safe distance he maintained between himself and the poor of the nation is nowhere better measured than in a speech to the reformed Parliament. Breathing his usual declamatory fire, speaking of the expenses he had had to face during elections thirty years earlier, he said, 'I assure you, Sir, I am indulging in no exaggeration. Honourable gentlemen may not believe it, but I can assure them there was a time when Lady Burdett had only one pair of horses to her carriage . . . ' As Disraeli remarked, it was the most patrician definition of poverty ever made.[9]

There is no question as to which member of the ruling class had made the most ineradicable mark on the working classes of the north of England. And, having made it, General the Hon Thomas Maitland, with a sense of release, left their country at the earliest opportunity. He was never to look back on this posting – it had taken less than a year out of his life – as other than an unwelcome interruption to an everywhere more spectacular career spent almost entirely in colourful locations. Equally there can be no doubt that his own assessment of his influence on England's internal socio-political events of 1812 is a considerable undervaluation.

Government itself, however, was not unaware of his contribution to national stability. He was quickly created baronet and offered a series of postings he would take with relief. They promised a warm climate and unpredictable people whose characteristics were more in tune with his own eccentricities. As Governor of Malta, then Commander-in-Chief of the Mediterranean, and finally as High Commissioner of the Ionian Islands, Maitland established himself, as he always had, as dictator. As in the north of England the uncompromising rule of 'King Tom' had a consistent and clear purpose – from the eradication of the plague on Malta to the suppression of revolution on Cephalonia.

Sir Charles Napier disliked Maitland from the moment he joined him in the Mediterranean. He could not bear his despotism, his coarse Scots habits, his bouts of drunkenness, or the young men he chose to have constantly dancing attendance. Nevertheless, in spite of himself, in the end, Napier was able to see the unusual strength of character of the man who now ruled all British dependencies in the Mediterranean. 'King Tom', said Napier, 'was a rock; a rock on which you might be saved, or, be dashed to pieces; but always a rock.'[10]

General Wroth Acland, left in command in Yorkshire by

Maitland, was eager to get away from the county and 'get nearer to my friends'.[11] Unlike Maitland, however, he fully realised how profound had been the experience of the past year. He would neither regret it, he said, nor forget it. He too was rewarded by a grateful government with a knighthood; he was given one of the first KCBs in 1815. Within a year he was dead of the fever – undoubtedly malaria – which had dogged him throughout the Luddite campaign.

But not all those who shaped its successful course were rewarded in the manner they had been led to think they deserved. Maitland, before sweeping out of Yorkshire, had not forgotten his favourite, Raynes, the captain who had been in effective command in the field. Putting up with the foul weather of the Pennines by night, the foul language of the people he meant to suppress by day, and the intense distaste ever afterwards of the senior officers he had displaced, it was Raynes, Maitland well knew, who had crucially dealt with the tedious practicalities of bludgeoning a loose but effective guerrilla army into submission.

But Raynes had had problems other than those given him by the Luddites. During the whole of the campaign his health had been far from good, and his wife, Sarah, they realised, was again pregnant. She had joined him at Rawfolds. As soon as the hanged Luddites were buried, Hammond Roberson baptised their newly born daughter.[12]

Maitland was more than ready to give Raynes ample acknowledgement for his services. With the campaign abruptly at an end, he ordered the militia captain to ride the 40 miles back to York both to make his farewell and to discuss his future. With a failed family business and no private income Raynes was extremely anxious about how he was to support his growing family after his release from his regiment. Apart from his good looks and his newly won reputation, he had not much to offer a potential employer. But Maitland could assure him that Lord Sidmouth had promised that the government would not forget the officers who had served the nation so well in the north. Any governmental post that brought him in even as little as £300 – £400, responded a relieved Raynes, would be welcome. Maitland said he saw no difficulties. But, he added, 'Now is the time – if you do not get it now, you never may.'[13]

Even this throwaway parting remark was yet another example of Maitland's accurate insight into the ways of his fellow men. During the next weeks, then months, then years, Raynes repeatedly petitioned higher and higher rank for the reward that had been promised. First the commanding officer of the Stirlingshire Militia; next the Regimental Colonel, the Duke of Montrose, who put Raynes's case to Lord Sidmouth and then to the Prime Minister. But by the end of 1813 all Raynes had received by way of remuneration was £200 for expenses – a figure well short of the monies he had spent on food for his men, forage for their horses, and payments to spies and informers when, throughout the previous year, he had been told to operate on his own initiative and from his own pocket.[14]

In April 1814 he was once again sick from the fever he had contracted as a young soldier in the Middle East – as with Acland the illness was probably malaria. At last, Raynes was granted an interview with Lord Sidmouth. It was a chilly and generally uncomfortable occasion. The Home Secretary eventually asked Raynes what government post he wanted. Raynes replied that the sort of thing he had in mind was a Commissioner of the Lottery. Sidmouth here interrupted him curtly to tell that he could not have that sort of reward. The interview petered out inconsequentially and with no promises of any kind having been made to Raynes.

By the time another year had passed, with neither cash nor job provided from any source within the ungrateful nation, Raynes had sunk to writing petulant letters to the people who might have helped most – including a much irritated Duke of Montrose. Finally in 1816 Raynes wrote several times to the Treasury of his pathetically sinking circumstances and succeeded in gaining another interview with Lord Sidmouth. The exchange would have been as cold as the first had it not been for the fury which welled up inside Raynes when the Home Secretary, having prepared nothing whatever to offer by way of job or sympathy, concluded with studied disregard for logic that there were three reasons why he was unable to give the militia captain any remuneration: his age, his state of health, and – perhaps as Sidmouth's nod to sensitivity – the fact that Raynes was a gentleman.[15]

A few weeks later, groping for some warm phrase or gesture, Sidmouth asked if, since there was nothing else for him, he might consider joining Sir Thomas Maitland in the Mediterranean. Raynes leaped at the chance.[16] Now pitiful and near destitute, he accepted the £100 Sidmouth offered him as a charitable donation to tide him over until the time that he could discuss the matter with Maitland during the brief visit the general was shortly to make to England.

Tragedy, however, had been destined to settle over Raynes's affairs from the time, three years earlier, that Maitland had given his parting advice. On the day fixed for Raynes to go from his Lincolnshire home to London to the interview, illness delayed him. By the time he reached the capital Maitland had sailed for Cephalonia.

He never saw Maitland again. Nor did he ever see or hear from Sidmouth. Reduced to using what little cash he had left on the private publication of an appeal to the public, his letters, requests, demands and complaints become less frequent and eventually he too is swallowed by the mists of history, thus experiencing, like the Luddites, the general fate of the poverty-stricken.

Time dealt kindly with the lawyers involved in the York Special Commission. Henry Hobhouse, 'the intelligent person' chosen by Lord Sidmouth to smooth the path of the trial, received ample reward for having rolled it to its powerful conclusion. He was created Under-Secretary of State in Sidmouth's own Home Department, where the Secretary 'regarded him ever afterwards with unabated confidence and friendship'. And J A Park's 'zeal and ability' were so approved of by Lord Sidmouth that he 'recommended him on more than one occasion' to the Prime Minister. He was, before long, elevated to Judge of the Common Pleas.[17]

Henry Brougham, most of whose clients had lost at least their freedom at York, left the city not noticeably disappointed, and certainly not shifted from the steeply rising slopes of his career. The fees he was able to command were rising in parallel – 'in one year I made in a stuff gown above £7000,' though others guessed the sum to be considerably higher.[18] His autobiography, charting the crowded political path to the summit of his profession as Lord Chancellor, is that of a man deeply immersed in the colourful history of his time. One hundred and sixty pages of it are devoted to his involvement with the Prince and Princess of Wales and their tedious quarrels. Less than three pages are given over to the trial of the Luddites at York. And though the names, work and workplaces of William Cartwright and William Horsfall are properly noted, nowhere does he mention so much as the surname of any one of the seventeen of his clients who lost their lives as a result of it.

In the small Yorkshire valleys where the wealthier class had borne most of the initial brunt of the year of upheaval and the poor had experienced most of the final catastrophe, the gentlemen had had much reassessment of their lives to consider.

In the Colne valley Joseph Radcliffe had been given clear signals that in the emerging industrial society, its newly created class division vividly displayed, he would remain a perpetually loathed figure.

The first sign was not new, but no less frightening than on earlier occasions. Within hours of Mellor's conviction, a gun had been loosed off into Milnsbridge House. Radcliffe immediately tried to have his military guard increased by a direct appeal to Sidmouth. The Home Secretary, however, nervously deflected the decision to Maitland.[19] Still convinced that the mass hangings would change the whole atmosphere of the country, Maitland refused to take any provocative action on behalf of the magistrate. In any case he regarded him as an irritating old man.

Radcliffe, according to his own reckoning, had put his life on the line. Not only had those in power not recognised his services with the baronetcy he hankered after, he was now even refused the safeguards he deserved of right. Petulantly, he complained to a friend that he had no intention of demeaning himself by begging for this favour from Maitland. 'If my situation is not worth protection,' he said, 'it can not be expected I should remain here, risking my life as I have hitherto done for the good of my country.'[20]

But Maitland's prediction had been correct. As soon as the news of the hangings had spread across the countryside, the stunned workers had withdrawn into a shell of passivity. With the announcement of an amnesty for those willing to swear the Oath of Allegiance to the Crown, Luddites had begun to filter in from the villages. The response was slower than seen in Lancashire and Cheshire in the previous autumn, but nevertheless numbers mounted day by day, showing resistance was at an end. Radcliffe's magistrate neighbours, Mr Scott and the Reverend Mr Coulthurst, administered the oath to almost sixty before February was out. Significantly, however, not a single worker had appeared at the door of Milnsbridge House.[21] The hatred for Radcliffe was unusual and intense, and he knew it.

In the end he decided that a judicious temporary absence from the Colne valley might be as effective a method as any of diverting attention from himself and his family, as well as providing – not unreasonably, considering the life he had led in the past year – a holiday. In April he set off on the Grand Tour.[22]

By the time he returned, not only did he have to acknowledge that the guard, which had been removed from his house, was truly no longer needed, the mood of the workers in the mills and finishing shops of the valley had undergone a remarkable transformation.

This was not the sole attitudinal change Radcliffe registered. His letters, to the soft-hearted Lord Fitzwilliam as well as to the stonier centred Lord Sidmouth, in which he had repeatedly and unashamedly drawn attention to the sacrifices he had made on behalf of his country, suddenly to his delight, began to show the blessed response he sought. In September 1813, the Home Secretary wrote to confirm that it was the intention of HRH the Prince Regent, to confer the dignity of a baronet on him. And on this occasion there was no Thomas Maitland waiting to spike the guns of the aspirant aristocrat. Joe Pickford was now fully transmuted to Sir Joseph Radcliffe, Bt. His ascendancy was nothing if not a triumph of persistence.

He had five more years to live. But in that time Milnsbridge was to begin to change drastically from the place of rural peace he had first found. Factories were creeping up the valley from Huddersfield. They multiplied with each inventive throb of the age. Not only could he see their chimneys, he could smell their acrid smoke and hear their endlessly turning looms. The buildings were beginning to jostle Milnsbridge House itself. His heir, his grandson, would quickly abandon it to the encroaching sea of commerce. He would move to a house 20 miles outside the Luddites' county where Radcliffe baronets could live beyond the reach of their loathing.

Symbolically, the wounds local people had tried and failed to inflict on Joseph Radcliffe were suffered by Milnsbridge House itself. By the end of the nineteenth century, the mills, and the streets of workers' cottages they spawned, had spread themselves into an untidy town literally covering the valley's bottom. Their blackened stone walls had pushed themselves in on every side, some to within feet of the simple but elegant Georgian mansion.

Today it is a cruelly time-worn carcass, the old body smothered by the streets of the manufacturing town. Concrete lamp-posts stand at its corners. Its once gentle-angled roof has been removed to expose what is left of its innards to the sky. Its lower floor houses an engineering works. A sliding green door covers the remains of its classical portico. No memorabilia recall the man whose property it once was.

Among the ranks of the middle class, fame was unpredictably reserved for the name of the man who, during the worst of the troubles, had sunk his public profile to the level of invisibility. The Reverend Patrick Brontë and his rapidly expanding family were to stay in the house on the heights above Rawfolds for less than three years. He would move first to the nearby parish of Thornton, and then – with seven carts of furniture and six children – shift a few more miles to Haworth. There, into old age, he would continue to test-fire from his bedroom window one of the pistols he had bought to ward off marauding Luddites. It was from him that his eldest surviving daughter, Charlotte, first heard of the events of the year of trauma, 1812, and put them in her novel *Shirley*. This, perhaps, is the reason why the chief male characters of the novel bear such little similarity to their real-life equivalents.

Hammond Roberson, the uncompromising cleric on whose character Patrick Brontë had tried to model himself, remained for the rest of his life in the Spen valley in the parish he had created. His great ambition, the building of the great church on the knoll across the valley, was complete. It now stood as a triumphant symbol of the ascendancy of the Established Church over the powers of dissent, disbelief, wickedness and violence in the valley around.

Until he died at the age of eighty-four he was a familiar, spare, upright military figure, riding the valley on his grey mare. He was buried in an inconspicuous corner of his own churchyard in a plot overlooked by tall sycamore and beech. From the moment of the consecration of the burial ground he had insisted that every headstone in it should be of the same size, topped by the same undecorated stone chevron.

His own was to be no different from any other: 2 feet 6 inches high in a small plot of grass. It still stands, in pleasing simplicity, identical to its neighbours, on parade with egalitarian soldiers of the Lord.

A mile up the valley William Cartwright's mill continued the business for which it had been built, powered now by steam rather than the water of the beck. The cropping machines which had triggered the events of the year stayed in use for a relatively short time, quickly outmoded by more subtle and more efficient technology.

For a few days after the hangings there had been sporadic acts of violence against some of the workers who had remained faithful to Cartwright.[23] Then the violence had died as quickly as it had grown. The workers returned to their lives and their work, neither of which would ever be as it had been. The small agricultural cloth-making household units of the hillsides above – each so easily identifiable by its tenter of white cloth – would be gone within a few years, replaced by the enlarged factory units of which Cartwright's, now one of dozens, had once been an ambiguous symbol of modernity.

The familial relationships created by the workshops of the small Masters which had endured for so long and given the area its unusual social stability and homogeneity were crumbling. In their place were now the more tenuous and politically uncomfortable bonds between factory owner and industrial worker, the latter still with many years' wait before he and his family would benefit materially from the products of the new technology.

The idyll, such as it was, was over.

But the extent of the change in the life, the livelihood and the class structure of the valley in which he was such an influential member was not William Cartwright's immediate concern. The self-pitying streak which was an unquestionable part of his character dominated his attitude to the consequences of Rawfolds for years to come.

The chief satisfaction he could draw from the affair was that, by the local middle classes at least, he was lionised. The spring of 1813 was warmed by a public testimonial from the inhabitants of the West Riding. It told him how heartily the signatories approved of 'your conduct in defence of your property and person against the unprincipled attack made upon Rawfolds Mill in the dead of night of the 11th April, 1812'.[24] It was accompanied by a subscription.

But it was not enough. In contrast to Joseph Radcliffe, whose deep-felt need was for esteem, Cartwright's was for money. It was this that had motivated him to use the ingenious products of the new technology so productively and so provocatively in the woollen industry. When, at the risk of his life, he defended both his invested capital and his right to employ that technology, then continued to defend them at the behest of government, he expected to be rewarded pound for pound for his trouble and losses. His letters, protesting the paucity of the compensation for his willingness to face near ruination – though what he had been given probably amounted to several thousand pounds – were still reaching the Home Office in 1815, still echoing the moaning cries for help from any quarter he had begun uttering in the days immediately after Rawfolds.

Caught up, like the workers who served him in the turmoil of technological advance, Cartwright eventually emerged richer but apparently no happier. Nor does there appear to have been contentment in his immediate family. One of his offspring was later to commit suicide, shooting himself in the glasshouse built to hymn technological achievement, the Crystal Palace.

William Cartwright died two years before Hammond Roberson. They were buried on the same slope of the same churchyard. After Roberson's body had been placed under its simple 2-foot 6-inch headstone, William Cartwright's memorial was completed. It was enlarged to 6 by 3 feet and surrounded by iron rails cast in the new foundries of the industrial valley.

Notes

Introduction

[1] Asa Briggs has discussed 'Private and Social Themes in *Shirley*' in the *Brontë Society Transactions*, 13, part 68, 1958.
[2] Brontë, C, p. 157.
[3] Thompson, p. 609.

Chapter 1   The Stage

[1] Defoe, p. 491.
[2] *Ibid.*, p. 492.
[3] Landes, p. 45.
[3] Fitzwilliam mss. 47/49; James, p. 285.
[5] Smith, p. 465.
[6] Gaskell, E, p. 1.

Chapter 2   The Gentlemen

[1] Peel (1893), p. 177.
[2] Wesley wrote this in 1777 of his visits to Birstall. See Cradock, pp 76–7.
[3] Nussey, J, *The Yorkshire Archaeological Journal*, 53, 1981, p. 97.
[4] *Ibid.*
[5] Charlotte Brontë to W S Williams, Sept 21st, 1849, quoted in Gaskell, E, p. 327.
[4] Brontë, C, pp. 45–6.
[7] Pobjoy, p. 135.
[8] Letter in possession of J Nussey, Phoebe Roberson to Sarah Morgan, April 25th, 1788.
[9] *Ibid.*

[10] *Ibid.*
[11] *Ibid.*
[12] *Ibid.*
[13] Brontë, C, p. 220.
[14] Cradock, p. 163.
[15] Pobjoy, p. 119.
[16] Sykes and Walker, p. 223; Radcliffe mss., *II*, 416.
[17] Sykes, p. 92; Radcliffe mss., *II*, 416.
[18] Radcliffe mss., *II*, 416.
[19] Samuel Bamford, quoted in Hammond, p. 9.
[20] Radcliffe mss., 39. 52.
[21] Radcliffe mss., F 45/119.
[22] Radcliffe mss., F 45/118, Radcliffe to Pelham, April 5th, 1803.
[23] Radcliffe mss., Radcliffe to Fitzwilliam, May 23rd, 1801.
[24] Radcliffe mss., *I*, 667 /c/23.

Chapter 3   The New Men

[1] Some historians speak of 'the myth of the Industrial Revolution'. Those who use this description of one of the most clearly marked episodes in the course of Western civilisation seem to me to be wilfully hiding their heads in the sands of time. The facts of this Revolution, unlike so many facts in the history of earlier technology and indeed in history in general, are clearly visible. I recommend that anybody tempted by the theory of the 'myth' should consult Tables VI and VII, pps. 734–43, in *A Short History of Technology* by T K Derry and T I Williams. There the extraordinary period of invention and technological application centred on Britain and occupying an unusually short time span is clearly and graphically displayed.
[2] Quoted in Derry and Williams, p. 281.
[3] Gaskell, E, p. 85.
[4] Halifax Ref Library, quoted in Thompson, p. 599.
[5] Engels, p. 205 (written in 1844–5).
[6] James, p. 333 (written in 1857). The Cartwright referred to in this passage is Edmund Cartwright, inventor of the weaving machine.
[7] Sykes (1898), p. 217.

Chapter 4   A Man of the People

[1] Brontë, C, p. 42.
[2] Diary of John Greenwood. In possession of Mrs Mary Preston, Haworth.
[3] Lock and Dixon, p. 18.
[4] Lock and Dixon, p. 242. Mary Burder to Patrick Brontë, August 8th, 1823.
[5] Lock and Dixon, p. 65.
[6] Yates, pp. 41–7.

[7] Gaskell, E, p. xii.
[8] Taylor to Nussey, April 19th, 1856 (quoted in Lock and Dixon, p. 462).
[9] *Leeds Mercury*, August 10th, 1811.
[10] *Leeds Mercury*, December 15th, 1810.
[11] Yates, p. 73. Yates collected this story from Joseph Tolson's grandson.
[12] *Ibid.* p. 76.

Chapter 5   The Workers

[1] Frank Peel, 'Old Cleckheaton', *Cleckheaton Guardian*, January–April, 1884, writing of the 1830s.
[2] Gaskell, E, p. xi.
[3] HO 42. 129.
[4] Sykes and Walker. The tale is developed in *Ben O'Bill's, the Luddite*.
[5] HO 42. 192, evidence of Benjamin Walker.
[6] *Ibid.*, evidence of Martha Mellor.
[7] Committee on the Woollen Trade, 1806, p. 296.
[8] Daumas, *II*, p. 220.
[9] Report from Assistant Hand-loom Weaver's Commissioners, 1840, part (ii), p. 439.
[10] *Ibid.*

Chapter 6   The Power of the Worker

[1] Radcliffe mss., F45/112, Fitzwilliam to Pelham, September 27th, 1802.
[2] Radcliffe mss., F45/112.
[3] HO 42.66, Fitzwilliam to Pelham, October 3rd, 1802.
[4] Radcliffe mss., F45/112, Fitzwilliam to Pelham, September 27th, 1802.
[5] HO 40.66, Cookson to Fitzwilliam, August 21st, 1802.
[6] Radcliffe mss., F45/112, Fitzwilliam to Pelham, September 27th, 1802.
[7] Committee on the Woollen Trade, 1806, p. 239.
[8] Committee on the Woollen Trade, 1806, p. 232.
[9] Accounts and Papers, 1812, x.25, quoted by Darvall, p. 19.
[10] Fitzwilliam mss., F47/49. *A Statement in support of the Petitions from the Merchants and Manufacturers in the Woollen Trade of the West Riding of Yorkshire*, April 13th, 1812.

Chapter 7   A Question of Technology

[1] Peel (1888), p. 50.
[2] Daumas, *III*, p. 617.

Chapter 8   1811

[1] From the diary of Joseph Rogerson, September 16th, 1811.
[2] Farr, p. 343.
[3] Farr, p. 349.
[4] Darvall, p. 15.
[5] Smith, p. 173.
[6] Farr, p. 349.
[7] Felkin, p. 236.
[8] Felkin, p.437, quoting Blackner's *History of Nottingham*.
[9] HO 42.120, Conant and Baker to Ryder, February 9th, 1812.
[10] *Ibid.*, *Nottingham Journal*, November 16th, 1811; Darvall, p. 68.
[11] Conant and Baker, *loc.cit.*
[12] *Ibid.*
[13] Ryder, speaking in House of Commons, February 14th, 1812, Parl. Debates, *xxi*, 1812, p. 808.
[14] *The Times*, February 1st, 1812.
[15] *Leeds Mercury*, December 26th, 1811.
[16] Byron to Lord Holland, February 5th, 1812, quoted in Marchand (1973), p. 165.
[17] *Nottingham Journal*, December 28th, 1811.

Chapter 9   Decision

[1] Brontë, C, p. 82.
[2] Booth, p. 18.
[3] Brontë, P, *Cottage Poems* (Holden, Halifax, 1811).
[4] Sykes (1906), p. 301.
[5] Committee on the Woollen Trade, 1806, p. 240.
[6] *Ibid.*, pp. 289, 297.
[7] Peel (1888); Sykes and Walker.
[8] HO 42.126, Maitland to Beckett, August 29th, 1812.
[9] For example, see *Leeds Mercury*, November 23rd, 1811.

Chapter 10   Trouble

[1] HO 42.119, Bulkeley to Ryder, January 1st, 1812.
[2] *Ibid.*
[3] HO 40.120.
[4] *Ibid.*, Lloyd to Bulkeley, February 11th, 1812.
[5] HO 40.1.
[6] *Ibid.*, Fletcher to Beckett, April 11th, 1812.
[7] *Leeds Mercury*, February 22nd, 1812.
[8] Peel (1888), p. 202.
[9] *Leeds Intelligencer*, January 20th, 1812.
[10] Raynes, p. 11.

[11] Fitzwilliam mss., F46/71.

[12] Pellew, *III*, p. 80.

[13] Felkin, p. 231.

[14] *Nottingham Review*, December 20th, 1811.

[15] *Leeds Mercury*, February 29th, 1812.

[16] Radcliffe mss., Beckett to Radcliffe, February 26th, 1812.

[17] *Ibid.*

[18] HO 42.120.

[19] HO 40.1/7, deposition of William Hinchcliffe, February 28th, 1812.

[20] *Ibid.*, deposition of John Sykes, March 6th, 1812.

[21] *Ibid.*, deposition of Samuel Swallow, March 6th, 1812.

[22] Lock and Dixon, p. 102.

[23] Gaskell, p. xii.

[24] HO 42.121, petition to Radcliffe signed by Roberson and others, February 29th, 1812.

[25] Radcliffe mss., 126/25, Radcliffe to Beckett, March 15th, 1812.

[26] Radcliffe mss., 126/27.

Chapter 11   The Power of the Law

[1] The Imperial Calendar, quoted in Ziegler, p. 315.

[2] Cmd. 309 (1806), Report of Royal Commission, quoted in Ziegler, p. 316.

[3] *The Times*, July 1st, 1812.

[4] HO 79.1, HO to Conant and Baker, January 29th, 1812.

[5] Byron to Hodgson, March 5th, 1812, quoted in Marchand (1957), p. 320.

[6] Parl. Debates, *xxi*, 1812, pp. 966–74.

Chapter 12   Preparing for the Worst

[1] Radcliffe mss., 126/19, Roberson to Radcliffe, March 9th, 1812.

[2] HO 42.120. Lloyd to Bulkeley, February 11th, 1812.

[3] *Ibid.*

[4] *Ibid.*

[5] HO 42.119, Fletcher to Beckett, January 21st, 1812.

[6] Radcliffe mss., 126/10, Radcliffe to Beckett, March 4th, 1812.

[7] Radcliffe mss, 126/8, Radcliffe to Beckett, March 3rd, 1812.

[8] Radcliffe mss., 126/22, Grey to Radcliffe, March 13th, 1812.

[9] Radcliffe mss., 126/13, Beckett to Radcliffe, March 6th, 1812.

[10] Radcliffe mss., 126/24, Beckett to Radcliffe, March 4th, 1812.

[11] HO 42.121, Grey to Ryder, March 8th, 1812.

[12] Radcliffe mss., 126/26.

[13] *Nottingham Journal*, February 1st, 1812.

[14] Longford, *I*, p. 329.

Chapter 13 The Enemy Within

1. Fitzwilliam mss., Walker to Fitzwilliam, July 9th, 1812.
2. Raynes, p. 20.
3. Raynes, p. 11.
4. Fitzwilliam mss., pp. 46–73.
5. Howell, p. 1077.
6. Peel (1888), p. 14.
7. Peel (1888).
8. Sykes (1906).
9. Peel (1888), p. 54.
10. HO 42.121, Grey to Ryder, March 25th, 1812.
11. Fitzwilliam mss., F45 (a)–(e).
12. Howell, p. 1160.
13. HO 40.2/3, Cartwright to Acland, September 5th, 1812.
14. Howell, p. 1161.
15. Peel (1888), p. 54.
16. Ferret, p. 22.

Chapter 14 Lines of Communication

1. HO 42.121, Grey to Ryder, March 16th, 1812.
2. *Ibid.*, Grey to Ryder, March 25th, 1812.
3. *Cowdroy's Manchester Gazette*, April 18th, 1812.
4. HO 40.1/1, Fletcher to Beckett, April 6th, 1812.
5. *Manchester Exchange Herald*, April 14th, 1812.
6. HO 43.21.
7. HO 42.21, Beckett to Clay, April 9th and 16th, 1812.
8. Liddell, p. 96.
9. Oman, V, p. 255. Wellington to Liverpool, April 7th, 1812.
10. HO 43.20, Beckett to Radcliffe, March 14th and 19th, 1812.
11. HO 40.2/2.
12. Radcliffe mss., 126/19, Roberson to Radcliffe, March 9th, 1812.
13. HO 42.122, Brown to Ryder, April 10th, 1812.
14. *Leeds Mercury*, April 4th, 1812.
15. See Baines and Howell's accounts of the Special Commission, York, 1813.
16. HO 40.2/3, Cartwright to Acland, September 5th, 1812.
17. HO 42.122, Cartwright to Raynes, April 23rd, 1812.

Chapter 15 Rawfolds

1. Details of the Rawfolds attack are taken from the reports of the Special Commission, York, 1813 by Baines, Hansard, Howells and Rede, none of which differ in material fact, and from HO 42.122, Cartwright to Raynes, April 23rd, 1812; HO 42.128, deposition of

Jonathan Dean, October 26th, 1812; HO 42.129, deposition of William Hall, October 22nd, 1812; deposition of Benjamin Walker, October 22nd, 1812; deposition of Joseph Sowden, October 24th, 1812; and from Peel (1888).

2 Peel (1888) tells the story that one athletic young Luddite named Rayner slipped past Hall and Rigg and, in 18 minutes, ran the 4 miles back to his home village. He arrived outside the village church in time to stand alongside the sexton listening to the clock strike thirteen – the clock having been improperly repaired that day. Subsequently the boy used the sexton as witness in an alibi to Joseph Radcliffe to prove he could not have been at the Dumb Steeple assembly.

It makes a good tale. However, Rayner's name appears in none of the letters or depositions written by Radcliffe, suggesting that this, like a few other stories told to Peel, was invented by local enthusiasts who collected and embroidered Luddite alibis.

3 Baines (1813), p. 40.
4 Brontë, C, p. 359.
5 Peel (1888), p. 104.
6 Lock and Dixon, p. 111.
7 *Leeds Mercury*, April 18th, 1812.

Chapter 16   The Tide of Sympathy

1 HO 40.2/3, Cartwright to Acland, September 5th, 1812.
2 HO 42.122, Campbell to Grey, April 16th, 1812.
3 *York Courant*, April 20th, 1812.
4 *Leeds Intelligencer*, April 27th, 1812.
5 HO 42.122, Fenton to Grey, April 16th, 1812.
6 Fitzwilliam mss., Fenton to Fitzwilliam, April 16th, 1812.
7 *York Courant*, April 27th, 1812.
8 HO 42.20, Beckett to Villars, April 13th and 17th, 1812.
9 HO 40.1/2, Lloyd to Ryder, April 13th, 1812. HO 40.1/1, Lloyd to Ryder, April 16th and 18th, 1812.
10 HO 40.1/2, Lloyd to Ryder, April 16th and 18th, 1812.
11 HO 40.1/1, Prescot to Ryder, April 27th, 1812; Broughton to Ryder, April 27th, 1812.
12 HO 42.122, Clay to Ryder, April 14th, 1812.
13 *Cowdroy's Manchester Gazette*, April 25th, 1812.
14 *Ibid.*, April 25th, 1812.
15 HO 42.122, Clay to Ryder, April 20th, 1812; Radcliffe mss., Fox to Radcliffe, April 21st, 1812.
16 HO 42.122, Hay to Ryder, April 21st, 1812.
17 HO 40.1/4, Fletcher to Beckett, April 22nd, 1812.
18 HO 40.1/2, Garside to Ryder, April 21st, 1812.
19 HO 40.1/4, Fletcher to Beckett, April 11th, 1812.
20 HO 40.1/2, Broughton to Ryder, April 27th, 1812.

[21] HO 43.20, Beckett to Wright, April 21st, 1812; HO 40.1/4, Chippendall to Anon., April 23rd, 1812; HO 40.1/1, Fletcher to Beckett, April 23rd, 1812.

[22] HO 42.122, Grey to Ryder, April 20th, 1812.

[23] HO 43.20, Beckett to Hordern, April 23rd, 1812.

[24] HO 40.1/1, Chippendall to Fletcher, April 23rd, 1812.

Chapter 17   Shots in the Dark

[1] *Cowdroy's Manchester Gazette*, April 25th, 1812; Farr, p. 344.

[2] *Leeds Mercury*, April 25th, 1812. *York Courant*, April 27th, 1812.

[3] Peel, (1888), p. 133.

[4] HO 40.1/7, deposition of George Whitbread, April 15th, 1812. Radcliffe mss., Radcliffe to Beckett, April 19th, 1812.

[5] HO 40.1/1, deposition of Isaac Rayner.

[6] HO 40.1/1, HO 40.1/7, Manufacturers' petition to the Home Secretary, April 29th, 1812; HO 42.123, Campbell to Grey, May 1st, 1812.

Chapter 18   Awful Times

[1] HO 42.129, examination of Benjamin Walker by Joseph Radcliffe, October 22nd, 1812.

[2] Baines (1813), p. 12.

[3] Radcliffe mss., 126/38, letter dated April 27th, 1812.

[4] Accounts of the murder of Horsfall are taken from the York Special Commission transcripts.

[5] Baines (1813), p. 15.

[6] HO 42.122, deposition of Mason Stanhope Kenny, April 30th, 1812; Baines (1813), p. 11.

[7] Baines (1813), p. 16.

[8] HO 40.1/1, HO 40.1/7, Manufacturers' petition to the Home Secretary, April 29th, 1812.

[9] Radcliffe mss., 126/38, letter dated April 27th, 1812.

[10] *Leeds Mercury*, April 25th, 1812.

[11] HO 40.1/7.

Chapter 19   Radical Reformer

[1] Cartwright to Mrs Cartwright, February 1803, quoted in Cartwright, p. 303.

[2] See Burdett, p. 38; *The Times*, May 6th, 1807.

[3] See Burdett, p. 42.

[4] A full description of the events is given in Burdett, p. 108.

[5] HO 42.123, Higgins to Beckett, May 2nd, 1812.

[6] HO 40.1/2, Lloyd to Ryder, May 2nd, 1812.

[7] *Cowdroy's Manchester Gazette*, May 2nd, 1812.

Chapter 20   Maitland

[1] Anglesey, p. 56.
[2] Napier, W, *I*, p. 285.
[3] See Napier, C, p. 152.
[4] Napier, C, pp. 151–2.
[5] *Ibid*.
[6] *Loc. cit.*, p. 150.
[7] Napier, W, *I*, p. 285.
[8] Raynes, p. 1.
[9] HO 40.1/1, Maitland memorandum, May 9th, 1812.
[10] Darvall, p. 1.

Chapter 21   In Manchester

[1] *Manchester Exchange Herald*, June 2nd, 1812.
[2] HO 42.123, Maitland to Ryder, May 4th, 1812.
[3] HO 40.1/1, from Maitland's orders to his COs, May 1812.
[4] HO 42.123, Maitland to Ryder, May 4th, 1812.
[5] *Ibid.*, May 6th, 1812.
[6] Parkinson, p. 13.

Chapter 22   Death of a Minister

[1] HO 42.123, deposition of W G Bowling, May 13th, 1812.
[2] Thornbury, p. 176.
[3] From Perceval's peroration of his speech at the trial of Peltier, the French editor in London, for his libel against Napoleon (1802), quoted in Thornbury, p. 175.
[4] *The Times*, May 12th, 1812; *The Courier*, May 13th, 1812; Thornbury, *loc. cit.*
[5] Aspinall, p. 1.
[6] HO 42.123, Stockdale to Castlereagh, May 12th, 1812.
[7] HO 43.20, Goulbourn to O.C., S. Hants Militia, May 13th, 1812.
[8] HO 42.131, Town Clerk of Nottingham to HO, May 14th, 1812.
[9] HO 40.1/1, Fletcher to Hobhouse, May 14th, 1812.
[10] HO 40.2/1, Nelthorpe to Acland, May 19th, 1812.
[11] HO 40.1/1, Stevenson to Dyott, June 16th, 1812.
[12] HO 42.123, Blacow to McMahon, May 27th, 1812.
[13] HO 40.1/4.
[14] HO 42.121, Bellingham's petition to the House of Commons.
[15] HO 42.122, Bellingham to Ryder, April 13th, 1812.
[16] HO 42.123, Butterworth to Ryder, May 18th, 1812.
[17] *The Courier*, May 18th, 1812; *Manchester Exchange Herald, Cowdroy's Manchester Gazette*, May 23rd, 1812.
[18] Marchand (1973), p. 176.

Chapter 23   Officer in Command

[1] HO 40.1/1, Hay to Beckett, May 16th, 1812.
[2] *Ibid.*, Maitland to Ryder, May 9th, 1812.
[3] *Ibid.*
[4] HO 42.123, Grey to unidentified recipient, Wakefield, May 13th, 1812.
[5] Radcliffe mss., 126/60 Radcliffe to Maitland, May 8th, 1812.
[6] Radcliffe mss., 126/91.
[7] Radcliffe mss., 126/49, Radcliffe to Gordon, May 2nd, 1812. HO 40.1/7, Radcliffe to Ryder, May 5th, 1812.
[8] Radcliffe mss., 126/45, Allison to Radcliffe, May 1st, 1812.
[9] HO 42.132, Campbell to Grey, May 9th, 1812.
[10] HO 40.1/1, Maitland to Ryder, May 15th, 1812; HO 42.123, Fitzwilliam to Ryder, May 16th, 1812; *ibid.*, Maitland to Ryder, May 16th, 1812.
[11] Fitzwilliam mss., F45/142, Fitzwilliam to Ryder, May 16th, 1812.
[12] HO 42.123, Perceval to Ryder, May 6th, 1812.
[13] HO 42.123, statement of Thomas Whittaker.
[14] *Manchester Mercury*, June 6th, 1812. *Cowdroy's Manchester Exchange Herald*, June 6th, 1812. Hammond, p. 294.
[15] *Leeds Mercury*, June 6th, 1812.
[16] HO 42.123, Hobhouse to Beckett, May 30th, 1812.
[17] *Ibid.*
[18] HO 42.123, Hobhouse to Beckett, May 30th, 1812.

Chapter 24   'The Doctor'

[1] *The Times*, May 22nd, 1812.
[2] Pellew, *III*, p. 78.
[3] *Memoirs of Thomas Moore* (ed. Lord John Russell), Lady Donegal to Moore, May 1812, quoted in Ziegler, p. 306.
[4] Brougham, *II*, p. 15.
[5] HO 40.1/1, Broughton to Sidmouth, June 17th, 1812.
[6] *Ibid.*, Lloyd to Beckett, May 21st, 1812.
[7] *Ibid.*, Chaplain of Chester Gaol to Keeper of Gaol, June 22nd, 1812.
[8] HO 40.1/4, letter dated June 16th, 1812.
[9] HO 40.1/1, report dated June 17th, 1812.
[10] HO 42.123, undated notice.
[11] HO 40.1/1, Maitland to Sidmouth, June 19th, 1812.
[12] HO 42.124, Maitland to Sidmouth, June 30th, 1812.
[13] HO 40.1/1, Maitland to Sidmouth, June 19th, 1812.
[14] HO 42.124, Maitland to Sidmouth, June 19th, 1812.
[15] HO 40.1/1, Maitland to Sidmouth, June 22nd, 1812.

[16] *Ibid.*, Maitland to Sidmouth, June 22nd, 1812.

[17] *Ibid.*, Maitland to Sidmouth, June 16th, 1812. HO 43.20, Beckett to Maitland, June 29th, 1812.

[18] HO 40.1/5, Maitland to Sidmouth, June 19th, 1812.

[19] HO 42.124, Maitland to Sidmouth, June 17th, 1812.

[20] *Ibid.*, Sidmouth to Maitland, June 20th, 1812.

[21] *Ibid.*, Maitland to Sidmouth, June 17th, 1812.

[22] HO 40.2/1, Nelthorpe to Acland, June 19th, 1812.

[23] HO 40.1/1, Maitland to Sidmouth, June 20th, 1812.

[24] Heape, p. 31.

[25] Jeffery, *III*, p. 4.

[26] *Manchester Exchange Herald, Manchester Mercury*, June 2nd, 1812.

Chapter 25 Raynes

[1] *The Times*, May 27th, 1812.

[2] Raynes gives a detailed account of his activities in his privately published *An Appeal to the Public – containing an account of the services rendered during the disturbances in the North of England in the year 1812.*

[3] HO 40.2/1, Maitland to Acland, June 22nd, 1812.

[4] Raynes, p. 31.

[5] HO 40.2/1, Maitland to Nelthorpe, June 24th, 1812. Not all Maitland's instructions to his regimental commanding officers were clear. Many were not only scribbled in haste and difficult to decipher, they were ambiguous. Given some of the surviving examples of Maitland's handwritten communications, it is not difficult to see how, forty years later, a British general would send a light cavalry brigade charging to its destruction down the wrong Balaclava valley.

[6] Raynes, p. 36.

[7] Raynes, p. 10.

[8] HO 40.2/2, Raynes to Acland, July 5th, 1812.

Chapter 26 Goodbye, Grey

[1] HO 40.1/1, Maitland to Sidmouth, June 16th, 1812; HO 42.124, Sidmouth to Maitland, June 20th, 1812.

[2] HO 42.125, depositions of Clifton householders to Sir George Armytage, July 15th, 1812.

[3] HO 40.1/1, John Cartwright to Wood, June 11th, 1812.

[4] *Ibid.*, Wood to Fitzwilliam, June 11th, 1812.

[5] Wentworth Woodhouse mss., F46/26, Grey to Wood, June 20th, 1812.

[6] HO 40.1/1, Wood to Fitzwilliam, June 7th, 1812.

[7] Pellew, III, p. 88, Lany to Rolle, June 19th, 1812.

[8] Parl. Debates, *xxiii*, 1812, p. 951 *et seq.* and p. 1028 *et seq.*
[9] *The Times*, July 10th, 1812.
[10] HO 40.2/1, Maitland to Acland, July 1st, 1812.
[11] HO 42.125, Maitland to Sidmouth, July 2nd, 1812; HO 42.123, Maitland to Beckett, July 4th, 1812.
[12] HO 42.125, Hay to Beckett, July 7th, 1813.
[13] *Ibid.*, Lloyd to Beckett, July 8th, 1812.
[14] *Ibid.*, testimony of Joseph Barrowclough, July 7th, 1812.
[15] *Ibid.*, Maitland to Beckett, July 11th, 1812.
[16] *Ibid.*, Maitland to Beckett, July 20th, 1812.
[17] *Ibid.*, Maitland to Beckett, July 20th, 1812.
[18] Howell, p. 1078 *et seq.*
[19] Pellew, *III*, p. 84, Seale to Sidmouth, June 30th, 1812.
[20] HO 42.125, Seale to Sidmouth, July 11th, 1812.
[21] *Ibid.*, Maitland to Seale, July 17th, 1812.
[22] *Ibid.*, unsigned letter, July 15th, 1812.
[23] Fitzwilliam mss., F46/77.
[24] HO 42.125, Maitland to Seale, July 17th, 1812.
[25] HO 42.125, Maitland to Sidmouth, July 18th, 1812.
[26] *Ibid.*, Maitland to Sidmouth, July 19th, 1812.

Chapter 27   On Oath

[1] *Cowdroy's Manchester Gazette*, August 1st, 1812.
[2] Fitzwilliam mss., F46/122, deposition of Thomas Broughton, August 26th, 1812.
[3] HO 40.2/1, Raynes to Acland, August 10th, 1812.
[4] Raynes, p. 56.
[5] Raynes, p. 58.
[6] HO 42.126, Maitland to Beckett, August 3rd, 1812.
[7] HO 42.125, Maitland to Sidmouth, July 14th, 1812.
[8] HO 42.126, Maitland to Beckett, August 15th, 1812.
[9] Raynes, p. 58.
[10] HO 40.2/1, Prescott to Beckett, August 29th, 1812.
[11] HO 42.126, Maitland to Beckett, August 29th, 1812.
[12] *Ibid.*, Lloyd to Beckett, August 24th, 1812.
[13] *Ibid.*, Lloyd to Beckett, August 27th, 1812.
[14] *Ibid.*, Maitland to Beckett, August 27th, 1812.
[15] *Ibid.*, Maitland to Beckett, August 19th, 1812; *ibid.*, Montgomery to Sidmouth, August 21st, 1812; *ibid.*, Lawson's deposition to Beckett, August 22nd, 1812; *ibid.*, Lawson's interview with Cannon, August 25th, 1812.
[16] *Ibid.*, Maitland to Beckett, August 29th, 1812.
[17] *Ibid.*, Maitland to Beckett, August 27th, 1812.
[18] *Ibid.*, Maitland to Sidmouth, August 22nd, 1812.
[19] HO 42.125, Maitland to Sidmouth, July 24th, 1812.

[20] Raynes, p. 58, Acland to Raynes, August 23rd, 1812.
[21] HO 40.2/3, Maitland to Acland, August 28th, 1812.
[22] Raynes, p. 68.
[23] HO 42.126, Maitland to Beckett, August 31st, 1812.
[24] HO 40.2/3, Maitland to Acland, August 25th, 1812.
[25] HO 42.126, Maitland to Sidmouth, August 24th, 1812.

Chapter 28   An Anonymous Letter

[1] *The Times*, September 1st, 1812.
[2] HO 40.2/3, Cooper to Acland, September 11th, 1812.
[3] Raynes, p. 93.
[4] HO 42.127, Radcliffe to Sidmouth, September 2nd, 1812.
[5] HO 42.126, Radcliffe to Sidmouth, August 3rd, 1812.
[6] HO 42.126, Radcliffe to Sidmouth, August 16th, 1812.
[7] HO 40.2/7, Acland to Maitland, August 25th, 1812.
[8] HO 42.126, deposition of David Hepworth, August 22nd, 1812.
[9] HO 42.127, Maitland to Beckett, September 3rd, 1812.
[10] *Ibid.*, Maitland to Beckett, September 8th, 1812.
[11] HO 40.2/3, Wollaston to Acland, September 4th, 1812.
[12] *Ibid.*, Cartwright to Acland, September 5th, 1812.
[13] HO 40.3/1, Roberson to Acland, September 7th, 1812.
[14] HO 40.2/3, Cooper to Acland, September 17th, 1812.
[15] HO 40.2/7, Acland to Maitland, September 15th, 1812.
[16] Raynes, p. 93.
[17] HO 40.2/3, Raynes to Acland, September 12th, 1812.
[18] *Ibid.*, Raynes to Acland, September 11th, 1812.
[19] *Ibid.*, Raynes to Acland, September 12th, 1812.
[20] HO 42.127, Lloyd to Beckett, September 14th, 1812.
[21] HO 40.2/3, Raynes to Acland, September 12th, 1812. Raynes calls the clergyman involved 'Robinson' (also the name of one of the informers) but he clearly means Roberson.
[22] HO 40.2/6.
[23] HO 40.2/5.
[24] Howell, p. 1035.
[25] HO 42.126, Lloyd to Beckett, August 29th, 1812.
[26] Fitzwilliam mss., F46/53, Maitland to Fitzwilliam, September 6th, 1812.
[27] HO 42.127, Lloyd to Beckett, September 14th, 1812.
[28] *Ibid.*, Lloyd to Beckett, September 14th, 1812.
[29] *Ibid.*, Lloyd to Beckett, September 14th, 1812.
[30] HO 40.2/3, Maitland to Acland, September 13th, 1812.
[31] *Ibid.*
[32] HO 42.127, Maitland to Beckett, September 13th, 1812.
[33] *Ibid.*, Allison to Sidmouth, September 14th, 1812.
[34] *Ibid.*, Lloyd to Beckett, September 17th, 1812.

35 HO 42.2/2, unsigned and undated letter.
36 HO 42.128, Lloyd to Beckett, October 18th, 1812.
37 HO 40.2/8, Acland to Maitland, October 11th, 1812.
38 Peel (1888), p. 189.

Chapter 29   King's Evidence

1 HO 42.129, examinations of Joseph Oldham and John Kinder by Joseph Radcliffe, October 10th, 1812; Howell, p. 998 *et seq.*; Baines (1813), p. 5 *et seq.*
2 HO 42.129, examinations of Thomas Durrance, Martha and Joseph Mellor by Joseph Radcliffe, October 11th, 1812.
3 *Ibid.*, examination of James Varley.
4 HO 40.2/8, Acland to Maitland, October 11th, 1812.
5 HO 42.128, Lloyd to Addington, October 20th, 1812.
6 Peel (1888), has it that Walker, after hearing of the offer of a reward of £2,000 for information leading to the murderers' arrest, sent his mother to Joseph Radcliffe. The Home Office papers show this not to be the case. The well-being of her son, and not money was her motive for secretly seeking advice, and it was he, not she, who incriminated himself.
7 HO 42.129, examination of William Thorpe by Joseph Radcliffe, October 19th, 1812.
8 HO 40.2/8, Acland to Maitland, October 18th, 21st and 22nd, 1812.
9 HO 42.129, Allison to Beckett, October 29th, 1812.
10 *Ibid.*, examination of William Hall by Joseph Radcliffe, October 22nd, 1812.
11 HO 42.128, Lloyd to Under-Secretary of State, October 24th, 1812.
12 HO 42.129, examination of Joseph Sowden by Joseph Radcliffe, October 24th, 1812.
13 HO 40.2/8, Acland to Maitland, October 22nd, 1812.
14 HO 42.128, Lloyd to Under-Secretary of State, October 24th, 1812.
15 Radcliffe mss., 126/91, Addington to Radcliffe, October 21st, 1812.
16 Radcliffe mss., 126/93, Radcliffe to Fitzwilliam, October 27th, 1812..

Chapter 30   The Turning Tide

1 HO 42.28.
2 Raynes, p. 94.
3 HO 40.2/2, Nadin to Acland, October 11th, 1812.
4 HO 40.2/7, Acland to Maitland, October 1st, 1812.
5 HO 40.2/3, Raynes to Acland, October 7th, 1812.
6 Fitzwilliam mss., 46/97, statement of Benjamin Walker, November 8th, 1812.
7 Radcliffe,mss., 126/96, October 30th, 1812.

8 Radcliffe mss., 126/92, October 26th, 1812.
9 HO 43.21, Beckett to Radcliffe, October 20th, 1812.
10 HO 42.129, Radcliffe to Sidmouth, November 11th, 1812.
11 *Ibid.*, Lloyd to Beckett, November 4th, 1812.
12 HO 40.2/3, Maitland to Acland, October 9th, 1812.
13 Fitzwilliam mss., 46/94, Maitland to Fitzwilliam, November 5th, 1812.
14 *Ibid.*, Maitland to Fitzwilliam, November 5th, 1812.
15 HO 42.129, Maitland to Fitzwilliam, November 3rd, 1812.
16 *Ibid.*, Maitland to Sidmouth, November 4th, 1812.
17 Quoted in Pellew, *III*, p. 90, Sidmouth to Babington, November 13th, 1812.
18 HO 40.2/3, Allison to Acland, October 31st, 1812.
19 Radcliffe mss., Hobhouse to Radcliffe, February 6th, 1813.
20 HO 42.123, Mellor to Eddie, November, 30th, 1812.
21 Burdett, appendix, speech to the electors of Westminster, October 8th, 1812.
22 Fitzwilliam mss., 46/94, Maitland to Fitzwilliam, November 4th, 1812.
23 HO 40.2/3, Raynes to Acland, November 7th, 1812.

Chapter 31   Retreat and Retrenchment

1 Cradock, p. 199.
2 Peel (1893), p. 396.
3 HO 42.130, Cartwright to Sidmouth, December 2nd, 1812.
4 HO 40.2/8, Acland to Beckett, December 19th, 1812.
5 Fitzwilliam mss., 46/107, Allison to Fitzwilliam, December 9th, 1812.
6 Sykes, p. 288, Fitzwilliam to Radcliffe, December 15th, 1812.
7 Fitzwilliam mss., 46/109, Radcliffe to Fitzwilliam, December 17th, 1812.
8 HO 42.130, Maitland to Beckett, December 23rd, 1812.
9 Radcliffe mss., 126/109, Sidmouth to Fitzwilliam, December 25th, 1812.
10 Radcliffe mss., 126/110, Fitzwilliam to Radcliffe, December 27th, 1812.
11 HO 42.130, Maitland to Beckett, December 21st, 1812.
12 HO 42.125, Lloyd to Beckett, July 30th, 1812. HO 42.128, Radcliffe to Sidmouth, October 1st, 1812.
13 HO 40.2/4, Hobhouse to Acland, December 24th, 1812.
14 HO 40.2/8, Acland to Maitland, December 26th, 1812.

Chapter 32   Defence

1 HO 40.2/3, Raynes to Acland, January 4th, 1813.
2 HO 42.129, Fitzwilliam to Sidmouth, November 9th, 1812.

³ HO 42.123, Hobhouse to Beckett, January 5th, 1813.
⁴ *Ibid.*, January 10th, 1813.
⁵ Pellew, *III*, p. 91.
⁶ Brougham, *III*, p. 40; *cf.* Sykes (1898), p. 362.
⁷ This account of the trial is based on the reports of Baines (1813) and Howell (1823).
⁸ HO 42.123, Hobhouse to Beckett, January 4th, 1813.
⁹ Baines, p. 2; Howell, p. 966.
¹⁰ HO 42.132, Hobhouse to Beckett, January 4th, 1813.

Chapter 33   Trial

¹ Baines, p. 52; Howell, p. 971.
² Rede, p. 462.
³ HO 42.132, Hobhouse to Beckett, January 5th, 1813.
⁴ Baines, p. 5; Howell, p. 997.
⁵ Mr Justice Le Blanc, nevertheless, made errors. It is interesting that Howell reports that Le Blanc, in his summing up, noted that the last witness called was a William Hirst. Baines, however, who published his part-verbatim report on the day following the trial, gives the evidence of an additional witness, Joseph Rushworth, not mentioned by Le Blanc; *cf.* Howell, p. 1031; Baines, p. 22.
⁶ HO 42.132, Hobhouse to Beckett, dated January 6th, 1812 (i.e. 1813).

Chapter 34   Retribution

¹ Baines, p. 27; Howell, p. 1035.
² *Leeds Intelligencer*, January 18th, 1813, letter from G Brown to the editor, dated January 16th, 1813.
³ HO 42.132, Hobhouse to Beckett, January 9th, 1813.
⁴ Baines, p. 49; Howell, p. 1064.
⁵ Baines, p. 50; Howell, p. 1074.
⁶ HO 42.132, Hobhouse to Beckett, January 9th, 1813.
⁷ HO 42.2/3, Hey to Ackworth, February 20th, 1813.

Chapter 35   This Deluded County

¹ Baines, p. 33; Howell, p. 1092.
² Howell, p. 1124.
³ Baines, p. 58; Howell, p. 1137.
⁴ Baines, p. 55; Howell, p. 1147.
⁵ HO 42.132, Hobhouse to Beckett, January 12th, 1813.
⁶ Baines, p. 61; Howell, p. 1159.
⁷ Howell, p. 1159.
⁸ Howell, p. 1161.
⁹ Baines, p. 62; Howell, p. 1161.

[10] Baines, p. 64; Howell, p. 1163.
[11] HO 42.132, Hobhouse to Beckett, January 13th, 1813.

Chapter 36 The Last of the Luddites

[1] HO 42.123, Cartwright to Blackburn, January 12th, 1813.
[2] *Ibid.*, Hobhouse to Beckett, January 13th, 1813.
[3] Sterling, vol. *II*, p. 131. The words are wrongly supposed to have been spoken by Baron Wood, who was not at York, rather than by Baron Thomson.
[4] *York Herald*, January 23rd, 1813.
[5] *Leeds Mercury*, January 23rd, 1813.
[6] *York Herald*, January 23rd, 1813.
[7] HO 40.2/3, Lacy to Acland, January 21st, 1813.
[8] *Ibid.*, Cartwright to Acland, January 30th, 1813.
[9] HO 42.132, Hobhouse to Beckett, January 13th, 1813.
[10] HO 40.2/3, Allison to Acland, January 16th, 1813.
[11] *Ibid.*, Maitland to Acland, January 13th, 1813.
[12] Raynes, p. 124; Acland to Raynes, January 16th, 1813.
[13] HO 40.2/3, Maitland to Acland, January 15th, 1813.
[14] *Ibid.*, Cooper to Acland, January 16th, 1813.
[15] *Ibid.*, Raynes to Acland, January 19th, 1813.
[16] *Ibid.*, Lacy to Acland, January 18th, 1813.
[17] *Ibid.*, Bruce to Acland, January 17th, 1813.
[18] Raynes, p. 124.
[19] HO 40.2/3, Maitland to Acland, January 13th, 1813.

Chapter 37 The Law of Technology

[1] See, for example, Kipling and Hall, p. 47.
[2] Darvall, p. xvi, quoting MacIntyre.
[3] HO 42.132, Maitland to Sidmouth, February 18th, 1813.
[4] HO 40.2/3, da Chesterton to Acland, January 9th, 1813.
[5] Annual Register, *lv*, 1813, p. 98.
[6] HO 42.132, Hobhouse to Beckett, January 11th, 1813.
[7] Howells, p. 1168.
[8] Parl. Debates, *xxxv*, 1817, p. 322.
[9] HO 79.3, Sidmouth to Lascelles, October 12th, 1812.
[10] Gaskell, P, p. 6.
[11] *Ibid.*, pp. 161–2.
[12] Quoted in Lipson, p. 206.
[13] Engels, p. 74.
[14] Darvall, p. x.
[15] See *Leeds Mercury*, January 2nd, 1813.

[16] Thompson, p. 601.
[17] Daniel Boorstin in *The Republic of Technology* has written eloquently on the subject.
[18] Quoted in Felkin, p. 51.
[19] Derry and Williams, p. 106; Daumas, II, p. 234.
[20] *Science*, *223*, 1984, p. 1368; *ibid*., *229*, 1985, p. 601.
[21] Daumas, *II*, p. 215.
[22] By Gordon Moore, Fairchild's director of research.

Chapter 38   Ever After

[1] HO 40.2/3, Mitchell to Cooper, February 2nd, 1813.
[2] HO 42.153, October 18th, 1816.
[3] Sykes (1898), p. 287.
[4] Radcliffe mss., F46/84, examination of Benjamin Batty by Joseph Radcliffe, January 22nd, 1813.
[5] *Ibid*., examination of Major Thomas Hankin by Joseph Radcliffe, January 22nd, 1813.
[6] Cartwright, p. 47.
[7] For example, see letters in HO 42.125.
[8] From a speech in support of the Corn Laws, February 22nd, 1842, quoted in Patterson, *III*, p. 655.
[9] Patterson, *III*, p. 667.
[10] Napier, C, p. ix.
[11] HO 40.2/9, Acland to Maitland, March 7th, 1813.
[12] J Nussey, personal communication. The Christening is recorded in the Birstall register of baptisms, January 24th, 1813.
[13] Raynes, p. 138.
[14] *Ibid*., p. 141.
[15] *Ibid*., p. 174.
[16] *Ibid*., p. 181.
[17] Pellew, III, pp. 91–2.
[18] Brougham, II; Hawes, p. 175.
[19] Radcliffe mss., 126/121, Beckett to Radcliffe, January 26th, 1813.
[20] Radcliffe mss., 126/124, Radcliffe to Lascelles, January 28th, 1813.
[21] HO 40.2/3, Lacy to Acland, January 17th, 1813; *ibid*., Coulthurst to Raynes, February 27th, 1813; Radcliffe mss., Radcliffe to Maitland, February 1813.
[22] HO 40.2/9, Acland to Maitland, February 23rd, 1813; *ibid*., March 7th, 1813.
[23] HO 40.2/3, Raynes to Acland, February 28th, 1813.
[24] May 17th, 1813. The original is in the Brontë museum, Howarth.

Bibliography

Primary Sources and Contemporary Publications

Fitzwilliam Papers (Sheffield City Libraries)
Home Office Departmental Papers (Public Record Office)
Radcliffe Papers (Leeds District Archives)

Baines, E, *History, Directory & Gazetteer of the County of York* (Baines, Leeds, 1822)

Baines, E, *Proceedings under the Special Commission at York* (Baines, Leeds, 1813)

Burdett, F, *Memoirs of the Life of Sir Francis Burdett* (Sherwood, Neely and Jones, London, 1810)

The Crown Calendar for the Yorkshire Summer Assizes, 1812 (W Storey, Petergate, York)

Howell, T, *State Trials, xxxi*, 1813, p. 959 *et seq. Proceedings under Commissions of Oyer and Terminer and Gaol Delivery, for the County of York* (Hansard, London, 1823)

Maitland, T, *Substance of Sir Thos. Maitland's Address to the Legislative Assembly of the Ionian Islands* (Reynell, London, 1822)

Raynes, F, *An Appeal to the Public – containing an account of the services rendered during the disturbances in the North of England in the year 1812* (London, 1817)

Rede, L, *York Castle in the Nineteenth Century* (Saunders, Leeds, 1831)

Walker, G, *The Costume of Yorkshire* (Longman et al., London, 1814)

I am grateful to the Archivist, Leeds District Archives, for access to the Radcliffe Papers, and to the Director of Libraries and Information Services, Sheffield and to Olive, Countess Fitzwilliam's Wentworth Settlement Trustees for access to the Fitzwilliam Papers.

Newspapers

London *Times*
London *Courier*
Edinburgh Evening Courant
Leeds Mercury
Leeds Intelligencer
Leicester Chronicle
Cowdroy's Manchester Gazette
Manchester Exchange Herald
Manchester Mercury
Nottingham Journal
York Courant
York Herald

Reports of Parliamentary Committees

Report on the State of the Woollen Manufacture in England and on the Use of Machinery, 1806
Report of the Committee on the Petitions of Several Weavers, 1811
Report of the Committee of Secrecy of the House of Lords into the Disturbances in the Northern Counties, 1812
Report of the Committee of Secrecy of the House of Commons into the Disturbances of the Northern Counties, 1812

Secondary Sources

Adams, A (ed.), *A Memoir of Edmund Cartwright* (Adams and Dart, Bath, 1971)

Advance 2 (UMIST, April 1967)

Anglesey, The Marquess of, *A History of the British Cavalry, Vol. I, 1816–1850* (Leo Cooper, London, 1973)

Aspinall, A (ed.), *The Diary of Henry Hobhouse* (Home and van Thal, London, 1947)

Aspinall, A, *The Early English Trade Unions* (Batchworth Press, London, 1949)

Baines, T, *Yorkshire, Past and Present* (William Mackenzie, London, 1876)

Berg, M, *The Age of Manufacturers (1700–1820)* (Fontana, London, 1985)

Bernal, J, *Science and Industry in the Nineteenth Century* (Routledge & Kegan Paul, London, 1953)

Bernal, J, *Science in History* (Watts, London, 1954)

Beveridge, W, *Full Employment in a Free Society* (Allen and Unwin, London, 1944)

Boorstin, D, *The Republic of Technology* (Harper and Row, New York, 1978)

Booth, P, *History of Gildersome & the Booth Family* (Lund, Bradford, 1920)

Bibliography

Braudel, F, *The Structures of Everyday Life* (Collins, London, 1981)

Briggs, A, *How They Lived, 1700 – 1815* (Blackwell, Oxford, 1969)

Briggs, A, 'Private & Social Themes in *Shirley*', *Brontë Soc. Trans., 13* part 68, 1958, p. 203

Briggs, A, *The Collected Essays of Asa Briggs* (Harvester Press, Sussex, 1985)

Briggs, A, *The Power of Steam* (Michael Joseph, London, 1982)

The Brontës, Their Lives, Friendships & Correspondences (Shakespeare Head Press, Oxford, 1932)

Brontë, C, *Shirley* (Penguin, London, 1981)

Brontë, P, *Cottage Poems* (Holden, Halifax, 1811)

Brougham, H, *The Life & Times of Henry Lord Brougham* (Blackwood, Edinburgh, 1871)

Brown, H and Hopkins, S, *A Perspective of Wages and Prices* (Methuen, London, 1981)

Cadman, H, *Gomersal Past and Present* (Hunters, Armley, Leeds, 1930)

Cardwell, D, *Technology, Science & History* (Heinemann, London, 1972)

Carmadine, D, 'The Present and Past in the English Industrial Revolution 1880–1980', *Past and Present, 103*, 1984, p. 131

Cartwright, F (ed.), *The Life and Correspondence of Major Cartwright* (Colburn, London, 1826)

Cooper, B, *Transformation of a Valley* (Heinemann, London, 1983)

Cooper, G, *Fifty Years Journalistic Experiences and Chronicles of a Typical Industrial Area* (Siddall, Cleckheaton, 1938)

Cowgill, J (ed.), *A Historical Account of the Luddites* (Cowgill, Huddersfield, 1862)

Cradock, H, *A History of the Ancient Parish of Birstall, Yorkshire* (Society for Promoting Christian Knowledge, London, 1933)

Crump, W (ed.), *The Leeds Woollen Industry, 1780–1820* (The Thoresby Society, Leeds, 1931)

Darvall, F, *Popular Disturbances and Public Order in Regency England* (OUP, London, 1969)

Daumas, M, *A History of Technology & Invention* (John Murray, London, 1980)

Defoe, D, *A Tour Through the Whole Island of Great Britain* (Penguin Books, Harmondsworth, 1971)

Derry, T and Williams, T, *A Short History of Technology* (OUP, London, 1960)

Engels, F, *The Condition of the Working Class in England* (Granada, London, 1969)

Farr, E, *The History of England* (George Virtue, London, n.d.)

Fay, C, *Life and Labour in the Nineteenth Century* (CUP, Cambridge, 1947)

Ferrett, M, *The Brontës in the Spen Valley* (Hub Publications, Bakewell, 1978)

317

Felkin, W, *A History of the Machine Wrought Hosiery and Lace Manufactures* (Longmans Green, London, 1867)

Fielden, J, *The Curse of the Factory System* (Cass, London, 1969)

Fitton, R and Wadsworth, A, *The Strutts and the Arkwrights* (Manchester University Press, Manchester, 1958)

Fores, M, 'The Myth of a British Industrial Revolution', *History*, *66*, 1981, p. 181

Forshaw, C (ed.), *The Poets of the Spen Valley* (College Press, Bradford, 1892)

Gaskell, E, *The Life of Charlotte Brontë* (OUP, London, 1961)

Goodall, A, *Spenlandia* (Stanley Press, Dewsbury, 1953)

Habakkuk, H, *American and British Technology in the Nineteenth Century* (CUP, Cambridge, 1967)

Hammond, J and Hammond, B, *The Skilled Labourer, 1760–1832* (Longmans, Green, London, 1919)

Hawes, F, *Henry Brougham* (Cape, London, 1957)

Heape, R, *Buxton under the Dukes of Devonshire* (Robert Hale, London, 1948)

Heaton, H, *The Yorkshire Woollen Industry from the Earliest Times up to the Industrial Revolution* (OUP, Oxford, 1920)

Heaton, H, 'The Economic Background of *Shirley*', *Brontë Soc. Trans.*, *viii*, part 42, 1932, p. 3

Hills, R, *Richard Arkwright & Cotton Spinning* (Priory Press, London, 1973)

Hobsbawn, E, *Labouring Men* (Weidenfeld and Nicolson, London, 1964)

James, J, *History of the Worsted Manufacture in England* (Longman, London, 1857)

Jeffrey, R (ed.), *Dyott's Diary* (Constable, London, 1907)

Journal of the Society for Army Historical Research, *19*, 1940, p. 75

Kendrick, T, *The Ionian Islands* (Haldane, London, 1822)

Kipling, L and Hall, N, *On the Trail of the Luddites* (Pennine Heritage Network, Hebden Bridge, 1982)

Landes, D, *The Unbound Prometheus* (CUP, Cambridge, 1969)

Liddell, R, *The Memoirs of the Tenth Royal Hussars* (Longmans Green, London, 1891)

Lilley, S, *Men, Machines and History* (Lawrence and Wishart, London, 1965)

Lipson, E, *The History of the Woollen and Worsted Industries* (Black, London, 1921)

Lock, J and Dixon, W, *A Man of Sorrow, The Life Letters and Times of the Rev. Patrick Brontë* (Hodgkins, London, 1979)

Longford, E, *Wellington, The Years of the Sword* (Weidenfeld and Nicolson, London 1969)

Marchand, L, *Byron* (John Murray, London, 1957)

Bibliography

Marchand, L, *Famous in My Time. Byron's Letters & Journals* (John Murray, London, 1973)

Martin, P and Olmstead, A, 'The Agricultural Mechanization Controversy,' *Science*, 227, 1985, p. 601

Morison, E, *Men, Machines and Modern Times* (MIT Press, Cambridge, Mass., 1966)

Napier, C, *The Colonies: the Ionian Islands* (Boone, London, 1833)

Napier, W, *The Life and Opinions of General Sir Charles James Napier* (John Murray, London, 1857)

Nelson, B, *The Woollen Industry of Leeds* (Thornton, Leeds, 1980)

Nussey, E, 'Reminiscences of Charlotte Brontë', *Scribner's Monthly*, ii, 1871

Nussey, J, 'Hammond Roberson of Liversedge (1757–1841)', *Yorkshire Archaeological Journal*, 53, 1981, p. 97

Oman, C, *A History of the Peninsular War* (OUP, Oxford, 1902–30)

Pacey, A, *The Maze of Ingenuity* (Allen Lane, London, 1974)

Parkinson, R, *On the Present Condition of the Labouring Poor in Manchester* (Simpkin, Marshall, London, 1841)

Patterson, M, *Sir Francis Burdett and his Times, 1770–1844* (Macmillan, London, 1931)

Peel, F, *Spen Valley: Past and Present* (Senior, Heckmondwike, 1893)

Peel, F, *The Risings of the Luddites* (Senior, Heckmondwike, 1888)

Pellew, G, *The Life of Sidmouth* (John Murray, London, 1874)

Pobjoy, H and M, *The Story of the Ancient Parish of Hartshead cum Clifton* (Ridings Publishing Co., 1972)

Randall, A, 'The Shearmen and the Wiltshire Outrages of 1802', *Social History*, vii, 1982, p. 283

Rudé, G, *The Crowd in History, 1730–1848* (John Wiley, London, 1964)

Singer, C (*et al.*), *A History of Technology (Vols. I–V)* (Clarendon Press, Oxford, 1958)

Smith, A, *The Wealth of Nations* (Penguin Books, Harmondsworth, 1977)

Stephenson, T, *The Pennine Way* (H M Stationery Office, 1980)

Stirling, A, *Annals of a Yorkshire House* (Bodley Head, London, 1911)

Sykes, D, *Huddersfield & its Vicinity* (Advertiser Press, Huddersfield, 1898)

Sykes, D, *The History of the Colne Valley* (Walker, Staithwaite, 1906)

Sykes, D and Walker, G, *Ben o' Bills, The Luddite* (Simpkin, Marshall, Hamilton, Kent, London, 1898)

Tames, R, *Documents of the Industrial Revolution, 1750–1850* (Hutchinson, London, 1971)

Thomis, M I, *The Luddites* (David and Charles, London, 1970)

Thomis, M and Holt, P, *Threats of Revolution in Britain 1789–1848* (Macmillan, London, 1977)

Thompson, E, *The Making of the English Working Class* (Pelican Books, Harmondsworth, 1968)

Thornbury, W, *Old Stories Retold* (Chatto and Windus, London)

Tomlinson, V, 'Letters of a Lancashire Luddite Transported to Australia, 1812–1816', *Trans. Lancs. and Cheshire Antiquarian Soc.*, *77*, 1967, p. 97

Turner, J (ed.), *Rev. Patrick Brontë, A.B., His Collected Works & Life* (Harrison, Bingley, 1898)

Wells, R, *Insurrection. The British Experience, 1795–1803* (Alan Sutton, Trowbridge, 1983)

Whyte, F, and Hilliard Atteridge, A, *A History of the Queen's Bays (The 2nd Dragoon Guards), 1685–1929* (Cape, London, 1930)

Williams, T (ed.), *A History of Technology (Vols. VI and VII)* (Clarendon Press, Oxford, 1978)

Yates, W, *The Father of the Brontës* (Spark, Leeds, 1897)

Ziegler, P, *Addington* (Collins, London, 1965)

Index

Acland, Maj Gen Wroth P 150,
    182, 184, 186, 190–1, 200, 202,
    203, 204, 205, 206, 207, 208, 212,
    216, 218, 222, 228, 235, 269, 274,
    289
Addington, Henry (*see* Lord
    Sidmouth)
Addington, Hiley 173, 217, 219
Africa 150
Agent-Solicitor 192
Aire valley 277
Allison, Jonas 212, 224, 229, 233,
    269
America, United States of 49, 174,
    175, 198, 222, 286
American Constitution 52
American Declaration of
    Independence 141
American War of Independence
    51
Ancoats Lane 201
Annual Register 274
Archangel 161
Arkwright, Richard 24, 28
Armitage, Ann 260
Armstrong, Betty 130–1
Armytage family 10–11, 18, 19
Armytage, Sir George 11, 20, 22,
    36, 64, 76, 98, 105, 187, 191
Armytage, Sir John 11, 14
Arnold 58, 59

Ashton and Oldham canal 21
Ashton-under-Lyne 122, 123, 124,
    176, 198
Ashworth, Mary 14
Atkinson, Thomas 134, 138, 139
Attorney General 156, 157, 219
Austen, Jane 19, 63

Badajoz 104
Baden-Powell, Robert 14
Baines, Edward 2–3, 66–7, 105,
    117, 139, 235, 240, 243, 247, 251,
    263, 265, 267
Baines, John (jnr) 193, 252–5, 263
Baines, John (snr) 52, 66, 93, 193,
    211–13, 252–5, 263
Baines, Zachariah 93, 211–12,
    253–5, 263
Balderstone, James 74
Bamforth, Mary 41
Bank of England 69
Barnsley 124
Barrowclough, Cpl 191–2
Batley, John 238, 268
Battersby, William 244
Bayley, Mr Justice 84, 168, 231,
    233, 234
Bays (see Dragoon Guards, 2nd)
Beckett, John 74, 77, 79, 80, 221, 237
Bellingham, John 156–62, 165, 174
Ben o'Bill's, the Luddite 3

Bent, Mr 86
Bentley, John 211
Berkshire 178
Berkshire Militia 151
Beveridge, Sir William 2
Birmingham 15, 16, 25, 89, 102, 120, 124
Birstall 91, 270
Birstall and Batley Militia 84
Black, James 25
Blackburn, Mr 233, 237, 266
Blackstone Edge 5, 277
Blakeborough, William 253
Bolton 100, 123, 124, 132, 146, 158, 198
Booth, John 94, 109, 114, 115, 116, 117, 118–19, 127
Boulton, Matthew 25–6
Bow Street Runners 78, 89, 144
Bower, John 245
Bowling, W G 156
Bradford 49, 179, 204, 234, 279
Bramah's water closet 24
Branwell, Maria 228
Brighton 103
Brighton Pavilion 103
British Army 147
British Empire 276
Brontë, Charlotte 2, 12–13, 14, 17, 27, 32, 33, 55, 63, 67, 115, 227, 294
Brontë, Patrick 31–7; change of name 31; early life 32–3; and Hammond Robertson 32, 33; and William Nowell's alibi 34–6; at Hartshead Church 36–7, 56, 64, 76; threats to 76–7; carries pistols 77; and Rawfolds attack 110, 117; courtship 228; publicity to Nowell's alibi 243–4; moves to Haworth 294
Brook, James 257–9
Brook, John 257–9
Brook, Mary 116
Brook, Thomas 109, 113, 114, 116, 257–9, 267
Brooke family 109
Brooke, Joseph 260
Brougham, Henry 157, 174–5, 201, 233–4, 237, 240, 242–6, 250, 254–5, 258, 291
Broughton, Reverend H D 121, 125, 175
Brown, Mr 105
Bruce, Major 270
Brussels carpets 26
Buckinghamshire Militia 151, 153
Buckworth, Reverend John 32, 34, 35, 36, 37
Bulwell 59
Burder, Mary 32
Burdett, Lady 288
Burdett, Sir Francis 68, 95, 127, 140–6, 157, 160, 175, 176, 177, 190, 194, 196, 225, 273, 287–8
Burdett, William James 146
Burton, Mr 122
Bury 198
Buxton 180–2, 190, 193, 222
Byron, Lord 61–2, 81–3, 161–2

Calder, river, 76
Calder valley 8, 10, 19, 66, 119, 132, 203, 227, 228, 273, 277, 282
California, University of 280–1
Cambridge 31, 32
Campbell, Col Charles 95, 99, 100, 101, 103, 119, 166
Carlisle 120, 124
Carr, John 180–1
Carron iron works 24
Cartwright, Dr Edmund 28, 42, 140
Cartwright, John 187
Cartwright, Major John 68, 95, 140–5, 196, 273, 287
Cartwright, William, meets Charlotte Brontë 2, 27; character of 27; and factory systems 28, 29; and finishing frames 30, 67; and Patrick Brontë 31; Rawfolds mill 41, 42,

44; and finishing process 43;
investment in machinery 49;
employs croppers 65;
mechanises 67; threats to 73, 76;
joins special constabulary 85;
finishing machines attacked 94;
prepares defence of mill 105,
106; Rawfolds defence 109–17;
Rawfolds aftermath 118, 127–9;
possibility of assassination 137;
communications with Home
Office 138; prepares for more
Luddite attacks 187, 194, 206–7;
seeks compensation 227–8; and
York trial 256–9, 266; sceptical
of Joseph Mellor 268; noted by
Brougham 291; later years
294–6; grave of 296
Castlereagh, Lord 144, 158, 200
Catholic Question 81
Cawston 12
Cephalonia 148, 288, 291
Ceylon 149
Ceylon, Governor of 165
Chancellor of the Exchequer 156
Charles I 60
Chartist gatherings 286
Chatham, Earl of 144, 157
Cheadle 124
Cheshire 8, 69, 70, 71, 72, 89, 93,
94, 120, 147, 152, 182, 186, 197,
199, 202, 204, 208, 220, 273, 292
Chester 120, 146, 175, 199
Chester Assizes 168
Chester Castle 121, 168
Chester Gaol 176
Chester Special Commission
168–9, 170, 171, 233
Chesterfield 16
Childe Harold 81, 83
Church Missionary Society 32
Church of England 32, 64, 94, 153
Church of Scotland 153
Ciudad Rodrigo 89, 104
Civil War 11
Clay, Col J G 101, 102, 103, 121–3

Cleckheaton 17, 114
Clerk of the Arraigns 263
Clifton 36, 187
Clough, Billy 114, 115
Coalbrookdale 24, 25
coal cutter 280
coal pick 280
Cobbett, William 140
Cobbett's Weekly Register 143
Cockhill, Thomas 114
Colne, river 8, 76
Colne valley 8, 10, 19, 29, 37, 39,
45, 51, 54, 65, 66, 71, 72, 85,
100, 127, 132, 171, 191, 203,
205, 208, 216, 249, 273, 282,
286, 292
Combination 47
Combination Acts 47, 48, 52
Commissioner of the Lottery 290
Committee of Huddersfield
Manufacturers 286
Committee for Suppressing the
Outrages 75, 105
Committee on the Woollen Trade
48
Cooke, William Peabody 26–7, 29
Cookson, William 47
Cooper, Alfred 203
Cooper, William 197
Corfu 148
Cornish Mines 26
Cottage Poems 64
Coulthurst, Reverend Mr 292
County Down 32
Coutts, Sophia 141
Coutts, Thomas 141
Covent Garden 142
Coventry 124
Crabtree, Samuel 197
Crompton's mule 24
Crosland Moor 74
Crown Inn 71, 75
Crowther, Joseph 229, 261, 267
crucible steel 24
Crystal Palace 296

Cumberland Militia 102, 106, 107, 112, 121, 122, 125, 127, 128

Danzig 281
Danzig, Municipal Council of 281
Darvall, F O 3
da Vinci, Leonardo 44
Dawgreen 34
Dawson, Mr 35
Dean, Jonathan 109, 112, 256–9, 267
Defoe, Daniel 277
Denbigh Militia 125
Derbyshire 42, 141, 180
Derbyshire, Lord Lieutenant of 60
Dewsbury 12–13, 31, 32, 33, 34, 36, 37
Dickinson, Joshua 108
Dirom, General 101, 103, 153
Disraeli, Benjamin 288
Dixon, Alec 114, 115
DNA 279
Doncaster 62, 124
Dragoons, 2nd (Royal North British) (*see* Scots Greys)
Dragoons, 15th 120
Dragoons, 18th Light 21
Dragoon Guards, 2nd (The Queen's Bays) 88, 106, 114, 115, 135
Drake, Joseph 109, 258, 286
Drumballyroney 33
Dublin 200
Duckworth, George 253
Dumb Steeple 98, 108
Dunbar 222
Dungeon Wood 213, 215, 246
Durrance, Thomas 215, 243
Dyott, General William 102, 103, 120, 151

Eaden, John 252, 263
Earl of Chester's Yeomanry Cavalry 121

East Devon Militia 189, 193
East India Company 149
Eccles 122, 124
Eddie, Thomas 224
Eddystone Lighthouse 24
Eden, Sir John 181
Eden, the Misses 181
Education Acts 282
Edward VI 280
Egypt 150, 279
Elizabeth I 40, 280
Elland 207, 234, 270
Engels, Friedrich 28, 277
'Enoch' 30
Erskine, Hon Mr and Mrs 181
Established Church 31, 37, 294
Eton 168
Etruria 24
Exchange St, Manchester 102
Exchequer, Baron of the 235

Factory Acts 282
factory system 28–9, 41, 46
Fenton, Lt Col Frank 119–20, 123
Fisher, Joseph 211, 238, 268
Fisher, Mr 41, 71, 245
Fitzwilliam, Lord 21–3, 35, 46–7, 72, 167, 168, 188–9, 221, 223, 225, 228, 229, 230, 232, 293
Fleming, Lady 181
Fletcher, Col Ralph 86, 87, 100, 101, 124, 126, 158
Flockton 210
flying shuttle 42
Foot Regiment, 28th (*see* Stirlingshire Militia)
Foot Regiment, 30th (Cambridgeshire Militia) 34
foot treadle 41
Foster, James 100
Frame Breaking Act 116
framework knitting machine 58–62
France 141, 273, 280
Freemasonry 93

French Revolution 48, 51, 52, 141, 176
Friendly Society 48, 186
Full Employment in a Free Society 2
Fuller's Earth 42
fulling 42

Garside, Thomas 123–4
Gascoyne, Gen Isaac 157, 161
Gaskell, Mrs E 8, 32, 33, 40
Gaskell, Peter 276
'General Ludd' 77
George III 18, 57, 155, 158, 176, 212
George Inn 89, 105, 138, 244, 246, 287
gig-mill 44, 47, 53, 206, 280
Gildersome 100
Gildersome Baptist Church 63
Glasgow 194
Gloucestershire 129
Golcar 75
Gordon, Major 87, 130, 166
Gossling, John 192–3, 211–13, 252–4
Gott, Benjamin 46–8, 53, 65, 67
Grange Moor 100
Great Britain 30
'Great Enoch' 110
Greece 279
Green, Thomas 211
Grey, Lieutenant General the Hon H G 87–8, 91, 95, 99, 100, 103, 119, 125, 165, 166, 167, 168, 188, 194–5, 201, 203
Guilds 44

Habeas Corpus Act 178
Haddington Burghs 149
Haigh, James 109, 114, 116, 130, 256–9, 268
Haigh, Samuel 191
Halifax 7, 22, 48, 50, 52, 73, 94, 98, 107, 118, 179, 193–4, 203, 204, 206, 211, 231, 252, 270, 277

Halifax Cloth Hall 51
Halifax Militia 115
Hall, William 40, 66, 110, 114, 134–5, 136, 218, 243, 257, 286
Halliley family 35, 37
Hamilton, Lady 80
Hammond, Barbara 3
Hammond, J L 3
Hampshire 178
Hankin, Major 287
Hargreaves's spinning-jenny 24
Harris, Benjamin 179
Harrison's no. 4 chronometer 24
Hartley, George 206
Hartley, Samuel 107, 109, 110, 111, 115, 117, 118, 127
Hartley, William 26, 267
Hartshead 17, 36, 56, 64, 117, 228
Hartshead Moor 37, 76, 94, 111
Haworth 8, 294
Hay, Reverend William 101, 123, 153, 154, 163, 191, 255
Healds Hall 18, 26, 27, 36, 114, 208, 227
Heathcote, Sir John 181
Heckmondwike 16, 17
Heckmondwike Herald 2
Hepworth, David 206
Hey, James 229, 261, 268
Hey, Job 260, 268
Hightown 110, 114, 116, 228
Hill, John 260, 267
Hinchcliffe, John 209–10, 249–50, 272
Hinchcliffe, William 75
Hirst, John 109, 110, 111, 257–9
Hirst, Joseph 74
Hobhouse, Henry, early career 168; at Chester Special Commission, 168–9; relations with Lloyd 169; recommends new Acts 170–1; and action against Luddites 174; and Lloyd 191; reviews evidence 231; and York trial 232–3, 235–42, 247, 249, 251, 252, 255,

258, 269; recommends
mechanisation 274–5; attitude
to Luddism 283; created Under
Secretary of State 291
Holland 44
Holland, Lord 61
Hollingsworth, Edward 59–60
Holme, river 8
Home Office 57, 59, 74, 78–80, 86,
87, 99, 120, 121, 123, 124, 125,
139, 140, 146, 164, 174, 178, 188,
206, 210, 219, 221–2, 230, 233,
261, 275, 295
Honley 234, 242, 245
Hood, Robin 10, 98
Horbury 100
Horsfall, John 75, 242
Horsfall, Reverend Abraham 136,
242
Horsfall, William, in Colne valley
29; and the Taylor brothers 30;
and Patrick Brontë 31; at
Huddersfield cloth market 39;
and finishing process 43; and
mechanisation 55, 67; defence
of mill 105; character of 106;
murder of 134–9, 165, 189, 191,
205, 206, 213, 215, 217, 229–37,
240–9, 262, 272, 286; noted by
Brougham 291
Houghton, Rowland 242
House of Commons 42, 48, 60, 80,
83, 127, 143, 145, 146, 156, 168,
175, 190, 196
House of Lords 61, 81, 83
Hoyle, Nathan 229, 261, 267
Huddersfield 7, 12, 17, 19, 21, 30,
39, 50, 71, 73, 75, 87–8, 91, 94, 98,
99, 100, 105, 107, 109, 115, 118,
119, 125, 127, 128, 130, 135, 136,
138, 164, 165, 166, 179, 180, 202,
203, 204, 210, 213, 216, 219, 229,
231, 232, 233, 235, 242, 244, 245,
246, 250, 269, 270, 277, 286, 287
Huddersfield and Halifax
Volunteers 22

Huddersfield Cloth Market 134,
135
Huddersfield Committee
for Preventing Unlawful
Depredations of Machinery and
Shearing Frames 138
Hull 125
Hullock, Mr 242
Hunsdon, Lord 280
Hunt, John 233–4
Hunt, Leigh 233–4
Hussars, 10th 103, 106
Hussars, 15th 189
Hyde Park 144

Income Tax 173
India 149, 150
Industrial Revolution 9, 12, 24, 25,
58, 89, 207, 249, 259, 277, 279,
282, 286
Ionian Islands, High
Commissioner of 288
Ireland 30, 124, 273
Ireland, Viceroy of 21

Jackson, Abraham 129
Jackson, Martha 34
Jackson, Samuel 34–5, 244
jack-wires 58
James, John 28
Jones, John Gale 143
Jubson, James 21
Judge of the Common Pleas 291

Keighley 8
Kenny, Mason Stanhope 135–6
Kent 150
Kersal Moor 153
Kinder, John 209, 213, 215–16, 243
Kirk Heaton 260
Kirklees 10–11, 17, 18, 76, 98, 109,
110
Kirklees House 189
Kirkstall Abbey 228

Lacey, Major R 270

Lamb, Lady Caroline 162
Lancashire 8, 20, 21, 22, 69, 70, 71,
  72, 85, 86, 87, 89, 93, 94, 95, 102,
  120, 123, 147, 152, 158, 163, 164,
  175, 176, 177, 186, 189, 199, 200,
  201, 204, 220, 232, 233, 273, 277,
  292
Lancashire cotton trade 49
Lancashire Militia 121
Lancaster 201, 210, 230–1, 232,
  234, 235
Lancaster Assizes 168
Lancaster Castle 146
Lancaster Special Commission
  170, 190
Lascelles, Lord 275
Lauderdale, Earl of 147
Law, Solomon 185–6
Lawrence, Sir Thomas 102
Lawson, Sgt James 200
Le Blanc, Sir Simon 169–70, 233,
  235, 238–65
Lee Fair 34, 244
Lee, Reverend William 58, 280
Leeds 17, 46, 47, 49, 65, 71, 72, 75,
  80, 91, 95, 98, 99, 100, 105, 110,
  112, 125, 166, 179, 180, 204, 214,
  231, 232, 234, 270, 277
Leeds and Liverpool canal 21
Leeds Mercury 2, 60, 66–7, 68, 71,
  77, 82, 105, 117, 139, 199, 235,
  247, 267, 276
Lees, James 198
Leicester Chronicle 159
Leicester, John 121
Leicestershire 42, 89
Leicestershire, Lord Lieutenant
  60
Lepton 130
Leveson Gower, Lord 161
Leyden 43
Lichfield 15, 103, 120
Life Guards 144, 157
Lightfoot, Reverend Mr 183
Lincolnshire 291
Linthwaite 75

Lisbon 81
Littletown 114
Liverpool 71, 89, 101, 103, 157, 159,
  161, 200, 234
Liverpool, Lord 104, 156, 172, 222,
  276
Liversedge 17, 41, 94, 105, 109, 127,
  243, 262
Lloyd, John S, patronised by
  Warren Bulkeley 69–70;
  response to Luddite attacks 85–
  6, 87; Lancashire activities 92,
  94, 101; Stockport activities
  120–1; relations with Maitland
  153, 154, 164, 166; makes arrests
  168, 170; relations with
  Hobhouse 169; interrogates
  prisoners 176, 191; relations
  with Raynes 191, 199;
  resented by Radcliffe 192;
  abused by Radcliffe 205;
  reconciled with Radcliffe
  208–9; first breakthroughs
  209–14; elicits evidence of
  murder 215–18; rewarded 220;
  offers services to HO 221–3;
  warns of Bayley's leniency 231;
  at York trial 233, 238, 242, 243,
  251, 253, 258, 268
Lloyds 161
Lockwood 88, 109, 270
London 42, 81, 144, 145, 174, 176,
  177, 179, 180, 190, 200, 222, 230,
  281
Longroyd Bridge 39, 51, 66, 76, 94,
  98, 108, 134, 135, 218, 270
Lord Chancellor 7, 233, 291
Louth Militia 151, 153
Lovat, Lord 200
Lowmoor 94, 115
Lud, Ned 73
Luddite, origin of name 73; oath
  93, 100, 137, 171, 200, 252–3;
  leadership 124, 176–8, 196, 205;
  Grand Council 200; causes of
  Luddism 278–84

Lumb, John 211, 238–9, 265

Macclesfield 122, 124, 158
machine wrecking in West of
  England 47
Madras 149
Maitland, Lt Gen the Hon
  Thomas, early career and
  character 147–52; in
  Manchester 153–5, 159, 163–4,
  175; and Lloyd 153, 154, 164;
  moves into Yorkshire 164–8;
  works with Sidmouth 174; view
  of sources of unrest 176–8;
  relations with Sidmouth 178–9,
  180, 184; at Buxton 180–1; and
  Raynes 184; and military
  commandos 186; policy in
  Yorkshire 187–95; ascendency
  over Grey 187–95; policy in
  Lancashire and Cheshire
  196–9; and James Lawson
  199–201; policy of fear
  202; policy in Yorkshire
  203–14; and Halifax spies
  210–14; appraises
  interrogations 216; causes of
  revolt 221–2; and zeal of
  magistrates 222–3; predicts end
  to illegal oaths 225; and
  Cartwright 228; intolerance of
  Radcliffe 229–30; plans Special
  Commission 230–1; and York
  trial 235, 249, 250–2, 253, 261,
  268; withdraws troops 268–9;
  and Luddite funerals 269–70;
  and satisfactory outcome of
  campaign 274; leaves Yorkshire
  283, 288; advises Raynes 289;
  and Raynes planned
  attachment in Mediterranean
  290–1; refuses protection to
  Radcliffe 292
*Making of the English Working
  Class, The* 2
Malta, Governor of 288

Malthus, Thomas 282
Manchester 19, 42, 70, 71, 89, 100,
  101, 102, 121, 122, 123, 124, 125,
  132, 134, 150, 153–5, 163–4, 170,
  180, 200, 220, 255, 285
Manchester Exchange 101–2, 120
Manchester Exchange Herald 82
Manchester Police Office 163
Marriage of Figaro 13
Marsden 29, 44, 54, 55, 65, 75, 76,
  94, 105, 134, 135
Marsh 74
Martial Law 178, 179
Marx, Karl 44
M'Donald, John 192–3, 211–13,
  252–5
Mediterranean 288
Mediterranean, Commander in
  Chief of 288
Mellor, George, death of 38; early
  life 39; and John Wood 39;
  working conditions of 40–1;
  apprenticeship 44, 51, 53; at the
  Crispin Inn 52; cash savings
  65; leads croppers 66–8; at John
  Wood's shop 71, 76; and John
  Baines 93; involved in oath
  taking 94; organises croppers
  98, 100; leads Rawfolds attack
  108–17; organising abilities
  132–3; and Radcliffe 133–4;
  attacks Horsfall 134–7; failure
  to advance leadership 160;
  leads small-scale attacks 206;
  interrogated 209; arrested 214,
  220, 225; evidence against
  215–19; guilt of 224, 231; and
  Brougham 234; arraignment of
  237; trial of 241–49; execution
  250–1, 261, 267; and York trial
  252, 256, 258, 259; possible
  innocence of 272; limited
  abilities of 273; inevitability of
  Rawfolds failure 283;
  association with George Inn
  287

Mellor, Joseph 209, 213, 215–17, 225, 243, 246, 268
Mellor, Martha 41, 215–16, 243, 246
Methodism 31
Meuse, river 56
Middle East 290
Middleton 122, 124
Millbridge 19n, 204, 208, 232, 262, 285
Milnes, Charles 192, 253
Milnsbridge 19, 19n, 22, 71, 75, 84, 135, 165, 166
Milnsbridge House 20, 39, 129, 130, 193, 204, 210, 214, 215, 218, 220, 260, 292, 293
Milton, Lord 35
mining machine 280
Mitchell, John 285
Molyneux, Charles 107
Montrose, Duke of 290
Moscow 230
Mosley, Lady 181
Mosley, Sir Oswald 181
Mottram 183
movable type 280
Moxon, Samuel 238
Moxon, William 238
Mozart, Wolfgang Amadeus 13
Mulgrave, Lord 156

Nadin, Joseph 153, 163, 192, 201, 220
nap 43, 44
Napier, Sir Charles 148, 149, 288
Napoleon 49, 56, 57, 124, 175, 230, 274
Naylor, Sarah 116
'Ned Lud' 59
Newgate 143, 158, 161
New Mill 234
Newstead Abbey 61
Newton 179
Newtown 179, 197–9
Non-Intercourse Act 49
Norfolk 7, 12, 18

North America 276
Northamptonshire 89
Northwich 7, 121
Nottingham 59, 67, 69, 70, 71, 73, 77, 81, 95, 103, 141, 158, 280
Nottingham Assizes 84
Nottingham General Hospital 61
Nottingham Journal 62, 82, 90
Nottinghamshire 57, 60, 73, 80, 86, 89, 95, 168, 274
Nowell, William 34–6, 244

Oastler, Richard 277
Oath of Allegiance 292
O'Bucks, Ben 41
Ogden, John 109, 256–9, 267
Old Bailey 161
Oldham 20, 124
Oldham, Joseph 215
On the Present Condition of the Labouring Poor in Manchester 155
O'Neill, Earl 181
Order of the Buffaloes 93
Orders in Council 49, 52, 53, 58, 71, 174, 175, 177, 234, 274
Osborne, Lord Sydney 149
Ottiwells House 29
Ottiwells mill 29, 105
Oxford 141, 168

Paine, Tom 52
Pall Mall 158
Palmerston, Lord 32, 35
Park, J A 233, 237, 238–44, 253–66, 286, 291
Parkin, Earl 211–12, 238
Parkinson, Canon 155
Parliament 48, 49
Parliamentary Secret Committees 189–90
Parr, Henry 135, 241–2
Paull, John 142
Peel Frank 2, 3, 66, 94, 285
Peninsula 89, 104, 126, 147, 150, 151, 163

Pennines 6, 29, 87, 119, 120, 122,
164, 178, 183, 200, 204
Perceval, Spencer 49, 57, 101, 104,
139, 143, 144, 156–62, 168, 174–5
Piccadilly 142, 144
Pickford, Joseph (*see* Radcliffe,
Joseph)
Picton, Sir Thomas 90
Pitt, William 81, 172
Pococke, Bishop 6, 12
Pontefract 234
Portugal 57, 81
Prescott, Reverend Charles 69–71,
199
Preservation of the Public Peace
Bill 189–90
Preston 66
Pride and Prejudice 63
Priestley family 14
Priestley, John 11, 14
Priestley, Joseph 11
Priestley, Dr Joseph 11, 20
Prince of Wales 57, 62, 291
Prince Regent 63, 88, 101, 102, 103,
125, 139, 158, 161, 172, 176, 196,
229, 230, 233, 275, 293
Prince Regent Arms 201
Princess of Wales 156, 291
printing press 280
Privy Council 125, 161
Pule, Abraham 107, 118, 206

Queen's Bays (*see* Dragoon
Guards 2nd)

Radcliffe, Joseph, early life 18–
20; early activities in West
Riding 20–3, 24; and
Milnsbridge House 29, 39;
signs for illiterates 38; for
'Church and King' 52; activities
as magistrate 53, 72, 73, 74;
travels in West Riding 71;
contacts Wilberforce 74;
response to Luddite attacks
74–7, 84–5, 86, 92, 94, 95;

relations with Home Office 78,
80; urges Ryder to action 77,
87–9, 99, 104; and Hammond
Roberson 105; threats to 129,
139; interrogates Luddites
130–1, 165, 191, 193, 225; and
George Mellor 133–4; and
Horsfall's murder 134–9;
defends Milnsbridge House
166; at Lieutenancy meeting
167; fears magistrates'
clemency 168; resentment of
Lloyd 192; fearful for life 205;
combines with Raynes and Lloyd
208–10; successful
interrogations 212–19;
attempted murder of 204, 220;
seeks commendation 221;
annoys Maitland 222; under
strain 227; seeks ennoblement
229; warns of Bayley's leniency
231; and York trial 235, 236,
238, 239, 242, 243, 249, 251;
created baronet 256, 258, 269,
292–3; need for esteem 295
Radcliffe, William 19
Ramsden Canal 76
Ramsden's screw-cutting lathe
24
Rawdon 99
Rawfolds 2, 3, 27, 29, 72, 100, 106,
107, 108–17, 118, 119, 120, 124,
125, 127, 130, 131, 133, 137, 187,
189, 192, 204, 205, 206, 207, 216,
217, 228, 256–60, 263, 264, 286,
287, 289, 294, 295
Raynes, Captain Francis,
Lancashire activities 92–3;
relations with Maitland 150,
184–5; and action against
Luddites 174; first encounter
with Luddites 182–6; and
military commandos 186;
relations with Lloyd 191;
Cheshire activities 197–9, 202;

Index

Yorkshire activities 204; in
Spen valley 207–8; and
Radcliffe 208; rewarded 220; at
Liversedge church 227;
observes York road 232; and
York trial 262; observes
funerals 269–70; reports rising
optimism 274; seeks
recompense 289–91
Raynes, Sarah 289
Reading 172
Reform Bill 287
*Reports on the Employment of
Children in Factories* 277
Rhine, river 56
Richmond Park 173
Rigg, George 110
Rights of Man, The 52
Riot Act 102, 119, 123, 144, 158
Risings of the Luddites, The 2
Roberson, Hammond, residency
in Spen valley 1–2, 11, 36, 94;
origins 12; and Charlotte
Brontë 12–13; organises
Sunday Schools 13; courtship
and marriage 14–18; and Joseph
Pickford 20; activities in West
Riding 24, 26; and Patrick
Brontë 32, 331; at Hartshead 36,
64; for 'Church and King,' 52;
illness of wife 63; inheritance of
Phoebe's mother's money 62–3;
threats to 76; response to
Luddite attacks 73, 84–5, 91;
defence of Spen valley 104–5;
and Rawfolds attack 114–16;
seeks more troops 194; reports
Gildersome attack 206–7;
assists Raynes 208; builds
Liversedge church 227; and
James Starkey 262; and
Luddite funerals 270; baptises
Raynes's daughter 289; grave
294, 296
Roberson, Phoebe 14, 18, 26, 36,
63, 207, 227

Roberttown 115
Robinson Crusoe 6
Rochdale 124
Rochdale canal 21
Rocket Corps 151
Rome 279
Royal Artillery 257
Royal Family 146, 176
Royal Horse Artillery 151
Royal Horse Guards 151
Royton 19, 20
Russell, Lt Col 184
Russia 39, 134, 161, 274
Ryder, Richard, speaks on
Midlands riots 60, 151;
encourages Lloyd 70; response
to Wilberforce 74; urged to
action by Radcliffe 77; as MP
79; inertia of 79, 80, 146, 160,
166, 179; seeks information
from Lloyd 86; requests from
Radcliffe 87–9; searches for
Luddite leaders 95; and
information sources 100, 101;
limited powers 103; and
Birmingham riots 120; and
Lloyd's methods 121; response
to riots 123, 124, 125; and
Atkinson 138; death threat 139;
apprised of Manchester
situation 153–5; and Perceval's
assassination 156, 158, 159, 168;
communications with Maitland
163–4; and new Acts 171; leaves
Government 172; suspicions of
Burdett 190

Saddleworth 122, 124, 179, 232
St Ann's Square 102
St Crispin Inn 52, 66, 72, 93, 94,
98, 108, 192, 252, 263
St James's Park 144
St John's College, Cambridge 32
St Mark's, Liverpool 159
San Domingo 149
Scheldt, river 56

Schofield, John 209–10, 218, 249–50
science 25, 279
Scotland 222
Scots Greys (2nd Dragoons) 72, 75, 102, 121, 122–3, 151, 287
Scott, Mr 292
Seale, Major J H 193–5
Secretary at War 35
Sedan 43
shearmen 51
Shears Inn 66, 72, 94
Sheepridge 206
Sheffield 25, 71, 89, 100, 119–20, 124, 125, 188, 194, 234
Sheffield Militia 119, 120
Shirley 2, 13, 27, 32, 63, 294
Sick Club 48, 186
Sidmouth, Lord, appointed Home Secretary 172–4, 175, 178; relations with Maitland 174, 178–9, 180, 184, 202, 222, 223; and Luddite leadership 177; attitude to Luddite attacks 188; corresponds with Seale 193–4; dismissal of Grey 194–5; and James Lawson 200; and Radcliffe 205, 221 and state of poor 223–4; and Cartwright 228; refuses Radcliffe's baronetcy 230; and satisfactory outcome of campaign 274; refusal to assist croppers 276; and Hobhouse's view of Luddism 283; interviews Raynes 289–9 recommends Hobhouse and Park 291; confirms Radcliffe's baronetcy 293
silicon chip 282
Sinkinson, Pearson and Co 62
Skipton 120, 124
Slingsby, Sir Thomas Turner 167
Smeaton, John 24
Smith, Adam 7, 57, 236
Smith, Hannah 170, 233

Smith, Thomas 41, 66, 108, 135–7, 217, 237, 241–9, 251, 256, 258, 261
Smith, William 157
Solicitor General 179, 219
South Crossland 88
South Devon Militia 193
Sowden, Joseph 137, 243
Sowerby 270
Spain 81
Spen, river 8, 110
Spen valley 8, 10, 37, 42, 45, 53, 64, 72, 76, 77, 84, 94, 98, 110, 127, 132, 171, 187, 203, 204, 208, 227, 256, 270, 273, 282, 286, 292, 294
spinning 41, 42
spinning-jenny 278
Squirrel Hall 14
Star Inn 115, 116, 135
Starkey, James 208, 262
steam engine 24, 25–6, 44
steam loom 85, 278
steam mill 279–80
Stirlingshire Militia (28th Foot Regiment) 150, 151, 153, 182, 184, 270, 290
stocking loom 280
stocking trade 57–62
Stockport 69, 70, 85, 100, 120, 121, 122, 124, 169, 176, 179, 198, 199, 220
Stuart-Wortley, J 172
Swallow, John 211, 238, 268
Swallow, Samuel 76
Sykes, D F E 3, 94
Sykes, John 75

Take Your Choice 141
Tate, John 48
Tattersall, Richard 129–30
Taylor brothers 76
Taylor, Enoch 29, 44, 45, 54, 55, 65, 110
Taylor Hill 88
Taylor, James 29, 44, 45, 54, 55, 65
teaseling 43, 44

technology, irreversibility of 279–84

technology, law of 272–84

tenterhooks 43

Thackray, James 34, 35

Thompson, E P 2–3

Thompson's mill 99

Thomson, Sir Alexander 233, 235–6, 238–65, 286

Thorn Bush Farm 64

Thornhill, Capt 179, 191, 202, 211

Thorpe, John 244, 246

Thorpe, William 41, 65, 66, 71, 94, 108, 110, 133, 135–7, 169, 170, 217–18, 237, 241–9, 251, 256, 258, 261, 294

The Times 60, 80, 203

Tintwhistle 124

Tolson, Joseph 36–7

Tower of London 143–5, 160

Trade-Union Act 282

Treasury 290

Tucker, Josiah 25

Tyburn, York 267

type-setting 280

Unlawful Oaths Act 198

Unlawful Oaths Bill 190

Upper Agbrigg Militia 105

Varley, James 213, 216, 262

Venn, Henry 12

Vickerman, Francis 88, 105

Voluntary Defence Associations 207–8

Wakefield 49, 74, 98, 105, 167, 168, 201, 203, 204, 234

Wakefield Grammar School 42

Wakefield House of Correction 35

Walker, Benjamin 66, 108, 109, 114, 116, 135–7, 209, 217, 220, 242, 245, 246, 258, 286

Walker, G H 3

Walker, John 109, 112, 257–9, 267

Walker, Mrs 217

Walker, Richard 91, 92

Waller, Mr 72

Wareham, Mr 14–16

War Office 35

Warren Bulkeley, Viscount 69–70, 85, 86

Warrener House Inn 135, 241

Washington Government 49

Watch and Ward Act 104, 154, 193, 199, 207, 287

water wheel 42, 44

Waterhouse's factory 107, 206

Watt, James 24, 25–6, 28

Wealth of Nations, The 7

weaving 41–2

Wedgwood, Josiah 24

Weightman, George 95

Wellington, Duke of 13, 57, 81, 89–90, 104, 126, 147, 150, 151, 155

Wentworth Woodhouse 21, 188

Wesley, John 11

West Houghton 170

West Indies 149

West Kent Regiment 125

West Lincolnshire Militia 151

West Norfolk Militia 151, 159, 179

West Riding 7, 8, 12, 22, 38, 49–50, 51, 65, 67, 72, 88, 95, 104, 108, 119, 138, 165, 167, 188, 202, 203, 218, 221, 229, 235, 295

West Riding, Lord Lieutenant of 46

West Riding Yeomanry 120

West Suffolk Militia 151, 204

Westminster 53, 95, 140, 174, 225

Westminster Bridge 24

Westminster, City of 142

Westminster School 141

Whitbread, Samuel 140, 194

White Hart Inn 244, 246

Whitechapel 249

Whitehall 126, 219

Whittaker, Thomas 169, 170

Wilberforce, William 32, 35, 74, 140, 190

Wilkinson's boring mill 24

Williams, Mr 258
Wilmslow 122, 124
Wilson, Reverend Thomas 17
Wiltshire 51, 141, 179
Wiltshire Militia 151
Wimbledon Common 142
Windsor 144
Womersley, John 244
Wood, John 39–41, 51, 65, 66, 67, 68, 76, 134, 136, 206, 209, 213, 243, 245, 257
Wood, Mathilda 39–40
Wood, Sir Francis 167, 188
woollen cloth 42–3
Woollen District 30
woollen industry 7
Woolwich 257
Worsley–Manchester canal 24
worsted 7, 28, 42

Yeomanry Cavalry 60
York 91, 95, 103, 168, 188, 203, 214, 231, 232–73, 287, 289, 291
York Assizes 223, 286
York Castle 11, 21, 72, 120, 131, 208, 211, 214, 216, 219, 221, 224, 229, 232–73
York Castle Chaplain 251
York County Hospital 251
York Courant 119
York, Duke of 125
York Herald 267
York Special Commission 2, 223, 231, 232–74, 286, 291
Yorkshire 46, 71, 80, 85, 94, 95, 99, 100, 102, 127, 129, 132, 147, 152, 164–8, 170, 175, 176, 177, 187–95, 201, 203, 204, 205, 208, 209, 220, 221, 222, 225, 227, 230, 233, 234, 238, 274, 275, 277, 286, 281, 284, 285, 289, 291
Yorkshire woollen manufacture 49